W9-CIG-359

URIEL'S
MACHINE

URIEL'S MACHINE

THE PREHISTORIC TECHNOLOGY THAT SURVIVED THE FLOOD

CHRISTOPHER KNIGHT
& ROBERT LOMAS

BARNES
& NOBLE
BOOKS
NEW YORK

This edition published by Barnes & Noble, Inc.,
by arrangements with Christopher Knight and Robert Lomas.

2004 Barnes & Noble Books

M 10 9 8 7 6 5 4 3 2 1

ISBN 0-7607-5342-3

Printed and bound in the United States of America.

Dedicated to the memory
of two great archaeologists:

Professor Alexander Thom.
Whose patient analysis proved the existence
of the megalithic yard.

Professor Michael O'Kelly.
Who so brilliantly resurrected Newgrange,
the first wonder of the world.

LIST OF FIGURES

ACKNOWLEDGEMENTS

Dr Jack Miller, for pointing us in the right direction.

Professor Philip Davies, for his valued comments.

Tony Batters, for his unstinting enthusiasm.

Alan Butler, for sharing his astronomical insights, mathematical speculations and sense of wonder.

Ian Sinclair of the Niven Sinclair Study Centre and Library at Noss Head Lighthouse, Caithness for his encouragement and for his hospitality on the night he stood with us and watched the midnight sun briefly dip below the northern horizon at St Clair Grirnigo Castle.

Dr. Julian Thomas of Southampton University for his help regarding the dating of Bryn Celli Ddu.

Alan Wilson for his help regarding the survival of a Druid tradition in South Wales.

Fred Olsen for sharing his great knowledge about early transatlantic voyages.

Bill Hamilton of A M Heath; for being a great agent.

Mark Booth and Liz Rowlinson of Century for their professional guidance.

Roderick Brown for his thoughtful editing.

The staff of Newgrange, Skara Brae and Maes Howe for their friendliness and helpfulness.

Our Masonic brethren of Ryburn Lodge for their support and understanding.

Oxford University Press for allowing us to reproduce Professor Thom's diagram from his landmark book *Megalithic Sites in Britain*.

The Catholic Herald, for their hilarious reviews that keep us smiling.

ILLUSTRATION ACKNOWLEDGEMENTS

Plan of Skara Brae, by permission of Historic Scotland
Plate 3 – by permission of Historic Scotland
Plate 4 GRJ Lomas
Plate 5 – by permission of the Trustees of the National Museum of Scotland
Plate 6 – by permission of Inverness Museum
Plate 8 GRJ Lomas
Plate 10 GRJ Lomas
Plate 18 GRJ Lomas
Plate 19 GRJ Lomas
Plate 21 Copyright 1994 Jeffery Newbury by permission of *Discover* magazine
Other photographs from the authors' own collection.

Contents

PROLOGUE

In the course of researching our last two books, we discovered that many standard explanations of historical events are little more than conventions assembled from limited information. We also found that there are veins of information about the past held within obscure texts such as the peculiar rituals of Freemasonry, some of which contain arcane knowledge of events over a vast period of time.

As Freemasons ourselves, we have assembled all of the available evidence within these rituals and found that they tell the story of the Jewish leaders from the biblical Flood down to the period of the Knights Templar. These old rituals make frequent reference to a worldwide Flood, and even today there is an entire order dedicated to preserving a verbal tradition about Noah, the builder of the Biblical Ark who survived the deluge, and his grandfather Enoch. There are lists of characters from the pre-Flood civilization such as Tubal-Cain who, Masons are told, invented agriculture and the ploughshare. The earlier rituals of the Ancient Scottish Rite of Freemasonry have not been in general use since 1813, when they had entire degrees devoted to Enoch, who was told by an angel called Uriel that he must preserve the secrets of civilization because a global disaster was imminent.

Masonic documents dating from the early 17th century, known as the Old Charges, tell how everything dear to mankind existed before the disastrous Flood and had to be reconstructed by the survivors. This is the same world-engulfing flood that biblical and Babylonian sources claim occurred at some point long before writing was invented.

Having discovered that the oral traditions of Freemasonry are the unwitting repository of so much accurate information of the past, we wondered if the idea of a global flood could be more than a legend. This spurred us to look into what is known of prehistory, and we were pleased to find that some of the greatest scholars in this area have already found what we discovered – that existing ideas are largely wrong. Professor Colin Renfrew, Disney Professor of Archaeology at Cambridge University, expressed it perfectly when he said:

The study of prehistory today is in a state of crisis.

To commence our new research, we posed ourselves three big questions:

1. Is it physically possible for the entire world to flood; and if so, what evidence is there that such a terrible thing has happened within human racial memory?

2. The oral traditions of Freemasonry claim that there was an advanced civilization before the coming of the Flood. Are these accounts just myth, or do they record a memory of a lost people?

3. Could all of this help us to construct a new paradigm of prehistory?

Perhaps we would never have started this complex mission, but for two things: The suggestion of leading geologist Dr Jack Miller of Cambridge University that a world flood is very possible; and the problems that Jupiter experienced in 1994.

Chapter One

THE PROBLEM OF PREHISTORY

THE COLLAPSE OF THE FIRST PARADIGM

Mankind is an enigma in search of its own solution.

The little planet we occupy has orbited a minor star on the fringes of a rather average galaxy in a universe of unimaginable vastness for over 4.5 billion years, yet our particular species of primate arrived on the scene very recently indeed. It is humbling to realize that, when we liken the age of the earth to the life-span of an average person, mankind has existed for less than the time it takes to say '*Homo sapiens*'.

Most people imagine that mankind evolved slowly and progressively from humble primate to advanced technologist, but there is no accepted theory for the development of the world we inhabit today. As we have already mentioned, Lord Renfrew, when Disney Professor of Archaeology at Cambridge University, stated that the study of prehistory is in a state of crisis:

> *Archaeologists all over the world have realized that much of prehistory, as written in the existing textbooks, is inadequate. Some of it quite simply wrong . . . What has come as a considerable shock, a development hardly foreseeable just a few years ago, is that prehistory as we have learnt it is based upon several assumptions which can no longer be accepted as valid. Several commentators have spoken recently of a 'revolution' in prehistory, of the same fundamental*

nature as a revolution in scientific thinking. It has been suggested, indeed, that the changes now at work in prehistory herald the shift to a 'new paradigm', an entire new framework of thought, made necessary by the collapse of the 'first paradigm'.[1]

The previously accepted paradigm of the origins of civilization assumed that advanced ideas sprang out of nowhere approximately 10,000 years ago. Across the world organized communities suddenly emerged, dogs became domesticated, boats were built, animal husbandry began, crops were planted, cities started to be erected and trading commenced.

This is all very recent indeed when we consider that manufactured stone tools recently found in the Gona River region of Ethiopia have been dated at between 2.5 million and 2.6 million years old. Knowing that tool technology has been around for such a huge period of time, the question we have to ask is: Why, after at least 100,000 generations of stagnating technology, did these 'ignorant cavemen' turn so suddenly into smart social creatures that gave rise to the great civilizations of the world? Roger Lewin, writing in *New Scientist* magazine, focused on the strangeness of the situation:

The invention and spread of agriculture is central to the history of humanity. For more than 100,000 years, humans subsisted in widely varied environments by foraging for food. Then, in a brief moment of prehistory starting about 10,000 years ago, people began to domesticate animals and plants in half a dozen 'centres of origin' in the Old and New Worlds.

Clearly, something is very wrong. The old theory of the development of civilization was formed out of assumptions made by Victorian observers and then built on by various experts at the beginning of the 20th century. The paradigm that became accepted grew and changed over time but a number of key points in human development were generally accepted until very recently. These beliefs included:

- Around 40,000 years ago modern man (*Homo sapiens sapiens*) appeared.

[1] Renfrew, Colin: *Before Civilization*, Penguin, 1978

- Around 12,000 years ago, Asiatic hunter-gatherers wandered across a land-bridge that then connected the Bering Strait, and settled an empty America.

- Around 10,000 years ago, organized farming communities began, dogs were domesticated, boats were built and trading started.

- Around 5,000 years ago, cities were invented in Sumer, and from there all the arts of civilization – architecture, specialization of labour, writing, mathematics, astronomy and record-keeping – spread out to civilize the rest of the world.

Over recent years archaeology has undergone a major revolution, with new scientific methods of analysis now available to replace the hypotheses of experts. Particularly important has been the huge improvement in our ability to date artefacts, which has shown that the key points above are simply incorrect. As a result, there is now a vacuum in our knowledge of prehistory.

OUT OF THE APES

So, where did human life start? Well, current thinking suggests that we started out as a microscopic blob that caught a cold!

Lynn Margulis of Boston University developed a theory that life as we know it first started as a disease, and that the genes we carry within us contain a symbiotic parasite.[2] The very first life on earth was simple single-celled creatures which were too inefficient biologically ever to develop into complex modern life-forms such as mammals. However, when they were infected by a simple bacterium, the combined inner chemistry of the two organisms allowed them to extract energy from oxygen. The breathing single-cell entities now had access to enough energy to grow into new organisms that were made up of many cells.

This breathing combination of cell and parasite has been immensely efficient at producing the essential components of cell growth. Every multi-cellular plant and animal on the planet today has mitochondria which can all be traced back to those original infected host cells, and both the human egg

2 Wills, Christopher: *The Runaway Brain*, Flamingo, 1994

and sperm cells contain mitochondria. During fertilization, the mitochondria of the sperm are not incorporated into the fertilized egg and consequently, mitochondrial genes are transmitted to offspring only by the mother, whose fertilized egg contains about 200,000 molecules of mitochondrial DNA (mDNA).

Over time, mutations occurred, so that the mitochondrial chromosomes of various human families gradually diverged and differences became more and more distinct over thousands of years. Because mDNAs do not recombine with each other, every human female retains an inbuilt coded record of her evolutionary history back to the dawn of our species, and beyond.

Geneticist Wesley Brown of the Howard Goodman Laboratory of the University of California realized that it should be theoretically possible to use mDNA to trace back all the linkages in the human species until he found the great-grandmother of all mitochondrial chromosomes, from which all others had descended. It also occurred to him that, in the process, he might reach so far back in time that the creature carrying the ancestral chromosome would not be human at all. Brown built his mitochondrial family tree and was surprised to pinpoint a relatively recent common female ancestor for all living humans. According to his calculations, every person on the planet today evolved from a small, mitochondrially monomorphic point somewhere between 180,000 and 360,000 years ago. In simple terms, this means that there was a single female from which all of mankind is descended. Understandably, Brown dubbed this unknown woman 'Mitochondrial Eve'.[3]

This was a staggering result. Human evolution is known to have taken many millions of years, yet just 200,000 or 300,000 years ago, there was a woman from whom all 6,000,000,000 people today have sprung. Allen Wilson, the leader of the research group which made this discovery, has always emphasized that this 'Mitochondrial Eve' had a small but unknown number of companions of both sexes who had contributed copies of their nuclear DNA to our gene pool but the implication is clear: all races of man are very close family members.

Our extended family is also much closer than most people realize. Molecular biologists have now identified from the study of DNA that our genes are about 98 per cent the same as the African apes. Sociologists have

[3] Wills, Christopher: *The Runaway Brain*, Flamingo, 1994

also established that every aspect of human social behaviour, from child beating to ice-cream craving is linked to some hidden evolutionary motive with a counterpart among every mammal, from lemurs to zebras.[4] Yet clearly we are very different.

Anthropologist James Shreeve explained the problem well when he said:

> *The fact is, human beings – modern humans,* Homo sapiens sapiens *– are behaviourally far, far away from being 'just another animal'. The mystery is where, how, and why change took place. There are no answers to be found in the vast bulk of hominid time on the planet. The gartel has been raised higher. An 'all-important transition' did occur, but it happened so close to the present moment that we are still reeling from it. Somewhere in the vestibule of history, just before we started keeping records on ourselves, something happened that turned a passably precocious animal into a human being.*[5]

The first creature officially categorized as 'man' – *Homo erectus* – appears to have migrated out of Africa between 1.7 and two million years ago, spreading out across the warm temperate zones of southern Europe and Asia as far as Indonesia. By 300,000 years ago, our ancestors had reached the colder areas as far north as the British Isles.

THE CAVEMAN MYTH

The image of ancient man is confused in the minds of many people today. Mention prehistoric man and the old stereotype of an excessively hirsute brute may come to mind.

But the truth could not be more different. Until very recently, fully modern man was considered to be only some 40,000 years old, and to have appeared from no known origin at about the same time that Neanderthal man disappeared. However, recent archaeological finds have shown that humans physically identical to ourselves co-existed with Neanderthal man for as long as 90,000 years. The debate as to whether our ancestors interbred with Neanderthals has been ongoing for many years.

Several scholars have argued that there must have been sexual relationships between two such similar forms of man; it would be against

[4] Shreeve, James: *The Neanderthal Enigma*, William Morrow and Co., 1995
[5] Shreeve, James: *The Neanderthal Enigma*, William Morrow and Co., 1995

human nature for there not to have been. Others have speculated that there might have been sexual encounters, but the two subspecies may have been too distant to produce offspring from such matings.

An answer to the vexing question of our relationship to Neanderthals seems to have been provided by the study of mDNA.

In 1997, ancient DNA was extracted from a Neanderthal specimen from the Feldhofer Cave of the Neander Valley near Düsseldorf in Germany. Matthias Krings, working in Svante Pääbo's laboratory at the University of Munich succeeded in piecing together a nucleotide sequence for 379 base pairs of maternally inherited mitochondrial DNA preserved in a 3.5-gram section of the specimen's right humerus. The results were then meticulously replicated by Anne Stone, working in Mark Stoneking's laboratory at Pennsylvania State University. When the Neanderthal mDNA sequence was compared with the corresponding region in modern humans and chimpanzees, the overall Neanderthal-human difference was approximately three times greater than the average difference among modern humans, but only about half as large as the human-chimpanzee difference. Because the Neanderthal sequence was so unlike any modern human sequence, many experts thought it highly unlikely that Neanderthals contributed to the human mDNA pool.[6]

So the evidence suggests that Neanderthals and modern humans diverged genetically between 500,000 and 600,000 years ago – around twice as far back in time as the 'Eve' bottleneck. Mark Stoneking and his colleagues expressed the bottom-line conclusion by saying:

> *These results indicate that Neanderthals did not contribute mitochondrial DNA to modern humans; Neanderthals are not our ancestors.*

Neanderthals may not be our ancestors, but neither were they were the near-ape ignoramuses of frequent depictions. In fact, a better way of thinking about these 'other' people has been well-expressed by one expert as follows:

> *If Neanderthal Man could be reincarnated and placed in a New York subway – provided that he were bathed, shaved, and dressed in*

[6] 'Book of the Year (1998): Anthropology and Archaeology', *Britannica Online*. <http://www.eb.com:180/cgi-bin/g?DocF=boy/98/L02405.html>

modern clothing – it is doubtful whether he would attract any more attention than some of its other denizens.[7]

If we accept that this is not a reflection on the subterranean population of New York, it does make an important point about our tendency to expect other, earlier forms of man to be rude and crude. The current definition of 'civilization' is rather restrictive and probably says more about the perceived supremacy of Europeans of the 19th century who applied the label 'savages' to any group who differed from their own Christian, technology-based world.

The reality is that Neanderthals had a slightly *larger* brain than the average modern human. Furthermore, they existed for a staggering 1.5 million years before disappearing some 25,000 years ago. They therefore had an immense amount of time to develop their own form of sophistication. Anyone who doubts that they were fully human needs only to study the beautiful works of art that they left behind, or take in the clear signs of ritual and social structure. It is now beyond doubt that later Neanderthals buried their dead with great care, often scattering the deceased with red ochre as well as supplying them with both tools and meat, presumably to assist their passage to 'the place beyond the grave'. The deceased were sometimes arranged in artificial postures known as 'flexed' or 'crouch' burials, in which the knees were drawn upwards and tied tight to the torso in a foetal position. We can not help but wonder whether this might have been connected with a belief in rebirth – placing the deceased in the position for arrival in the next world, or even their next worldly incarnation.

What might have been in the minds of these parallel people? – A people who once owned the earth, but of whom so little now remains? They must have loved life and respected death. Some Neanderthal bodies were buried wearing caps and cloaks covered in ornate beads, carved bracelets, pendants and, occasionally, pairs of mammoth tusks.[8] It struck us that items like these must have been of considerable value and the decision to bury them with the dead indicates powerfully the existence of religion, with an expectation of need in some kind of afterlife – otherwise, why waste precious manufactured items by leaving them in a grave? We know that many cultures, such as the Ancient Egyptians, equipped their deceased for the journey to the 'Duat' –

[7] Strauss, W.L. and Cave, A.J.E.:- 'Pathology and Posture of Neanderthal Man', *Quarterly Review of Biology*, 32 (1957), pp.348-363
[8] Walker, Alan and Shipman, Pat: *The Wisdom of the Bones*, Alfred A. Knopf, Inc., 1996

the land of the dead – so why should the same not apply to the Neanderthals?

There is also evidence of sheer human emotion. Some Neanderthal burial sites contain large amounts of ancient pollen around the body that can only have been created by the scattering of a copious number of flowers over the departed friend or relative.[9] The slender evidence we have of Neanderthal culture also shows signs of human love and caring. A 60,000-year-old site in Iraq's Zagros Mountains (that is, 30 times further back into history than the birth of Jesus Christ) provides an excellent example. Amongst the remains of nine Neanderthals, one skeleton shows clear signs that the individual had been severely injured many years before death, leaving him with head injuries, a withered arm and blindness in at least one eye. The substantial gap of time between being physically devastated and his eventual death demonstrates that he must have been fed and cared for by others. We can only conclude that Neanderthal groups must have developed a structure of social responsibility.

It is possible that Neanderthal culture may have reached a level not unlike certain current human groups, such as the Australian Aborigines, who shun technology, preferring their old ways based upon empathy with their environment.

For our previous books we had spent years researching the history of the Jewish people and we were fascinated to discover that the land that is now Israel has been an active centre for man for more than 100,000 years. Some of the earliest known remains of modern man were found in a cave at Qafzeh, just a stone's throw from the town centre of Nazareth. This cave contains the remains of both Neanderthals and modern man, but it is the sequence of layers of earth and the order of the fossilized skeletons that is so fascinating. Our direct ancestors were found at the deepest levels whilst the Neanderthals were found much higher up, proving beyond doubt that 'modern man' was there tens of thousands of years ahead of our fellow hominids.

Dating such old artefacts is not straightforward but there are techniques which give good results. The usual method of dating organic material is to measure carbon 14 content, but this ceases to be useful with artefacts that are 50,000 years old or more. However, other methods such as thermoluminescence (TL) and electron spin resonance (ESR) can be used to date older material.[10]

[9] Shreeve, James: *The Neanderthal Enigma*, William Morrow and Co., 1995
[10] Aitken, M.J.: *Science-based Dating in Archaeology*, Longman, 1990

In the early 1980s, Hélène Valladas, an archaeologist at the Centre for Low-Level Radioactivity of the French Atomic Energy Commission, used the TL method to date the human skeletons at Qafzeh as being an amazing 92,000 years old. Then Henry Schwarcz of McMaster University and his colleague Rainer Grün of Cambridge applied the ESR method to conclude that the skeletons were no less than 100,000, and more probably 115,000 years old.[11] It suddenly became very difficult for anyone to dispute that the first-known modern humans had been at the site of Nazareth 5,000 generations before the birth of Jesus Christ!

The Old Testament states that the first man created by God was Adam and it provides a genealogy through to Abraham. The Gospel of Matthew, in the New Testament, gives the genealogy from Abraham to Jesus himself. In all it adds up to 61 generations, but even allowing for the great ages attributed to some biblical characters, it seems that an awful lot of people have been forgotten somewhere down the line.

These fossilized skeletons found in that cave on the outskirts of Nazareth are anatomically identical to ourselves today. As in the case of the Neanderthal on the New York tube, if one of their children could be snatched by a raider in a time machine, that child could be brought up in a normal manner and potentially educated through university to exactly the same level as any person in the modern world.

Quite simply, all of the available evidence indicates that our species has not evolved for over 100,000 years. This raises the difficult question of why human social and technological development appears to have stagnated for so long. Tim White of the University of California, Berkeley, put the point very neatly when he said:

> *Nothing happens for hundreds of thousands of years. And that's normal for an animal. Human behaviour isn't like that. One thing you can count on about humans. They change.*

According to standard theory, virtually nothing changed until approximately 10,000 years ago. Then wham – everything changed!

Why?

[11] Schwarcz, H.P.:- 'ESR Dates for the Hominid Burial Site of Qafzeh in Israel', *Journal of Human Evolution* 17, 1988

THE BUILDING OF EARLY SOCIETIES

In the summer of 1998 Chris was driving between Qumran, on the Dead Sea and Jerusalem. The road rises from the lowest point on earth, 1,350 feet below sea level, to cross the Judaean Desert towards the ancient city of Jerusalem. However, a far older city lay just a few miles off Israel's Highway One, but one that was effectively out of bounds for Chris to visit. Indeed, when he had hired the car, the lady from Avis explained that the car insurance would be void if it were taken into this Palestinian city. This was a great pity because Jericho is now known to be the oldest living city in the world, having been almost continuously occupied for the last 11,000 years.

The original, small settlement had been constructed next to a perennial spring but around 10,000 years ago it suddenly developed into a town covering ten acres.[12] At around this time a huge stone wall and a 30-foot high tower with an internal staircase were constructed. This project would have required many workers, plus people to supply them with food, and it has been estimated that there may have been as many as 3,000 people living there.

For the first 2,000 years the small population is known to have kept wild animals, such as the gazelle, the fox and small ruminants, for its food supply. However, once the stone-built city had been established, the diet of the much increased population shifted in favour of new breeds of domesticated animals such as goats, sheep, pigs and cattle.

The reason for the development of a city at this location is not known but archaeological remains indicate that trade was very important to its inhabitants as far back as 10,000 years ago. Yet not so long ago, the academic world believed that the oldest cities in the world lay in Mesopotamia, with the 5,000-year-old city states of Sumer – the most famous being Ur, the city of Abraham.

Nonetheless, even back in 1929, when Sir Leonard Woolley wrote a book about his excavations in Mesopotamia, he expressed some doubts about the origins of the cities of Sumer.

> *There is nothing to show to what race the first inhabitants of Mesopotamia belonged . . . At a date which we cannot fix, people of a new race made their way into the valley, coming, whence we do not know, and settled down side by side with the old inhabitants. These*

[12] Oliphant, Margaret: *Atlas of the Ancient World*, Ebury Press, 1992

> *were the Sumerians . . .The Sumerians believed that they came into the country with their civilization already formed, bringing with them the knowledge of agriculture, of working in metal, of the art of writing –'since then,' said they, 'no new inventions have been made' – and if, as our excavations seem to show, there is a good deal of truth in that tradition . . . later research may well discover . . . where the ancestors of our Sumerians developed the first real civilization.*[13]

To this archaeologist the Sumerian cities appeared to spring out of nowhere with all their arts of civilization fully developed.

Surely, Woolley had to be right. Many of his contemporaries were happy to identify a hard-edged moment when civilization began, but things are rarely that simple. All change takes time and usually leaves a trail of incremental development. While there was undeniably a watershed in human development just under 10,000 years ago, some groups of people were undoubtedly advanced long before that.

For instance, in the village of Dolni Vestonice near the town of Mikulov in the Czech Republic is the site of a 26,000-year-old factory and trading station that has been fully described by James Shreeve. The remains of five buildings have been identified, outlined by traces of post-holes, limestone blocks and mammoth bones, as well as by the dense layers of artefacts on their floors. The largest of these ancient buildings is 50 feet by 30 feet, with five regularly distributed hearths around which are littered implements made of stone, bone and ivory, as well as manufactured ornaments. Outside are the remains of a substantial fence, and beyond that, a vast accumulation of mammoth bones piled up in a marsh.[14]

At one time it was thought that the mammoth remains were the carcasses of animals hunted down by the Palaeolithic villagers, but experts – such as Olga Soffer of the University of Illinois[15] – now believe that the people built their village next to the site of a natural mammoth graveyard. Like modern elephants, it seems that when older mammoths suffered from worn teeth they migrated to marshy land where there was softer vegetation. Eventually, too weak to leave the swampy ground, they would die there. Their bones made excellent building materials and, perhaps more importantly, once the

13 Woolley, L.: *Ur of the Chaldees, Seven Years of Excavation*, Pelican, 1929
14 Shreeve, James: *The Neanderthal Enigma*, William Morrow and Co., 1995
15 Shreeve, James: *The Neanderthal Enigma*, William Morrow and Co., 1995

inhabitants got their fires hot enough, the mammoth bones also made excellent fuel thanks to a calorific value higher than coke.

This source of high-energy fuel appears to give a clue to the real purpose of the site. Just yards away from the location of the huts is a disused quarry which reveals sheer, 100-foot-high walls of loess – a fine-grained, clay-like deposit that was once used for brickmaking. However, Shreeve points out that 26,000 years ago the inhabitants were using the same loess for quite a different purpose. Higher up the slope from the ancient buildings is a circle of posts thought to be the remains of a round hut, some 20 feet in diameter. At its centre was a horseshoe-shaped kiln made from earth and limestone.

More than 10,000 pieces of fired clay have been found, including large numbers of irregular pellets and fragments of heads and feet of animal figurines, some still bearing the fingerprints of their creators. Other ceramic objects, including parts of human figures, were also found in and around this factory.

The word 'factory' does appear to be appropriate. Surely no single community could possibly have need for such a prodigious output of pot figurines, so it seems reasonable to conclude that these goods were manufactured for the purpose of some kind of trade. The available evidence appears to confirm that people headed to this location from as far as 200 kilometres away. Furthermore, geological examination of the high quality stone tools found at the Dolni Vestonice site shows that they are not made from local raw materials: more than 80 per cent are flints traceable to distant sources, as much as a few hundred kilometres away in the north, the east and the south-west.[16]

The odd thing about this early Stone-Age ceramics factory is the very high level of what, at first, appears to be waste. Every amateur potter knows that it is essential to remove air bubbles and trapped water from a lump of clay before fashioning it into the desired form, and then allow it to dry out to a 'leather' hard state before firing. If this is not done, the item will almost certainly explode in the kiln, due to thermal expansion of the trapped air or water. The 10,000 items found at Dolni Vestonice are fragments of figures – a lion's head here, a woman's torso there – but not even a half-complete figure has been found around the kilns. This led the team investigating the site to look at the broken sections under an electron microscope at the

[16] Shreeve, James: *The Neanderthal Enigma*, William Morrow and Co., 1995

Smithsonian Institute in Washington DC. They found that the ceramic items in the huts had been broken after manufacture but those in the kilns had exploded from thermal shock whilst being fired.

This absence of any complete figure amongst all the finds suggested to the team that there was something wrong. However, experimentation with the local loess showed that it was unusually resistant to thermal shock, which made it even more puzzling that these ancient potters failed so often. Pamela Vandiver of the Smithsonian was clearly puzzled when she said, 'One would have to try very hard to explode objects moulded from this stuff.' Then Olga Soffer concluded, 'Either we are dealing with the most incompetent potters the world has ever seen, or else these things were shattered on purpose.'[17]

The team deduced that the figures may never have been intended to be kept – their dramatic destruction in the horseshoe-shaped kiln could actually have been the desired result. Perhaps the moment of violent disintegration was the climax to some religious or magical ritual. It struck us that if this were the case, the figures could have been used rather as a voodoo doll is sometimes used today, whereby a small model is made in the likeness of an opponent and then subjected to maltreatment, in the expectation that the living individual will suffer accordingly. If so, the desired outcome really was to see the modelled image explode miraculously and satisfyingly in the flames; if the figurine survived the test, it was taken to the accommodation huts below and discarded as a failed attempt to gain power over another. The skilful potter would have been able to control the result, and it seems probable that these craftsmen were viewed as priests or shamans who produced the outcome that they thought the 'customer' deserved.

Nonetheless, whatever was going on at this site 26,000 years ago, it points to a society that was far more advanced than it had any right to be, according to standard theories of human development.

ROCKING THE CRADLE OF CIVILIZATION

Not so long ago Europe was considered to have a far younger civilization than those of the Middle East or Asia. Prehistorians of the early 20th century thought that all major advances in Europe were directly caused by influences from the Near East, brought to the West either by migrating peoples or by trading.

[17] Shreeve, James: *The Neanderthal Enigma*, William Morrow and Co., 1995

Typical of this attitude to the chronology of prehistoric Europe was Gordon Childe's 1939 article entitled 'The Orient and Europe', in which he laid down the stages that explained Europe's civilization as a natural spread from the East:

> *1) Civilization in the Orient is extremely ancient.*
>
> *2) Civilizations can be diffused.*
>
> *3) Elements of civilization must have diffused from the Orient to Europe.*
>
> *4) The diffusion of historically dated Oriental types provides a basis for bringing prehistoric Europe within the framework of historical chronology.*[18]
>
> *5) Prehistoric European cultures are poorer than contemporary European cultures, i.e. civilization is later in Europe than in the East.*

There was at that time no way of dating the megalithic structures of Europe, so everyone assumed that all European prehistory was later than the 3000 BC dating of the start of Egyptian records. Then, in 1955, a physicist called William Libby discovered the technique of radiocarbon dating and upset the whole house of cards.[19] Libby was awarded a Nobel Prize for the development of this technique of independently dating artefacts.

His idea is simple in concept but quite difficult in practice. It is based on the fact there are three different types of carbon atom. By far the most common type is carbon 12, but a very small number of carbon atoms have extra neutrons in the atom. These isotopes, as they are called, come in two types: carbon 13 and carbon 14. Carbon 14 is radioactive, formed when cosmic rays hit nitrogen atoms high in the atmosphere. This radioactive atom behaves just like any other carbon atom. It combines with oxygen to make carbon dioxide, is taken up by the photosynthesis of plant life and is

[18] Childe, V.G.: 'The Orient and Europe', *American Journal of Archaeology*, vol. 43, p.10, 1939

[19] Libby, W. R.: *Radiocarbon Dating*, University of Chicago Press, 1955

then in turn eaten by animals and taken into their bodies. This cycle continues as long as a plant or animal is alive.[20]

However, the carbon 14 atom is unstable. It was originally formed from a nitrogen atom, and occasionally a carbon 14 atom will give up the extra energy it received from the cosmic rays and revert to being just an ordinary nitrogen atom again. About one per cent of all the carbon 14 atoms in a sample turn into non-radioactive nitrogen every 83 years. So after 5,730 years the original number of atoms in the sample will have reduced by half. This is called the half-life of the isotope. It also implies that after 11,460 years, the number of atoms will have reduced to one quarter of the original number. Thus, every 5,730 years, the number of remaining radiocarbon atoms halves. It is this known rate of decay which enables radiocarbon measurements to be used to date objects.

If it is known what proportion of the carbon atoms in an object were originally radioactive, it is quite straightforward to work out, from the proportion left, how long the carbon 14 atoms have been turning back into their original nitrogen. Libby originally assumed that because the rate of cosmic ray bombardment was roughly constant, a state of dynamic balance would be created in any living object where the decay of atoms would be matched by the intake of fresh radiocarbon. This equilibrium level would be a balance between the loss by radioactive decay and the production by cosmic rays. A living organism would be continually exchanging its carbon atoms with those of the global reservoir and so its level of radiocarbon would stay the same. Once this cycle stops, either when the organism died or in the case of wood when the cellulose molecules of the growth rings formed, then the concentration of radiocarbon atoms starts to decline. By measuring the remaining radiocarbon in a sample, it is possible to tell when it stopped exchanging carbon with its environment. The technique is a very effective dating methodology up to about 60,000 years, when there are no longer enough radiocarbon atoms left to take an accurate measurement.

REDATING THE MEGALITHIC SITES OF EUROPE

By the end of the 1960s, many radiocarbon dates had been obtained for prehistoric sites all over Europe, and the results started to pose problems for

[20] Aitken, M.J.: *Science-based Dating in Archaeology*, Longman, 1990

the conventional view that rough stone structures of western Europe were crude copies of the architecture of Sumer and Egypt. These new radiocarbon dates pushed the date back to well before 3000 BC, which was a little early for Childe's Oriental theory but still within the dates of the earliest Sumerian cities.[21]

However, one scientist, Professor Hans Suess of the University of California, was not happy with the standard assumptions about radiocarbon dating, particularly Libby's assumption about the rate of uptake of radiocarbon. He thought the effects of burning coal and oil (fossil fuels) since the Industrial Revolution would have changed atmospheric radiocarbon. Fossil fuel releases carbon 14 which decayed millions of years ago, so diluting the carbon 14 proportion and making items seem younger than they really are.

In addition, atmospheric nuclear weapons testing during the Cold War period caused the creation of several tons of carbon 14, which would also change the estimates of the age of objects.[22] Suess created a new calibration curve for carbon 14 on the basis that once a tree has formed a growth ring the wood in that ring stops replacing its carbon 14 and so the radiocarbon clock starts to tick. Using a technique called Dendrochronology, which is counting the growth rings on trees, he could accurately date the time the growth ring was formed and then measure its carbon 14 content. Assessing the wood of bristlecone pines, the world's oldest trees, he constructed an accurate calibration curve for the concentration of carbon 14 in the atmosphere for the past 10,000 years.[23] His calibration curves for the period of the Cold War he confirmed using samples of malt whisky and – for the Industrial Revolution, samples of vintage wine![24]

This new, highly accurate calibration curve has been used to redate the megalithic stone monuments of western Europe, and they were found to be far older than the Sumerian and Egyptian cities. The implications of this were devastating for Gordon Childe's view of prehistory given earlier. Indeed, summed up by Colin Renfrew: the understanding of prehistory was completely changed:

> *'Suddenly and decisively the impressive megalithic tombs of western Europe are set earlier than any comparable monuments in the world.*

[21] Mackie, E.: *The Megalith Builders*, Phaidon Press, 1977
[22] Aitken, M.J.: *Science-based Dating in Archaeology*, Longman, 1990
[23] Suess, H.E. and Berger: R., *Radiocarbon Dating*, University of California Press, 1970
[24] Aitken, M.J.: *Science-based Dating in Archaeology*, Longman, 1990

There are no stone-built monuments anywhere approaching them in antiquity. Perhaps even more remarkable, some of these underground burial chambers, with their roofs of stone, are preserved entire, so that we can enter them and stand inside a stone chamber which looks today just as it did more than 5,000 years ago . . . Now the paradox is with us again: that such impressive monuments were created many centuries before the Pyramids by barbarians who lacked even the use of metal. The urgent task confronting us is to explain just how these monuments did come to be built, if it was not by colonists from the early civilizations of the Near East.'[25]

As we have mentioned, the European 'barbarians' had built and worked the pottery complex of Dolni Vestonice many thousands of years before Jericho, the oldest Middle Eastern city, had even been thought of. As the facts uncovered by archaeology were tested by the new scientific dating methods, the European paradigm of prehistory crumbled slowly into nothingness.

But other academic disciplines were turning their attention to the problems of understanding prehistory, with equally disturbing effects.

THE POWER OF LANGUAGE

It seems obvious that people as organized as those at the figurine factory at Dolni Vestonice must have had language in order to facilitate such a complex interaction among a large number of individuals. No one can be sure when language first began, and even the mechanism behind this key human skill is hotly debated. William Noble and Iain Davidson of the University of New England have argued that all human languages can be traced back at least 32,000 years, based on the assumption that it was only then that iconic objects such as sculptures and cave paintings first appeared.[26]

They argue that until people were able to use symbols to represent reality, they would not be capable of developing language, as language itself is only an advanced form of symbolic representation. So the earliest evidence of language has to be evidence of symbols used in painting and sculpture. Their dating of the earliest use of symbols is now known to be rather modest, as

[25] Renfrew, C.: *Before Civilization*, Jonathan Cape, 1973
[26] Wills, Christopher: *The Runaway Brain*, Flamingo, 1994

many works of art several thousand years older than this have since been discovered.

There is enough evidence available for us to know that humans have been making modelled images for a very long time indeed. Ivory artefacts are known to have been made throughout Europe and elsewhere more than 40,000 years ago, and complex figures such as a man with a lion's head carved from mammoth ivory has been carbon-dated at between 30,000 and 34,000 years old. At the time that the factory at Dolni Vestonice was in full swing 'Venus' figurines were popular from what is now western France to central Russia. One such 'Venus' figure, found in the ashes of a hearth of a hut at Dolni Vestonice, was a typically heavy-breasted and big-hipped representation of the female form. The purpose of such statuettes cannot be known for sure but many authorities believe that they may have represented a goddess figure of procreation and wellbeing.

Extremely ancient though these 'Venus' figures are, they are young compared with one found at Berekhat Ram by Israeli archaeologists. A stone that had been naturally formed to have an appearance of a female figure bears marks to show that its shape was improved by a human hand more than 230,000 years ago![27]

The ability to communicate abstract thoughts through speech must surely have been the most important advance in all of human development. Steven Pinker, a psycholinguist at the Massachusetts Institute of Technology (MIT), has a clear view about the nature of language:

> *People know how to talk in more or less the sense that spiders know how to spin webs . . . language is no more a cultural invention than is upright posture.*[28]

Probably the most prominent proponent of language being an innate ability, rather than a cultural one, is fellow MIT man Noam Chomsky. He challenged the prevailing wisdom of behaviourists back in 1957 when he published his book, *Syntactic Structures*. The behaviourists' view was that nothing could exist in the mind that hadn't been created by personal experience. Chomsky asserted that because many of the sentences that

[27] Rudgley, R.: *Lost Civilizations of the Stone Age*, Century, 1998
[28] Pinker, Steven: *The Language Instinct*, Harper Perennial Library, 1995

humans utter are a novel combination of words, it follows that the brain must contain a program that can assemble an infinite number of sentences from a finite lexicon, rather than being shaped just by experience. He also observed that children rapidly learn grammatical structure without formal instruction and are able to interpret novel sentences well before they are two years old. Children must therefore be innately equipped with a common plan to grammars of all languages. Chomsky called this a 'Universal Grammar'.

This inbuilt ability for the application of grammar is not restricted to speech, for many people who cannot talk can still hold fluent and complex conversations at normal speed using sign language. These non-verbal languages for the deaf or dumb are not a simple manual translation of dominant spoken language but fully fledged languages in their own right, with their own syntax, grammar and vocabulary.

A team led by Laura Petitto of McGill University recently made an interesting discovery when conducting a study of deaf children born to signing families. They found that deaf babies 'babbled' with their hands in just the way that normal babies did with their mouths. These babies learned in the normal manner, starting with repeated hand movements instead of regularly repeating the same sound such as 'la, la, la, la'. Petitto concluded that there must be something very fundamental about language acquisition.[29]

There is clearly much more to language than the ability to generate modulated sounds from a voice box. If it is indeed as natural for humans to speak as it is to walk upright, our species must be further away from primates than we ever imagined. Steven Pinker is a champion of natural selection, arguing that spoken language began to emerge very early in human prehistory before evolving to a point where it became a fundamental human instinct. He turned prevailing logic smartly on its head by reasoning that humans did not develop language because they evolved big brains; our brains got bigger as a result of the growing demands of the elaborate structures that underlie language. In short, language is at the root of all our higher cerebral achievements.

Surely, Pinker has to be right. In our own experience it is certainly true that some mentally handicapped people with very low IQ levels learn to walk upright and speak their native tongue to a reasonable degree, even though

[29] Walker, Alan and Shipman, Pat: *The Wisdom of the Bones*, Alfred A. Knopf, Inc., 1996

they never master infinitely less complex acquired skills, such as washing or dressing themselves. This observable fact seems to confirm Pinker's claim that language operates at an instinctive level just as much as walking on two legs. We must all be born with some kind of cognitive matrix into which the vocal sounds of any language can slot quickly and easily, so all a child has to learn is the sounds themselves rather than the mechanism for using them. This would explain why young children can learn a second, or even a third, language at amazing speed if placed in an environment that requires it.

If Steven Pinker is right about our brain size being due to the demands of language, *Homo sapiens sapiens* and our cousins *Homo sapiens neanderthalis* must have been communicating with speech for a very long time indeed. We know that our own ancestors had brains the same size as ours today (normally between 1,300 and 1,500 cc) over 100,000 years ago, and Neanderthals had slightly larger brains. So it seems reasonable to estimate that rudimentary language may have occurred twice as far back in time; more than 200,000 years ago. If this was the case, it compounds the puzzle of why it took humans so long to develop the social structure that we call civilization.

It was once thought that we could never know much about the history of mankind before the advent of writing, but new techniques are extending our knowledge rapidly. One of the most important methods of understanding the movements of ancient peoples is the study of the interconnectivity of different spoken languages.

It has been estimated that there may be as many as 10,000 different languages in the world today. Most people probably imagine that these languages exist because populations were fairly isolated and each region built its own communications system independently of everyone else. However, nothing could be further from the truth.

It is 200 years since Sir William Jones discovered that Sanskrit is related to Latin and Greek, which led to the identification of a group of related languages now known as the Indo-European group of languages. Indo-European is the linguistic superfamily that includes nearly all of the languages spoken in modern Europe. One leading figure, Joseph Greenberg, has proposed a macro-family he has called Eurasiatic, covering Indo-Eurpean, Uralic-Yukaghir, Altaic, Chichchi-Kamchatkan and Eskimo-Aleut which he suggests is the common ancestor of the languages of most of Europe and North America. This 'ancestral-language' concept has been further developed by other linguists such as Vadislav Illich-Svtych and Aron

Dolgopolsky to show links with Dravidian, Kartvelian, Nilo-Sharan and Niger-Kordofanian. They have dubbed this root language Nostratic.[30]

The startling conclusion of this work is that the Middle East, Europe and America all originally shared a common language. Dolgopolsky observed that in the languages based on Proto-Indo-European there are many common words associated with agriculture and husbandry, suggesting that Proto-Indo-Europeans were a Neolithic people with a food-producing economy. By contrast, the Proto-Nostratic lexical stock did not have these words at all but did have terms associated with hunting and food-gathering, suggesting that agriculture and animal husbandry were more recent than the point at which the Proto-Nostratic people left south-west Asia prior to the Neolithic revolution.[31]

To use the words of anthropologist Richard Rudgley, the consequences of the Nostratic hypothesis are mind-boggling. The root language must be more than 10,000 years old and is likely to be nearer to 15,000 years old. It is simply amazing that such correspondences should exist as far afield as the deserts of southern Africa, the Amazon rainforest, the Arctic and the cities of Europe – all still retaining links from a remote time when they were all part of the same tongue.[32]

Linguist Merrit Ruhlen has gone one step further and proposed that a common language once spanned the entire world. He said of this foundation language, which he calls Proto-Global:

> *What if Bengtson and I are right, and the linguistic similarities we have uncovered really do represent traces of a single earlier language family? . . . What seems to me the most probable explanation for the linguistic data, as they are presently known, is that current linguistic diversity derives from the appearance of behaviourally modern people forty or fifty thousand years ago. While anatomically modern humans may have appeared in Africa before 100,000 BC these people did not behave like us. That in itself may indicate their more rudimentary linguistic skills. Several scholars have in fact suggested that the 'sapiens explosion' as it is sometimes called, involved the development of fully modern human language as recently as 40,000 years ago.*[33]

30 *New Scientist*, 17 October 1998

31 Dolgopolsky, D.: 'Linguistic Prehistory', *Cambridge Archaeological Journal,* 5/2, 1995, pp.268-71

32 Rudgley, R.: *Lost Civilisations of the Stone Age*, Century, 1998

33 Ruhlen, M.: 'Linguistic Evidence for Human Prehistory', *Cambridge Archaeological Journal,* 5/2, 1995, pp.265-8

As a final thought on the use of linguistics to infer information about prehistory, the technique has been promoted by Colin Renfrew, who is quoted as saying that to ignore these linguistic findings would be to miss out on a completely new tool for the prehistorian to use. After looking at the detailed findings of Ruhlen *et al.* Renfrew proposed his own date of 15,000 BP (i.e. Before Present; 1950, defined as the base year for radiocarbon date) as the earliest likely date for Nostratic.

THE ANCIENT HISTORIES

Alexander Marshack is one of many observers who have focused on the problem of man's amazingly recent and uneven development. As a science writer, he became interested in the origins of civilization when commissioned by NASA to write an historical perspective of the progress of man culminating in the moon landings of 1969. Over the next 30 years he became an expert on prehistoric science and the origins of scientific artefacts. Back in 1972 Marshack wrote:

> *Searching through the historical record for the origins of the evolved civilizations, I was disturbed by the series of 'suddenlies'. Science . . . had suddenly begun with the Greeks . . . bits of near science, mathematics and astronomy had suddenly appeared among the Mesopotamians, the Egyptians, the early Chinese and much later in the Americas. Civilization itself had appeared suddenly with the cuneiform of Mesopotamia and the hieroglyphs of Egypt; agriculture . . . had apparently begun suddenly some ten thousand years ago with a relatively short period of time . . . near agriculture; art and decoration had begun suddenly some thirty or forty thousand years ago during the Ice Age, apparently at the point during which modern man walked into Europe to displace Neanderthal man.*[34]

The biggest problem of all is the apparent explosion of technology that appears to have suddenly arrived just under 10,000 years ago. How could unconnected people around the world so suddenly, and so simultaneously, develop agriculture and start to build cities? Where could these people have

[34] Marshack, A.: *The Roots of Civilisation*, McGraw Hill, 1972

got the 'blueprint' for their science and social order? There are an awkward questions that many scholars have carefully avoided because there are only three answers, all of which are equally uncomfortable:

1. External stimulus. Visitors from outer space landed on Earth and taught our forefathers the wonders of agriculture and science.

2. A random series of events. It was just a huge coincidence that mankind across the globe spontaneously developed all of these great advances at the same time.

3. Pre-existent knowledge. The knowledge of such advanced matters had already evolved naturally over a far greater period of time, but for some reason the archaeological evidence is missing.

The idea that extraterrestrial visitors have been here before is in vogue at the moment, with several popular writers putting forward this argument. Although many people – including ourselves – have difficulty with this general hypothesis, it would be wrong to dismiss it as a complete impossibility. However, even if there has been extraterrestrial contact in the past, there are no grounds to attribute all human success to an unknown alien contact.

The suggestion that people around the world spontaneously emerged from ignorance to intellect in an evolutionary 'blink of an eye' is wholly unscientific and at odds with new information. The fact that this supposed solution has been accepted for generations has blunted our critical faculties. If such a theory was put forward today for the first time, it would be immediately rejected by all serious scholars on the grounds of its extreme statistical improbability.

Most of what we have been taught about the distant past of mankind is based upon the opinions of 19th- and early 20th-century scholars who studied the remaining physical evidence of extinct peoples and then created a 'best-shot' impression of what must have been the case. Their conclusions sometimes went way beyond the limitations of the available evidence, yet their often imaginative views became accepted as fact. The general approach of scholars of the Victorian period was at best Europeanist, and at worst cultural racism. One English naturalist recorded his disgust at a group of Fuegians who were shouting at him from a canoe:

> *Viewing such men, one can hardly make one's self believe that they are fellow creatures, and inhabitants of the same world. We often try to imagine what pleasures in life some of the lower animals can enjoy: how much more reasonably the same questions may be asked concerning these barbarians!*

Surprisingly, these words were written by a young man called Charles Darwin – who later went on to become one of the most forward thinking men of his age.

The prejudices of the Anglo-Saxon world are slowly breaking down; indeed, in some areas 'political correctness' is arguably over-compensating for the arrogancies of the past 200 years. There are now some very balanced people leading the thinking in anthropology and archaeology, but in the general world something of a split has appeared between 'establishment' people and 'New Agers'. Those in the first group assume that standard explanations are somehow intrinsically factual, and prefer to dismiss ideas which are not incremental developments of their existing world-view as over-imaginative folly. The people on the other side of the philosophical fence often deride current mainstream views as blind conventions or even conspiracies of disinformation, whilst revering the ancient past as a lost 'golden age' when true wisdom prevailed.

In our opinion, it is unhealthy to lean too strongly in either direction, because both approaches have value. There are now a number of objective and open-minded experts who are confident enough to admit that recently accepted ideas are more likely to be wrong than right. So, if some of the old ideas of 'official' historians are now being reviewed or even discarded, perhaps it is time to reconsider the possibility that there might be some truth in ancient folk histories. These stories occur in all established cultures, having been preserved over great periods of time by means of oral tradition from generation to generation.

As we demonstrated in our previous books, the rituals used today by Freemasons are the only major living oral tradition of the Western world. They are based on once-secret information that is older than anything in the New Testament, having been taken directly from Jewish traditions that predated the fall of Jerusalem in AD 70. Although they have been deliberately changed by English Freemasons for political reasons over the last 300 years, the story of a major near extinction event, the biblical Flood, has always been at the very heart of these rituals. The first line of our first book, *The Hiram Key*, quoted the *Daily Telegraph* of 1871 which said: '. . . Freemasonry dates from before the Flood . . .'

Before they were deliberately censored by English Freemasons in the 18th and 19th centuries, the higher rituals of Freemasonry unequivocally stated that they preserved the arcane knowledge of the Jewish High Priesthood, which was ancient even at the time of King David and King Solomon.[35] As we have already mentioned, these Masonic rituals, which are memorised word-for-word by Freemasons, still make frequent reference to a worldwide Flood, and an entire order is dedicated to preserving verbal traditions about Noah, the builder of the biblical Ark that survived the deluge. There are also lists of characters from a civilization that is said to have existed before the catastrophic deluge, such as Tubal-Cain – the man who, Masons are told, invented agriculture and the ploughshare.

The oldest records of rituals are those of the original Ancient and Accepted Scottish Rite of Freemasonry, which have not been in general use since 1813. Throughout these old rituals there is frequent reference to the biblical character called Enoch, with Masonic degrees devoted entirely to him, telling his story as the man who was told by the angel Uriel that he must save the secrets of civilization from a global disaster.

Stories of a global flood are so widespread across the world that it is hard to dismiss them all as mere coincidence. Could there actually have been such a monumental disaster that wiped out a previous civilization – as described in ancient Freemasonic ritual? Such a cataclysm could certainly make sense of the apparent contradiction in the emerging evidence of man's early development.

However, we could not understand how all of the world could possibly be flooded when it has a fixed amount of water. Soon, though, thanks to a chance conversation with Dr Jack Miller, a leading geologist from Cambridge University, we would have our attention directed towards an entirely different field of study.

Our analysis of the failings of prehistoric theory seemed to be pointing towards the pre-existence of knowledge. Given that modern techniques of post-rationalizing supposed histories from the remnants of past peoples have so spectacularly failed, perhaps it is time to examine the 'official' histories of real people to reconstruct our origins.

[35] Knight, C. and Lomas, R.: *The Hiram Key*, Century, 1996

Across the world there are ancient oral traditions that claim to record extremely distant events. They have been studied by anthropologists but largely ignored by archaeologists, who seem to believe that unearthing artefacts is the only legitimate means of understanding distant peoples. Many oral traditions contain symbolic elements that may themselves be clues to real events, so it might be wrong to dismiss such stories as tribal myths.

Given all this information, our starting point had to be the ancient stories of Enoch contained in the rituals of Freemasonry, the Bible and other Jewish texts.

CONCLUSION

Technological developments over the last 30 years have thrown our understanding of prehistory into disarray.

Neanderthal man, often depicted as our ancestor, diverged genetically from the modern human race between 500,000 and 600,000 years ago. About 300,000 years ago the human population was reduced to a very small number, so much so that one single female from this time became a common ancestor to all living humans.

New archaeological discoveries have found art objects as old as 250,000 years, suggesting that language itself may be older than had once been thought. This is confirmed by linguists who have shown that language has long been innate in humans.

Technological development is older than most people realise. There is hard evidence of a 26,000-year-old manufacturing economy in Europe.

Improvements in the technology of dating have shown the megalithic stone structures of western Europe to be far earlier than the cities of Sumer and Egypt.

Experts believe that there was a single global language which may have existed as recently as 15,000 years ago.

Ten thousand years ago there was a sudden, world-wide leap forward in technology which cannot be explained in terms of normal incremental change.

It seems possible that the development of human technology is subject to occasional catastrophic changes which interrupt an underlying process of steady incremental change.

Chapter Two

THE ANCIENT STORY OF ENOCH

WHO WAS ENOCH?

In 1996 we published our first book, *The Hiram Key*, which put forward an argument that Rosslyn chapel in Scotland was not a Christian building at all, but a Knights Templar-inspired copy of the ruined Jerusalem Temple. We also argued that it was built to house important scrolls that are known to have been placed under the Jerusalem Temple prior to AD 70 and which, we maintained, were subsequently excavated and moved to Scotland in AD 1140. A number of leading scholars from British and American universities have agreed with our assessment that the building is a deliberate copy of the Herodian Temple.

In the summer of 1996 we visited Rosslyn in the company of Dr Jack Miller, a head of studies in Geology at Cambridge University, and Edgar Harborne, a very senior Freemason and a one-time research fellow at Cambridge in Military Science.

Jack was extremely interested in the geology of the stone used in the construction of Rosslyn, which he identified as being of exactly the same stratum as that found in Jerusalem. He also demonstrated that our opinion about the west wall being a copy of a ruin, had to be correct. After spending our first evening together looking over the Chapel in detail we retired to the Roslin Glen Hotel for a meal and a few drinks. As the evening progressed we told Jack how we had found that the rituals of Freemasonry contained a great deal of historical information, despite the fact that the United Grand

Lodge of England continues to insist that their rites are simply invented nonsense.

We then told Jack that we had been unable to understand why the biblical character of Enoch, and the Flood itself, were so central to the oldest forms of Freemasonry. The story of the Flood was, we said, clearly fictitious, so . . . Jack's response was immediate and unexpected. 'Why do you think that the story of the Flood is fiction?'

'Well . . . because there isn't enough water to flood the whole world – unless it is just a reference to their Sumerian "world" of the Tigris-Euphrates basin,' replied Chris, looking both surprised and intimidated by Jack's odd question.

'You're thinking in terms of a closed system,' Jack said, holding his hands to form a sphere. 'You need to change your frame of reference. There is some new work on this subject which I think will give you a new way of thinking about the biblical Flood.'

We were amazed and excited to hear that yet another part of Freemasonic legend might be based in historical fact. Jack promised to dig out some references from geological journals and forward them to us.

As soon as we received this information, we knew we had to study the curious figure of Enoch and the stories of the Flood in as much detail as possible.

ENOCH IN THE BIBLE

There is not a great deal of information about Enoch in the Bible, but what there is mostly occurs in the first part of Genesis.

The first five books of the Bible, which start with Genesis, are called the *Torah* in Judaism, although Christian Old Testament scholars refer to them as the *Pentateuch*. These stories are generally taken as a collection of myths, saga material, cult legends, legal texts and poems all woven together into a written document, possibly as late as the 6th century BC.

The formalization of the written *Torah* brought together ancient Jewish oral traditions and attempted to explain how the God who made heaven and earth had selected the Jews as His chosen people. The problem facing this group of compilers was the question of how the various stories might fit together into a cohesive whole. Various groups had each preserved their own traditions and these had to be incorporated into the new, official big picture.

The first reference to Enoch occurs in Genesis 4:16-23 where the following genealogy is given from Adam to Enoch and on to Noah, the man who built the ark to survive the Flood:

Adam

Cain

Enoch

Irad

Mehujael

Methusael

Lamech

Noah

The next reference to Enoch occurs in Genesis 5: 21-29, and here it gives a very different genealogy for him. The originators of this tradition might not have been happy to have this hero be descended from Cain, the first murderer who killed his brother Abel. He was therefore given a different lineage through Seth, the third son of Adam and Eve, and was said not to have suffered death, but to have walked with God before being taken directly into heaven by Him.

It is interesting to note that Methuselah, the longest living of them all, appears to have perished in the Flood.

These are the only two references to Enoch in the Old Testament, but there are a further three references in the New Testament. In Chapter 3 of the Gospel of Luke, there is a genealogy of Jesus, via his father Joseph right back to Enoch, and therefore to Adam. This genealogy has struck many people as being an odd thing to quote, because if Jesus was born the son of God and a earthly virgin, then the genealogy of his adoptive father has no relevance at all.

In this genealogy, Jesus is linked to a number of important characters who are held to be of great importance in Freemasonry, in particular to

Zerubbabel, David, Boaz, Noah, Lamech and Enoch. Luke's Gospel also tells us that Jesus' mother, Mary, was from a priestly bloodline with direct descent from Aaron (the Egyptian high priest) who was the brother of Moses. Luke 1:5 says that Elizabeth, wife of Zacharias and mother of John the Baptist, is of the line of Aaron:

> *There was in the days of Herod, the king of Judaea, a certain priest named Zacharias, of the course of Abia: and his wife was of the daughters of Aaron, and her name was Elizabeth.*

Then, in Luke 1:36, when Gabriel is telling Mary she is about to give birth to Jesus, we are told that Mary is a cousin to Elizabeth and so also of the line of Aaron:

> *And, behold, thy cousin Elizabeth, she hath also conceived a son in her old age:*

We learn a little more about the mysterious figure of Enoch from the New-Testament book of Jude. In Jude 1:13-14 there we are told that Enoch prophesied a great catastrophe which would befall mankind if they did not stop behaving in an ungodly manner:

> *Raging waves of the sea, forming out of their own shame, wandering stars, to whom is reserved the blackness of darkness for ever. And Enoch also, the seventh from Adam, prophesied of these saying, Behold the Lord commeth with ten thousand of his saints.*

Obviously the author of Jude does not accept the tradition that Enoch was third from Adam, via the murderer Cain, but agrees with the genealogy which Luke attributes to Jesus via his father Joseph. Yet here we are told that Enoch prophesied about raging waves of the sea and wandering stars, which are *not* mentioned in the Old Testament.

The third reference to Enoch in the New Testament is in Paul's Letter to the Hebrews where in 11:5 he says:

> *By faith Enoch was translated that he should not see death; and was not found, because God had translated him: for before his translation he had this testimony, that he pleased God.*

THE MASONIC ENOCH

Although the average Freemason is unaware of it, the story of Enoch and the global Flood is of great importance to Masonic ritual. The earliest known written Masonic reference to Enoch comes from two manuscripts known as the *Indigo Jones* and the *Wood* manuscripts. Although these documents were written down at the beginning of the reign of James I of England, the Ancient Charges that they contain are generally agreed to be several hundred years older.

King James VI of Scotland had been made a Freemason at the Lodge of Perth and Scoon in 1601, and in 1603 he became King James I of England. It was he who authorized a new English translation of the Bible, known as the King James Version, to avoid what he described as 'popish errors' in previous translations. The sequence of events was as follows:

1601 James VI becomes a Freemason

1603 James VI of Scotland became James I of England

1604 James announces the creation of a new translation of the Bible.

1607 The author of the *Indigo Jones Manuscript* writes down the verbal tradition of the Origins of the Mason's Craft in one of the earliest versions still known of what Freemasons call the Old Charges.

1610 J. Whytestones writes down a broadly similar version of the Old Charges and history of the Craft which he says he has transcribed from an older document, which has since been lost.

1611 The King James Bible is published and authorised for public worship.

This traditional history of the origins of the Craft of Masonry appeared at just the time that the teachings of Freemasonry had been brought to England by James and his Scottish Court. It places great importance on the achievements of the Pre-Flood peoples and claims that all the seven sciences of the *quadrivium* – Grammar, Rhetoric, Logic, Arithmetic, Geometry, Music and Astronomy – were highly developed before the time of the Flood; and that the people who developed them foresaw the coming of the Flood and preserved the details of these sciences on two pillars, one built to withstand fire and the other to withstand water. In addition, both documents claim that the Egyptians did not develop civilization for themselves but instead found these secret pillars after the Flood and used the knowledge they contained to create their vast achievements.

The *Indigo Jones Manuscript* gives details of the steps taken to preserve the knowledge of science through the expected disaster:

> *YOU ask me how this Science was Invented My Answer is this: That before the General Deluge, which is commonly Called NOAH'S Flood, there was a Man called LAMECH, as you may read in IV. Chapter of Genesis; who had two Wives, the One called ADA, the other ZILLA; BY ADA, he begat two SONS, JABAL and JUBAL, by ZILLA, he had One SON called TUBALL and a Daughter called Naamah: These four Children found the beginning of all crafts in the World: JABAL found out GEOMETRY, and he Divided Flocks of Sheep, He first built a House of Stone and Timber.*
>
> *HIS Brother JUBAL found the ART of MUSICK He was the Father of all such as Handle the Harp and Organ.*
>
> *TUBAL-CAIN was the Instructer of Every Artificer in Brass and Iron, And the Daughter found out the ART of Weaving.*
>
> *THESE Children knew well that GOD would take Vengeance for SIN either by Fire or Water; Wherefore they Wrote their SCIENCES that they had found in Two Pillars, that they might be found after in Two Pillars, that they might be found after NOAH'S Flood.*
>
> *ONE of the Pillars was Marble, for that will not Burn with any Fire, And the other stone was Laternes for that will not drown with any Water.*
>
> *OUR Intent next is to Tell you Truly, how and in What manner these STONES were found whereon these SCIENCES were Written.*
>
> *THE Great HERMES (Surnamed TRISMAGISTUS, or three times Great) Being both King, Priest and Philosopher, (in EGYPT) he found One of them, and Lived in the Year of the World Two Thousand and Seventy Six, in the Reign of NINUS, and some think him to be Grandson to CUSH, which was Grandson to NOAH, he was the first that began to Learn of Astrology, To Admire the other Wonders of Nature; He proved, there was but One GOD, Creator of all Things, He Divided the Day into Twelve Hours, He is also thought to be the*

first who Divided the ZODIACK into Twelve Signes, He was scribe to OSYRIS King of EGYPT; And is said to have invented Ordinary Writing, and Hierogliphiks, the first (Anno Mundi. MDCCCX.) Laws of the Egyptians; And Divers Sciences, and Taught them unto other Men.

The earlier document, known as the Wood Manuscript, claims in its preamble to be newly translated from an earlier document by J. Whytestones for John Sargensonne in 1610. It tells a similar story to that of the *Indigo Jones Manuscript*.

These 4 children knew well that god would take vengeance for sin either by water or fire. Wherefore they wrote the sciences which they had found, in two pillars of stone that the sciences might be found after Noah's flood.

One of the pillars was of marble which would not burn with any fire and the other pillar was of a stone called Laterus which would not dissolve, sink or be drowned in any water.

Our intent is to declare unto you truly how and in what manner these pillars of stone (before declared) were first found wherein the Sciences (before mentioned) were written.

The great Hermerius the which was Cush his son the which Cush was Sem his son the which Sem was Noah his son.

The said Hermerius was afterward called Hermes who was the father of the wise men. The which Hermes found one of the said Pillars of Stone, in the which stone he found the sciences written. And the said Hermes taught the said sciences unto men at the making or building of the Tower of Babylon thus was the science of masonry first found and very much esteemed.

In the part of Freemasonry known as the Ancient and Accepted Scottish Rite, there is a degree known as the Royal Arch of Enoch, which tells a similar story. A Masonic historian of the early part of the 20th century found the old ritual and compared it with the ritual currently in use. He described how the Thirteenth Degree, called 'The Royal Arch of Enoch', relates that Enoch, foreseeing that the world would be overwhelmed with some disaster, either through flood or fire, determined to preserve at least some of the knowledge at that time possessed by man. He therefore engraved certain records on two columns, one of brick and the other of stone. These columns were preserved through the Flood, and subsequently discovered, one by the Jews, and the other by the Egyptians.

He then goes on to say that the ritual relates the discovery by the Jews of fragments of this column during the building of King Solomon's Temple, which occurred about 3,000 years ago. In the ritual, the workmen clear the ground on the site (which was already the site of a more ancient Enochian Temple) and find the top of a vaulted arch. A keystone is removed and one of the masons is lowered down by rope to discover certain relics.[1]

The story is continued in the next degree, which is called the Scotch Knight of Perfection. Again it describes how the principal pedestal used in the lodge room represents Enoch's pillar, which, being found in the ruins by Solomon's masons, was put together for that purpose. On a table is placed bread and wine and a gold ring for the newly admitted brother. The companions, when seated, form a triangle, and 24 lights are placed, three and five in the west, seven in the north, and nine in the south. The legend is retold that King Solomon formed a 'Lodge of Perfection' made up of certain worthy Masters, and that, whenever this Lodge met, nine Knights of the Ninth Arch tiled (guarded with drawn swords) the nine arches which led to the Sacred Vault. None was permitted to pass without giving the passwords of the different arches.

According to this Masonic tradition, a number of ancient Masters at the time of Solomon were jealous of the honours conferred on the members of the Thirteenth and Fourteenth Degrees, and claimed the same honors. This was refused, and Solomon told them that those whom he had advanced to the Degree of Perfection had wrought in the difficult and dangerous work of the ancient ruins, had penetrated into the bowels of the earth, and had brought out treasures to adorn the Temple. He then told the petitioners to go in peace and aspire to perfection by good works. The discontented Masters determined to go to the ancient ruins and search in the bowels of the earth, that they might have an excuse for making a further application to the king for the honours they coveted. The next morning they removed the 'Cubicle Stone' and descended into the cavern with a ladder of ropes by the light of torches; but no sooner had they all reached the bottom than the whole nine arches fell in upon them. When Solomon heard of this accident

[1] Ward, J.S.M.: Freemasonry and the Ancient Gods, 1921

he sent three of his officers – Joabert, Giblim, and Stolkin – to make inquiries as to what had happened. On reaching the spot they could find no remains of the arches, nor could they whether that any of those who had descended had escaped. They then carefully examined the spot, but found nothing, save a few fragments of masonry inscribed with hieroglyphics, which Solomon declared were fragments of one of the pillars of Enoch.

The story now moves on to explain the fate of this antediluvian pillar of scientific knowledge. A special group of masons is created to protect the pillar and its teachings and to recognise one another they wear a gold ring depicting the pillar.

We have already established in our previous books that the rituals of Freemasonry began with the secret traditions of the Jews who wrote the Dead Sea Scrolls and with the hereditary high priesthood of Jerusalem.[2] The stories of Enoch contained in Freemasonic oral tradition are therefore almost certainly very ancient indeed, and are possibly the only surviving strand that continues the tradition of Enochian artefacts found when the first Temple of the Jews was built on the site of a ruined prehistoric structure.

The layout of the various antediluvian vaults that were said to be found on Mount Moriah are still shown in Freemasonry. The visualisation from verbal descriptions is depicted in Freemasonry; see Figure 1.

Whilst the Bible does not connect Enoch with the Flood, the 1st century historian of the Jews, Josephus, does. This man, who is believed to have trained with the Qumram community, states that Enoch recorded astronomical data on two pillars.

The old rituals of the Ancient Scottish Rite say that the Jerusalem high priests who survived the destruction of AD 70 gave rise to great families in Europe who, 1,000 years later, formed the Order of the Knights Templar. Could their more detailed knowledge have come from these families or from the Qumranian scrolls that the Templars unearthed when they excavated under the Temple Mount in Jerusalem between 1118 and 1128?

There is a further reference source for Enoch which makes very similar claims as Freemasonry. It is an ancient Jewish book that was lost to the Western world for more than 1500 thousand years until it was rediscovered by a leading 18th-century Freemason.

[2] Knight C. and Lomas, R.: *The Second Messiah*, Century, 1997

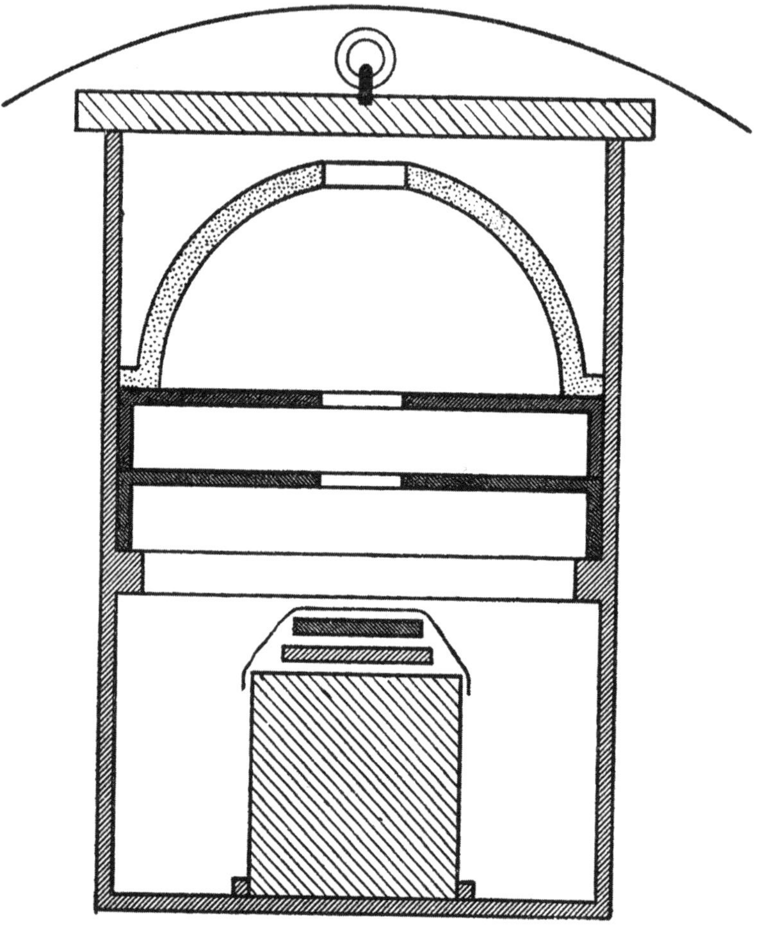

Figure 1. *The stylized Masonic layout of Enoch's vault.*

AN ANCIENT TEXT REDISCOVERED

James Bruce was born on 14 December 1730 at Kinnaird House, near Larbert in Falkirk. His family were descended from Robert the Bruce and had been involved with the Knights Templar and the beginnings of Scottish Freemasonry in the 15th century. In 1747 he went to Edinburgh University to read Law and whilst there he became a Freemason at Lodge Cannongate Kilwinning. Apparently he took more interest in his Freemasonry than he did in his studies of the Law, progressing through the various degrees of the

Ancient and Accepted Rite where he learnt about Enoch's contribution to Freemasonry and civilization.

Bruce dropped out of university and went to London, where he met and fell in love with Adriana Allan, the sister of a successful wine merchant. He married her in February 1754, after a brief but intense courtship. Unfortunately, his new wife suffered from consumption, and in the September the young couple set off to spend the winter in Provence, hoping that Adriana's health would benefit from the milder weather. They got as far as Paris when Adriana was taken seriously ill and died within a matter of days.

James was devastated, and he returned to Scotland where he devoted himself to studying Freemasonry and its links with his family. Then, in 1757 he set off on a trip to visit some of the sites in Europe that had been connected to the Knights Templar.

The following year his father died and he returned to Falkirk to take over the running of the family estate at Kinnaird. He was not really interested in the life of a gentleman farmer and within two years he had signed an agreement with the Carron Company to allow coal to be mined on his estate. By 1761 he was receiving an annual fee of £250 and ten per cent of the value of all coal extracted, which guaranteed him sufficient funds to dedicate his life to a study of the Templars and the origins of Freemasonry.

Bruce obviously took to the good life and described himself without modesty:

> *My ancestors were among the kings of the country in which I was born, and to be ranked among the greatest and most glorious that ever bore the crown and title of king. This is the truth and nothing but the truth.*[3]

Through his Freemasonry he had made the acquaintance of Lord Halifax, who offered him the post of Consul-General at Algiers, which he took up in February 1762. Bruce saw this as a major opportunity to travel extensively in North Africa, a trip which was to take over 12 years to complete. There were many things he wanted to study including the Falashas, the black Jews of Ethiopia, and their links with the Knights Templar – who had built extensively across this otherwise forgotten land.

[3] Bruce, J.: *Travels to Discover the Source of the Nile*, vol. IV

Bruce was not an outstanding consul, and he left the post in August 1765 to travel around the Mediterranean. He planned to visit Armenia (the supposed landing place of Noah's Ark) to observe a transit of Venus. Unfortunately he lost his telescope *en route*, and so, instead he set off to travel up the Nile to Ethiopia.

The story of Bruce's travels is full of adventure and discovery, but there is one particularly interesting tale that makes clear just how proficient he had become in astronomy.

Having developed quite an ability as a medical doctor, Bruce was invited to treat some of the women of the Sheikh of Beyla's household. However, the Sheikh decided that he did not like this handsome, six-foot-four foreigner touching his women, and accused Bruce of improper behaviour. Bruce realized that he was in serious danger, but his knowledge of the heavens and quick thinking saved his neck. He told the Sheikh that he was innocent of any wrongdoing, and to prove his case he would invoke the power of the Almighty to send a sign to confirm his claim. Bruce then made a prediction of a strange event that would occur the following Friday:

> *If the afternoon of that shall pass like those of common days, I am a worthless man and an impostor; but if on that day after four o'clock a sign be seen in the heavens that shall be thought by all of you unusual and extraordinary, then I am an innocent man.*[4]

It was fortunate for Bruce that on that day a total eclipse of the moon was due to occur at about ten minutes past four. He waited until the moon had risen and the earth's shadow was well on its way across the disc before turning to his accusers with a skyward-pointing finger. He later recounted the occasion:

> *'Now look at that,' said I; 'in some time after this the moon shall be so totally swallowed up in the darkness, that a small shell shall only be seen at the edges.' They were frightened at the denunciation, rather that at any thing they observed, till a little before the eclipse became total. A violent apprehension then fell upon them all; and the women from their apartments began to howl, as they do on all melancholy occasion of misfortune, or death. They were in the inner square.*

[4] Bruce, J.: *Travels to Discover the Source of the Nile*, vol. IV

> *'Now,' continued I, ' I have kept my word; it will soon be clear again, and will do no harm to man or beast.' It was agreed among them that I should not go home till it was totally at an end. I consented to this.*[5]

Having escaped unpleasant reprisals, Bruce continued his journey by visiting an area inhabited by ascetic monks near the city of Axum. His diary described it as an unwholesome, hot and dangerous country entirely inhabited by holy men who voluntarily spent their lives in penitence, meditation and prayer.

> *They first shave their hair and put on a cowl, renouncing the world for solitude and taking vows. These monks are held in great veneration; are believed by many to have the gift of prophecy, and some of them to work miracles, and are very active instruments to stir up the people in time of trouble.*[6]

We cannot know for sure whether Bruce went looking for the lost *Book of Enoch*, or simply stumbled across it as a consequence of his Templar quest, but it was here that he made the most important discovery of his life. Bruce certainly understood the great importance of the *Book* and as a good linguist (speaking several languages including Tigre, Amharic and Arabic) he was able to translate his find into French and English before returning to Europe.

He was honoured in France after he presented his translation of the *Book of Enoch* to the king, and on his return to London was celebrated as a traveller and elected a Fellow of the Royal Society.

The Masonic historian J. S. M. Ward believed that the version of the *Book of Enoch* that Bruce found must have been greatly corrupted, compared with the ancient original, because it contained magical and astrological formulae. In recent years Bruce has been vindicated with the finding of nine further copies of the *Book of Enoch* at Qumran within the Dead Sea Scrolls. These damaged fragments, which were buried sometime prior to AD 68 and discovered after 1947, show that the astronomical and astrological material in the book had been there from at least as early as 200 BC.

[5] Bruce, J.: *Travels to Discover the Source of the Nile*, vol. IV

[6] Bruce, J.: *Travels to Discover the Source of the Nile*, vol. IV

THE BOOK OF ENOCH

Ward's disquiet at the content of the *Book of Enoch* is entirely understandable. It does indeed contain fairly weird information including what appears to be astronomical knowledge and descriptions of an observatory on a mountain top, and it warns of a coming catastrophe and details some of the preparations that need to be made.

Michael Black, the biblical scholar who has published the most up to date analysis of the *Book of Enoch*, says this about it:

> *What the book presents to the reader is a bizarre variety of disparate and overlapping traditions, containing units of narrative and discourse. . . . The* Book of Enoch *is like an intricately devised jigsaw puzzle, or rather a collection of such puzzles, in which, after the main component pieces have been put together to make a whole picture, there still remain elements unaccounted for which baffle the most ingenious attempts to fit them into a coherent whole . . . there is no Ariadne's thread to lead [the reader] through the Enochian labyrinth.*[7]

The *Book of Enoch* is widely considered to be a collection of works by different authors and some parts are still believed to be missing. The first chapter starts by informing the reader that a great judgment will be sent upon the Earth in the form of a deluge, and only a handful of selected members of the human race will survive. Worryingly, our hero, speaking after the deluge, also warns that there is *another* judgment yet to come. This seems to the prophecy that Jude warned about, showing that some writers of the New Testament had access to this book.

The following four chapters are a homily, focusing on the harmony and regularity of nature. They provide a discussion on how the study of the harmony of nature can help in the understanding of God, and how the regular motions of the stars and the natural rhythms of the seasons are evidence of God's work. This unusual world-view, and the actual words chosen, are remarkably similar to those used by Freemasons, even in the much-amended modern rituals.

Freemasons repeatedly use the words 'harmony', 'nature' and 'regularity', as well as having a lodge structure created around the seasons and the movements of stars: the ceilings of English Masonic Temples are covered in stars. Freemasons come from all monotheistic religions and God is therefore

[7] Black, M.: *The Book of Enoch or I Enoch, A New English Edition*, Leiden, E.J. Brill, 1985

not given a name, but He is referred to as 'the Great Architect of the Universe'.

What could be more Enochian?

The next two chapters recount the story of the strange alien beings that they call the Watchers. This is the story of a group of advanced people who take the daughters of men as wives. The progeny of these matings are a group of misfits, called the Giants or Nephilim, who apparently rampage throughout the land. The misdeeds of the Nephilim are given as the reason why God decides to send the deluge. Some recent readers of the *Book of Enoch* have stated that they believe the Watchers must be extraterrestrials, but we find no reason to rely on this speculation. The book says they had many skills which they taught to men, that they sometimes lived for periods amongst men but returned to a distant place where they lived with their leader, who is described as God the Most High. From the descriptions, it sounds to us as those people were an advanced group who were not part of mainstream society.

Chapters 17-36 tell of Enoch's journeys taken in the company of various beings, who are described as angels or sometimes as Watchers. During these journeys Enoch is told about the coming deluge and shown various geographical features which seem to have the air of reality about them.

The following 35 chapters are concerned with the parables of Enoch. These are mainly eschatological discourses about Enoch's understanding of the nature of the Last Judgement and the form it will take.

Chapters 72-82 are entirely astronomical in character, dealing with the movements of the sun, the moon and the stars. The conventional interpretation of this section is that it is primitive and inaccurate in its approach to astronomy. One expert, Otto Neugebauer, was particularly dismissive:

> *This work is concerned with astronomical concepts of a rather primitive character (variation of the length of daylight, illumination and rising amplitude of the moon, wind direction, etc.), dominated by simple arithmetical patterns.*

This section also introduces heavenly tablets, containing secrets in to which only Enoch has been initiated, and explains how he passes this information on to Methuselah to write down for future generations.

Next, we are told about the dreaming visions experienced by Enoch. This part is made up of four sections which recount the history of the world as a sequence of parables concerning the actions of various animals. It starts at the beginning of time with Adam and Eve and goes as far as its authors' own era, referring to the Maccabaean Revolt of the second century BC. It then moves into the future with a vision of the New Jerusalem and the arrival of a second Adam.

The final section is the 'Epistle of Enoch', which deals with Enoch's advice to Methuselah and his family, and describes the miraculous birth of Noah, which is told in even greater detail in the 'Tales of the Patriarchs' in the Dead Sea Scrolls. The 'Apocalypse of Weeks' tells of a vision of a final judgement before the coming of a new heaven and a new earth, and the closing section is a long tirade against sinners.

This book was once highly revered by the early Christians. We can see this from the writings of Paul in his letter to the Hebrews. He is trying to convince them that blind faith is more important than reason.

> *Hebrews 11:1 Now faith is the substance of things hoped for, the evidence of things not seen.*

To support his contention that 'What I want to believe must be true, if I only have enough faith', he tries to draw support from Old Testament figures who would carry weight with his readers. He quotes Abraham, Sarah, Jacob, Joseph, Moses, working his way through all the Jewish Patriarchs to support his view – but it is Enoch whom Paul uses as a well known example of goodness, which he claims was achieved by faith, in verses 5-6:

> *By faith Enoch was translated that he should not see death; and was not found, because God had translated him: for before his translation he had this testimony, that he pleased God. But without faith it is impossible to please him: for he that cometh to God must believe that he is, and that he is a rewarder of them that diligently seek him.*

The early Christians held the *Book of Enoch* in high regard, but it is easy to see how a Biblical scholar such as H. L. Goudge can describe it as a 'stupid book'.[8] However, casual reading of any book of the Bible would cause a logical and rational person to take a similar view.

[8] Campbell, J.Y., The Origin and Meaning of the Term Son of Man, *JThS* XLVIII (1947) p.148.

As we read this non-biblical Jewish book, we could see that there simply has to be a connection of some kind with Freemasonry. The bottom line is this: the Masonic story of Enoch already existed before the *Book of Enoch* was rediscovered by Freemason, James Bruce. No one outside of Ethiopia had known about it for more than 1,500 years, yet Freemasons knew stories contained in that lost book.

James Bruce was a member of a family which was descended from the Jewish high priesthood at the time of Christ and indeed earlier. He might well have been aware of it, even though he did not have a copy. The Knights Templar had been highly involved in Ethiopia during the 13th century, and it is possible that they found it, or already had it, and used it for their rituals. If so, this would add further confirmation to our thesis that the rituals of Freemasonry developed out of pre-rabbinical Judaism via Templarism.

We were soon to find a great deal more that would substantiate the case for Freemasonry being a modern day Enochian cult. But first we needed to consider further the physical reality of the global Flood that we now believe Enoch was describing. Cambridge geologist Jack Miller had given us information that turned us towards extraterrestrial giants; the kind that travel fast and hit hard.

CONCLUSION

Freemasonry records an ancient tradition that says that a man called Enoch foresaw a worldwide Flood and tried to preserve civilization. An ancient Jewish text known as the *Book of Enoch,* which had been lost around the second century AD, but which was found by an 18th-century Freemason, *does* contain such an account. This book provides detailed information about the movements of the sun, moon and the stars, taught to Enoch by an angel called Uriel, and, also tells about a strange group of beings called the Watchers, who bred with local women to produce giants as their children.

Chapter Three

VULNERABLE EARTH

OUR BATTERED NEIGHBOUR

Man has probably gazed up at the moon in awe for as long as our species has existed. A shaped and engraved bone plaque found in a rock shelter in south-west France has been identified as an accurate lunar calculator, and carbon dating has established that it is between 32,000 and 34,000 years old.[1]

The moon's surface features are clearly visible to the naked eye, and when Galileo first sketched the moon through his telescope almost 400 years ago, he interpreted its surface as being covered with seas, mountains and extinct volcanoes. Since then, 184 of the largest craters have been given names, some classical such as Plato, Pliny and Ptolemy, and large flat areas were given romantic names such as *Mare Tranquillitatis* (the Sea of Tranquillity) and *Mare Nectaris* (the Sea of Nectar). However, we now know that our near neighbour has no seas, and the scars we see are the result of countless collisions over billions of years. The largest of the many visible craters is almost 300 kilometres across and four kilometres deep; a huge indentation for a body that is one-50th the volume of the earth.

In the scheme of things, our planet and its moon are little more than specks of dust in a boundless but largely empty universe. Three-and-a-half billion years ago, when the Earth was still relatively young, it was regularly

[1] Cunliffe, B.: *Prehistoric Europe*, Oxford University Press, 1998

struck by chunks of space debris hundreds of kilometres wide that were travelling at speeds of around 100,000 kilometres per hour. Each one of these massive collisions would have excavated a crater the size of Texas, and the blast stripped away most of the atmosphere, replacing it with a global furnace of vaporized rock at a temperature of 3,000°C. Any primordial life that may have existed would have been instantly snuffed out as the boiling oceans turned to vapour and a lethal pulse of sterilizing heat seared a kilometre down into the ground.[2]

Less than 100 major impact craters have been positively identified on earth but that does not mean that we have been any more fortunate than the moon. The surface of our world is more than two-thirds covered by water, and vegetation covers large parts of the rest, concealing the fact that our planet has been hit by 20 times more objects than the moon. Our turbulent atmosphere and the shifting of the planet's crust has simply hidden the ancient scars from view. It has been estimated that over the last billion years alone, the Earth must have been hit by at least 130,000 comets or meteors that were big enough to produce craters of over a kilometre wide. Around 50 of these were so massive that they left basins greater than 1,000 kilometres in diameter.[3]

Thankfully, there have been no first-magnitude impacts in recent times, and this period of stability has allowed the Earth to evolve life on its surface to a point where its offspring now have the ability to travel to other planets. Dr David Hughes of Sheffield University wrote reassuringly about previous extraterrestial impacts:

> *We are still here. Humanity and the animal kingdom still inhabit the earth. Craters have been produced, catastrophes have occurred, but we are not extinct. Things were worse in the past and we survived.*[4]

However, just because we have enjoyed a period of relative tranquillity, we should not be complacent about the threat of extraterrestrial impacts – substantial chunks of the heavens could collide with our little planet at almost any time.

[2] Davies, P.: *New Scientist*, 12 September 1998

[3] Hughes, D.: 'Focus: Visitors from Space', *Astronomy Now*, November 1997, pp.41-44

[4] Hughes, D.: 'Focus: Visitors from Space', *Astronomy Now*, November 1997. pp.41-44

COMETS AND METEORITES

There are two types of body which have collided with the earth and created impact craters: comets and meteorites. Whilst meteors are made up of various minerals, comets are almost entirely ice interspersed with bits of general space debris frozen within them. Most are formed in a region of space called the Oort Cloud – a vast haze of dust, rock and ice that surrounds our solar system like a nebulous doughnut ring. Others are comets of unknown origin, such as Comet Hyakutake which passed through our solar system in 1996, originating from deep in interstellar space.

Comets are probably the most remarkable of the heavenly bodies that can be seen with the naked eye. They can make sudden and often unexpected appearances in our skies and a large comet, such as the recent Hale-Bopp, will produce a magnificent spectacle in the night sky. The orbits of most comets are sharply inclined to the plane of the earth's orbit around the sun, which makes the path of the comet seem abrupt and capricious compared with the steady movements of the stars and planets. Comets that rush past the Earth show off at least two lengthy tails, which are not indicators of the object's direction of travel because they always point away from the sun. The tails occur when a comet approaches the sun, which heats it up to the point that its ice vaporizes and the gaseous water streams off in the solar wind. Comets only become visible from Earth when a luminous gas tail is created, so any that are more than 300 million miles from the sun are impossible to spot.

Those that originate in the Oort Cloud are drawn into the sun's gravitational field, where they become captured in an elliptical orbit swinging around the star in long repetitive loops. Comet Hale-Bopp, for example, is on such a long orbit that it can only be seen by the naked eye once every 4,000 years or so. Halley's Comet, one of the best known of these periodic comets, was first recorded by Chinese astronomers in 240 BC and was also mentioned by Josephus, the Jewish historian, who states that he saw it as a broadsword-shaped star over Jerusalem during the time the city was under siege in AD 70.[5]

One of the most famous visits of Halley's Comet was during another famous battle when the Normans invaded England and defeated King Harold at Hastings in AD 1066. The comet's appearance was recorded on

[5] Flavius Josephus: *The Jewish Wars,* Folio Society, 1971

the Bayeux Tapestry which was commissioned by Matilda, the wife of William the Conqueror. It shows the flaming comet above King Harold who is tottering on his throne and is surrounded by frightened courtiers. The text above the comet relates, 'They are in awe of the star'.

Whilst these periodic comets travel in elliptical orbits as part of the solar system, others come from interstellar space, and once they have rounded the sun they disappear, never to return. Once a comet has been spotted and three precise measurements of its position in the sky, relative to the background stars, have been taken, its orbit can be calculated. But this is not easy to achieve, and of 1,028 recorded comets more than half have not been observed closely enough to decide whether they are periodic or not.[6]

The local area of our galaxy, the Milky Way, must contain an unimaginable number of these giant ice cubes. The famous 16th century astronomer Johannes Kepler was right when he commented: 'There are as many comets as there are fish in the sea.' Kepler was the first person to put forward a rational explanation of the comet's tail when he said that these tails were due to some sort of repulsive force emanating from the sun and driving the gaseous matter of the head out into a long streamer.

Meteors are a very different sort of object. Looking up on a clear moon-free night even the most casual observer can sometimes notice brief bright streaks of light flashing across the sky from east to west. These are small particles of rock or cosmic dust which fall into the Earth's upper atmosphere and are burnt away by friction with the upper air. On average, a sky watcher will normally see a meteor, or 'shooting star', about once every six seconds during a prolonged period of observation. However, at some times of the year this frequency increases greatly when the Earth passes through areas of space which contain large amounts of debris, causing what we call 'meteor showers'. These meteors are very small indeed, some little more than grains of sand, and they do not present any danger as they burn up long before they hit the ground. But occasionally, larger lumps of space rock do come too close for comfort and they are a cause for concern.

The ancient Greeks wrote about something they called 'thunder stones'; large stones which survived their explosive arrival from heaven. These alien stones were always considered to be special, particularly if the stone was large. One thunder stone which fell in Thracia in 476 BC was said to be 'as

[6] Moore, P. and Mason, J.: *The Return of Halley's Comet*, Patrick Stephens, 1984

large as a chariot' and in the 18th century one weighing 1,600 lbs was reported from Russia.[7] Many of these larger meteorites are objects which have been disturbed from a region of space called the Asteroid Belt, which is a large ring of broken rocks circling the sun between the orbits of Mars and Jupiter. Their origin is unknown but a study of collected meteorites suggests they are about 4,600 million years old and so must have been formed at the same time as the solar system came into being.[8]

A small percentage of the Earth's daily intake of meteorites weighs a kilogram or more and at this size could survive the entry and crash to the ground. Meteorites with an original mass of around 100 tons tend to bore into the surface upon impact, whilst any much larger than this will explode upon striking the ground because of their huge momentum. Even small incoming meteorites cause significant detonations as they have 100 times the explosive capacity of TNT per unit of mass due to their high kinetic energy, which increases with the square of the velocity.[9]

A HISTORY OF EARTH IMPACTS

It is now widely thought that the impact crater on Mexico's Yucatan Peninsula marks a disaster that changed the course of evolution. This 65 million-year-old crater has led a number of scientists, such as Luis and Walter Alvarez, to conclude that it explains why dinosaurs and most varieties of marine invertebrate species suddenly disappeared at precisely this time. Detailed geochemical studies conducted around the world have shown that a clay layer of the period has a very high iridium content of the type that is found in meteorites. Such an impact would have thrown enough dust into the atmosphere to reduce incoming solar radiation for years, causing a rapid reduction in global temperatures – which would explain why so many larger species became extinct simultaneously.

In astronomical terms, the global holocaust that appears to have ended the reign of the dinosaurs has to be considered to be relatively recent, but lesser events have continued to occur with a worrying frequency. An example is the explosion in the atmosphere that occurred above a remote area of Siberia called Tunguska early in the morning of 30 June 1908. The local Tungus tribesmen and fur traders reported how they saw an enormous fireball

[7] Gerber, P.: *Stone of Destiny*, Canongate Books, 1997
[8] Grady, M.: *Astronomy Now*, November 1997, pp.45-49
[9] Hughes, D.: 'Focus: Visitors from Space', *Astronomy Now*, November 1997, pp.41-44

streaking across the sky followed by a series of violent explosions from the direction of the trading town of Vanavara. When the area was inspected, it was found that more than 2,000 square miles of forest had been totally flattened by the blast that had ripped downwards from the sky. Subsequent analysis of tree resin from the surrounding area has shown unduly large traces of iron, calcium, aluminium, copper, gold and zinc, indicating that the impacting object was a small stony meteorite of average density. Luckily little damage was done on this occasion but had the collision occurred just a few hours later, the rotation of the earth would have caused the meteor to cremate the entire population of Moscow.

It is not always possible to tell the difference between a comet and a meteorite crater, but occasionally chemical traces such as those at Tunguska and at the Barringer Crater in Arizona indicate that the object was mineral and not water.[10] The head of a comet is 99 per cent ice, and the vast amounts of energy produced at the moment of impact with a body such as the Earth will instantly turn the comet into super-heated steam and leave little behind to identify the cause of the explosion. Detailed calculations by Dr David Hughes of Sheffield University have shown that impacts on the Earth large enough to cause craters are 200 times more likely to be meteors than comets.

Comets have fascinated man for many thousands of years, but the first serious studies we know of were carried out by Sir Isaac Newton, Sir Edmond Halley and Marquis Pierre Laplace. It was Laplace who showed that these beautiful objects were not the messengers of God's wrath, as previous ages had usually assumed, but astronomical bodies obeying the universal laws of gravitation. As astronomers began to understand the orbits of comets, it soon became clear that some must occasionally cross the Earth's orbit, which led scientists to speculate about the possibility of an Earth collision. In 1796 Pierre Laplace described what he thought would happen if a comet struck the Earth:

> *... the axes and rotational movement will be changed, the seas forsaking their age-old positions and rushing towards the new equator; most of the human race and the beasts of the field will be drowned in this universal deluge or destroyed by the violent shock imparted to the terrestrial globe, entire species annihilated, every monument to human endeavour overthrown.*[11]

[10] Hughes, D.: 'Focus: Visitors from Space', *Astronomy Now*, November 1997, pp.41-44

[11] Laplace; Pierre Simon: *Exposition du Système du Monde*, 1796

This view of a cometary impact was not generally accepted by later astronomers and even as recently as 1959 the possibility of a collision was considered negligible.

> *An actual collision would take place only if the two orbits intersected exactly, and if the Earth and the comet arrived at this point simultaneously. The perfect timing and positioning required make the possibility of collision extremely slight.*[12]

Then something happened to change this cosy view of spaceship Earth. In March 1993, at the Palomar Observatory in southern California, astronomers Eugene and Carolyn Shoemaker and fellow comet-hunter David Levy identified a new lump of dirty ice far out in deep space. They catalogued it as D/1993 F2, but it soon became better known to the rest of the world as Comet Shoemaker-Levy 9.

A NEARBY DISASTER

The team were already famous comet spotters. Carolyn was the reigning world champion with 32 comet discoveries, her husband Eugene was credited with 29, and David Levy with 21. The six-mile-diameter comet was pulled into Jupiter's gravitational field and swung around the giant planet like a weight on the end of a bolas. The stress was too much for the comet and it broke up into fragments, which continued on their way to orbit the sun for one last time. Eugene Shoemaker and David Levy calculated that the cometary fragments would return and probably hit Jupiter, a planet that intercepts the vast majority of the interstellar comets that would otherwise collide with the Earth.[13]

No one had ever predicted the collision of two solar system bodies before, and all experts agreed that the outcome was going to be visible from Earth. Accordingly, terrestrial observatories and many spacecraft, including Voyager 2, the Hubble Space Telescope, Ulysses and Galileo all turned their attention to the anticipated display.

When the impacts came in mid-July 1994, the results were far more spectacular than anyone had imagined. The line of comet fragments returned

[12] *Larousse Encyclopaedia of Astronomy*, 1959 ed.
[13] Gribbin, J. and Plagemann, S.: *The Jupiter Effect*, New English Library, 1980

like a string of 21 glowing pearls to crash into the Jovian atmosphere at speeds in excess of half a million kilometres an hour.[14]

Although each fragment had a diameter of no more than 2.5 kilometres, they created plumes of debris many thousands of kilometres high and fireballs larger than the planet Earth. Hot bubbles of super-heated gas created scars on the face of the wounded planet that were visible for more than a year.

An event that had been the subject of many a science fiction story had just entered the realm of hard scientific fact. It was suddenly clear that the universe is a far more dangerous place than anyone had previously thought.

Once the initial euphoria died down, astronomers everywhere started to consider the first obvious question: if this can happen to Jupiter in the tiny time-frame of our lifetimes, could an impact like this happen to earth? The answer seemed unavoidable. It was put very succinctly by the co-discoverer of Shoemaker-Levy 9, astrophysicist David Levy: 'It is not a question of if we will be hit . . . it is when.'

Comet Shoemaker-Levy 9 woke the world up to the probability that large comet impacts are relatively regular occurrences, perhaps happening at frequencies measured in thousands, rather than millions of years. Whilst we have been living in a period of relative stability, there is no guarantee that it will continue.

Comets which have orbits in the same plane as the orbit of the major planets, including Earth, are much more likely to collide with us. The great mass of Jupiter affects a comet in one of two ways. It can divert the comet into a hyperbolic orbit, sending it off into space, or it can capture it into a tight elliptical orbit round the sun, making it a member of the Jupiter family of comets. This is what was about to happen to Comet Shoemaker-Levy 9, but its flight path was changed so abruptly that it was shattered to pieces under the strain. This event has shown us that it is possible for Jupiter to capture a comet, break it into fragments and deflect those fragments onto a collision course with the Earth. If a comet was diverted by Jupiter into a collision trajectory with the Earth, the maximum warning we would get would be about half an orbital period of a Jupiter family comet, which equates to between eighteen months and five years.

Since the impact of Shoemaker Levy 9 with Jupiter, scientific interest in the subject of extraterrestrial impacts has continued to increase, and in 1997 a

[14] http://nssdc.gsfc.nasa.gov/planetary/comet.html

major computer simulation was run to investigate just what would happen to our planet if it were struck by a comet. David Crawford of Sandia National Laboratories in Livermore, California, used the brand-new Intel Teraflops super-computer to model the effects of a billion-tonne comet smacking into deep ocean. This most powerful of computers ran for 48 hours to complete the simulation. The results showed that even a 'small' comet striking earth would create an explosion ten times as powerful as all the nuclear weapons in existence at the height of the Cold War.

This modest hypothetical comet was 10,000 times smaller than Comet Hale-Bopp, which came so close to the Earth recently. Yet when it hit the virtual ocean, the computer reported an explosion which instantly vaporized nearly 500 cubic kilometres of sea water and generated a colossal tsunami wave that would have completely overrun lower-lying land areas such as Florida. The resulting data also proved that after the initial effects had subsided, the atmosphere was left with enough vapour to darken the planet's skies for years, devastating world agriculture. After the consequences of comet impact simulation had been digested, David Crawford observed: '*It's a low-probability, high-consequence event. If one did hit, your chance of becoming a victim would be high.*'[15]

The realization that mankind is vulnerable to cosmic disaster has created popular interest in rogue planets, asteroids and comets. Naturally everyone, from Houston to Hollywood, has focused on the possibility that the Earth might be hit by a comet at some point in the future.

But what effects would it have had on our history if our planet was struck in the not-so-distant past? Our interest was aroused because the realisation that solar system collisions might be relatively frequent events seemed to provide a potential explanation for one of the greatest mysteries of the past: the sudden appearance of civilization.

EARTH IMPACT

Seventy-one per cent of the Earth's surface is covered by the oceans and an incoming comet is therefore more likely to crash into the sea than strike land. This would make it very hard to find evidence of any recent impact. Even cratering of the land is not always a simple thing to detect, and it is only since

[15] *Astronomy Now*, November 1997.

the use of space surveying from orbiting shuttles that evidence of similar events to the impact of Comet Shoemaker Levy 9 with Jupiter have been found on Earth.

The most recent discovery was made by the Shuttle *Endeavor* in two missions flown during April and October of 1994. During investigation of a previously known impact site at Aorounga in northern Chad, using Spaceborne Imaging Radar, two new craters were found close by. NASA geologist Adriana Ocampo speaking at the Lunar Planetary Science Conference in Houston in 1996 commented:

> *The Aorounga craters are only the second chain of large craters known on Earth and were apparently formed by the break-up of a large comet or asteroid prior to impact.*
>
> *The pieces were all similar in size – less than a mile in diameter – and the craters are all similar in size – about seven to ten miles wide.*

The NASA scientists think that the Chad craters were made about 360 million years ago, about the time of an early extinct event which as recorded in the fossil record. Ocampo said about the extinction events:

> *These impacts in Chad weren't big enough to cause the extinction, but they may have contributed to it. Could the impacts have been part of a larger event? Were they, perhaps, part of comet showers that could have added to the extinction? Little by little, we are putting the puzzle together to understand how earth has evolved.*[16]

If Ocampo is right and these craters are part of much larger series of related impacts, then the other impacts are very likely to have been in the sea, so that traces of the craters have been eroded by the water.

THE EFFECTS OF A SEA IMPACT

In 1982, two members of the Department of Planetary Sciences at the University of Arizona, Donald Gault and Charles Sonett set out to try to understand what would happen if an asteroid or comet were to hit an ocean.

[16] Isbell, D. and Hardin, M.: *Chain of Impact Craters Suggested by Spaceborne Radar Images,* http:/www.jpl.nasa.gov/sl19/news80.html

They used information from nuclear tests and combined it with laboratory data using NASA's Vertical Gun Ballistic Range to fire pyrex spheres into a tank of water at muzzle velocities of 2.7 kms/sec. They followed this up by using a light gas gun set up to achieve impact velocities of 5.6 kms/sec. These impacts were recorded with a high-speed film camera and the mechanisms of wave formation were studied in great detail.

Gault and Sonett found that the impact would have a number of effects. Firstly, it would cause a large ejecta plume of vaporized matter made up of seawater, comet material and rock from the sea bed. This gaseous plume would be sucked high into the atmosphere by the reduced pressure left by the comet's passage down.

The energy released by the initial impact would throw an enormous ring of water upwards and outwards, resulting in a very powerful and destructive tsunami-type wave. These waves can travel for enormous distances with very little loss of energy. They found by experiment that the first wave was pushed along by the substrate of water which is forced out by the passage of the impactor, leading to wave speeds of 640 kilometres per hour.

The next outcome is caused by the gigantic hole in the ocean left by the initial vaporization. The impact site temporarily becomes a circular wall of water several kilometres high, with a base pressure of around 5,000 tonnes per square metre the situation is massively unstable. As the high pressure waters rush back into this hole a second tsunami wave, of around 60 per cent of the power of the first one, is generated.

The mechanics of water waves are well understood, and standard formulae exist for calculating the speed and height of waves once they are produced by any means including a comet impact.[17] When a comet strikes water, an enormous amount of energy is transferred from the high-speed object into the wave. This can take the form of potential energy, resulting in the wave being very high, or of kinetic energy, which means the wave moves very quickly.

It is both amazing and frightening, but it is a fact that the initial height of the first wave will be the same height as the depth of the water at the impact point. If the strike was in a deep part of the Atlantic or Pacific, it would result in a wave five kilometres high, with an initial speed around 640 kph! In the open sea the wave crest would settle down quite quickly to a low level of perhaps just a few metres. But as the wave comes towards the shallower

[17] Stoker, J.J.: *Water Waves, the Mathematical Theory with Applications*, John Wiley & Sons, 1992

seabed of a continental shelf it would rear up back close to its original height, as the kinetic energy of motion is converted back into the potential energy of height.

Using these energy relationships it is possible to make an estimate of the initial breaking distance of a wave on a shore. For example, a wave 5 kilometres high, moving at about 700 kph, would take 17 minutes to break. This means that a comet-induced tsunami wave of this size will remain as a high standing, crested wave for a distance of around 200 kilometres before it becomes a turbulent torrent that will continue deep inland.

That is not the end of the story because behind the first wave is the second wave – less powerful than the first, but still absolutely massive. The second wave would also drive deep inland and add power to the destructive penetration of the first wave.

THE EVIDENCE FOR THE ENOCH IMPACTS

The paper that Jack Miller sent to us was authored by Edith and Alexander Tollmann, a husband-and-wife team of geologists based at the Institute of Geology at Vienna University, Austria. They have compiled some very significant information which they believe demonstrates that the Earth was indeed hit by a comet in the Holocene Period, around 10,000 years ago.[18] They drew on the wealth of published academic information about Earth-impact events and produced a detailed synthesis of important global geological events which are known to have occurred in the older Holocene period, for which there is no adequate explanation.

Our interest was heightened when we read that the Tollmanns actually quoted the legend of Enoch regarding the seven stars that appeared as great burning mountains descending towards Earth. These they interpreted as seven cometary fragments.

They looked first at the distribution of small glassy objects called tektites, which are found scattered in S-shaped patterns over large parts of the earth's surface. These smooth stones are chemically similar to some types of commonly occurring igneous rock, but they have always posed a puzzle to geologists because they appear in sites where the bedrock is not the same as the tektite composition. The other characteristic of tektites is their irregular

[18] Tollmann, E. and A.: *Terra Nova*, 6, pp.209-217, 1994

but rounded shapes, which suggests that they have been formed by molten rock being ejected into the atmosphere and then freezing into flattened and rounded spheres. It has recently been generally recognized that they are remnants of high energy cometary impacts on the Earth, and many are very old. It was analysis of these older tektites which provided clues to Alveraz to help understand the dinosaur extinction from the Cretaceous-Tertiary impact.

In 1970, tektites were found embedded in fossilized wood in Australia which was carbon dated and found to have an age of 9,520 plus or minus 200 years BP.[19] The Tollmanns also noted that the tektite scatter over Vietnam had been dated using stratigraphic methods to about the same age.[20] This dating had been confirmed when tektites were found in seabed cores taken from sediment layers in the Indian Ocean known to be approximately 10,000 years old.[21]

The Tollmanns deduced that all of the seven major impacts must have occurred in deep ocean sites, although there were smaller pieces such as a

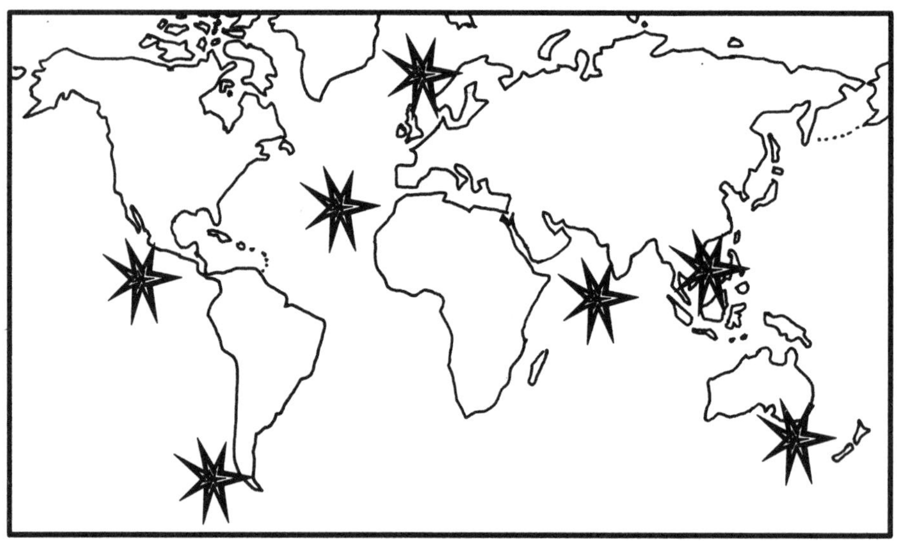

Figure 2. *The seven impact sites of the 7640 BC comet, after Tollmann.*

[19] Glass, B,P.: 'Australasian Microtektites and the Stratigraphic Age of the Australites, *Bull. Geol. Soc. Am. 89*, 1978, pp.1455-1458

[20] Izokh, E.P.: 'Age-paradox and the Origin of Tektites,' *Sec. Int. Conf. Nat. Glasses*, Charles University, Prague, 1987, pp.379-384

[21] Prasad, N. Sh. and Rao, P.S.: 'Tektites Far and Wide', *Nature*, 1990, 347, pp.340

splinter which impacted in Kofels in the Otz Valley of the Austrian Tyrol.

However, they found more evidence to help them fix the date. They knew that the air explosion of the meteorite over Tunguska in 1908 had caused a blip in the radiocarbon calibration curve which was identified using dendrochronology – the study of tree growth rings to determine the age of the tree. The Tunguska impact had destroyed over a third of the ozone layer, allowing more ultraviolet radiation to penetrate the lower reaches of the atmosphere. This resulted in an increase in the production of carbon 14 in the atmosphere, causing a very clear variation in the calibration curve.

They reasoned that a cometary impact would always have the effect of destroying large chunks of the ozone layer, and the Flood comet would have been no exception. Looking at the radiocarbon calibration curve produced by Kromer and Becker,[22] the Tollman's were struck by the pronounced peak in radiocarbon which occurred 9,500 years BP. This could only have been caused by a massive destruction of the ozone layer, such as one would expect from a comet impact.

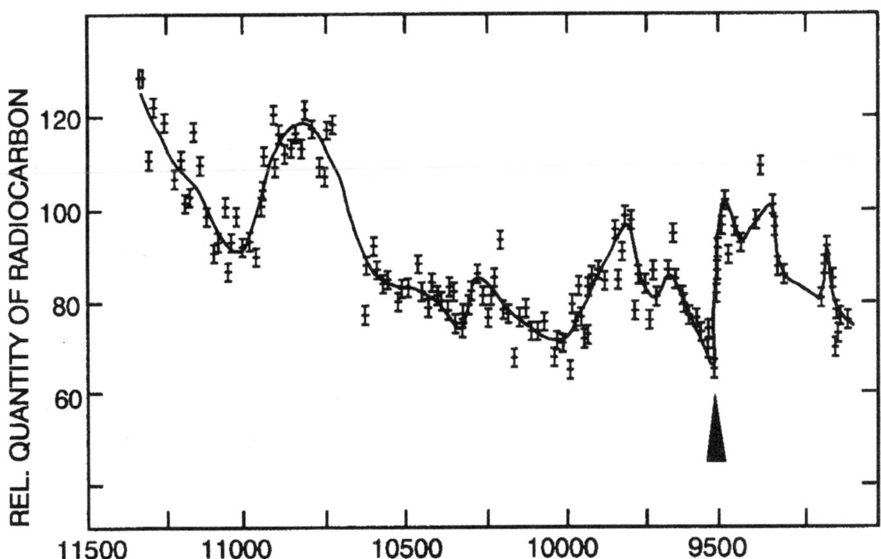

Figure 3. *The radiocarbon blip in the dendrochronological record about 9,500 BP.*

[22] Kromer, B. and Becker, B.: 'Tree Ring Carbon 14 Calibration at 10,000 BP,' *Proc. NATO Advanced Research Workshop*, Erice, 1990

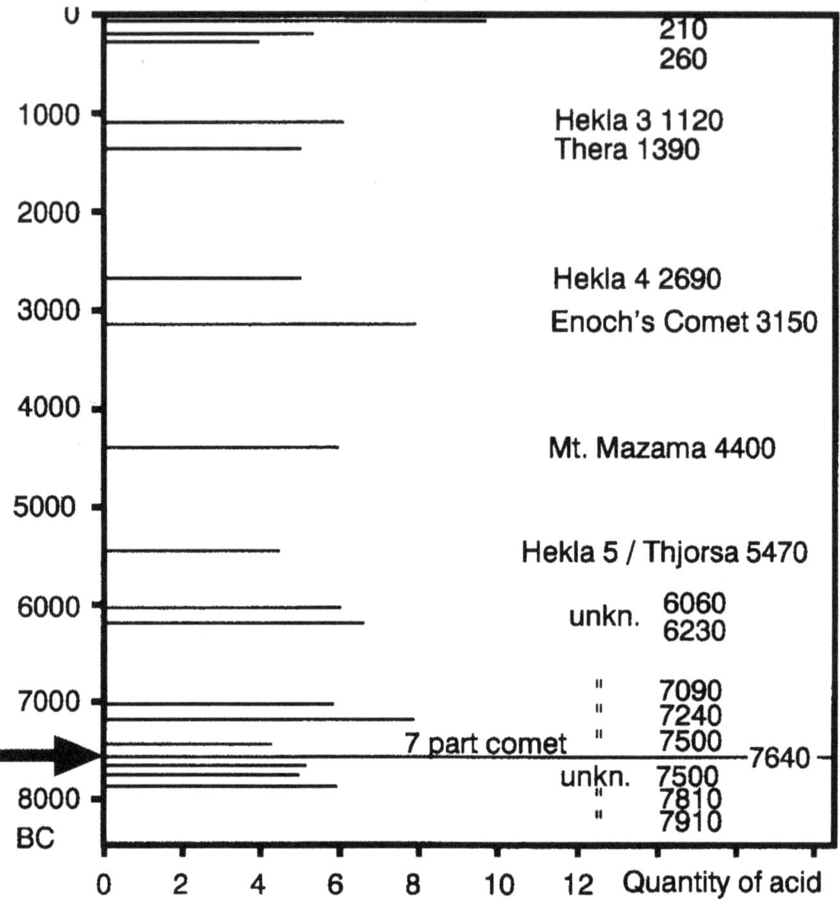

Figure 4. *Peaks of nitric acid shown in world-wide ice-core samples, with a major peak at 7640 BC.*

We already knew that the fossil record showed mass extinctions, caused by the impact of earlier comets and followed in most cases by the appearance of genetically different species. The Tollmanns had argued that evidence from the archaeological record which shows that over 10,000 species became extinct at the Pleistocene/Holocene boundary, which is generally dated to *circa* 10,000 years ago, dated the worldwide Flood to 7640 BC.[23]

Could the appearance of several domesticated species shortly after the impact of this particular comet be related to the temporary lack of the protection caused by the depletion of the Earth's ozone layer?

[23] Dubrovo, I.: 'The Pleistocene Elephants of Siberia', *Megafauna and Man*, University of Flagstaff, 1990, pp.1-8

The descriptions of 'bloody rainfall', which occur in many of the Flood legends around the world, seemed to the Tollmanns to be a perfect description of the impact-generated nitric acid formed from nitrogen burnt by the energy of the impact. Records of acid build-up in the atmosphere are available from ancient ice sheets at the polar regions, and in 1980 an experiment was carried out on a series of ice cores dating back 9,890 years from the perma-ice at Camp Century in north-west Greenland. A marine impact of a high energy comet fragment produces large quantities of acid, both hydrochloric and sulphuric, from the sea water, but in addition, vast amounts of nitric acid are formed from the burning up of the nitrogen in the atmosphere during the passage of the comet. Looking at the graphs showing nitric acid concentration in the layers of the ice cores, the Tollmanns saw a enormous peak occurring.

The Tollmann's had another piece of evidence that pointed to a very serious cometary impact in 7640 BC.

They knew from studies of impact mechanisms that after a high energy collision there would be a tremendous build-up of carbon dioxide, something we call today a 'greenhouse effect'. This should have caused a enormous increase in the temperature of the Earth – in current jargon, 'global warming'. In recent years archaeologists have developed a way of studying ancient climates, called palynology, which is the study of pollen trapped in sediment layers. This new science has established that from just after the 7640 BC impact until about 3000 BC, the Earth went through a very warm phase, where the sea temperature increased by a staggering 4.5 degrees centigrade compared with the average level before the impact.[24]

This warming of the oceans of the world must have increased the speed of ice melting at the end of the last Ice Age and created the world we enjoy today. The ice melting produced an increase in sea water and average sea levels rose by between 90-120 metres. This warm climate continued for thousands of years until it slowly returned to normal about 2200 BC. At this time the British Isles became separated from Europe by the new North Sea and the English Channel. Even northern Scotland enjoyed a Mediterranean-style climate.

[24] Tollmann, E. and A.: *Terra Nova*, 6, 1994, pp.209-217

SAND, SALT AND SEASHELLS

At the time of the comet impacts, Britain and Ireland were still connected to mainland Europe and this entire region would have carried the brunt of the tsunami waves from the mid- and north-Atlantic strikes. It seems almost certain that the entire land-mass of the British Isles was deep underwater for a brief time.

Surely, we thought, there must be some geological evidence of such a cataclysmic event. We soon found it.

The first evidence concerns a layer of white sea-sand which has been found at various sites all over Scotland as far apart as Fife and Inverness. Archaeologist Caroline Wickham-Jones drew attention to it, reasoning that it had to be due to an enormous tsunami wave which seemed to have swept right across large parts of Scotland.[25]

This sand layer was just what we would expect, but we needed to know if its dating was anywhere near the comet strike we were investigating. In the late 1960s the remains of a Neolithic site was found when ground was being excavated for the foundations of a new Mcdonalds fast-food restaurant in Castle Street, Inverness. The complete excavation report by Jonathon Wordsworth,[26] which we found at Inverness Museum, identifies that charcoal from a fire found above the sand layer was radiocarbon dated at 5,325 BC, plus or minus 470 years. These dates are uncorrected radiocarbon years, and have to be adjusted to find the true calendar dating. Once this radiocarbon date is calibrated, it suggests that this fire was lit above the sea sand layer around 7000 BC.

Such a dating is about as precise as we could have wished for, and as tsunami waves on this scale are extremely rare events, it is more than reasonable to connect this sand layer with the inundation caused by Enoch's cometary impacts.

The wave that struck Scotland must have also covered the rest of Britain, and we soon found evidence that the seawater wave was truly massive. In North Wales, beds of sand and gravel with geologically recent sea shells can be found on mountains such as Moel Tryfan which is over 400 metres above sea level, showing that North Wales was briefly covered by sea water at a point in the recent past.[27]

[25] Wickham-Jones, C.R.: 'Scotland's First Settlers', *Historic Scotland*, 1994
[26] Inverness Museum, Private Communication, 1998
[27] Geikie, A.: *Text-book of Geology*, quoted in Filby, F.A.: *The Flood Reconsidered*, Zondervan, 1971

A book by Professor J. Prestwich describes how he has found similarly recent deposits throughout Europe.[28] In South America Charles Darwin reported that he was amazed to find unfossilized seashells high up in the Andes.

We had now found a convincing array of evidence from a number of experts that the Flood happened almost 10,000 years ago, but we were soon to find even more.

THE POWER OF MAGNETS

It was well after midnight when the phone rang.

'Hello Robert,' Chris said, secure in the knowledge that there is only one person who would call him at such an hour.

'I've just found something really exciting.'

'Good,' Chris replied without any particular emotion, knowing that Robert was capable of finding excitement in the most obscure technical detail.

'There was something niggling me about what Gault and Sonett said when they were studying the effects caused by high velocity impacts by extra-terrestial bodies into the sea. They noted that an impact from a meteor or a comet would have a hell of an electromagnetic effect as it entered the Earth's atmosphere.' Robert then quoted from their work.

> *The entry is likely to be associated with a strong electromagnetic signature. This will move outward away from the source at the speed of light jointly with the strong thermal and optical radiation fields, once it clears the immediate high-temperature neighbourhood. However, an electromagnetic component associated with the magneto-hydrodynamic bow-shock wave will accompany the bolide to the surface.*[29]

'Do you see the point?' Robert asked without pausing, before he continued. 'The heat generated by the movement of such a large object at high speed

[28] Prestwich, J.: *On Certain Phenomena Belonging to the Close of the Last Geological Period*, quoted in Filby, F.A.: *The Flood Reconsidered*, Zondervan, 1971

[29] Gault, D.E. and Sonett, C.P.: 'Laboratory Simulation of Pelagic Astroidal Impact: Atmospheric Injection, Benthic Topography, and the Surface Wave Radiation Field. Geological Implications of Large Asteroids and Comets on the Earth', *Spec Papers Geol Soc A.*, 190, pp.69-92

through the atmosphere must cause a plume of intense electro-magnetic radiation. This will ionize the air and push those ions along at enormous speeds, creating a magneto-hyrodynamic shock wave which would cause an enormous plasma tail.'

As a non-physicist, Chris tried to translate this scientific jargon into lay-speak. 'Are you telling me the friction of an incoming comet with the atmosphere generates a powerful electric current?' he asked.

'Exactly,' said Robert. 'But the important point is that the current also causes an enormous magnetic field at right angles to itself . . . a magnetic field much stronger than the Earth's natural magnetic field. Gault and Sonnet have suggested this mechanism could induce remnant magnetization effects, which should be measurable.'

'I see what you mean. I imagine that's why incoming spacecraft lose radio contact when they enter the atmosphere?' Chris said.

'That's right.'

'Are you telling me that there might be a source of evidence for an electromagnetic impact event which could date the entry of the Flood comet?' Chris enquired.

'I think there could be,' said Robert. 'Do you remember magnetostratigraphy?'

'That's the method of dating of the soils beneath ancient kilns and fires, isn't it?' Chris could see where Robert was heading.

'Yes. In fact, anywhere that a ferrous-loaded substrate congealed, it will have preserved the alignment of the Earth's magnetic field at the time.'

'Are you expecting some sort of blip in the Earth's magnetic field record when the Flood comet passed through the atmosphere?' Chris asked.

'If the Flood impact really happened, it'll be rather more than a blip,' Robert answered. 'I'm going to pull out the data tomorrow, and see what's there.'

A great deal is now known about the mechanism which causes the Earth to behave like a giant magnet. Our planet has a solid mantle which covers a fluid core, which in its turn has a further solid core. The solid outer mantle and the solid centre core have this fluid buffer between them and within the fluid layer are large amounts of ferrous material. The whole structure is therefore effectively an enormous rotating dynamo. The iron-rich molten core rotates in the electrostatic field of the sun, which causes eddy currents to flow in the molten ferrous material of the core. This large rotating electric current in turn creates a magnetic field which is at right angles to itself, and because the current flow is around the equator, this magnetic field points towards the poles of the Earth's axis.

The magnetic effect is produced by the movement of the ferrous fluid within the rotating container of the Earth's mantle, but just as water carried in a cup will slop about, so does the rotating ferrous fluid and causes the Earth's magnetic field to move. Under extreme conditions it may even go into reverse, particularly if the hand holding the cup is jolted.

Robert's guess was that any major Earth impact event would cause just such a jolt.

There is a tendency for any rotating ring of current to wobble on its axis of rotation in a manner which can be largely predicted. This is called the precession of the dipole, and accounts for what is known as the secular variation of the magnetic North.[30]

Over the past five million years, the Earth's magnetic field has completely reversed four times. The mechanism which causes this is not fully understood, but the magneto-archaeological record shows that on four separate occasions, for periods of several thousand years, the magnetic field has died away almost to zero. This change is never very rapid and usually takes place over many thousands of years, showing that the system is very sluggish in its reactions. When it restarts, there seems to be an equal probability that it could go in either direction. When the field dies away and then builds up in the same direction, archaeologists refer to it as an aborted reversal.

Nobody really understands how this happens, but the effect on the Earth during these periods is important to life-forms, because the planet's magnetic field acts as a shield, deflecting most of the more energetic particles from the sun away from the surface. When the current dies, these potentially destructive particles penetrate the earth's atmosphere in much larger quantities, which must have genetic consequences for life on the planet. Such events could explain the rapid evolutionary changes that occurred during the Cambrian Period and which have puzzled evolutionists.[31]

In order to date a magnetically orientated substrate a calibration chart showing variations in the direction of the Earth's magnetic field has been created from the available data. It was this data that Robert needed to study in order to prove, or disprove, his theory.

[30] Aitken, M.J.: *Science-based Dating in Archaeology*, Longman, 1990
[31] Gould and Eldridge: *Punctuated Equilibria: an Alternative to Phyletic Gradualism, Models in Paleobiology*, 1990, pp.42

The phone on Chris's desk rang.

'I have Dr Lomas for you,' announced the receptionist.

'Well?' Chris asked without wasting time on a greeting. 'Did you find anything?'

Robert's reply was slow and deliberate. 'The calibration graph generally shows the very smooth wobble which is to be expected from the precession of the magnetic generator. However, in the last 10,000 years there have been two exceptions when the direction of the magnetic field has changed abruptly and in a manner which suggests an outside impulse. There is a clear perturbation at around 3150 BC, which probably means a cometary impact, but there is a significantly larger one around 7000 BC. Knowing that the system is highly damped with a time-constant of over 1,000 years suggests that there must have been a very large current pulse affecting the system between 7000 and 8000 BC.'

'Spot on,' said Chris.

So it *does* appear that the impacting comet that caused the global Flood also caused a tremendous pulse of electromagnetic energy, strong enough to disturb the rotating current loop of the Earth's core.

LONG-TERM EFFECTS ON THE ENVIRONMENT

At the time of the comet impact in 7640 BC, the world was in the grip of a million-year Ice Age, which was just starting to retreat. Up until this time the entire span of human history had been spent in the cold, so that the population was concentrated towards the equatorial regions.

At the time of the Flood comet-strike, Egypt and the Sahara Desert of North Africa were forested and inhabited by elephants, giraffes and aquatic animals.[32] The Sphinx, if it existed at that time, would have faced a large freshwater lake. There are those who claim that the Sphinx in Egypt is 13,000 years old, and we find no reason to believe that this is in any way impossible.[33]

During Ice Ages, the average temperature of both the atmosphere and the sea can vary by as much as 9°Celsius. Since the formation of the earliest rocks of the Earth, the average global temperature has been in the range of

[32] *Geographical Magazine*, December 1964
[33] Hancock, G. and Bauval, R.: *Keepers of Genesis*, Heinemann, 1996

15°-25°Celsius. At the lower temperature ranges the polar ice caps become much larger and extend much nearer to the equator than they do at the moment. Ice Ages seem to occur roughly every 150 million years and last for about one million years. At the end of the Pleistocene period, about 10,000 years ago, the ice sheets which had covered Europe and North America had just started to withdraw as the climate warmed up. This was towards the end of the Quaternary Ice Age (roughly the last two million years), which some scientists believe may not yet have completely ended. Indeed, there is a debate going on at the moment about whether the melting of the polar ice caps is due to global warming caused by man, or is simply the natural cycle of the Earth's average temperature.

In 1920, a Yugoslavian astronomer by the name of Milutin Milankovitch suggested a cause for Ice Ages when he noted that the Earth's orbit is not completely stable. He also recognized that the average temperature of the Earth depended on how much energy it was able to absorb from the sun's radiation. Milankovitch, using his studies of the orbital variations of the Earth, plotted heating curves extending back for 600 million years at two latitudes he considered important, which were 45° and 75° North.[34]

At first some of his predictions of the earliest Ice Ages did not seem to fit, but as geologists developed more accurate dating techniques his theory became more generally accepted.[35] The accuracy of Milankovitch's predictions has now been widely confirmed – with one remaining problem. He observed that the last Ice Age retreated far too quickly, and then seemed to lose impetus and cool down again about 4,000 years ago before resuming its steady upward slope.

According to the normal pattern of Ice Ages, we should still be involved with the last one. Rhodes W. Fairbridge writing in *Microsoft Encarta 97*, comments:

> *Studies indicate that Milankovitch's cycles do not fully account for the timing of events in the recent glacial/interglacial cycle.*

Something happened to change the normal pattern.

Milankovitch's observations were based on the fact that the orbital variation of the Earth causes changes in the amount of energy intercepted

[34] Milankovitch, M.M.: *Canon of Insolation and the Ice-age Problem*, Koniglish Serbisch Akademie, Beograd, 1941
[35] Imbrie, J. and Imbrie, K.P.: *Ice Ages*, Harvard University Press, 1986

from the sun. The summer radiation flux in the high northern latitudes, particularly 65°N and above, is very important. Much of the northern hemisphere is made up of land-mass, which causes a continental climate that is prone to greater extremes of hot and cold. The southern hemisphere is encircled by a continuous seaway so it has a far more maritime climate which does not exhibit extremes. If the land and sea were uniform in both hemispheres, the orbital effects would be cancelled out. As matters are, if the northern high latitudes receive less than a critical value of solar flux over the year a spiral of cooling follows and the world moves into an Ice Age. If more than the critical solar flux is received, the climate starts to warm and the ice melts. This theory is called climate control by 'orbital forcing' and it has been extensively studied.[36]

The time delays in the system are slow, of the order of 8,000 years. This figure has been determined over the last 500 million years using increasingly sophisticated methods of dating events and climate changes. It is the strange short-term perturbations in the recorded climate changes, compared with the predictions of the Milankovitch model, which strongly support the Tollmanns' argument that there was an external energy input superimposed on the basic temperature change. The cause of the perturbations was surely the 7640 BC cometary strike. This explains the sudden sea temperature rise of over 4.5°C in the northern latitude, followed by a downwards trend back to the expected temperature curve around 2000 BC.

So the Earth was already in a stage of warming up from the last Ice Age when the comet struck. This had two effects.

Firstly, the impact ejected an enormous amount of debris into the atmosphere, which caused an effect similar to a 'nuclear winter'. For the survivors it must have seemed like an endless night which eventually gave way to a very cold and misty dawn, followed by years of hard winters and short cool summers. It has been estimated from computer simulations that it would take ten years for the dust to settle and the amount of sunlight reaching the Earth's surface to return to normal levels.[37] This ten-year winter must have contributed to the extinction of more than 10,000 species at this time, a fact well attested to in the archaeological record and one which has been a longstanding puzzle for biologists.

[36] Imbrie, J. and Imbrie, K.P.: 'Modeling the Climate Response to Orbital Variations', *Science*, 207, 1980, pp.943-953

[37] Turco, R.P., Toon, O.B. *et al*, 'Nuclear Winter: Global Consequences of Multiple Nuclear Explosions', *Science*, 222, 1983

At this point in the cycle of events, another problem occurred. During the impact and consequent release of energy, enormous amounts of so-called 'greenhouse gases' were produced. In particular, carbon dioxide was created in large quantities by the wildfires which burned after the pulse of heat from the impact.[38] As the dust settled, the long-lived greenhouse gases created a heat shield in the atmosphere which stopped the Earth reradiating its heat out into space and caused the type of global warming which is of such concern to us today.

The melting of the ice that occurred caused the sea to rise some 120 metres, which meant that any coastal towns would have been lost from sight beneath the waves. Researcher and author Michael Baigent reviewed the literature on undersea archaeology in his book *Ancient Traces* and provided a number of maps showing the effect of this sea-level change on the shape of the coastline of America, complete with supporting evidence that revealed sub-sea finds of preserved mammoth and mastodon teeth from layers of ancient peat on these sunken lands. Carbon dating for peat from these sites gives a calendar date of around 9000 BC.[39]

Every piece of the jigsaw was slotting into place.

Thanks to the direction given to us by Dr Jack Miller, we now knew that the Flood was real and that it almost certainly happened in the autumn of 7640 BC. Armed with this knowledge, we decided to revisit the Flood legends world-wide, to see what they would tell us.

CONCLUSION

Modern scientific investigations show that the Earth has been hit many times by objects such a comets and meteorites. Large impacts have a considerable effect on the environment and cause long-term changes in both climate and geography. These impacts continue to occur – in 1908, a meteorite exploded in Siberia, devastating large areas of uninhabited forest. In 1994, a large comet appeared from outer space, was broken up by the gravitational field of Jupiter, orbited once around the sun and smashed into Jupiter, causing enormous scars on the giant planet. This event has made scientists aware that the Earth is also vulnerable to similar collisions.

[38] Melosh, H.J., Schneider, N.M., Zahnle, K.J. and Latham, D.: 'Ignition of Global Wildfires at the Cretaceous/Tertiary Boundary', *Nature*, 348, 1990
[39] Baigent, M.: *Ancient Traces*, Viking, 1998

Laboratory work on the effects of impacts shows that tidal waves of more than five kilometres high and travelling at up to 640 kph can be caused. Waves of this size would over run much of the Earth's land area. The debris forced into upper atmosphere by the impact would cause a short-term nuclear winter and a longer term global warming effect. It would also leave traces of nitric acid, magnetic fingerprints, tektite trails and radiocarbon blips which could be used to date the event.

This type of evidence shows that there have been two large impacts in the last 10,000 years: a seven-fold impact into all the world's major oceans around 7640 BC, and a single impact into the Mediterranean about 3150 BC.

Chapter Four

ANCIENT MEMORIES

NOAH'S ACCOUNT OF THE FLOOD

The Jewish *Torah* (and therefore the Pentateuch of the Christian Old Testament of the Bible) contains two versions of the Flood story, each telling a similar but a significantly different tale of Noah and his ark. The stories are believed to have been taken from different oral traditions which have been identified as running through the whole of the *Torah*. These intertwined traditions have been teased apart by scholars, who have labelled them as the J (Jahveh or Yahweh) tradition, the E (Elohim) tradition; and the P (Priestly) tradition. It is believed that the J tradition originated in the south of Israel and the E tradition in the north.

There are differing claims for the duration of the inundation, but more importantly, J refers to rain being the cause of the flood, whereas P says that 'fountains of the deep' rose up and hit the land before the rains started. This fundamental difference in the cause of the Flood could be put down to preferences in storytelling, but it is possible that they are *both* correct because they are from witnesses who saw *different* events. The two oral traditions were combined into a single story less than 3,000 years ago, so it is highly likely that they came from diverse sources. If they do stem from fundamentally different eyewitness accounts, the people concerned must have been well apart – one much much further inland than the other.

It is generally believed that the Old Testament versions of the Flood story are closely related to the much earlier Babylonian and Sumerian stories of the

Flood. The standard view is that either the story of Noah was taken directly from the Babylonian stories or they both came from a common source.

The Flood story is introduced in the Book of Genesis, the first book of the Bible, which sets out to explain where man came from. It starts by telling how a supreme deity made the world and then created Adam and Eve, who soon fell from grace and were driven from the garden of Eden. The story of the brothers, Cain and Abel, follows, and a genealogy from Adam through to Noah is provided. Then, in Genesis 6:4, there is a strange account of the interbreeding between a race of giants, described as the 'sons of God', and human women.

> *There were giants in the earth in those days; and also after that, when the sons of God came in unto the daughters of men, and they bare children to them, the same became mighty men which were of old, men of renown.*

This brief passage is the first of many ancient Jewish references which record that it was once widely believed that the offspring of matings between an unknown group called the 'Watchers' and human women were giants who became leading figures at some time in the distant past.

Next, Genesis states that the creator God decided to destroy the entire world but tells Noah of the coming deluge, instructing him to build an ark of gopher wood to carry him, his family and breeding pairs of every animal. Then follows the description of the Flood which destroys life on the Earth completely.

The Flood lasts for 40 days according to the J tradition, and 150 according to the P tradition, which is the only one to name the place where the ark finally came to rest.

According to the P tradition, the ark was 300 × 300 × 30 cubits and consisted of three storeys; it also states that the landing point of the ark after the waters subsided was Mount Ararat, in Urartu, which is now known as Armenia. This extremely mountainous country, to the east of Turkey, has an average elevation of nearly 1800 metres and Mount Ararat is, at its highest point, more than 4 kilometres above sea level. If this description is correct, the ark could conceivably have been carried to such an elevation only by the tsunami wave that was generated by the impact in the Indian Ocean (see Figure 5, page 71). It would have travelled up the Persian Gulf and north-westwards across the low-lying land of Mesopotamia.

If we assume for the moment that there is some truth in this story, it suggests that the ark met the impact wave high up on the Zagros Mountains, above the land later known as Sumer, and was carried in a straight line until the wave lost its power. We had wondered how anyone could launch a ship into an oncoming tsunami wave, but it could be possible if the wave had travelled over sufficient land to break down into a chaotic swirl. If the vessel had been built on a high mountain like this, the rising sea water might be

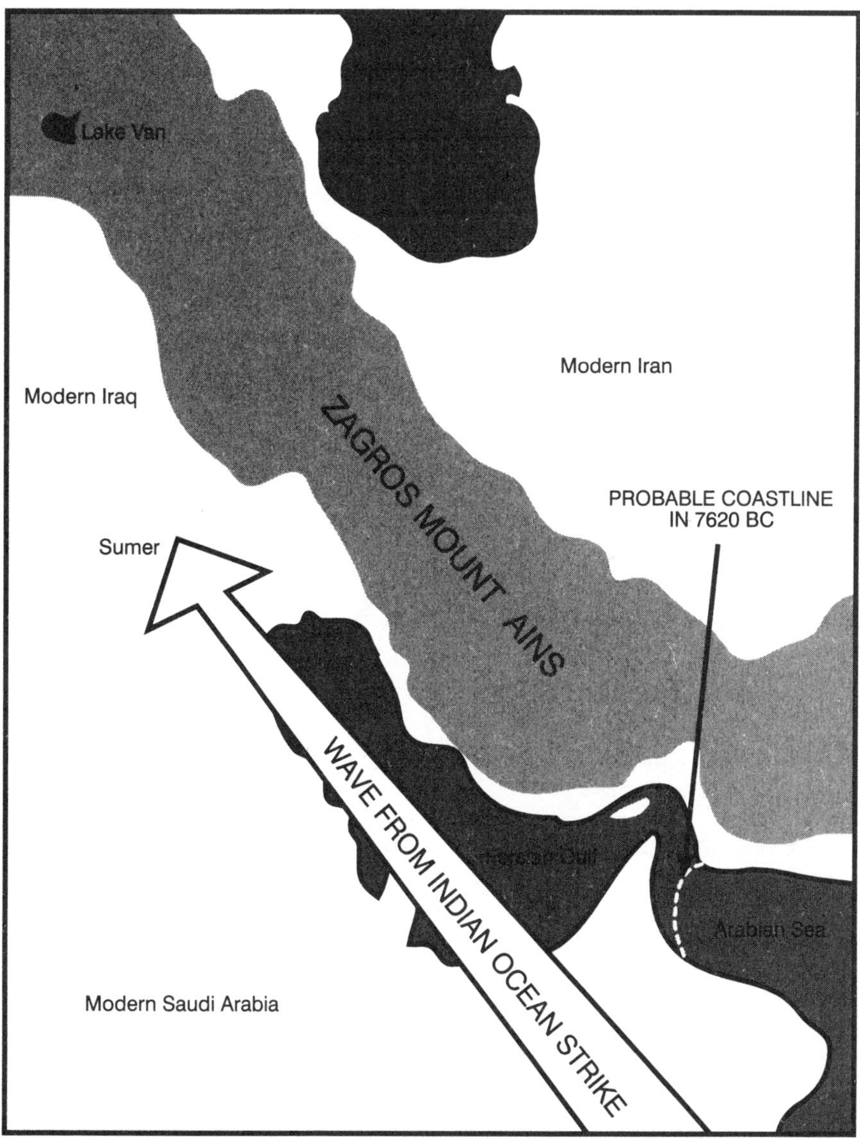

Figure 5. *How Noah's Ark could have been carried to Mount Ararat.*

Figure 6. *Masonic Tracing Board showing comet, Venus, rainbow and cave motifs.*

moving vertically upwards, rather than rushing forward like a wall. It is therefore possible to imagine that a launch could be achieved in such circumstances, without the vessel necessarily being dashed to matchwood.

To sum up, then, the height of the land and its alignment with the wave epicentre and the claimed final resting point of the ark do make sense.

THE RAINBOW MESSAGE

We found it particularly interesting that the P tradition of the *Torah* says that God sent the rainbow as a sign that He will never again flood the world.

It takes very little imagination to appreciate how terrifying the aftermath of the Flood must have been for the survivors. The perpetual night caused by the clouds of water vapour and dust particles blotting out the sun must have seemed like the end of the world. People must have feared that the sun and the moon had been destroyed in the cataclysm, and that the cold blackness was going to last for ever. When the sun finally broke through between the dense clouds of the nuclear-style winter, the rays of sunlight would have been passing through the continuing rains that must have still been sweeping the planet. This would have refracted the light and caused multiple rainbows to appear almost everywhere. Such a manifest display of beautiful colour from the heavens after the blackness, heralding the return to warmth, must have seemed like a welcome message from God.

Rainbow imagery also appears in Masonic symbolism and is associated with falling comets and the Flood. This image (Figure 6, page 72) is taken from an old Masonic 'tracing board' that was used to instruct Freemasons in the ancient traditions of the Order. At the top a hand appears from the sky holding a dagger, which is known to be an extremely old symbol for a comet.[1] Around the hand sea waves are depicted, possibly symbolizing the top of the waters when the floodwaters struck. In the centre we are shown a rainbow containing the five-pointed star which is a representation of Venus, the morning star which symbolizes rebirth in Judaism, Freemasonry and many other ancient traditions. Below the rainbow is the burning bush, from which God is said to have spoken to Moses in the Sinai, and below that is an underground cavern which must have been the only sanctuary during the dark, cold and very wet months after the comet impact.

[1] *Larousse Encyclopaedia of Astronomy*, 1959 ed.

Another medieval illustration shows a stylized comet impact by showing a hand with a dagger that has a comet complete with a long tail at its tip. The ten, apparently severed, heads around the comet are all quite different, and may be meant to symbolize the races of man.

The Babylonian tradition does not mention rainbows, but it does add considerable realistic detail to the story, which makes it worth studying.

Figure 7. *Medieval drawing of a comet.*

GILGAMESH'S FLOOD

The *Epic of Gilgamesh* is an important Babylonian legend thought to be more than 5,000 years old, although it was first written in cuneiform script on 12 clay tablets about 2000 BC. According to the story, Gilgamesh is a semi-divine but tyrannical king of Uruk (now the Iraqi city of Al Warka), who seeks out one of his own ancestors, Utnapishtim, who knows the secret of immortality, because he is the last of the people from before the Flood. The story of the Flood that Utnapishtim provides is very similar to the biblical accounts.

Utnapishtim, who had the title 'Atrakhasis' (meaning 'unsurpassed in wisdom'), is said to have attained immortality and deification by passing through the waters of the Flood. The Sumerian king-lists from the city of Larsa give the names of ten kings who reigned before the Flood, and the length of their reigns ranges from 10,000 to 60,000 years each, making the biblical Methuselah seem like a young man.

It has been conjectured by biblical scholars that the huge ages attributed to the kings in the Sumerian lists may be the product of astrological speculations, which applied measurements derived from the observation of the stars to the calculation of mythical regal periods. In the same way, the numbers in the priestly king-lists may have been arranged to correspond with a chronology which assigned a fixed number of years from the Creation of the World to the foundation of Solomon's Temple, and divided this period into epochs, the first of which from the Creation to the Flood is said to have contained 1,656 years.[2]

The king-list ends with the words: '*After the Flood kingship was sent down from on high*'. This states that a new group of rulers had to be found after the Flood. The seventh king in the Sumerian list was regarded as possessing special wisdom in matters pertaining to the gods, and as being the first of mankind to practise divination.

Sanskrit scholar Robert Temple believes that the *Epic of Gilgamesh* has been put together from a number of different sources, with fragments of it existing in five ancient languages.[3] The oldest material was ancient Sumerian, thought to have originated in a city named Eridu on the coast of the Persian Gulf about 2750 BC. Many scholars, including Temple, believe that it had existed as a verbal tradition before it was written down and that it was first formalized as a sacred drama.

[2] Hooke, S.H. 'Genesis' *Peake's Commentary on the Bible*
[3] Temple, R.: *He Who Saw Everything*, Century, 1991

So Utnapishtim, (or Ziusudra as he is also known) is the equivalent to the Biblical Noah. He was a king and priest of the Sumerian city of Shuruppak which is one of the original seven cities founded by the Seven Sages who the Sumarians believed were half-man, half-fish.[4] Gilgamesh's friend Enkidu, who shares many adventures with him, is called 'son of the fish' by a monster called the Huwawa. After they had founded the Sumerian civilization the fish-men, or Oannes as they were called, were said to have gone to the secret hideaway of the god Enki, who lived in a perfect cube under the sea.

The patron god of the Seven Sages was Enki who warned Ziusudra to construct an ark in which to save the seed of mankind. The ark is built as a replica of Enki's secret house beneath the seas, so was also in the form of a perfect cube. Here are the instructions Enki gave to Ziusudra, taken from Robert Temple's translation.

> *Tear down your hut of reeds, build of them an ark. Abandon things, seek life, give up possessions, keep your soul alive and take into the ark the seed of all living creatures. The ark you will build will have dimensions carefully measured. Its length and its width shall be equal and roof it as I have my subterranean watery abyss.*

Ziusudra explains to Gilgamesh how he followed the instructions.

> *On the fifth day I laid out the plan. The floor was on Iku. Its sides were ten gar high, each edge of its square measured ten gar (This is an area of approximately one acre) I delineated its exterior shape and fashioned it together thus dividing it into seven and the ground plan I divided into nine parts.*[5]

Ziusudra then tells Gilgamesh how he boarded the ark and made sure the door was safely closed before committing the navigation to his boatman Puzur-Amurri (a name which means the Western Star – possibly Venus in its evening position). He goes on to describe how the waters appear like a black cloud on the horizon. There is an enormous flash of light and then all is darkness as the waters of the seas rise up and overwhelm even the mountains. 'For six days and seven nights the flood wind blew.' Then at sunrise on the

[4] Hallo, W.W.: *Journal of Cuneiform Studies*, vol. 23, No 3, 1971, pp.57-67
[5] Temple, R.: *He Who Saw Everything*, Century, 1991

seventh day the sea grew quiet and the storm subsided, the flood ceased. Ziusudra continues:

> *I looked at the weather, it had gone quiet. All men had returned to clay, the land had been levelled like a terrace. I opened a dove flap and light fell on my face. I bowed and wept, tears flowing down my cheeks. I peered in every direction but the sea was everywhere. In each of the fourteen regions there emerged a mountain peak for that point.*[6]

Robert Temple makes the point in his translation notes that there are 14 mountain peaks associated with 14 major oracle centres known to the Egyptians, Minoans, and Babylonians. He also observes that Mount Tomaros where Deucalion (the Greek equivalent of Noah) landed is on exactly the same latitude as Mount Ararat where the Hebrew Noah is said to have landed.

Ziusudra then sends out a series of birds to see if the waters have really subsided. First he sends a dove, which returns, next a swallow, which also returns; and finally a raven, which does not return. Ziusudra then makes sacrifices to the gods. The most powerful of the gods, Ashtar, appears wearing jewels fashioned from lapis lazuli and is outraged that Enki has warned a human and saved his life. Enki then speaks out on behalf of Ziusudra, berating Enlil (the god responsible for causing the flood) for deciding to bring down a deluge without consulting the other gods and so killing the innocent along with the guilty.

In the epic, Ziusudra tells Gilgamesh that he must dive under the water to recover a special rose which holds the secret of eternal life. This we found interesting, because the five-petalled rose is a common symbol of the planet Venus and of resurrection and rebirth.

In his translation notes, Robert Temple comments that the Babylonian word for the Great Flood is 'Abubu', which he believes stems from the term 'Agh-hu-bua', meaning 'celestial inundation': literally the great deluge of the stars, perhaps put simply, the great rain of stars. He also comments on the meaning of the word used for the ark in the Genesis (Hebrew) version of the story – *teba*, which is an Egyptian word meaning box, chest or coffer. He adds that the perfect cube was used in the design of various temples which, according to the Bible, include the inner chamber of King Solomon's Temple.

[6] Temple, R.: *He Who Saw Everything*, Century, 1991

In the tablet describing how Gilgamesh is told by the tavern-keeper Siduri where to find the boatman, we learn the boatman uses 'stone things' and artefacts known as 'urnu-wigglers' to guide him across the Sea of Death. Gilgamesh threatens Urshanabi [or Puzur-Amun], the boatman to Ziusudra, by destroying his stone things and his urnu-wrigglers to force him to carry Gilgamesh across the Sea of Death to meet with the sole survivor of the celestial inundation.

Gilgamesh travels on through a long night and a short day to reach a garden of trees growing special living jewels and golden jewelled fruits. His journey is measured in a curious unit referred to as a 'beru' this has been translated as 'double hours', which are a twelfth part of a circle. On this journey he travels ten double hours in darkness and two double hours in light. If we take this at face value, the only latitude that could give 20 hours of normal darkness would be at least 65 degrees North or South of the equator – in other words, around the Arctic or Antarctic circles during mid winter!

Much of the *Epic of Gilgamesh* relates to events taking place in the movement of the stars. Some writers, such as Werner Papke, have interpreted it as entirely an astro-poem, in which all the events described have astronomical connotations.[7] The use of the strange unit of double hours in the description of Gilgamesh's visit to the garden of living jewels suggests a memory of an older tradition which was based on measurement units of a twelfth part of a circle.

THE FLOOD DESCRIBED IN THE DEAD SEA SCROLLS

The document styled as 1QapGen of the Dead Sea Scrolls, known as the *Tales of the Patriarchs*, adds to the story of the Flood. It tells us that the character called Enoch was involved along with Lamech and Noah. These were all names we knew well from Masonic ritual as well as from the Bible and so we read on with great interest.

Apparently Lamech was worried by the 'glorious countenance' of his son Noah. He thinks that his wife Bitenosh (which means 'Daughter of Man') might have been impregnated by one of the Watchers, but she reminds him of their lovemaking and assures him that she has never lain with any of the 'Sons of Heaven', and that Noah is indeed his true son. Lamech still isn't

[7] Papke, W.: *Die Sterne von Babylon*

quite sure, so he goes to his father, Methuselah, and asks his advice. Methuselah decides in turn to visit *his* father, Enoch, who had already been 'translated' (meaning, he had left Earthly life without experiencing death) to the highest heaven, a place called Parvain. (It is interesting to note that Enoch and Elijah are two of the only characters in the Bible who never died – including Jesus.)

So, because of this, Methuselah could still talk to Enoch as he sat with all the other Angels or Holy Ones discussing various matters of importance. Methuselah asks Enoch about Noah and is told how the Watchers came down from heaven to take human wives – but that Noah was not born of the Sons of Heaven, but of Lamech. The story goes on to tell how Noah was the most righteous of men and was to be given dominion over the whole Earth after the Flood.

The story is next taken up by Noah who tells how he landed in a vineyard on Mount Ararat after the Flood.

> *'Afterwards, I descended to the base of this mountain, I and my sons and grandsons . . . the devastation of the earth was large scale. Sons and daughters were born to me after the Flood. To Shem my oldest son was born first namely Arparchad, two years after the Flood. All the children of Shem were Elam, Ashur, Arparchard, Lud, Aram and five daughters. In addition the children of Ham were: Cush, Mizrain, Put, Canaan and seven daughters. The children of Jepheth were Gomer, Magog, Madai, Javan, Tubal, Moshok, Tiras and four daughters.*[8]

Noah goes on to describe how he restarted agriculture and planted new vineyards.

Another of the Dead Sea Scrolls, document 4Q370, contains a sermon about the Flood which tells of the sheer abundance of the world before the deluge. It also gives a detailed description of the Flood which starts with the earth being shaken just before the sea bursts from its depths:

> *So the Lord judged them according to all their practices, according to the designs arising from their evil hearts. He thundered against them in His might so that the very foundations of the earth were shaken.*

[8] 4Q531 Frag 1 Wise, M.: Abegg, M.: and Cook, E.: *The Dead Sea Scolls, a New Translation*, Harper San Francisco, 1996

Water burst forth from the depths, all the windows of heaven were thrown open, the depths poured out their awful waters, the windows of heaven emptied themselves of their rain. So they were destroyed by the Flood, every one of them perishing in the water for they disobeyed the commandments of the Lord. Therefore all on dry ground were blotted out, man and beast, bird and winged creature – all died; not even the giants escaped.[9]

A third fragment containing a sermon about the flood makes the point that all the Watchers and their half human offspring were destroyed in the flood. This did not tie in with the Book of Genesis, which says that these giants, born of the daughters of men, became men of renown after the flood.

OF GIANTS AND NEW ANIMALS

Returning to the Old Testament, we found yet another ancient Jewish story making reference to a race of giants produced by Earthly women. The most famous giant in the Bible is Goliath, who was slain by David's slingshot. We are told in I Chronicles 20:3-6 that he was a descendant of King Og of the Ammonites:

And he brought out the people that were in it, and cut them with saws, and with harrows of iron, and with axes. Even so dealt David with all the cities of the children of Ammon. And David and all the people returned to Jerusalem.

And it came to pass after this, that there arose war at Gezer with the Philistines; at which time Sibbechai the Hushathite slew Sippai, that was of the children of the giants: and they were subdued.

And there was war again with the Philistines; and Elhanan the son of Jair slew Lahmi the brother of Goliath the Gittite, whose spear staff was like a weaver's beam.

Why, we wondered, was it so important to the founders of the Jewish nation that David should be clearly seen to be replacing the last of the giants? Was it symbolically important that the old 'sons of God' had been replaced by a

[9] 4Q531 Frag 1 Wise, M.: Abegg, M.: and Cook, E.: *The Dead Sea Scolls, a New Translation*, Harper San Francisco, 1996

new order? David is certainly always cited as being the basis of Jesus' hereditary authority, despite the fact that he was the second king of the Jews.

II Samuel 21:20 tells us once again about David's battle with the giants, who are not only tall but have extra fingers.

> *And there was yet a battle in Gath, where was a man of great stature, that had on every hand six fingers, and on every foot six toes, four and twenty in number; and he also was born to the giants.*

There are references to these giants having survived the Flood in several books of the Bible including Genesis, Samuel, Deuteronomy and Joshua. They are also spoken of in various Apocryphal books such as the *Book of Judith*, the *Wisdom of Solomon*, the *Wisdom of Jesus the Son of Sirach* – and the *Book of Baruch*, which says:

> *There were the giants famous from the beginning, that were of so great stature, and so expert in war . . . But they were destroyed, because they had no wisdom, and perished through their own foolishness.*

It was the Dead Sea Scrolls that produced the most thorough account of these giants in a part of the *Book of Enoch* that had not been known before it was found amongst the damaged scrolls from Qumran. It is called, simply, the *Book of Giants*, and we now quote extensively from this exceptionally important fragmentary document, starting with a line that tells of some secret knowledge held by the giants and their ruthlessness towards men:

> *1Q23 Frag. 9 + 14 + 15 2[. . .] they knew the secrets of [. . .] 3[. . . si]n was great in the earth [. . .] 4[. . .] and they killed many [. . .] 5[. . . they begat] giants [. . .]*

The giants enjoy the fruits of the earth and watched normal people very closely:

> *4Q531 Frag. 3 2[. . . everything that the] earth produced [. . .] [. . .] the great fish [. . .] 4[. . .] the sky with all that grew [. . .] 5[. . . fruit of] the earth and all kinds of grain and all the trees [. . .] 6[. . .] beasts and reptiles . . . [al]l creeping things of the earth and*

they observed all [. . .] 8[. . . eve]ry harsh deed and [. . .] utterance [. . .] 9[. . .] male and female, and among humans [. . .]

The Watchers choose animals on which to experiment with unnatural breeding:

1Q23 Frag. 1 + 6 [. . . two hundred] donkeys, two hundred asses, two hundred . . . rams of the] flock, two hundred goats, two hundred [. . . beast of the] field from every animal, from every [bird . . .] [. . .] for miscegenation [. . .]

Their experimentations with animals and human women result in the creation of monstrous beings:

4Q531 Frag. 2 [. . .] they defiled [. . .] [. . . they begot] giants and monsters [. . .] [. . .] they begot, and, behold, all [the earth was corrupted . . .] [. . .] with its blood and by the hand of [. . .] [giant's] which did not suffice for them and [. . .] [. . .] and they were seeking to devour many [. . .] [. . .] [. . .] the monsters attacked it.

Corruption results from their terrible experimental breeding programme:

4Q532 Col. 2 Frags. 1 – 6 [. . .] flesh [. . .] al[l . . .] monsters [. . .] will be [. . .] [. . .] they would arise [. . .] lacking in true knowledge [. . .] because [. . .] [. . .] the earth [grew corrupt . . .] mighty [. . .] [. . .] they were considering [. . .] [. . .] from the angels upon [. . .] [. . .] in the end it will perish and die [. . .] [. . .] they caused great corruption in the [earth . . .] [. . . this did not] suffice to [. . .] they will be [. . .]

The giants begin to have a series of bad dreams and visions. Mahway, the giant son of the Angel Barakel, tells one of these dreams to other giants, how he sees a tablet holding a list of names, immersed in water. When it emerges, only three names remain. The dream represents the coming destruction by the Flood of all people except Noah and his family:

2Q26 [. . .] they drenched the tablet in the wa[ter . . .] [. . .] the waters went up over the [tablet . . .] [. . .] they lifted out the tablet from the water of [. . .]

4Q530 Frag.7 [. . . this vision] is for cursing and sorrow. I am the one who confessed [. . .] the whole group of the castaways that I shall go to [. . .] [. . . the spirits of the sl]ain complaining about their killers and crying out [. . .] that we shall die together and be made an end of [. . .] much and I will be sleeping, and bread[. . .] for my dwelling; the vision and also [. . .] entered into the gathering of the giants [. . .]

6Q8 [. . .] Ohya and he said to Mahway [. . .] [. . .] without trembling. Who showed you all this vision, [my] brother? [. . .] Barakel, my father, was with me. [. . .] Before Mahway had finished telling what [he had seen . . .] [. . . said] to him, Now I have heard wonders! If a barren woman gives birth [. . .]

4Q530 Frag. 4 [There]upon Ohya said to Ha[hya . . .] [. . . to be destroyed] from upon the earth and [. . .] [. . . the ea]rth. When [. . .] they wept before [the giants . . .]

4Q530 Frag. 7 [. . .] your strength [. . .] [. . .] Thereupon Ohya [said] to Hahya [. . .] Then he answered, It is not for us, but for Azaiel, for he did [. . . the children of] angels are the giants, and they would not let all their loved ones] be neglected [. . . we have] not been cast down; you have strength [. . .]

The giants realize that they cannot overcome the forces of heaven. Intriguingly, the *following* words are said to be spoken by someone called Gilgamesh.

4Q531 Frag. 1 [. . . I am a] giant, and by the mighty strength of my arm and my own great strength [. . . any]one mortal, and I have made war against them; but I am not [. . .] able to stand against them, for my opponents [. . .] reside in [Heav]en, and they dwell in the holy places. And not [. . . they] are stronger than I. [. . .] of the wild beast has come, and the wild man they call [me].

Gilgamesh is described as one of the giants, and Ohya reports how he has been 'forced' to have a dream:

> *[. . .] Then Ohya said to him, I have been forced to have a dream [. . .] the sleep of my eyes [vanished], to let me see a vision. Now I know that on [. . .] [. . .] Gilgamesh [. . .]*

The vision that Ohya is made to experience is of a tree that is uprooted by most of its roots, except three.

> *6Q8 Frag. 2 three of its roots [. . .] [while] I was [watching,] there came [. . . they moved the roots into] this garden, all of them, and not [. . .]*

The details of this next dream are obscure, but it bodes ill for the giants. The dreamers speak first to the monsters, then to the giants.

> *4Q530 Col. 2 concerns the death of our souls [. . .] and all his comrades, [and Oh]ya told them what Gilgamesh said to him [. . .] and it was said [. . .] 'concerning [. . .] the leader has cursed the potentates' and the giants were glad at his words. Then he turned and left [. . .] Thereupon two of them had dreams and the sleep of their eye, fled from them, and they arose and came to [. . . and told] their dreams, and said in the assembly of [their comrades] the monsters [. . . In] my dream I was watching this very night [and there was a garden . . .] gardeners and they were watering [. . . two hundred trees and] large shoots came out of their root [. . .] all the water, and the fire burned all [the garden . . .] They found the giants to tell them [the dream . . .]*

Enoch attempts to interpret these dreams.

> *[. . . to Enoch] the noted scribe, and he will interpret for us the dream. Thereupon his fellow Ohya declared and said to the giants, I too had a dream this night, O giants, and, behold, the Ruler of Heaven came down to earth [. . .] and such is the end of the dream. [Thereupon] all the giants [and monsters grew afraid and called Mahway. He came to them and the giants pleaded with him and sent*

him to Enoch [the noted scribe]. They said to him, Go [. . .] to you that [. . .] you have heard his voice. And he said to him, He will [. . . and] interpret the dreams [. . .] [. . .] how long the giants have to live. [. . .]

Then Mahway comes to Enoch and makes a request:

[. . . he mounted up in the air] like strong winds, and flew with his hands like ea[gles . . . he left behind] the inhabited world and passed over Desolation, the great desert [. . .] and Enoch saw him and hailed him, and Mahway said to him [. . .] hither and thither a second time to Mahway [. . . The giants await your words, and all the monsters of the earth. If [. . . has been carried [. . .] from the days of [. . .] their [. . .] and they will be added [. . .] [. . .] we would know from you their meaning [. . .] [. . . two hundred tr]ees that from heaven [came down . . .]

Enoch sends back a message of judgement, with hope for repentance:

4Q530 Frag. 2 The scribe [Enoch . . .] [. . .] a copy of the second tablet that [Enoch] se[nt . . .] in the very handwriting of Enoch the noted scribe [. . . In the name of God the great] and holy one, to Shemihaza and all [his companions . . .] let it be known to you that not [. . .] and the things you have done, and that your wives [. . .] they and their sons and the wives of [their sons . . .] by your licentiousness on the earth, and there has been upon you [. . . and the land is crying out] and complaining about you and the deeds of your children [. . .] the harm that you have done to it. [. . .] until Raphael arrives, behold, destruction [is coming, a great flood, and it will destroy all living things] and whatever is in the deserts and the seas. And the meaning of the matter [. . .] upon you for evil. But now, loosen the bonds bi[nding you to evil . . .] and pray.

So, the book starts by telling how the giants were the holders of great knowledge including all the hidden mysteries of nature and science. We are told that these Watchers exploited the fruitfulness of the Earth and also interfered with the breeding of many animals including donkeys, asses, sheep, goats and other types of animal. They carried out some strange breeding activities which are described as miscegenation, or the interbreeding of creatures of different species. Some of the results of their experiments were apparently monsters who turned on their masters.

We found all of this utterly remarkable. As a story, it is as spellbinding as any Greek myth or a yarn from the Arabian Nights. Yet there is one very significant difference: this story appears to be a memory of something that actually happened!

The very sudden appearance of new varieties of plants and animals around the time of the Flood is accepted because we know it happened. Our modern minds are conditioned to accept the obvious as though it is entirely natural. But these events seem to be anything but natural.

Shortly after the flood of 9,640 years ago, we know that the species of animals that we fondly call 'domesticated' suddenly came into being. Could these ancient Jewish texts be recording a racial memory of some carefully planned genetic engineering? In the town of Jericho, for instance, the evidence is quite clear.

Zoo-archaeologists can distinguish wild from domesticated animals by analysing bone remains. Experts will happily agree that 10,000 years ago the people of Jericho had corralled wolf, bezoar, Asiatic moufflon, wild boar, auroch and wild cat. But a few hundred years later they are just as sure that those same animals had been largely replaced by previously unknown creatures. Their replacements were respectively, the dog, the goat, the sheep, the pig, the cow and the domestic cat. The previous animals did not just turn cute and docile – they changed their form and their nature to become absolutely suited to human needs.

How?

Surely, there was too little time for normal evolution? By constrast, however, there may have been time to re-engineer the DNA characteristics of the core species that the surviving humans needed for the beginning of a new age. Why else did these fundamental, species-defining changes occur in such a short space of time?

Today we can, and do, cross nature's boundaries of breeding by artificial means; we call it 'genetic engineering'. Nature only allows breeding within a species, but man has found ways to create new varieties of animals and plants. In fact, recent developments are causing a similar outcry to that which the ancient records suggest happened in times before history officially began.

Many people today are unhappy about cloning experiments such as those carried out at the Roslin Institute near Edinburgh, where Dolly the sheep has seen herself replicated. Even those who are normally relaxed about genetic experiments are starting to see that we could be creating a disaster for mankind. In 1998 it became public knowledge that agricultural seed breeders have the ability to create infertile crop species: you can plant their hyper-efficient seed varieties, the seed and the crops will grow for you to process an abundant harvest – but try and plant some of the seed produced by these varieties and it will rot in the ground. These masters of genetic engineering have built into the plants' 'software' the right to use the designer species just once, ensuring themselves a returning customer every planting season.

But what if there is a catastrophe of some kind – a war or a natural disaster, such as a comet impact? People will starve as they desperately try to make sterile seed grow, and the survivors will tell, and retell, folk stories of the mistaken experiments of the giant companies that once thought they ruled the Earth.

Another example of how we have reached a dangerous stage in experimentation is attempting to remove nature's barriers to inter-species breeding. Genetic engineers can introduce foreign DNA into a fertile egg/seed. In normal sexual intercourse, the sperm of the foreign species would be rejected by the egg's natural protective outer coating. By mechanically bypassing this protection mechanism, cross-species miscegenates can be produced. This technique is already highly developed to manufacture genetically modified food and became the subject of serious opposition in 1998 when the British Government authorized the open-air planting of genetically modified oil-seed rape. All the environmental protection groups expressed fears about releasing genetically modified rape pollen into the wild, but before the crop could flower it was destroyed by a fire.

Could these ancient documents mean what they say? Did people have the ability to control inter-species breeding at some time in the extreme past? The automatic response is to say, 'This has to be impossible' – but if *we* can do it, it is *not* impossible. Why on Earth did these ancient people record such a strange idea in connection with a Flood, one that we are finding is not at all fictional?

ENOCH DESCRIBES THE SEVEN COMET FRAGMENTS HIT TIN 6 EARTH

Putting the story of the Book of Enoch into sequence, we see that in Chapter Six it tells us that there was an advanced but 'unholy' civilization before the global Flood, when earthly women had been impregnated by a group of 200 giants.

> *And it came to pass when the children of men had multiplied that in those days were born unto them beautiful and comely daughters. And the angels, the children of the heaven, saw and lusted after them, and said to one another: 'Come, let us choose us wives from among the children of men and beget us children.' And Semjaza, who was their leader, said unto them: 'I fear ye will not indeed agree to do this deed, and I alone shall have to pay the penalty of a great sin.' And they all answered him and said: 'Let us all swear an oath, and all bind ourselves by mutual imprecations not to abandon this plan but to do this thing.' Then sware they all together and bound themselves by mutual imprecations upon it. And they were in all two hundred; who descended in the days of Jared on the summit of Mount Hermon, and they called it Mount Hermon, because they had sworn and bound themselves by mutual imprecations upon it.*

Then it moves on to describe in perfect detail the events leading up to the cometary disaster that has been identified from a raft of geological records.

We are next told how these 'Watchers' taught ordinary men the hidden mysteries of nature and science:

> *And Azazel taught men to make swords, and knives, and shields, and breastplates, and made known to them the metals of the earth and the art of working them, and bracelets, and ornaments, and the use of antimony, and the beautifying of the eyelids, and all kinds of costly stones, and all colouring tinctures. And there arose much godlessness, and they committed fornication, and they were led astray, and became corrupt in all their ways. Semjaza taught enchantments, and root-cuttings, Armaros the resolving of enchantments, Baraqijal (taught) astrology, Kokabel the constellations, Ezeqeel the knowledge of the clouds, Araqiel the signs of the earth, Shamsiel the signs of the sun, and Sariel the course of the moon.*

Soon the archangels, displeased at what is happening, decide that the Earth shall be destroyed:

And then Michael, Uriel, Raphael, and Gabriel looked down from heaven and saw much blood being shed upon the earth, and all lawlessness being wrought upon the earth. Then said the Most High, the Holy and Great One spake, and sent Uriel to the son of Lamech, [i.e. Noah] and said to him: 'Go to Noah and tell him in my name 'Hide thyself!' and reveal to him the end that is approaching: that the whole earth will be destroyed, and a deluge is about to come upon the whole earth, and will destroy all that is on it. And now instruct him that he may escape and his seed may be preserved for all the generations of the world.

We are told that Enoch apparently goes away somewhere with the Watchers:

Before these things Enoch was hidden, and no one of the children of men knew where he was hidden, and where he abode, and what had become of him. And his activities had to do with the Watchers . . .

Enoch then describes the place where he was taken by the Watchers:

And they brought me to the place of darkness, and to a mountain the point of whose summit reached to heaven. And I saw the places of the luminaries and the treasuries of the stars and of the thunder and in the uttermost depths

. . .and behold there came forth from heaven beings who were like white men: and four went forth from that place and three with them. And those three that had last come forth grasped me by my hand and took me up, away from the generations of the earth, and raised me up to a lofty place, and showed me a tower raised high above the earth, and all the hills were lower. And one said unto me: 'Remain here till thou seest everything that befalls.'

Then the coming disaster is foreseen with a comet smashing down upon the Earth. The cause of the Flood is explicitly stated as being due to extraterrestrial impacts. The consequences of the comet hits is described:

I saw in a vision how the heaven collapsed and was borne off and fell to the earth. And when it fell to the earth I saw how the earth was swallowed up in a great abyss, and mountains were suspended on mountains, and hills sank down on hills, and high trees were rent from their stems, and hurled down and sunk in the abyss. And thereupon a word fell into my mouth, and I lifted up (my voice) to cry aloud, and said: 'The earth is destroyed'.

Then, the following words unequivocally describe the arrival of the seven lumps of comet that were bearing down upon the earth:

I saw there seven stars like great burning mountains, and to me, when I inquired regarding them, The angel said: 'This place is the end of heaven and earth: this has become a prison for the stars and the host of heaven. And the stars which roll over the fire are they which have transgressed the commandment of the Lord in the beginning of their rising, because they did not come forth at their appointed times. And He was wroth with them, and bound them till the time when their guilt should be consummated (even) for ten thousand years.'

Enoch then asks in apparent dismay why these seven flaming stars are bound for the earth:

And there I saw seven stars of the heaven bound together in it, like great mountains and burning with fire. Then I said: 'For what sin are they bound, and on what account have they been cast in hither?'

In a dream, Enoch foresees the moment of disaster:

And again I saw with mine eyes as I slept, and I saw the heaven above, and behold a star fell from heaven . . . And behold I saw many stars descend and cast themselves down from heaven to that first star . . . and behold all the children of the earth began to tremble and quake before them and to flee from them. And again I saw how they began to gore each other and to devour each other, and the earth began to cry aloud.

Then the seas rise up over the land, even into the mountains:

And the spirit of the sea is masculine and strong, and according to the might of his strength he draws it back with a rein, and in like manner it is driven forward and disperses amid all the mountains.

And thence I went towards the east, into the midst of the mountain range of the desert, and I saw a wilderness and it was solitary, full of trees and plants. And water gushed forth from above. Rushing like a copious watercourse [which flowed] towards the north-west it caused clouds and dew to ascend on every side And all the cattle of that enclosure were gathered together until I saw how they sank and were swallowed up and perished in that water sinking to the bottom with all the animals, so that I could no longer see them, and they were not able to escape, (but) perished and sank into the depths. And again I saw in the vision till those water torrents were removed from that high roof, and the chasms of the earth were levelled up and other abysses were opened. Then the water began to run down into these, till the earth became visible; but that vessel settled on the earth, and the darkness retired and light appeared.

These words were written down over 2000 years ago from an ancient oral tradition. That they describe a cometary impact upon the Earth is, we believe, beyond dispute. The idea of an extraterrestrial impact occurs in at least one other ancient account from the area of the Mediterranean. The so-called *Sibylline Oracles* contain information that is apparently linked to the events described in Enoch. These stories, attributed to female prophets called Sibyls, are generally thought to have taken their current form at about the same time that the *Book of Enoch* was written down, and likewise they are acknowledged to be much older. They were certainly mentioned by early classical Greek writers such as Plato, Plutarch and Heraclitus of Ephesus. Belief in the importance of the Sibyls persisted into the early Christian era, when they were briefly accorded an authority equal to the Old Testament prophets.

The passages that are particularly interesting refer to a star falling into the ocean causing winter to come immediately:

and from heaven a great star shall fall on the dread ocean and burn up the deep sea, with Babylon itself and the land of Italy, by reason of which many of the Hebrews perished.

. . . Be afraid, ye Indians and high-hearted Ethiopians: for when the fiery wheel of the ecliptic . . . and Capricorn . . . and Taurus among the Twins encircles the mid-heaven, when the Virgin ascending and the Sun fastening the girdle round his forehead dominates the whole firmament; there shall be a great conflagration from the sky, falling on the earth;

And then in his anger the immortal God who dwells on high shall hurl from the sky a fiery bolt on the head of the unholy: and summer shall change to winter in that day.[10]

ENOCHIAN JUDAISM

All of the information we had put together had convinced us that Enoch must have been far more important to the Jews of 2000 years ago than anyone had previously thought. The *Book of Enoch* was of great importance to the Qumran Community, with no less than nine fragmentary copies of the book among the Dead Sea Scrolls, and yet the work did not survive into Rabbinical Judaism or into Christianity past the first century AD. It seemed to us that there must have once been a great allegiance to the figure of Enoch which died with the Jewish nation during the war that broke out in AD 66. The Contemporary historian Josephus states that 1.3 million Jews died in this terrible conflict, leaving the way open for two new religions as the old Judaism of the Temple was crushed out of sight.

Chris decided to put the thought that the importance of Enoch was once far greater, to our good friend Professor Philip Davies, the well-known Biblical scholar and expert on the Dead Sea Scrolls. Philip is a generous man who always looks for reasons to support a new idea before he introduces the counter-view in a measured manner. However, his response was entirely positive.

'Ah, yes,' he said, nodding. 'The idea is not daft at all. In fact there is a definite school of thought emerging at the moment that there may have been two distinct forms of Judaism that can be detected in the Qumran scrolls.'

This was interesting news indeed. He then explained that he had just reviewed a new book for an academic publication that was based very much upon this idea.

[10] ***Sibylline Oracles.***

In his review of a book by Gabriele Boccaccini, Philip Davies stated that there was now widespread agreement that the documents found at Qumran reflect an earlier dispute between priestly traditions, and he believed that Boccaccini had made an impressive attempt at a new synthesis, building upon the work of his mentor P. Sacchi and upon the theories of the 'Groningen school' that the Qumran group must be distinguished from a parent movement whose ideas are equally well-represented in the Dead Sea Scrolls.[11] The rest of the review made fascinating reading:

> *Boccaccini postulates two rival priestly schools: the Zadokite and the Enochic, which differed doctrinally over the origin and nature of sin. The Enochians believed that evil originated from above and could not be removed from the earth; the Zadokites that sin could be avoided by following the Mosaic law. Other differences between them lay in their calendar, and in the espousal by Enochians of apocalyptic. The Qumran texts preserve features of both Judaisms, including compromises between the two views. Boccaccini traces from I Enoch, through Daniel, Jubilees and the Temple Scroll, a merging of the Enochic and Mosaic (Zadokite) traditions that occurred in the wake of the Maccabean war. In the Halakhic Letter (4QMMT) he sees a manifesto of the Enochic priesthood against a now disenfranchized Zadokite priesthood, and in the Damascus Document an attempt by followers of the Teacher of Righteousness to control the Enochic movement which was accommodating its views to those of the Zadokites. The Teacher's failure led to the founding of a community at Qumran which broke with the main Enochic movement, producing a dualistic and strongly predestination ideology. On several details here and there I disagree, but Boccaccini has an impressive and stimulating synthesis which makes an important advance in our understanding of what the Scrolls mean for ancient Judaism.*[12]

So, it seems that there were once two forms of Judaism; one looking to Moses for their inspiration and another, far older, looking to Enoch.

As amateur biblical historians, we had become convinced of the importance of the group led first by John the Baptist, then by Jesus and then

[11] Boccaccini, G.: *Beyond the Essenes*, Eerdmans (Grand Rapids), 1998

[12] Private communication, Professor Philip Davies.

by Jesus's, brother James. In our first book we put forward the idea that these leaders were hereditary priests and kings of Israel who thought the end of the present world was about to happen at the time of Jesus. To us, the evidence showed that the Qumran community had been deeply connected with an ancient form of Judaism, and that the so-called 'Jerusalem Church' had sprung from the Qumran community. Furthermore, we found that countless scholars had abundant evidence that Christianity in its current form had been more or less invented by St Paul in very Roman, rather than Jewish terms.[13]

However, there are clear strands of Enochian Judaism still surviving in the Christian Scripture, despite the fact that they are not understood by Christians. The last two books that squeezed into the New Testament are the most obvious Enochian works.

The very short Epistle of Jude was declared canonical at the Council of Carthage in AD 397, despite its gnostic tendencies. There are various theories as to the identity of the author, including that he was one of the brothers of Jesus, but one of the more likely possibilities is that it was written by Jude, the son of James (the brother of Jesus). This Jude was therefore nephew to Jesus and hereditary leader of the Jerusalem Church. Indeed, he became the bishop of Jerusalem when his father, James, was murdered in AD 62[14]. It is known that Jude drew upon *Enoch* and the *Assumption of Moses*, which were both of great importance to the Qumran community.[15]

Revelation is a curious book, which may have been written by a person who witnessed the destruction of Jerusalem. It is apocalyptic in the style of the books of Enoch and Daniel. This writer foresees another comet disaster coming because of man's failings. Revelation 8:7 to 9:1 is clearly predicting just a such an event as Enoch did when its author says:

> *The first angel sounded, and there followed hail and fire mingled with blood, and they were cast upon the earth: and the third part of trees was burnt up, and all green grass was burnt up.*
>
> *And the second angel sounded, and as it were a great mountain burning with fire was cast into the sea: and the third part of the sea became blood;*

[13] Knight, C.: and Lomas, R.: *The Hiram Key*, Century, 1996
[14] Boobyer, G.H.: 'Jude,' from *Peake's Commentary on the Bible*
[15] Knight, C. and Lomas, R.: *The Hiram Key*, Century, 1996

And the third part of the creatures which were in the sea, and had life, died; and the third part of the ships were destroyed.

And the third angel sounded, and there fell a great star from heaven, burning as it were a lamp, and it fell upon the third part of the rivers, and upon the fountains of waters;

And the name of the star is called Wormwood: and the third part of the waters became wormwood; and many men died of the waters, because they were made bitter.

And the fourth angel sounded, and the third part of the sun was smitten, and the third part of the moon, and the third part of the stars; so as the third part of them was darkened, and the day shone not for a third part of it, and the night likewise.

And I beheld, and heard an angel flying through the midst of heaven, saying with a loud voice, Woe, woe, woe, to the inhabiters of the earth by reason of the other voices of the trumpet of the three angels, which are yet to sound!

And the fifth angel sounded, and I saw a star fall from heaven unto the earth: and to him was given the key of the bottomless pit.

The disaster that Enoch apparently predicted did occur – but the prophecy contained in Revelation has not, as yet, happened.

The story of Enoch and the tradition that celebrated him appear to have died, on the surface at least. Remarkably, Freemasonry is possibly the last surviving strand of this very ancient tradition.

ENOCHIAN FREEMASONRY

As we have established, the tradition of Enoch survives in present-day Masonry in various ways. Another significant connection with Enoch is a Masonic Degree called The Princes Rose Croix of Heredom of the Ancient and Accepted Rite for England and Wales, which is now open only to Christian Freemasons. We believe that it was, in fact, an exclusively Enochian-Jewish rite that has been altered to introduce Jesus as the principal character in place of Enoch.

It has gone through various changes to remove unwanted elements over the last 150 years or so. In 1994 the ritual was amended a little, to make it even more acceptable to mainstream Christianity. The notes from this edition of the printed ritual say:

> *This new edition of the ritual contains very few alterations . . . the scripture reading which follows is a most difficult one- involving the hardly explicable 'until Shiloh come'.*

This is typical of the foolish tinkering that English Freemasons have conducted for centuries. They are like children playing with a irreplaceable ancient relic, unaware of the unbelievable damage they are inflicting on the archaeo-ethnological gem that has been entrusted to them by previous generations. They do not understand the ancient Masonic ritual so they change it to something entirely wrong, so that simple-minded souls do not get too confused. They can then get on with play-acting their corrupted rituals without the stress of having to understand what they were really meant to convey.

The continual nibbling away at the authentic ritual by ignorant Masons continues. In 1996 edition of the ritual, the opening notes show that the present rulers of the degree are extremely concerned to make sure that all the ceremonies are perceived as Christian and have changed the ritual to make sure this impression is maintained. The ritual now has the Sovereign say to the assembly:

> *Princes, the candidate for Perfection having stated that he professes the Trinitarian Christian faith and that he is willing to take an obligation in the name of the Holy and Undivided Trinity, we will proceed.*

This recent requirement is a confirmation of the outrageous scam that has been introduced to prevent any Jew or Muslim from progressing into the so-called higher degrees of the Ancient and Accepted Rite. Freemasonry has much to be proud of, but also a number of things of which it should be deeply ashamed.

In the ritual, the purpose of the degree is explained in this exchange between the master of the chapter (the lodge), who is addressed as Most Wise Sovereign, and one of the senior officers who is known as the Excellent and Perfect First General.

> ***Sovereign:*** *Excellent and Perfect First General – what is the hour?*
>
> ***1st General:*** *The ninth hour of the day.*

Sovereign: *Then it is the hour when the veil of the Temple was rent in twain and darkness overspread the earth, when the true Light departed from us, the altar was thrown down, the Blazing Star was eclipsed, the Cubic Stone poured forth blood and water, the Word was lost, and despair and tribulation sat heavily upon us.*

Since masonry has experienced such dire calamities it is our duty, Princes, to endeavour by renewed labours to retrieve our loss. May the benign influence of Faith, Hope and Charity prosper our endeavours to recover the lost Word for which purpose I declare this Chapter of Princes Rose Croix of Heredom duly open in the name of the great Emmanuel.

Although the ceremony as it is used today conveys a totally Christian message, enough of the original remains to strongly suggest that it was once telling the story of a visit to heaven by Enoch. Indeed, most of the references to Jesus are quite forced.

The Sovereign says to the newly 'perfected' candidate.

The eagle reminds us that the Saviour is God Himself; as He said to the Israelites of old; 'I bare you on eagles' wings and brought you unto myself.

The rose is an emblem of secrecy and silence. In the Song of Solomon we find reference to the Saviour under the mystical title of the Rose of Sharon.

The quote in the first part comes directly from Exodus 19:4 when Moses went up Mount Sinai and asked God for advice on what to say to the Israelites. The second part is a completely unsustainable interpretation of the Song of Solomon. Why is the rose an emblem of secrecy and silence? Despite the fertile imagination of some Christians, there is nothing in this work or in any part of the Old Testament that refers to Jesus Christ. How could it, unless one declares a belief in time travel or primitive magic?

The Song of Solomon has nothing to do with Jesus – we read it as simply a beautiful poem about a woman in love and a celebration of the coming of spring although some scholars see it as a love song between the sun and the moon.[16] But even to link this interpretation to Jesus would involve viewing

[16] Bailey, H.: *The Lost Language of Symbolism*, 1998

him as a type of stellar god which is unlikely to be the intention of the Masonic revisionists.

> *I am the rose of Sharon, and the lily of the valleys . . . I charge you, O ye daughters of Jerusalem by the roes and by the hinds of the field, that ye stir not up, nor awake my love, till he please.*

The degree of Sovereign Prince Rose Croix was once the 18th degree of the 33 degrees of the Ancient and Accepted Scottish Rite.

The ceremony consists of the candidate being taken on a journey through a series of rooms and eventually up a ladder to heaven. The officer who conducts the candidate is called Raphael. He meets the candidate in the Black Room. This is remarkably similar to the meeting between Enoch and Raphael when Enoch is given a tour of the seven heavens and taught the secrets of nature. Here is the description of Enoch's experience given in 1 Enoch 22: 1-3:

> *1 And thence I went to another place, and the mountain [and] of hard rock.*
>
> *2 And there was in it four hollow places, deep and wide and very smooth. How smooth are the hollow places and deep and dark to look at.*
>
> *3 Then Raphael answered, one of the holy angels who was with me, and said unto me: 'These hollow places have been created for this very purpose, that the spirits of the souls of the dead should*
>
> *4 assemble therein, yea that all the souls of the children of men should assemble here. And these places have been made to receive them till the day of their judgement and till their appointed period [till the period appointed], till the great judgement (comes) upon them.'*

The stage directions for the Rose Croix ritual tell how the Black Room and the Chamber of Death are to be arranged:

> *All the general lighting in the approaches to the Black Room and between the Black Room and Chamber of Death must be*

extinguished. Every precaution should be taken to prevent any extraneous lighting disturbing the candidate's journey through darkness.

A black veil is placed on the candidate's head so that it covers his face. The candidate is led into the Chamber of Death and seated facing the emblems of mortality. He is left for a while to meditate upon them. The Marshall retires from the Chamber of Death leaving the candidate alone to meditate on the emblems of mortality.

After a pause Raphael with sword at the carry enters the Chamber of Death admitting as little light as possible.

Notice that the guide for the candidate is none other than Raphael himself – Enoch's guide! It is he who explains to the candidate why he is there.

I come to conduct you from the depths of darkness and the Valley of the Shadow of Death to the Mansions of Light.

It can be no coincidence that Chapter 71 of the Book of Enoch begins as follows:

And I saw the holy sons of God. They were stepping on flames of fire: Their garments were white [and their raiment], And their faces shone like snow.

2 And I saw two streams of fire, And the light of that fire shone like hyacinth, And I fell on my face before the Lord of Spirits.

3 And the angel Michael [one of the archangels] seized me by my right hand, And lifted me up and led me forth into all the secrets, And he showed me all the secrets of righteousness.

4 And he showed me all the secrets of the ends of the heaven, And all the chambers of all the stars, and all the luminaries, Whence they proceed before the face of the holy ones.

5 And he translated my spirit into the heaven of heavens, And I saw there as it were a structure built of crystals, And between those crystals tongues of living fire.

There is one last clue in this degree which links it with Enoch and with the planet Venus. When the Rose Croix Chapter is closed, the following ritual dialogue is conducted between the Sovereign and the officer called the Excellent and Perfect Prelate.

Sov: *Excellent and Perfect Prelete, what is the hour?*

Prel: *It is the first hour of the third day, being the first day of the week – the hour of a Perfect Mason.*

Sov: *What is the hour of a Perfect Mason?*

Prel: *It is the hour when the Word is found and the Cubic Stone is changed into the Mystic Rose. The Blazing Star has reappeared in all its splendour; our altars are renewed; the true Light restored to our eyes; the clouds of darkness dispersed; and the New Covenant is given.*

The 'Mystic Rose' is not some unbelievably obscure reference to the Christian 'saviour' but to the mysterious properties of the planet Venus. These properties were central to an understanding of the hidden mysteries of nature and science (a central theme of Freemasonry).

THE METRONOME OF THE SOLAR SYSTEM

Venus is the second planet from the sun and the Earth is the third. Venus is the third brightest object in the sky, and so intense is its light that it casts a discernible shadow on a moonless night.

The orbit of Venus is such that it produces a very strange but interesting effect when viewed from Earth against the backdrop of fixed stars that we know as the zodiac. The planet appears to move in the form of a five-pointed star with the sun at its centre, taking a 40-year cycle to repeat the process. These movements are far more reliable than the proverbial Swiss clock. If one understands the position of Venus, one knows the time and date to a precision measured in seconds over hundreds of years (See Figure 16).

Figure 8. *Egyptian hieroglyphs that incorporate the five-pointed star to demonstrate knowledge.*

The relationship between the synodic Venus year and the Earth year repeats at nearly five Venus synodic years to eight Earth years. It's not quite exact, being about a third of a day out and of course this error grows. But it is a fact that after 14,597 days the relationships between Venus and the sun will repeat exactly. However, the event does not happen in quite the same place in the zodiac. Here again the cycles can help, because Venus can be guaranteed to occupy exactly the same zodiac position as it does today, in 14,607 days time. That is exactly 40 years less three full days. Ten days later Venus will have moved to exactly the same position relative to the sun that it had been 40 years earlier. There are also various shorter periods when matches occur, roughly every eight years. We would remember this relationship when we came to study the calendar implications of the *Book of Enoch*.

This remarkable periodic relationship between the position of the Earth to the sun (i.e. the time of the calendar year) and the appearances of Venus against the backdrop of the fixed stars, were used by astronomers to correct the civil calendar until the development of atomic clocks in this century gave us a more accurate means of keeping our calendar in line. Amazingly, the five-pointed star shape which describes this calendar pattern of Venus is still depicted at the centre of the ceiling of all English Masonic temples. The mystical five-pointed star is shown with a bright light at its centre to represent the sun and is superimposed with a letter 'G' (representing God, the Most High).

We are certain that it is no coincidence that the five-pointed star was the Ancient Egyptian hieroglyph for 'knowledge'. Anyone who understood the movements of Venus was in possession of the most important knowledge of science; a detailed understanding of the seasons from planting through the beneficial inundation of the Nile, to the perfect harvest.

In many traditions the Venus symbol of the five-pointed star is intimately related to the five-petalled rose, which is also a symbol of resurrection and virgin birth.

The symbol of the five-petalled dog rose is another symbolic representation of the synchronized Venus-earth cycle. Even the stamen ring at the centre can represent the sun at the focus of the Venus transits.

A further reason for the choice of the rose as resurrection symbol linked to Venus is the reproductive nature of the *Rosa Canina*, the common five-petalled dog rose. This plant has the ability to fruit without being pollinated by another plant. Most flowers reproduce by sexual means (cross-pollination) but the dog rose simply does not need a mate in order to produce a rose hip. Therefore, the plant can die and yet be born again, identical to its former self.

We believe this association with 'virgin birth' and 'resurrection' has

Figure 9. *How the star Venus maps onto the shape of a rose. The centre of the rose represents the sun.*

caused Christian Freemasons to believe, erroneously, that the references to the rose of Sharon in the Rose Croix degree is a reference to Jesus.

THE HANGING ANGEL

There is one further important connection that we should mention at this point. It is between the story of the Flood in the *Book of Enoch* and Rosslyn – the curious medieval building in Scotland that appears to mark the transition from Templarism to Freemasonry. Inside Rosslyn, at the precise centre of the heavily carved eastern wall, is an inverted angel suspended by a rope tied to his legs. Without doubt this is a representation of Shemhazai who was instrumental in causing the Flood.

According to the Jewish Enochian legend, the Antediluvians had committed many great sins which upset God so much that he regretted having made humans in the first place. Two angels called Shemhazai and Azazel came to God and asked for permission to come down to earth and live among men to try to redeem mankind. God gave them His permission, but as they mixed with the children of man they took to sin themselves, with Shemhazai felling in love with the beautiful Ishtar (the Babylonian goddess of love and war). She would only take him as a suitor on condition he told the secret name of God, and Shemhazai lusted after her so much that he told her the most secret Word. Ishtar then used the power of the Word to ascend to heaven to shine for ever and ever among the stars of the Pleiades. After being duped in this way, Shembazai and Azazel decided to choose wives from among the daughters of men and had children by them. They each had two daughters – Heyya and Aheyya, and Hiwwa and Hiija – who lead men into great sins. Hiwwa and Hiija dreamt that they saw angels with axes cutting down the trees of a great garden. Soon after this dream, God told Shemhazai and Azazel that he would send a great flood to destroy the world. Shemhazai repented of his sins but was afraid to face God and so he suspended himself between heaven and earth, handing by a rope, head downwards because he was afraid to appear before God (see plate 30). Azazel however did not repent but continued to lead the people of the Earth into greater and greater sins until God finally sent the Flood to destroy them.[17]

CONCLUSION

The Flood legends of the Bible seem to be based on memories of real events, but a number of different traditions have been combined into a confusing amalgam. The Sumerian story of Gilgamesh tells a very similar story but suggests the Ark is a cubical survival chamber rather than a boat. Some parts of the Gilgamesh story describe visits to places in the far north of the world to look for survivors of the Flood.

The Dead Sea Scrolls have added to the stories of the Flood by telling us more about the giants and the Watchers, and by showing that the *Book of Enoch* had been extremely popular the with Qumran Community.

The *Book of Enoch* describes events which geology has confirmed happened in 7640 BC. It transpires that Enoch was a far more important figure in early Judaism than had been previously realized, and modern biblical research shows that a separate form of Enochian Judaism existed up to the Roman destruction of the Temple.

There are also remains of Enochian degrees in Freemasonry which have been Christianized by 19th century Freemasons. The Enochian material seems to be closely involved with Venus symbolism, which is also present in the third degree of Freemasonry. English Freemason's lodge contains a symbol of the movements of Venus around the sun, the five-pointed star usually found at the centre of Temple, which forms the most accurate calendar system known to observational astronomy.

[17] Gaster, M.: *The Chronicles of Jarahmeel*, 1890

Chapter Five

A WATERSHED FOR MANKIND

THE AMERICAN WAVE

Chicago had been cold; around minus 9° Celsius. As Chris took off from O'Hare bound for Dallas-Fort Worth, his mind turned to the huge ice sheet that once ended at this point. Texas was enjoying a splendid February heat-wave of 26°, and the flight of around two hours was a welcome doorway from deep winter to high summer.

Three days later Chris was *en route* for San Francisco, where the climate was a cooler, but still very acceptable, 18° Celsius. As the plane swung westwards the first town to come into view was Clovis, New Mexico. This was the place where Stone Age man had manufactured thin, tapered points for spears that brought down mammoths as far back as 11,500 years ago. The finding of these artefacts gave rise to the term 'Clovis Horizon' to describe what was then considered to be the historical edge of human presence in America.

The thought was unavoidable. What happened to these people when the comet struck?

Given that modern passenger aircraft usually cruise at a height of around ten kilometres above sea level, it was easy to imagine what the huge tsunami waves must have looked like tearing across land masses and swamping mountain peaks. As the plane flew onwards across the deserts of New Mexico, Arizona, Utah and Nevada, it seemed that the mountain chains and the valleys were running almost north to south, and therefore were aligned with the direction of the comet strike in the Pacific where the depth of water is around fire kilometres deep. According to Robert's comments about impact waves, the tsunami that hit the coast of southern Californian and north Mexico could have been the best part of five kilometres high as the 'potential' energy of wave height at the coast was converted from to 'kinetic' energy of the breaking wave. The displaced ocean must have ripped over the places that are now Los Angeles and San Diego and hurtled north and east, obliterating all life in its terrible wake.

Could the sea's up-thrust have poured into the Great Basin of the western United States and even spilled over the Rocky Mountains to send unimaginable volumes of Pacific waters cascading down onto the Great Plains of the central USA? Perhaps, too, these floodwaters were met by the tsunami from the Atlantic comet strike as it surged westwards across the lowlying land from Florida to the Rio Grande?

Could it be the land that is now the United States of America was the comet's greatest victim?

As Chris looked down from the aircraft, he could visualize the giant rolling wave and appreciate for the first time the real scale of disaster that surely unfolded here less than 10,000 years ago. Mud-blackened waters smothering the entire landscape before returning to the ocean like a wild animal satiated with the blood of its victim. Once the waters reached equilibrium, again the valleys and lowlying areas must have been transformed into inland seas. The whole landscape must have looked like a giant rock-pool after the tide has ebbed away.

The Great Plains are flushed with regular rains and drained by a web of rivers that flow into the Gulf of Mexico, so the cleansing rain would have long ago removed the evidence of a sea incursion. But west of the Rocky Mountains, the land is arid with few rivers, and the only significant watercourse is the Colorado River running back to the Gulf of California.

An immediate thought was: What happened to those inland seas? The answer seemed obvious. There was nowhere for them to go except upwards. They must have simply evaporated away over many years. But if so, they must have left a mineral deposit behind. Chris looked out of the aircraft window to check his thought.

Yes, the ground below was white – white with salt.

Though too far north to be seen from this aircraft, the Great Salt Lake and the Great Salt Lake Desert were just 300 miles away, in north-western Utah. This is the largest salt lake in the western hemisphere and one of the saltiest stretches of water on the planet. The principal rivers flowing into the lake are the Bear, Weber, and the Jordan. No streams empty from the lake, so the only outlet for water is through evaporation.

Could these huge salt deposits be a result of comet tsunami? Chris seemed to remember that the lake is eight times saltier than the ocean, which suggested it could have been created from what had been an original volume of sea water eight times greater than today's lake settling in the area.

Immediately upon return to the UK, Chris checked out the known facts. He read that the dimensions of the lake can change drastically from year to year because of variations in the amount of water that flows into it. Today, it is normally about 120 kilometres long from north to south and about 50 to 80 kilometres wide, but over a 30-year period from 1962, its surface area increased by 237 per cent, from 2,500 to 6,000 square kilometres. This dramatic change in shoreline size was due to an increase in depth of just six metres.[1]

Apparently, the Great Salt Lake is considered to be a remnant of the glacial Lake Bonneville, which covered approximately 50,000 square kilometres during the Pleistocene Epoch (the period that ended about 10,000 years ago). The fascinating point here is that the prehistoric Lake Bonneville was then a large, deep freshwater lake that occupied much of western Utah and parts of Nevada and Idaho, and people at that time fished around these waters.[2]

If it was so recently a freshwater lake covering the current area of the Great Salt Lake (as well as all of the surrounding salt flats), the question has to be asked: where did all that additional salt come from around 10,000 years ago, if not from a huge sea incursion? The standard explanation is that it is due to tiny amounts of mineral salts in freshwater streams accumulating over the millennia. But in that case, how did this ancient lake only start to pick up mineral salt 10,000 years ago?

There is a further problem for the mineral salt build-up argument. The deposits in Utah are not just any salt – they are sea-salt. The Great Salt Lake has a chemical make-up similar to that of the oceans![3] The chemical composition of sea water is made up of a solution of salts including chlorine 55 per cent and sodium 31per cent, by weight of all the dissolved matter. Sea water also contains trace amounts of all the other elements, such as nitrate, phosphate, iron, manganese and gold.

1 *Grolier Encyclopaedia* (e media)
2 'Great Salt Lake,' *Microsoft® Encarta® 97 Encyclopedia*
3 'Great Salt Lake' *Britannica Online*. www.eb.com

It is also interesting to note that the topology of the eastern part of the Great Basin once acted as a container for a freshwater lake that covered about 50,000 square kilometres (thanks to melting glaciers), which was possibly its maximum capacity before the waters overran the edges of the natural basin. With that surface area, the lake would be just about eight times larger in volume than the current lake. Given that the basin floor is relatively flat and that the median depth is normally only 4.5 metres, it appears to confirm that there was eight times the volume of salt water present immediately after the flood. This calculation seems to confirm the reduction was due to evaporation, leaving water with a salinity approximately eight times that of the Pacific Ocean.

If we are right, and two tsunami waves did strike deep into the land that is now the United States, where is the evidence of such a relatively recent cataclysmic disaster? How could the various experts have failed to notice such an event?

The simple answer is that each set of specialists has indeed noticed the effects, but the whole picture simply has not been pieced together.

ANCIENT AMERICA

When did the first humans arrive on this continent?

In the 1920s anthropologists came up with the theory that the first humans walked onto the American continent a little more than 11,300 years ago across the Bering land bridge that once linked Siberia with Alaska, in three waves of migration. As ever, once someone with a grand title had spoken, the idea went unchallenged for decades. But now, anthropologists have had to reassess the whole thing. Richard Jantz, an anthropologist at the University of Tennessee at Knoxville now believes that the first settlers probably reached the Americas at least 25,000 years ago – the time when the figurine factory at Dolni Vestonice was in full production and the last Neanderthals were still living in southern Europe. According to Jantz, it seems likely that people arrived by boat as well as on foot and that east Asians may have been accompanied by Europeans.[4]

Richard Jantz believes that early American anthropology is in the middle of a paradigm shift. In 1927, the established anthropological dogma – which claimed that the New World had been uninhabited before simple foragers

[4] *New Scientist*; 17 October 1998

arrived some 2,000 years ago – disintegrated when a stone projectile point was found embedded between the ribs of a bison that had become extinct nearly 10,000 years ago. Five years later, archaeologists working in a gravel pit near the town of Clovis in New Mexico, unearthed further stone weapon tips associated with the bones of mammoths.

If these people were fresh immigrants who had just walked in across the northern land bridge, they would have to be super-human because much of North America was buried under ice sheets almost 2.5 kilometres thick, extending down to the Great Lakes. Because of the fluctuating size of the ice sheets covering North America, there were only two windows of opportunity for anyone to cross the land bridge: before 25,000 or after 12,000 years ago, and the age of the many 11,000-year-old sites, known as Clovis sites, gave rise to a firm conviction that the first Americans must have entered through the post-12,000 window. This window of opportunity became known as the 'Clovis Horizon' – the oldest possible point for people in America. Or so they thought.

The Clovis Horizon was breached by Thomas Dillehay and his team from the University of Kentucky who excavated a site at Monte Verde in southern Chile between 1977 and 1985. They found that about 30 people had lived on the sandy bank of a small creek, where they had eaten a variety of food (including the meat of the mastodon which has been extinct for almost 10,000 years). They had stone points and grinding stones, digging sticks and bola stones, which they used to catch small animals.[5]

The Monte Verde site is well preserved and radiocarbon dating sets its age at 12,500 years old, more than 1,000 years earlier than the Clovis Horizon. Dillehay had a hard time persuading sceptical archaeologists to take his claim seriously, but in January 1997 a team of nine doubting archaeologists arrived at the site and proceeded to check out Dillehay's findings. What they saw changed their minds. Dennis Stanford, an archaeologist at the Smithsonian Institute, said: '*It totally changes how we think of the prehistory of America. Our models clearly are not right.*'[6] Vance Haynes of the University of Arizona, who had inspected many less convincing claims for pre-Clovis sites, described Monte Verde as 'a paradigm buster'.

If the Clovis people were *not* the first Americans, the earlier ice-free window

[5] *New Scientist*; 17 October 1998
[6] *New Scientist*; 17 October 1998

of opportunity has to be looked at as the probable entry point. If the dates for the ice-free corridor *are* correct, people must have entered the Americas around 25,000 years ago – but, of course, that raises the question as to why there is no other known evidence of occupation prior to 9,300 BC.

The experts have been coming up with many theories as to what happened, and their major weapons have been the study of linguistics and mitochondrial DNA. The latest mDNA data has found a link between Native Americans and Europeans. A few years ago, a new mitochondrial lineage was discovered in Amerindians in the Central Great Lakes region in North America, which they called X. The same lineage has traces in European populations, but is totally absent in Asian ones. The experts have been able to demonstrate that the lineage cannot have been introduced by interbreeding after Europeans arrived in the Americas, because later forms of European mDNA are not present.

Douglas Wallace of Emory University in Atlanta voiced the apparently inevitable conclusion:

> *'It looks as if a European population moved up through Asia and was part of the wave of east Asian people who moved across the Bering land bridge,'*[7]

If this is true, this influx of Europeans must have occurred at least 25,000 years ago!

Wallace found five strands of genetic markers: four Asian, which he called A, B, C and D, and one European, which he designated X (see Figure 10). The strange thing about X is that it does not appear at all in Asia, and surely it should. It is difficult to imagine that a substantial group of hunter-gatherers just packed up their bags and marched singlemindedly across the largest land mass on earth. Surely we have to assume that they took at least 1000 years to span the 6,000 miles from Europe to the Bering Strait by natural migration from one hunting ground to another – always moving onward and eastward, towards the new dawn.

That being the case, how did they manage not to interbreed with the Asiatic peoples *en route*? A thousand years is a very long time indeed. Experts have tried to explain away the absence of the X lineage in Asia through 'genetic drift', a theory according to which these genes just

[7] *New Scientist*; 17 October 1998.

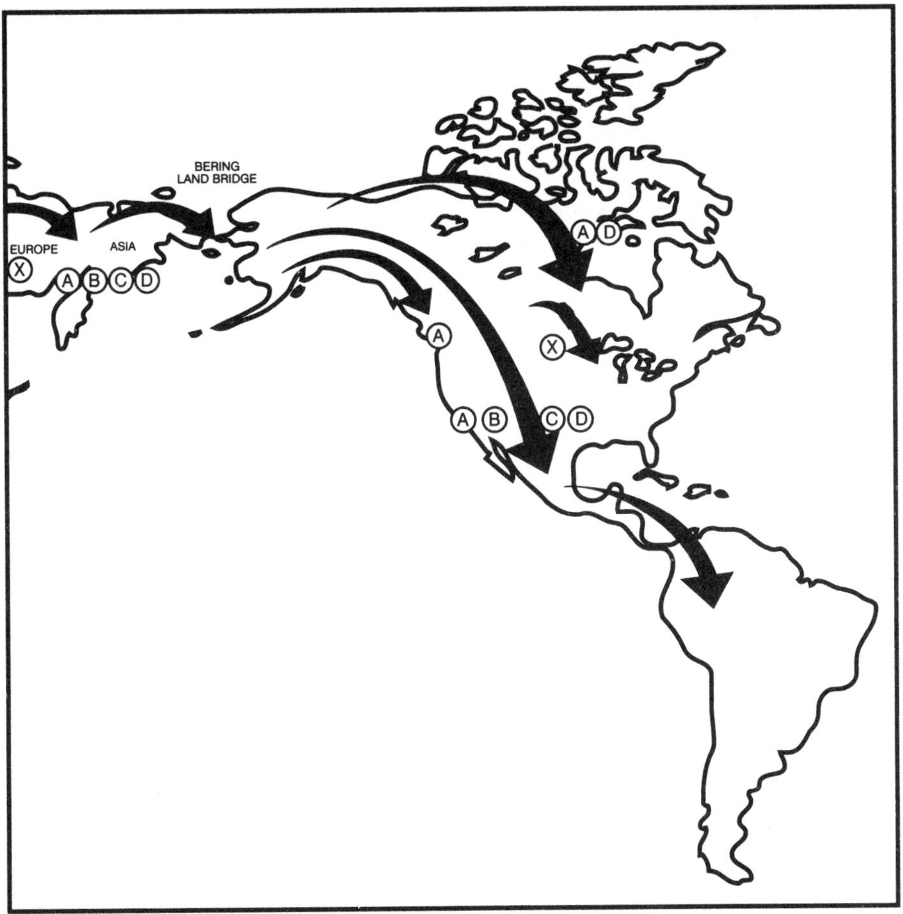

Figure 10. *Suggested migratory paths for the peopling of America from Europe and Asia.*

disappeared over time. This theory is widely accepted by genetic historians, but although it is accepted wisdom it does have an air of post-rationalization about it. It seems to us that there is an unnecessarily black-and-white approach being made by some people; according to them, Europeans *either* arrived post-Columbus, *or* they came at least 25,000 years ago across the Bering Strait.

What about the possibility that they arrived at some point, or points, between these two extremes? There is strong evidence to indicate that Europeans were in the Americas well before Columbus. As we have reported in one of our previous books, there is a tower at Newport, Rhode Island which appears to be medieval, and from its style may have been built by the Knights Templar, who we believe did visit America long before 1492. It was marked on Giovanni da Verrazano's map of 1524 as an 'existing Norman Villa'[8]. In the same book we described Rosslyn Chapel in Scotland, which has long been known for the American plants carved into its fabric several decades before Columbus set sail to America.

After the publication of *The Hiram Key* in 1996, we were contacted by a great number of people who wanted to add information to what we had found. One such person was the Norwegian shipping magnate, Fred Olsen. Mr Olsen has worked hand-in-hand for many years with his fellow countryman, anthropologist and explorer, Thor Heyerdahl. Heyerdahl is famous for his theories about migration patterns of various ancient peoples and amongst his many practical sailing experiments he managed to demonstrate that ancient Egyptians could have reached South America more than 4,000 years ago. (Recent evidence from Egyptologists in Germany and England supports this view as high levels of cocaine and tobacco appear to be present in a number of ancient Egyptian mummies.)

During the course of one lengthy telephone conversation, Fred Olsen informed us that many Norwegian sailors used the English seaport of Bristol as a base, and that they had told him that there were still records in that city of regular voyages to North America, long before the time of Columbus. On a visit to Bristol later that year we talked with Freemasons who told us of local records, held in the city's customs and excise archives, of a sailing master called John Cabot trading with a land across the Atlantic, which we now call North America. These registers date from the early 15th century – well before Columbus first sailed west. Such stories had been widely reported in the local history journals for Bristol and we were even shown a print of Cabot's ship, apparently a popular image in the Bristol area.

As the operator of a large number of ships, Fred Olsen had spent much of his life amongst sailors and collected their traditional lore for his friend Thor Hayerdahl. Mr Olsen told us that over the years he had collected research notes, which he passed on to Heyerdahl, and had recorded many early reports that had led him to believe that the Roman Church had a bishopric in what is now north-eastern Canada long before Columbus, the clerics having sailed there with fishermen and traders from Britain, in order to serve their spiritual needs. This does not seem a unreasonable claim, as there was

[8] Knight, C. and Lomas, R.: *The Hiram Key*, Century, 1996

a Bishop of Greenland established on the west coast of that island in AD 1329 by Pope John XXII.[9]

It was also his belief that a civilization that once thrived along the banks of the Mississippi was wiped out when pre-Columbian European traders brought the Black Death to America in the mid 14th century. This terrible disease, a form of bubonic plague, killed between a third and half of the Old World from China to the British Isles, and could have easily laid waste the people of Mississippi basin. We were later to remember this conversation when we came to look at early transatlantic links.

Fred Olsen also pointed out to us that European sailors reached the Americas without ever sailing more than 130 miles from land. They would sail from Orkney and Shetland, to Iceland, around the southern tip of Greenland, along Baffin Island, down the coast of Labrador to Newfoundland and Nova Scotia, never losing sight of land from the top of their masts. Once this very checkable fact sinks in, it seems almost ridiculous not to accept Mr Olsen's claim that Europeans were making journeys to

Figure 11. *Fred Olsen's 'sight-of-land' route to America.*

[9] Pohl, F.J.: *Prince Henry Sinclair*, Nimbus, 1967

North America hundreds, and quite possibly thousands, of years before Columbus.

To sum up, if all of the available evidence is looked at and probabilities are compared, pre-Columbian European mDNA in North America is far more likely to have arrived by sea from the East, not by land from the West.

A JAPANESE CONNECTION?

In July 1996 something very unusual started to unfold in the town of Kennewick, Washington State. Two young spectators at a boat race were wading the Columbia River to get a better view of the hydrofoil racing when they stumbled on a human skull in the muddy bed of the river. They reported the find to the local police and when Sergeant Craig Littrell investigated the site, he found an almost complete human skeleton. The officer sent the skull to the State Crime Laboratory for forensic examination, where the coroner instantly recognized that the individual had been dead for a very long time indeed. Anthropologist Jim Chatters was then called in to help solve the mystery.

The deceased was about five feet ten inches tall and was estimated to have been between 40 and 55 years of age when he died. The skull was long and narrow with a projecting nose, receding cheek bones, a high chin and square mandible. The back of the skull was not flattened by the use of cradle boards, a common feature of old American Indian skulls. In fact, the immediate impression was that these were European features, not those of a native American. Furthermore, the teeth were in very good condition, unlike most American Indian remains which always show tremendous wear because of the high fibre and grit content of their diet.

Chatters' first thought was that it was a drowning victim from some earlier period, but he also found a two-inch-long stone spear tip embedded in the right hip. When he later gave a newspaper interview, he said:

'I've got a white guy with a stone point in him. That's pretty exciting. I thought I had a pioneer'.[10]

But Kennewick Man, as the skeleton is now known, was not the sort of pioneer Jim Chatters had originally envisaged. He consulted Professor Catherine Macmillan of Washington University who agreed the skeleton was

[10] *Tri-City Herald*, 9 September 1996

Caucasian but commented that the spear point of this type would usually be dated between 7000 and 2500 BC. When this was reported to the coroner of Benton County, he asked for carbon-dating tests to be carried out. So a small section of the bone joining the left little finger to the wrist was sent to Dr Taylor of the University of California, who identified that the individual died in 9410BP or plus or minus 160 years (7414 BC).

There was sufficient surviving DNA to test against various populations around the world, including American Indians. Unfortunately these investigations at the University of California were halted following a court action over custody of the remains.[11] The skeleton was seized by the Army Corps of Engineers on the basis that it was pre-Columbian and therefore a 'Native American' body which, by law, had to be returned to the tribe of origin. Unfortunately the politics of political correctness triumphed over the needs of genuine scientific inquiry.

But how did an ancient European male come to be in the north-west USA, nearly 9,000 years before Columbus?

Whoever Kennewick Man was, it became clear that he had had a difficult time. He had survived, and recovered from a number of broken ribs, a broken arm and stone spear embedded into his right hip. The two-inch-long spear-point of grey volcanic rock had a split at its tip, which experts take as a sign that the missile had been travelling very fast at the time of impact. This was certainly more than a simple thrusting wound as it had been caused by a high-velocity projectile, possibly propelled by a throwing stick.[12]

His bones showed little signs of arthritis, suggesting that he rarely carried heavy weights during his life, and his teeth indicated that he had probably enjoyed a good diet of soft foods including a lot of meat. Jim Chatters reconstructed the facial features of Kennewick Man, and speaking on an *Equinox* TV programme broadcast by the BBC on 6 October 1998, commented that the nearest racial group seemed to be the Ainu people of Japan.

Now this idea struck us as particularly interesting, as the Ainu are something of an historical enigma in their own right.

They are a Caucasian people who occupy parts of the Japanese island of Hokkaido and the nearby Russian islands of the Kuriles and Sakhalin. They have short, sturdy bodies, a light complexion, wavy hair and some have blue

11 Slayman, A.L.: 'Battle of Bones', *Archaeology*, vol. 50, Number 1, January/February 1997
12 Jim Chatters reported in *Tri-City Herald*, 28 August 1996

eyes. The men have particularly heavy beards which they allow to grow. They are thought to be descended from an ancient circumpolar people who arrived in Japan some time over 7,000 years ago. A few isolated communities of upland Ainu are still identical in some respects to those of prehistoric times. Archaeologists have found ancient Ainu pit houses, ground-stone celts (prehistoric implements shaped like a chisel or ax-head), ground-bone projectile points, and grit-tempered, cord-marked pottery.[13] Some of the most striking finds were the clay and stone female figurines with mask-like faces and protuberant eyes – very similar to the extremely ancient 'Venus' figurines found in Europe, including the factory at Dolni Vestonice in the Czech Republic that we mentioned in Chapter One.

A number of ancient Ainu stone circles have also been found, similar to the megalithic sites of western Europe; a few still have slender upright stones at their centre. Japan also has a number of prehistoric monuments known as dolmens, which consist of several great stone slabs set edgewise in the earth to support a massive flat stone roof. The word 'dolmen' is believed to be Celtic in origin and these structures are normally considered to be typical of the Neolithic Period in the British Isles and Europe, although some have been found in northern Africa as well as Japan.

There is evidence that the Ainu were once highly accomplished sailors and it is said that they possessed complex navigational techniques that had been carefully guarded by certain special bloodlines. According to some elders, these select navigator families held an astonishing amount of astronomical knowledge in their heads, which had to be memorized from childhood and was built up throughout their lifetime.[14]

The Japanese government does not acknowledge the Ainu people as an indigenous and distinct people and their ancient language has been discouraged, so now only a handful of elders can speak it at all. This ancient language appears to be unrelated to any other, but a case has recently been put forward that there are many striking similarities between it and Basque, a western European language that had also been thought to be unique.[15]

Bear worship has always been central to the Ainu religion and it may well stem back to Palaeolithic bear worship, which appears to have been practised across many parts of the world. This 'primitive' practice was not

[13] Knez, Eugene I: 'Ainu,' - *Microsoft ® Encarta*, 97
[14] Nyland, Edo: http://www.islandnet.com/~edonon
[15] Nyland, Edo: http://www.islandnet.com/~edonon

tolerated by the new major religions and it has only been possible for anthropologists to study this religion in the peripheral areas of northern Europe and Siberia. So had the Ainu moved eastward through Siberia, even though the nearest people of their type are found almost 6,000 miles away?

Pottery had long been assumed to be a fairly late invention of the Neolithic age, but that theory was shattered in 1960 when a site belonging to the Jomon culture of Japan was excavated. This site at Natsushima near Yokosuka yielded pottery over 9,000 years old, and further discoveries soon followed, dated at *circa* 12,700 years old. The Jomon had previously been considered to be nothing but a primitive Stone Age culture, but in fact they had developed an advanced pottery-manufacturing industry which was over 3,500 years older than the oldest pottery to be found in China, making Jomon pottery the oldest-known pottery in the world.[16]

It seems that there could well be a connection between ancient Europeans, the aboriginal Ainu who settled in Japan, and people who inhabited parts of North America more than 7,000 years ago. So here is another example of the inadequacy of the old paradigm of prehistory.

AN AMERICAN DISASTER

Over the last 25 years, increasing evidence of some unprecedented catastrophe around 10,000 years ago has emerged in the field of palaeontology. Paul S. Martin from the University of Arizona expressed his amazement at the available evidence, in a paper entitled 'Who Or What Destroyed Our Mammoths?' when he wrote:

> *Animals that had been native for millions of years disappeared under circumstances that were suspiciously sudden . . . the loss of over thirty genera of large mammals including mammoths and mastodons, horses, camelids, tapir, ground sloths, sabertooth 'cats', and many other species of large animals in North America alone.*[17]

This powerful statement cannot be ignored. Many others are equally puzzled. The following comment from another specialist is a further expression of the apparent conundrum:

[16] Rudgely, R.: *Lost Civilisations of the Stone Age*, Century, 1998
[17] In Agenbroad, L.D., ed.: *Megafauna and Man*, Flagstaff University, Hot Springs, 1990

'At the end of the Pleistocene about 10,000 years ago, there was an extinction event that decimated the large terrestrial mammalian herbivores and carnivores of North America, South America and Australia. In North America alone, more than 32 genera of mammals became extinct. The cause of this extinction is debatable . . . Some scientists believe that these extinctions are the direct result of over-exploitation of large mammal herbivores for food by Ice-Age hunters. This model has been referred to as 'Overkill' or 'Blitzkrieg'. Others attribute the demise of the Pleistocene mammals to changing climatic and environmental conditions.'[18]

The 'Blitzkrieg' model is odd to say the least. Did the Clovis people have buffalo guns? Surely they would have needed much more than flint-tipped spears to have made such a huge impact on so many species of mega-fauna that once roamed in their millions. We know of no record of any species being hunted to total extinction by anyone. The early European settlers in North America tried to hunt the buffalo to death but didn't quite succeed, even with sophisticated guns. The only possible candidate for the distinction of being hunted to extinction is the dodo, and present research suggests that it died out because its could not adapt to its changing environment, not because it was hunted out of existence. Only today do we seemed to have developed far enough to in a position to force animals into extinction, which we are doing by sheer pressure of human numbers destroying the animal's natural environments. It seems unlikely a that few early hunters with simple stone weapons could wipe out so many species.

Let us try to find a more plausible explanation by putting together some apparently unconnected facts. Start by comparing the timing of agriculture and the creation of new varieties of 'domesticated' animals:

'The invention and spread of agriculture is central to the history of humanity. For more than 100,000 years, humans subsisted in widely varied environments by foraging for food. Then, in a brief moment of prehistory starting about 10,000 years ago, people began to domesticate animals and plants in half a dozen 'centres of origin' in the Old and New Worlds'.[19]

[18] Graham, R.W.: *Evolution of New Ecosystems at the End of the Pleistocene*, Research and Collector Center, Illinois State Museum
[19] Roger Lewin, *New Scientist* magazine

So, in the words of two unrelated experts, 'about 10,000 years ago, there was an extinction event', and 'about 10,000 years ago people began to domesticate animals and plants'. Surely, it is futile to pretend that the world did not fundamentally change at this time.

In this context, it is instructive to note that the Ute Native American people have an old legend that appears to be a tribal memory of the heat flash and tsunami effects of a major cometary impact:

> *. . . the sun was shivered into a thousand fragments, which fell to earth causing a general conflagration. Then Ta-wats fled before the destruction he had wrought, and as he fled the burning earth consumed his feet, consumed his legs, consumed his body, consumed his hands and arms – all were consumed but the head alone, which bowled across valleys and over mountains, fleeing destruction from the burning earth, until at last, swollen with heat, the eyes of the god burst and tears gushed forth in a flood which spread over the earth and extinguished the fire.*[20]

Further north on the American continent, a flood legend of the Canadian Chiglit tribe was recorded by French anthropologist M. Petitot:

> *The water having poured over the terrestrial disk, human dwellings disappeared, the wind carried them away. They fastened several boats to one another. The waves traversed the Rocky Mountains. A great wind drove them. Presently the moon and the earth disappeared. Men died of a terrible heat. They also perished in the waves. Men bewailed what happened. Uprooted trees floated about in the waves. Men having fastened boats together trembled with cold in the darkness which covered the waters. Alas, men were enclosed under the tent without doubt. Thereupon a man called the Son of the Screech-Owl threw his bow into the sea. 'Wind this is enough; be still,' he cried. He thereupon threw his earrings into the water. It was enough and the end had come.*[21]

[20] Edmonds, M. & Clark, E., *Voices of the Winds*, Facts on File Ink, 1989

[21] Petitot, M.: *Dialecte des Tchiglit*

Here, then, is a description that suggests that the wave did indeed overwhelm the Rocky Mountains and the sky was blacked out in a nuclear-style winter.

In fact, there are numerous tribal stories of the Great Flood from the mountains of the north-western United States. When the earliest Christian missionaries arrived, proudly bringing their own folk tales and associated myths, they were surprised to find that the story of Noah was already present. In 1878, the Reverend Myron Eells reported on the widespread nature of Flood stories:

> *'Those Indians had their traditions of a flood, and that one man and his wife were saved on a raft. Each of those three tribes also, together with the Flathead tribes, had their separate Ararat in connection with the event.'*[22]

Tribes of the Olympic Peninsula and the Yakima of Washington State tell stories of the enormity of the Flood. Mrs Rose Purdy, a member of the Skokomish tribe, recalled one such ancient story:

> *'Once a big flood came to this world. My people made ropes of twisted cedar limbs. They tied the ropes to their canoes and fastened the canoes to the mountain . . . When the world got flooded, the Shokomish people went higher and higher into the Olympic Mountains. The Olympics got flooded. Some of the ropes broke and they drifted away.'*[23]

The Indians of Oregon tell a story that the survivors of the Flood, surviving in a boat, came to rest on top of Mount Jefferson – the state's second highest peak. They believe that all of their tribe alive today descend from these survivors.[24]

In Northern California, there is an old tradition telling of animals that were chased by the rising waters to the very top of Mount Shasta which

[22] Clark, E.E.: *Indian Legends of the Pacific Northwest.* Berkeley: University of California Press, 1963.
[23] Clark, E.E.: *Indian Legends of the Pacific Northwest.* Berkeley: University of California Press, 1963
[24] Clark, E.E.: *Indian Legends of the Pacific Northwest.* Berkeley: University of California Press, 1963

stands at 14,162 feet (over 2.5 miles) above sea level. It says these animals are the ancestors of all animals in the world.

Interestingly, the Indians agree with the Jewish tradition when it comes to the reason for the Flood and regarding a warning given to a righteous man. According to a Yakima legend, good men shared the news:

> *One of the good men told the others, 'I have heard from the Land Above, the land of the spirits, that a big water is coming – a big water that will cover all the land. Make a boat for the good people. Let the bad people be killed by the water . . . The Earth will be destroyed by a big water if the people do wrong a second time.'*

The similarities between the North American and the Middle-Eastern stories are remarkable. There has been one flood long ago, when even the mountains were overrun by the waters. The cause of the disaster was a punishment from heaven, but a good man was forewarned of the impending doom. One legend is especially close to that of Noah, except the hero had no sons. This account deals with the obvious problem of finding food and safe drinking water after such an total cataclysm:

> *'God came down to the earth, and found it was very dirty, and full of bad things, bad people, mysteries, and cannibals. He thought he would make a flood to clean the earth, and drown all the bad people and monsters. The flood covered the tops of mountains; and all the people were drowned, except one man and his two daughters, who escaped in a canoe.*
>
> *When the water receded, they came ashore and found that the earth was clean. They were starving, and looked for food, but nothing edible could they see. No plants grew near by, only some trees of several varieties. They crushed a piece of fir with stones, and soaked it in water. They tried to eat it, and to drink the decoction: but it was too nasty, and they threw it away. Thus they tried pine, alder, and other woods, and at last they tried service-berry wood, which tasted much better. The women drank the decoction, and found that it made them tipsy. They gave some to their father, and he became quite drunk. Now they thought to themselves, 'How is the earth to be peopled?' And they each had connection with their father without his knowing it.*

As the water receded, they became able to get more and more food: but they still continued to drink the service-berry decoction, and, as their father was fond of it, they frequently made him drunk, and had connection with him. Thus they bore many children, and their father wondered how they became pregnant. These children, when they grew up, married one another, and thus was the earth re-peopled. The animals and birds also became numerous again.'[25]

The great height of the Andes Mountains that run down the western edge of the land mass must have given some protection from the worst effects of the tsunami waves. The South American peoples all have oral traditions about the Flood, both in the mountainous regions and in the tropical lowlands. The Flood is often associated with a divine punishment wiping out existing mankind in preparation for the emergence of a new race.[26]

In Peru, one legend tells of a man being caught by surprise when he checked his herd of llamas:

One day a herdsman found that his animals were all staring in the direction of the sun. When he lifted his hand to his eyes to look himself, he saw a cluster of stars which seemed to be surrounding the sun, even in daylight. The llamas then told the man that the stars which had appeared close together, were a sign that the world was about to be destroyed by a great deluge. The farmer took his family and his animals to the very top of a mountain and they had only just reached the summit when the waters of the sea rose up in a mighty wave and swamped the land. It was many days before the waters started to recede and while this was happening the sun was hidden by a great darkness.[27]

Various causes for the Flood are given by the peoples of South America. In Inca mythology it is said to have been provoked by the supreme god, Viracocha, who decided to destroy all mankind because they were not good

[25] Thompson, S.: *Tales of the North American Indians*, Bloomington: Indiana University Press, 1966

[26] Osborne, H.: *South American Mythology*, Hamlyn Press, 1968

[27] Bancroft, *The Native Races of the Pacific States of America*, quoted in Howarth, H.H.: *The Mammoth and the Flood*, Sampson Low, Marston, Searle and Rivington, London, 1887

enough. The Yaghan people of Tierra del Fuego believe that the Moon caused the deluge in revenge for a beating she received when men, who were not priests, discovered the secrets of initiation rites. The ancient inhabitants of the region of Quito in Equador, the Jivaro and Murato Indians, link the deluge with the killings by a supernatural boa.

The Ipurina say that the deluge was brought about by the overflowing of a kettle located in the sun. The inundation is said to have been caused by rains according to the Inca, Canari, Yaruro, Tupinamba and the Tempe. Others, such as the Canishana, Yagua, Witoto, Jivaro, Mura, Tupinamba and the Bororo, say simply that the waters overflowed, while the Canari and Araucanians specifically refer to the sea rising up and covering the land.

According to most tribes, the highest mountains in each country were the sites where people survived. In the Inca, Guanca and Aymara versions of the Flood legend the survivors found shelter in sealed caves, and later emerged to spread across the world. If this has some historical truth to it, it indicates definite forewarning to give time for such watertight structures to be created.

Why are there so many stories about an inundation, if it is not a memory of a real event? Where are the stories of a great forest fire, a terrible plague or some other human disaster? The answer keeps on repeating itself: the Flood is the most terrible event in the oral history of different peoples from across the globe.

INLAND SALT SEAS

We already knew that there was a layer of sea sand and sea shells deposited across the British Isles; but if North American salt lakes can be associated with the Flood, what about other places around the world? Further investigations revealed some amazing facts about the site given in the Bible as the place that Noah's Ark came to land.

The lakes Van and Urmia, near to Mount Ararat, are respectively 1,670 metres and 1,250 metres above sea level, and almost unbelievably, they are both salt lakes. Even stranger, there are still sea-sand 'beaches' much higher, at 2,150 metres in the mountains above the south of Lake Van.[28]

In the lowlying lands to the east of Mount Ararat lies the Caspian Sea –

[28] King, L.C.: *The Morphology of the Earth*

the largest landlocked body of water on the planet. We looked up the facts about this giant lake and were hardly surprised when we found that it is also a salt-water lake, containing salmon, sturgeon and herring as well as other marine animals such as porpoises and seals.

The question has to be asked: how does a giant landlocked, seawater lake come to exist so deep inside a continental land-mass, and how did large sea mammals get there? The nearest connection to the oceans is 800 kilometres south, in the Persian Gulf. Could it be that this is another remnant of a giant continental 'rock-pool' left by the comet Flood? Is it not possible that the oceanic animal life in this lake was carried there by a wave of unimaginable proportions? We could find no explanation from the experts.

We also found abundant evidence that the region to the north was once covered in salt water, while the Aral Sea, another lake some 480 kilometres further east in Kazakstan and Uzbekistan, is also a salt-water lake.

Indeed, the apparently impossible seems to go without explanation across the world. In South America, for example, Lake Titicaca is more than three kilometres up in the Andes, yet it contains marine fish such as the sea-horse.[29]

The most famous salt-water lake of them all is arguably the Dead Sea, to the east of Jerusalem: could it too be a 'rock-pool' remnant of the Flood? According to legend, this is the site of the cities of Sodom and Gomorrah which were destroyed for their evil ways. One Biblical expert says:

> *The ruins of Sodom and Gomorra lie in all probability beneath the waters at the southern end of the Dead Sea, and a nearby sanctuary with standing stones at Bab-edh-Dhra is mute evidence of this.*[30]

Some geologists, who are expert in the region, believe that the River Jordan and the alluvium plain of the area are to be associated with the end of the last Ice Age, and that they were formed during Neolithic times; i.e. something less than 10,000 years ago.[31] The time-frame fit continues to build a picture of the global Flood.

[29] Bellamy, H.S.: *Before the Flood: the Problem of the Tiahuanaco Ruins*, Faber & Faber, 1943
[30] May, H.G.: 'History of Israel', - 1, *Peake's Commentary on the Bible*
[31] Picard, L.: 'Structure and Evolution of Palestine', *Bull Geological Department*, Hebrew University, Jerusalem, 1943

THE DISASTER THAT SHAPED A NEW WORLD

Wherever people were during the autumn of 7640 BC, anybody who happened to be standing on our little planet and looking out towards the sun must have found it a strange and threatening time. Something terrible was happening in the heavens, because the great fiery disc that rose each day to warm the earth seemed to be under attack. The events that followed were so terrible that even today, nearly 10,000 years later, people still tell tales of how the sun seemed to be surrounded and overwhelmed by new bright stars which fell to earth as flaming mountains, of how the sea rose up in mighty waves and engulfed the land, and of how summer was driven away in fright and a darkness fell which lasted for months.

Accounts of this massive human disaster have been passed down by folk traditions across the globe, all telling remarkably similar stories. Until relatively recent times these ancient stories were generally considered to be accounts of an actual event, but during the 19th and 20th centuries it became increasingly fashionable to dismiss such oral traditions as the products of the imagination of primitive peoples, who had merely childlike intelligence. But it seems to us both foolish and arrogant to exclude such vital evidence when trying to reconstruct long-distant events. Of course, some of these stories may be mere invention, but others may contain important information that can be corroborated by other means.

Back in the mid 18th century, a Swiss scientist, Charles Bonnet, made a detailed examination of the available fossil evidence of extinct species and developed what he called a 'catastrophe theory of evolution'. The evidence told him that the earth must periodically suffer universal catastrophes which wipe out great numbers of creatures, but the survivors move up a notch on the evolutionary scale. Two schools of thought then developed, and for a long time the debate between 'castastrophists' and 'gradualists' continued fiercely. The gradualists eventually won, and their belief that everything develops smoothly, over great periods of time, has become accepted as the mainstream theory.

The reality is that a common theme to flood stories has survived across the planet, despite the fact that many of the people who tell of this disaster are believed to have had no contact with one another. The question has to be asked: why should they all invent what is essentially the same story?

It is true that the effects of the impacts would be remembered by survivors in different ways. Those who witnessed one of the massive tsunami waves – and lived to tell the tale – must have been on high ground well inland, or possibly out in deep ocean in a substantial boat. Others, deep inside a continental mass, would not be aware of the sea waves – but they would still have experienced flooding from the colossal rain generated by the impacts. Still others may have remembered the heat pulses or earthquakes and the cold, permanent night that lasted for months. And many will have told their children and grandchildren about the long cold winter that would not go away.

Nonetheless, legends recording a global flood exist in ancient cultures all around the world. The conventional academic assumption is that there can be no connection between these flood legends, because it is impossible for the waters of the earth suddenly and simultaneously to cover the entire planet. Of course, these anthropologists know little of geology or astronomy and they are therefore unaware that the world's waters could flood the land if an external object, such as a comet, enters the equation.

Remarkably, there are hundreds of such legends from every continent. In many cases, the ancient flood stories of indigenous peoples have been dismissed as spin-offs from the Noah epic, told by missionaries to the wide-eyed savages who they were trying to convert to Christianity.

Australia, however, is different. It is a remote continent with an aboriginal people who are thought to have had no contact with the rest of humanity for 40,000 years up to the time of Captain Cook, yet these people also tell of a great universal flood in the distant past. The Australian Aborigines never developed writing, which has ensured that their oral traditions are still intact. It is now accepted that some of their stories, particularly regarding the Rainbow Serpent, are at least 10,000 years old, so it is very reasonable to believe that they would have cultural memories of the comet generated flood.

One of the major impact sites was in the Tasman Sea (as shown on the map on page 56), and so the south of Australia must have been struck by a tsunami wave. This direct involvement and uncontaminated continuity of legend made the stories of the people especially interesting, so Chris went 'down under' to find out details of the legends.

As in Judaeo-Christian legend, there is an acceptance of a global flood that marks a literal 'watershed' in history. And very strangely, the Aborigines have Enoch-like stories of outside visitors who are far more advanced than themselves. They tell how long ago, there were spirit people they call the Nurrumbunguttias who lived on earth. Like the Watchers of Enochian legend, these people were said to have come down from the sky. These spirit people ruled the earth, but the sea rose up and flooded the land so that even the mountain tops were covered and the whole world was water. Many Nurrumbunguttias were drowned, but others escaped to the heavens to become gods in the sky. Then the sea went back to its own place and the land steamed hot so that the animals, birds, insects and reptiles could once again make their homes on the quick-drying plains.

Another fundamental story tells how the world was once dark and sorrowful as floods ravaged the land and animals took refuge in a cave high up in the mountains. From time to time, one of them would go to the entrance to see if the waters had subsided. There was nothing to be seen except the swirling of the waters under a sunless sky.[32]

It is probable that the sea incursions did not penetrate into the centre of Australia, and so, like those of some of the inhabitants of North America, many memories will record the other terrible consequences of the comet's impact.

There are many stories amongst the Aborigines of seven sisters who came from a great hole in the sky in the constellation of Orion. In one telling, these seven sisters are called the Water Girls. Terrible events unfold and a young man flees from the wrath of the sun goddess. He tells how he can smell his hair singeing and watched as trees cracked and burst into flame, indeed he says 'the whole world seemed to be on fire'.

The oral tradition of the death of the people at Marabibi tells how Yung-galya, the 'running star', appeared and a number of objects fell to earth, burning and removing the skin of the people. Yet another story of the seven sisters tells of flying stars which drop down and make holes in the ground.

Australian Aborigines living in southern Australia sing a traditional song of how the sky glowed an evil red and made the land hotter than the people could bear. Men were driven to kill their wives and children before committing suicide to escape the torment of being broiled alive.[33] Along with this story of immense heat, the Aborigines of Victoria tell of a great flood which covered all the country drowning everybody except one man and three women. They took refuge on an island of mud and when the waters went down they had children who repopulated the land.[34]

There are many explanations for the flood that are based on the idea of a split water-bag. Here is one from South Australia:

[32] Reed, A.W.: *Myths and Legends of Australia*

[33] Walk, L.: 'Das Flut-Geschwisterpaar als Ur und Stammelternpaar der Menschheit, Mitt osterr Gesz', *Anthropol Ethon, Prahist*, v.78/79, 1941

[34] Lang, A.: *Custom and Myth*, 1860

Yaul was thirsty, but his brother Marlgaru refused to let him have any water from his own full kangaroo-skin waterbag. While Marlgaru was out hunting, Yaul sought and found the bag. He jabbed it with a club, tearing it. Water poured out, drowning both brothers and forming the sea. It was spreading inland, too, but Bird Women came from the east and restrained the waters with a barrier of roots of the ngalda kurrajong tree.[35]

Another explanation for the event was an over enthusiastic rainmaker:

Djunban performed the rainmaking ceremony again, but he was grieving his sister and not concentrating on his task, and the rain came too heavily. He tried to warn his people, but the flood came and washed away all the people and their possessions.

Aboriginal stories largely exist to explain the world they see and events that happen to them. In Gippsland, Australian folk memory tries to explain these strange events and ascribe a reason to the catastrophe, suggesting that they were struggling to make sense of something unusual. The story tells how some boys of the Kurnai were playing and found a bull-roarer type of whistle known as a turndiun, which no woman was allowed to look at. Because the boys were foolish enough to show it to their mother, the whole earth crumbled away and a great flood covered the land, drowning all the Kurnai.[36]

The Glasshouse Mountains in Queensland are towering stacks that are the larva cores of long extinct volcanoes, where the outer earth has largely weathered away. The Aborigines have a legend to explain these mountains, one of which has a pronounced twist in its tall, narrow structure.

A man called Tibrogargan and his wife Beerwah had nine children who were called; Coonowrin, Beerburrun, the Tumbubadla twins, Coochin, Ngun Ngun, Tibberoowuccum, Miketeebumulgrai and Elimbah.

One day, when Tibrogargan was standing by the sea he noticed a great rising of the waters. Hurrying off to gather his younger children

[35] Berndt and Berndt: *The Speaking Land*, Penguin, 1989
[36] Lang, A.: *Custom and Myth*, 1860

in order to flee to the safety of the mountains in the west, he called out to his eldest son, Coonowrin, to help his mother, who was again pregnant.

Looking back to see how Coonowrin was assisting Beerwah, Tibrogargan was most angered to see him running off alone. He pursued Coonowrin and raising his club, struck his son such a mighty blow that it dislocated Coonowrin's neck, and he has never been able to straighten it again. When the great flood subsided and the family had returned to the plains, the other children teased Coonowrin about his crooked neck.

The Flood was such a reality to the Aborigines that they used its existence to create a story that explained these strange shaped mountains as the frozen remains of Tibrogargan and his family.

The Aborigines record the Flood in many ways, and it must have been experienced very widely by the 500 different tribal groups. Australia is a low-lying continent with about 95 per cent of its land at less than 600 metres above sea level, and its highest mountains, a relatively low 2,200 metres high. When it was struck by the tsunami wave from the Tasman Sea strike, it can only have been the sheer size of the land-mass that prevented the entire country being inundated.

Australia has a great deal of desert and some land, in the Great Artesian Basin of central southern Australia, is below sea level. In the vast Erye Basin lies Australia's largest lake which we found is another, shallow inland sea of salt water, whose shores are 150 metres below sea level. For much of the time, the lake is little more than a muddy waste covered with a 38 cm-thick layer of salt, and only on rare occasions does it fill completely to its maximum depth of 4 metres.

Could Lake Eyre be another remnant of a Flood 'rock-pool'?

Even the isolated islands of the Pacific have legends of a mighty flood which destroyed everyone and everything. This one comes from Tahiti:

Two men had gone out to fish. Roo was the name of one, Tahoroa of the other. They threw out their line and the hook caught in the hair of the god Ruahau. They thereupon cried out 'A fish' but on drawing in the line, they found that they had caught a man by the hair. At the sight of the god they jumped to the other side of the boat and there

> *remained stupefied with fright. The god asked them to explain. They said they had gone to fish and did not know that the god was there. Ruahatu then bade them unloose his hair from the hook which they did. He then asked them their names. On telling him he ordered them to return to shore and tell mankind that the sea would overwhelm the land, and that everybody would perish. He also bade them go the next day to the islet of Toa-marama, which would prove a place of safety for them. The god brought the deluge as he had prophesied and only Roo and Tahoroa and their families escaped.*[37]

A Fijian flood legend was reported by Reverend Lawry, an early missionary:

> *After the islands had been peopled by the first man and the first woman, a great rain took place, by which they were finally submerged. But before the highest places were covered by the waters, two large double canoes appeared. In one of these was Rokova, the god of the carpenters, in the other Rokola, his head workman, who picked up some of the people and kept them on board until the waters had subsided, after which they were again landed on the island. The persons thus saved, eight in number, were landed in Mbenga, where the highest of their gods is said to have made his first appearance. By virtue of this tradition the chiefs of the Mbenga take rank before all others and have always acted a conspicuous part among the Fijians.*[38]

The Chinese classic story of the Yihking tells how Fuhhi escaped from the waters of a great flood in a large box accompanied by his wife, his three sons and three daughters to become the founder of all Chinese civilization. This story, depicted in a Buddhist temple in China, was described by a traveller called Gutzlaff, in *Journal of The Asiatic Society*. He saw it as a direct parallel to the Biblical account of the flood.

> *'In beautiful stucco, the scene shows how Kwanyin, the Goddess of Mercy, looks down from heaven upon the lonely Noah in his ark*

[37] Lenormant, L.: *Les Origines de l'Historie*, quoted in Howarth, H.H.: *The Mammoth and the Flood*, Sampson Low, Marston, Searle and Rivington, London, 1887
[38] Lawry, R.: *Friendly and Feejee Islands*, quoted in Howarth, H.H.: *The Mammoth and the Flood*, Sampson Low, Marston, Searle and Rivington, London, 1887

> *amidst the raging waves of the deluge, with the dolphins swimming around as his last means of safety and the dove, with an olive branch in its beak, flying towards the vessel.'*[39]

In Chinese mythology, Ta Yü was the Tamer of the World Flood and one of China's saviour-heroes. He was reputed founder of China's oldest hereditary dynasty, the Hsia or Xia Dynasty, which began around 4,200 years ago. One legend recounts Ta Yü's extraordinary birth: a man called Kun was given charge of controlling the great deluge. To create some dry land in the flooded land, he built dams using some magical soil that he stole from heaven. This theft from heaven angered the Lord on High, who issued an order for his execution. After three years, Kun's miraculously preserved body was slit open and a son brought forth. This was Ta Yü who, with the aid of dragons, created outlets for the flooded land to drain back to the sea, and the world was once again fit for human habitation.

Elsewhere in Asia, India preserves a flood legend in the writings of the Satapata Brakmana, which forms part of the collection of literature known as the *Rig Veda* as well as in the *Mahabharata*. This story is told of the god Manu:

> *One morning they brought to Manu some water to wash in, and when he had washed a fish remained in his hand, which addressed him these terms; 'Protect me and I will save thee.'*
>
> *'From what wilt thou protect me?' he said.*
>
> *'A deluge will sweep away all creatures, it is from this I will protect thee,' the fish replied. 'While we are small we live in great danger, for fishes eat each other. Preserve me, therefore, in a bowl; when I grow too large for this put me in a larger basin, and when I am still larger turn me out into the ocean. Thus I shall be saved from destruction.'*
>
> *Presently it became a great fish and said to Manu, 'In the very year in which I shall attain my full growth the deluge will happen. Build thyself a ship and adore me. When the waters rise, enter into the ship and I will save thee.'*
>
> *After having thus brought it up Manu took the fish to the ocean. In the year it had pointed out, Manu built a ship and adored the fish and*

[39] Gutzlaff, A.: *Journal of the Asiatic Society*, vol. xvi, no. 79

> *when the deluge came he entered the ship. Thereupon the fish came to him swimming, and Manu fastened the rope of the ship to the fish's horn, and thus it made the ship pass over the Mountain of the North. The fish said, 'I have saved thee; fasten the ship to a tree, so that the water may not enter it whilst thou art on the mountain and when the waters settle down thou canst then descend.'*
>
> *As the waters settled Manu settled down too, and this was what was called 'the descent of Manu' on the Mountain of the North. The deluge had carried off all creatures and Manu alone remained.*[40]

Another version of this Indian legend appears in a poem called *Bhagavata Purana* which was translated and summarized by Sir William Jones in the 19th century.

> *Satyavrata, king of the fishermen was one day bathing in the River Critamala. Vishnu appeared to him in the shape of a small fish, which, passing from one water to another, gradually became larger, until Satyavrata ended by putting it in the sea. Then Vishnu addressed his astonished worshipper and said, 'In the course of seven days all creatures which have wronged me shall be exterminated by a flood, but thou shalt be saved in a great ship marvellously built. Take therefore all kinds of useful vegetables and grain for food, and a pair of all animals, and then do thou embark with the seven Rishies, thy wife and their wives. Embark without fear, and thou shalt see God face to face, he will answer all thy questions.'*
>
> *After having spoken he disappeared. In the course of seven days the ocean overflowed, and the earth was submerged by continual rain. Thereupon Satyavrata, who reflected on the divinity, saw a great ship floating on the waters. He entered it and followed out exactly the orders of Vishnu, who, having taken the shape of an immense fish, attached the ship to his immense horn by a great octopus, which served as a cable.*[41]

Across the world, then, the physical evidence and the human memory tell a very similar story of massive sea waves driving deep inland, followed by

[40] Muller, M.: *Translations of Sanskrit Literature*
[41] Klee, K.: *La Deluge*, (quoted in *The Works of Sir Wm Jones*), London, 1880

massive rains. Some legends refer to burning mountains falling to earth, and several of a great heat followed by darkness and periods of extreme cold. All of this information fits with the chain of events which the geological records indicate occurred in 7640 BC. Peoples of all continents have preserved these stories which have to be a racial memory of a world-shattering event.

In a matter of days, hundreds of major species of mammals disappeared from our planet, including the mammoth, sabre-tooth sloth, the American horse and camel, as well as the woolly rhinoceros. Inevitably, the majority of the human population across the planet must also have perished, due to the effects of the impact itself or from the long, cold years that followed when food was extremely scarce.

For us the case is proven – the Flood happened. Our next task was to find out what else we could deduce about the people who preceded the Flood, and to try to understand better how the world was rebuilt.

CONCLUSION

America's inland salt sea and salt deserts date from exactly the same time as the 7640 BC impact, and they are a remnant of the enormous waves it caused. The dating of the arrival of *Homo sapiens* in America has been continually pushed back. There is strong evidence to indicate that Europeans were in the Americas thousands of years before Columbus, and that they probably came by sea. A Caucasian skeleton found in Washington State, dating to circa 7400 BC, shows similar characteristics to those of the Ainu people who arrived in Japan over 7000 years ago, built stone circles and are known as skilful navigators. Japan is also home to the oldest pottery industry in Asia, associated with the Jomon culture.

Evidence from archaeologists shows that on the America continent about 7000 BC, there was a major event that decimated the large terrestrial mammalian herbivores and carnivores, wiping out large numbers of species. Legends from all over the American continent tell of an enormous, world-destroying Flood.

The land-mass of Europe and Asia also shows evidence of inland salt seas which date from 7640 BC. Flood legends persist worldwide, describing events which fit the geological events of that period. Enough evidence exists to show that a worldwide Flood really did happen.

Chapter Six

ENOCH AND THE ANGELS

THE PEOPLE OF ENOCH'S STORY

The story that Enoch tells contains three sets of beings who can be differentiated from the 'normal' inhabitants of his world, namely: angels, the Watchers; and their cross-bred offspring, the giants. As we shall see, the relationships between these three groups are complex and interesting.

Angels are well-known beings of Jewish and Christian myth that have developed into winged men who fly between heaven and earth to communicate messages from God. The word 'angel' comes from the Greek *aggelos*,which simply meant 'messenger', and was a direct translation of the Hebrew term for angel, *mal'ak*. At the time of Christ, angels became extremely popular creatures, although from Acts 23:8 we learn that the more pragmatic Jews, such as the ruling Sadducees, denied their existence. The Bible names only two angels, Gabriel and Michael, and both of these references are in the book of Daniel, which is acknowledged to be in the Enochian tradition.

Originally, the term 'angel' simply meant a god in the pantheon of heaven, but as the Jews became monethistic these other inhabitants of heaven had to be relegated to a secondary role that did not compromise Yahweh's unique position. The role of angels as gods themselves is suggested in Psalm 82:1. We found it interesting that the Bible attributes this psalm to Asaph because according to Masonic legend he was responsible for providing the music at the consecration of King Solomon's Temple.

God standeth in the congregation of the mighty; he judgeth among the gods . . . I have said, Ye are gods; and all of you are children of the most High.

When angels were reduced to being members of God's divine council, later references described these other-worldly creatures variously as 'sons of God', 'morning stars' or the 'host of heaven'. As time passed there was an increasing emphasis on God's transcendence and the angels became divine mediators, frequently being described as 'men' themselves (e.g. Joshua 5:13). This certainly fitted with information we had previously received from a man claiming direct descent from the first-century Jerusalem priesthood, who said that the term 'angel' was always applied to senior priests. Therefore when the angel Gabriel visited the Virgin Mary to tell her she was to conceive, he was there to inseminate her with his own 'holy' seed.[1]

A particularly interesting document is the *Book of Jubilees*, also once known as the *Apocalypse of Moses*, which is claimed to have been written down by Moses on Mount Sinai as an angel dictated to him. On the surface it is an account of histories of days past, but on another level this book is a calendar document, closely associated with Enoch, which lays out the importance of a 364-day year. It is now believed to have been composed in the second century BC by the Qumran Community, and fragments of it have been found amongst the Dead Sea Scrolls. The book makes several references to the Watchers and is concerned with the understanding of the trajectories of heavenly bodies.[2] It records how these Watchers instructed men:

For in his days the angels of the Lord descended upon earth – those who are named The Watchers – that they should instruct the children of men, that they should do judgment and uprightness upon earth.

From the descriptions we have come to the conclusion that, although the angels of legend were considered to be types of gods, the individuals who interacted with the proto-Jewish people were simply mortal men, and over time the myth turned them into supernatural beings. It seems probable to us that terms such as 'angel' were originally understood to apply to men who had great knowledge, and only later post-rationalization which made them

[1] Knight, C. and Lomas, R.: *The Second Messiah*, Century, 1997
[2] Eisenman, R. and Wise, M.: *The Dead Sea Scrolls Uncovered*, Element, 1992

deities. We have found this to be evident in the story of Jesus, who was considered to be a man by the Jews of the Jerusalem Church, but later people of the Roman Empire elevated him to the level of a deity.

Interestingly, it is widely accepted that the term 'Watcher' was once commonly used in Enochian-style literature to describe an angel.[3] This would suggest that Enoch's people saw that the Watchers were men, but their unusual powers that made them seem godlike.

Whilst the *Book of Enoch* makes many references to the Watchers, there are just two references to them in the *King James Bible.* A single phrase: '*A Watcher and an holy one came down from heaven*' is repeated twice in Chapter 4 of the Book of Daniel. According to Professor H. T. Andrews both a Watcher and a 'holy one' were considered to be classes of angel.[4]

Chapter 6 of the *Book of Enoch* tells us that the angels, the children of heaven, saw and lusted after the beautiful daughters of men and took them as wives. There is some confusion as to the difference between the Watchers and angels, but it is their offspring, the Nephilim, who are particularly interesting. The 'congenital deviants' born out of the mating of the Watchers and human women are described in the Old Testament, although the original Hebrew word 'Nephilim' was translated into Greek as 'giant'. In modern Christian Bibles the word Nephilim has been translated as 'giants', but in the Jewish version of Numbers 13:32-33, translated directly from the Hebrew, we read how small the Jews felt when confronted by these men of 'great stature':

> *And all the people that we saw in it are men of a great stature. And there we saw the giants, the sons of Anak, which come of the Nephilim: and we were in our own sight as grasshoppers, and so we were in their sight.*[5]

According to legend all but a few Nephilim were destroyed in the Flood, and the term 'sons of Anak' is a reference to the remnants of this strain of giants, who remained in the hill country of Palestine prior to the arrival of the Jews.[6] Biblical scholar S. H. Hooke believes that the destruction of these prehistoric giants in the Flood was an explanation for their disappearance:

[3] Barr J.: 'Daniel', *Peake's Commentary on the Bible* (1962 edition)
[4] Andrews, H.T.: 'Daniel', *Peake's Commentary on the Bible* (1920 edition)
[5] Cohen, A.: *The Soncino Chumash*, The Soncino Press, London, 1962
[6] Snaith, N.H.: 'Numbers', *Peake's Commentary on the Bible* (1962 edition)

> *In early Hebrew tradition the myth of the Nephilim was an aetiological myth intended to explain the existence of a vanished race of giants.*[7]

The word 'Nephilim' is of uncertain origin, but it has been observed by specialist scholars that the root Aramaic word *nephîlâ* is the name of the constellation Orion, and therefore, Nephilim would seem to mean 'those that are of Orion'.

As we had already noted, the Australian Aborigines identified that their own version of the Watchers (the Nurrumbunguttias) had come to earth from Orion. Given that the Australian Aborigines are thought to have been isolated from the rest of the world for 40,000 years, this must surely be coincidence – but there is yet another connection.

The ancient kingdoms of Upper and Lower Egypt became united into a single state at some time around 3100 BC. Their history was written down from this time, and everything prior to this point was remembered as Zep Tepi, which literally meant 'The First Time'. According to the ancient Egyptians, Zep Tepi had been an age when gods had ruled in their country, bringing the gift of civilization.[8] The Egyptians believed that there had been intermediaries between gods and men whom they called the Urshu, which translates as the Watchers.[9]

We have discussed these Egyptian Watchers with Graham Hancock, the well-known researcher and author, who has said:

> '*. . . they [the Ancient Egyptians] preserved particularly vivid recollections of the gods themselves, puissant and beautiful beings called the Neteru who lived on earth with humankind and exercised their sovereignty from Heliopolis and other sanctuaries up and down the Nile. Some of these Neteru were male and some female but all possessed a range of supernatural powers which included the ability to appear, at will, as men or women, or as animals, birds, reptiles, trees or plants.*
>
> *Paradoxically, their words and deeds seem to have reflected human passions and preoccupations. Likewise, although they were portrayed as stronger and more intelligent than humans, it was believed that*

[7] Hooke S.H.: 'Genesis', *Peake's Commentary on the Bible* (1962 edition)
[8] Grimal, N.: *History of Ancient Egypt*, Blackwell, Cambridge, 1992
[9] *The Gods of Ancient Egypt*, Vol. 1

> *they could grow sick – or even die, or be killed – under certain circumstances.*[10]

The writer, Zecharia Sitchin, states that the Egyptian recorded that these Watchers had come to their kingdom from a place called 'Ta-Ur' which he believes means something like a 'oldest, far-off land'.[11] We do not know how he has arrived at this interesting translation, but the word 'Ta' certainly meant 'land' in ancient Egyptian. However, the word 'Ur' is widely thought to mean 'city',[12] so that the implication is that 'Ta-Ur' was an ancient place where there is, or was, a land of integrated communities. Almost by definition, this place must have been distant from Egypt.

This meaning of the word 'Ur' caused us to reflect on the meaning of the name 'Uriel'. Because an 'el' ending of a Hebrew word meant 'of God', it seems reasonable to take this angel's name as giving the meaning 'city of god'.

So, these three ancient traditions present a coherent picture of the Watchers and their giant offspring, which says that they were men from a distant land where civilization had been long established. Their technical development was so advanced that to the native North African culture of the time, they appeared to be gods. The Watchers seem to have kept themselves relatively removed from the indigenous people, apart from producing the Nephilim by their mating with local women. The Jewish legends are impossible to date exactly, except that they must predate Moses and the Exodus, which is generally believed to have happened around the 13th century BC. The Egyptian records predate the begining of Egyptian history, so we can safely conclude that both stories refer to a time no less than 5,100 years ago (the legends refer to earlier times, but this is not necessarily the same as saying they originated then).

THE GIANT OF BASHAN

A famous giant of the Old Testament is King Og of the Ammonites, the leader of the people of Bashan, a land to the south-east of the Sea of Galilee,

[10] Hancock, G.: *Fingerprints of the Gods*, Heinemann, 1995
[11] Sitchin, Z.: *The Wars of Gods and Men*
[12] *The Oxford Companion to the Bible*, Oxford University Press

which was one of several kingdoms laid waste by Moses and his band of marauding Hebrews. The invading Hebrews put all the inhabitants of these lands to the 'ban', which meant total genocide; every man, woman and child being hacked to pieces upon the direct instruction of God. The event is proudly described in Numbers 21:33-35:

> *And they turned and went up by the way of Bashan: and Og the king of Bashan went out against them, he, and all his people, to the battle at Edrei. And the LORD said unto Moses, Fear him not: for I have delivered him into thy hand, and all his people, and his land; and thou shalt do to him as thou didst unto Sihon king of the Amorites, which dwelt at Heshbon. So they smote him, and his sons, and all his people, until there was none left alive: and they possessed his land.*

One of the principal cities of the ill-fated kingdom of Bashan was Edrei, which was an amazing underground city based on a complex of caves of hard, black basalt rock. Og may have been one of the last of the Nephilim who, perhaps as a result of his superiority, became king of the people of Bashan. We were impressed to learn that according to Arab tradition these people are believed to be connected with the remains of a megalithic culture found in the region around Palestine, the Lebanon and Jordan. This megalithic interpretation is heightened by the fact that King Og is said to have possessed a bedstead of great dimensions, described in Deuteronomy 3:11:

> *For only Og king of Bashan remained of the remnant of giants; behold, his bedstead was a bedstead of iron; is it not in Rabbath of the children of Ammon? nine cubits was the length thereof, and four cubits the breadth of it, after the cubit of a man.*

According to some experts, this 'iron bedstead' was a dolmen, a large igneous stone slab raised up upon other stones to form a table.[13] We found this to be very significant, because such prehistoric structures are normally associated with the megalithic culture of the British Isles. The size given for this stone slab of nine by four cubits is said to equal thirteen-and-a-half feet

[13] Hooke, S.H.: 'Genesis', *Peake's Commentary on the Bible*

by six feet, which is typical of the stones found in Britain. An example of such a dolman is to be seen at Llugwy on Ynys Mon (Anglesey).

This curious connection moved us quickly onto the next question: where did these people come from, and what power did they possess that caused them to be thought of as gods?

WHERE WAS THE *BOOK OF ENOCH* WRITTEN?

The section of the *Book of Enoch* known as the 'Book of the Heavenly Luminaries' records a man being given instruction in matters concerning astronomy, a subject he clearly does not understand. Enoch records the event using phrases such as:

> *Uriel, the holy angel, who was with me, who is their guide, showed me; and he showed me all their laws exactly as they are.*

> *And all these Uriel, the holy angel who is the leader of them all, showed to me, and their positions, and I wrote down their positions as he showed them to me, and I wrote down their months.*

> *For the signs and the times and the years and the days the angel Uriel showed to me.*

> *In like manner twelve doors Uriel showed me.*

> *And now, my son, I have shown thee everything, and the law of all the stars of the heaven is completed. And he showed me all the laws of these for every day, and for every season of bearing rule, and for every year, and for its going forth, and for the order prescribed to it every month and every week: as they were, and the appearance of their lights till fifteen days were accomplished.*

> *Such is the picture and sketch of every luminary which Uriel the archangel, who is their leader, showed unto me.*

> *And he said unto me: 'Observe, Enoch, these heavenly tablets, And read what is written thereon, and mark every individual fact.'*

Enoch tells how he was is taken by the Watchers, to a far away place for these lessons about the heavens. He tells us:

> *And they brought me to the place of darkness, and to a mountain the point of whose summit reached to heaven. And they showed me all the secrets of the ends of the heaven, And all the chambers of all the stars, and all the luminaries, Whence they proceed before the face of the holy ones.*

He goes on to describe how, throughout the course of the year, the sun moves around the sky, appearing to believe that there are many different openings in the sky, which he calls portals and windows, through which the sun appears at different times. Here is how he describes it:

> *And I saw six portals in which the sun rises, and six portals in which the sun sets. Six in the east and six in the west, and all following each other in accurately corresponding order: also many windows to the right and left of these portals.*
>
> *And first there goes forth the great luminary, named the Sun. The sun goes down from the heaven and returns through the north in order to reach the east, and is so guided that he comes to the appropriate portal and shines in the face of the heaven.*
>
> *In this way he rises in the first month in the great portal, which is the fourth [those six portals in the east]. And in that fourth portal from which the sun rises in the first month are twelve window-openings, from which proceed a flame when they are opened in their season. When the sun rises in the heaven, he comes forth through that fourth portal thirty, mornings in succession, and sets accurately in the fourth portal in the west of the heaven. And during this period the day becomes daily longer and the night nightly shorter to the thirtieth morning.*

Enoch describes in detail how the sun moves between these openings throughout a 364 day long year, made up of twelve 30-day months plus four extra days. We could not help being fascinated, whilst reading this description, by Enoch's obsession with carefully recording every little thing he has been told.

All these little asides have the ring of somebody trying to explain something that he might not quite understand, but realizes is important. The recognized expert on the 'Book of the Heavenly Luminaries' is Professor Otto Neugebauer, of the Institute of Advanced Studies at Princeton, and we started by reading his views on the subject.

Neugebauer states that most scholars think that the astronomical chapters of the *Book of Enoch* are a composition that stands alone, not having much direct contact with the other parts of the work, but he goes on to say that he believes its contents 'reflect faithfully the simple concepts that prevailed in the communities which produced the Enochian literature'. He also comments that it may well be possible that there was a single original treatise which could have recorded the astronomical views of the early Enochian sect, but adds that if such an original work had existed, it could have been modified and requoted throughout the long history of the works of Enoch. He supports this view with information that fragments of Enochian astronomy occurred in many other Ethiopian works.[14] He comments:

> *The statement that the astronomical part of the* Book of Enoch *is based on concepts extant in the Old Testament is simply incorrect: the Enoch year is not an old semitic calendaric unit; . . . there exists no linear scheme in the Old Testament for the length of daylight, or patterns of gates.*[15]

Neugebauer believes that all the Enochian views on astronomy are 'hemmed in by a rigid schematism unrelated to reality', a conclusion based on his interpretation of the word 'gates' (which Charles had translated as 'portals'). He also comments that the role of the stars is limited to their times of rising in the solar year, and that they are not linked to constellations or the movements of the planets. He remarks: 'The search for time and place of origin of this primitive picture of the cosmic order can hardly be expected to lead to definitive results.'

He then goes on to attempt to relate the use of a 30-day month to Babylonian and Egyptian calendars, but decides that the Enochian calendar is unique, commenting that his reading of the text suggests a linear pattern for the relative times of day and night which he plots as a triangular shape.

[14] Neugebauer O.: 'Ethiopic Astronomy and Computus', *Akad d Wiss*, 1979
[15] Neugebauer O., in Black, M.: *The Book of Enoch or I Enoch* Brill, E. J. 1985

Taking the points, which are described in the text, he proceeds to fit a linear function to the length of day, on the basis that the resulting linear zigzag function is a fundamental feature in Babylonian astronomy – as described in cuneiform texts referring to large, or double hours (in Chapter Four we discussed Robert Temple's assessment of these units in Tablet Nine of the *Epic of Gilgamesh*). He then admits his borrowing from early Babylonian material cannot be used to date the composition, and his failure to make any sense of the work led him to conclude that: 'The whole Enochian astronomy is clearly an *ad hoc* construction and not the result of a common Semitic tradition.'

His suggestion that Enoch is using a Babylonian linear zigzag function to describe the length of day would lead to his conclusion that Enoch's schemata is unrelated to reality, but Professor Neugebauer was overlooking a key piece of information which can help in the search for the place of origin. His failure to locate where the work had been written was discouraging at first, but we decided to try a different type of analysis of the material to see where it would lead us.

It is clear from the Book of Enoch that its author was not a mathematician, but he is giving information about the relative length of day and night which can be translated into a latitude, given the clues about season, as we will now demonstrate.

At the equator, day and night remain approximately 12 hours each throughout the year, and there are no seasons. As one moves north or south of the equator, the ratio of light to darkness changes until the poles are reached, and extreme summer days have no darkness and winter ones no daylight. For most places on the planet there are only two days of equal light and darkness in the year; the equinox around 21 March, and the other equinox around 21 September.

We wondered whether we could get any clues from Enoch's information, bearing in mind we should be able to calculate a minimum distance from one of the poles. The lengths of daylight recorded in the 'Book of the Heavenly Luminaries' seem to be done by a crude observation, because the times are not given in hours but in ratios, for example:

> *On that day the day is longer than the night by a ninth part, and the day amounts exactly to ten parts and the night to eight parts.*

The only unit used is an eighteenth part of a day, which means that the scale of measurement Enoch is using is very inexact. Because all his measurements are taken on a scale which quotes only complete units of 1 hour 20 minutes (i.e. an eighteenth of 24 hours), he has to round up or down to the nearest unit to state a figure for the continuously changing hours of daylight. This means the closest he can measure time, no matter how accurate his estimates are, is plus or minus 40 minutes.

The length of day and, even more importantly, its rate of variation can be used to work out the possible latitudes at which the observation was made. The fact that Enoch's units of measurement can be up to 40 minutes wrong in either direction translates to a possible error of latitude of five degrees either way, which represents about 320 miles.

There is an additional complication to consider in that he is describing a journey which covers quite a wide area – north, south, east and west – and it is fairly safe to assume that he was unaware that the length of day and night varies according to the latitude of the observer. A person who normally spends his entire life in a small area would not have any idea that their own day and seasons are not a constant everywhere. He may have faithfully recorded observations taken at different latitudes as if he had stayed in one place. If this happened, it would explain some of the mismatches we observed in his data.

Tacitus, the Roman historian of the first century AD, was greatly surprised at how much longer the days were in the northern parts of Britain.

> *Their day is longer than in our part of the world. The nights are light, and in the extreme north so short that evening and morning twilight are scarcely distinguishable. If no clouds block the view, the sun's glow, it is said, can be seen all night long, it does not set and rise, but simply passes along the horizon. The reason must be that the flat extremities of the earth cast low shadows and do not raise the darkness to any height; night therefore fails to reach the sky and its stars.*[16]

He does not, however, show any understanding of the phenomena of day-length varying wth latitude, but tries to explain it in terms of going too near the edge of a flat-disc earth. Tacitus was a highly educated Roman citizen

[16] Tacitus: *The Agricola* and *The Germanis*, Penguin Classics, 1948

and yet even he was unaware of the change of length of day with latitude. It is therefore hardly surprising that Enoch did not understand how the length of day which he is trying so hard to report, was changing.

Thus, Enoch makes a similar statement to that of Tacitus, in Chapter 72

And the sun goes down from the heaven and returns through the north in order to reach the east, and is so guided that he comes to the appropriate portal and shines in the face of the heaven.

If the educated Tacitus was unaware of this phenomenon until he received reports from an expedition which sailed round the Isles of Orkney, how did Enoch learn of it? The answer is, he seems to have been taken to a site in the far north. Indeed he says as much, even complaining of the cold weather in Chapter 34, adding detail to confirm this:

And from thence I went towards the north to the ends of the earth, and there I saw a great and glorious device at the ends of the whole earth.

And here I saw portals of heaven open in the heaven: through each of them proceed north winds: when they blow there is cold, hail, frost, snow, dew, and rain. And out of one portal they blow for good: but when they blow through the other two portals, it is with violence and affliction on the earth, and they blow with violence.

Hail, frost, snow and violent winds seems a fair description of the northern latitudes in winter. It certainly doesn't fit the Middle East.

THE EVIDENCE OF THE LENGTH OF DAY

At first reading, the *Book of Enoch* appears to describe extremely accurately where it was written. Enoch says he can measure the length of day exactly, and so we sat down and translated the dates into the modern calendar, saying that on 21 May the ratio of day to night is 11:7 (or the length of day is 14.67 hours). On the solstice (21 June) the day is 16 hours; 30 days later (21 July) the ratio of night to day is 11:4 (i.e. 14.34 hours); and 30 days later again (21 August) is 10:8, i.e. (13.34). We felt that from this information we should be able to work out where he was, but we were soon disappointed.

Assuming that the day length is absolutely correct on 21 May as 14.67

hours, fixes his latitude at 43° north or south of the equator. But then, assuming that the day length is also absolutely correct on 21 June as 16 hours, fixes his latitude at about 51° north or south, while on 20 August (60 days after the solstice) day length of 13.34 hours fixes his latitude at around 43° north or south.

So where was he? The first thing we could be reasonably certain of was that his latitude must be north of the equator, because the only land at these latitudes to the south would place him in Chile, Argentina, Tasmania or New Zealand – which all seemed equally improbable.

The latitude brackets that we had from this information were certainly surprising because, even if he had recorded the length of day in different places, the most southerly possibility was on a line that includes Naples, Barcelona and Istanbul. This means that he was at least 1,100 kilometres to the north of Qumran, where the document is believed to have been first written down. On the other hand, he could have been as far north as Paris.

So, the lengths of day that Enoch describes could not possibly fit any *single* place on earth. They all gave different answers, and we could not choose to trust one and reject the others. All we could assume is that he had made an

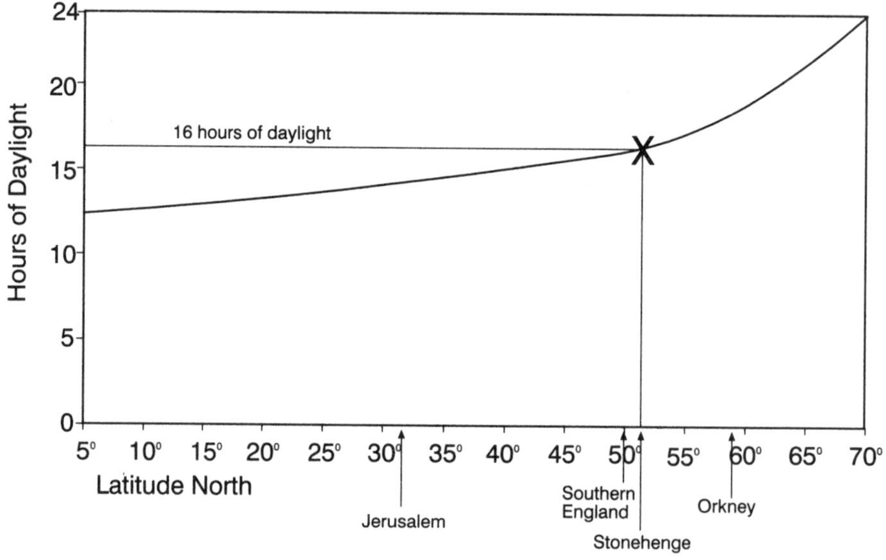

Figure 12. *Enoch describes the length of day at the solstice as 16 hours. The chart shows this statement is true at the latitude of Stonehenge.*

honest mistake with his length of day estimates, or had not recorded them all at the same latitude, so we decided to try another approach to the problem.

We took it that Enoch was doing his best to describe something that he had truly experienced, and whilst he may not have got the absolute time right, he may have estimated the *rate of change* of the length of day more accurately.

We decided to test this assumption.

The change in length of day between 21 May and 21 June that Enoch describes is 1.33 hours (one eighteenth part of a day), which places him at 60°N.

The change in length of day between 21 June and 20 August is 2.66 hours (two eighteenth parts of a day), this places him 59°N.

If we assume that he is estimating absolute day length to an accuracy of one eighteenth part of a day and that his timing points are exactly every 30 sunrises as stated, then he could be anywhere between 43°N and 60°N. But we knew that we could improve this guess by looking at the consistency of his measurements.

If he got the day length right, he is between 41°N and 51°N, with an absolute error in his measurements of plus or minus four degrees of latitude. So now we knew he didn't measure the absolute day length very accurately, but he was comfortably within the theoretical error of his measurement system, which was plus or minus five degrees.

If he got the *rate of change* in length of day right, he is between 59°N and 60°N, with an absolute error of half a degree of latitude. So if he was not better at estimating changes than absolute values, then at the very least he was more self-consistent, and was well within his error limit of plus or minus 5°. But he was wildly out on his day length at the solstice, by *more* than the error of his measuring unit.

Not to be defeated, we continued because there are two other reasonable assumptions we could make about his measurements:

1. He was making an average assessment of the length of day which is about right, but he didn't really understand the day/night curve underlying it. We used a mathematical technique, known as the 'least squares method', to fit the nearest real day/night curve (i.e. one that could really happen) to Enoch's data, and found that the curve for a latitude of 52°N fits best. With his inherent error of five degrees, this puts him somewhere between 47°N and 57°N.

2. If we assume that he has been accurate with his length of day, but has been mistaken in his time, (i.e. he is describing the length of day accurately but he is not really sure of his date or position) then we can get a better fit to the real shape of the daylight curve and an estimate of mean latitude as 55°N. With his inherent error, this gives a range of 50°N to 60°N.

When we take the inherent measurement error of Enoch's method into account, it leads to a series of estimates of his latitude, all based on different assumptions tending to a range of between 51°N and 59°N (55° plus or minus 4°).

This probability calculation is mathematically sound and suggests that Enoch's position was somewhere between the latitude of Brussels and Stockholm, or the south of England and the northern tip of Scotland.

By any standards this was strange for an ancient Jewish document.

We looked along the line of latitude of 59°N to see how many candidate countries there were. It runs through the Orkneys, then going west touches the lower tip of Greenland before going on through Labrador across Hudson Bay, then on through Canada and Alaska, to cross Siberia to Sweden and Norway and complete its great circle. As we studied the globe, however, we could not avoid noticing that the *Book of Enoch* was describing a location which fitted the range of latitudes occupied by a group of people known, rather unpoetically, as the Grooved Ware People. These people built some of the most important astronomically aligned megalithic structures in the world. They built such sites as the rings of Brodgar and Stenness, Maes Howe and Callenish in the north of Scotland, Newgrange, Knowth, Dowth in the Boyne Valley of Ireland, Barclodiad y Gawres and Bryn Celli Ddu in north-west Wales; and Stonehenge, Avebury, Silbury Hill and Durrington Walls in the south of England.

Was it just a coincidence that the 'Book of the Heavenly Luminaries' is a dissertation on ancient astronomy, and that the latitudes Enoch inadvertently describes appear to coincide with the world's earliest-known astronomical observatories?

Because so little is known about these ancient people, they are defined by the style of ceramic artefacts that they left behind them. This class of pottery is known as 'Grooved Ware' for the simple reason that it is decorated with a large number of grooves on the surface of the pots. These vessels are typically flat-bottomed and are covered by a repeating lozenge pattern which has also been found on certain buildings of the period.

Most Grooved Ware sites seem to have used the motif only on pottery. However, the Orcadian artefacts known as Skaill knives, which are triangular-shaped, flaked-stone hand knives, were often decorated with this same grooved pattern which was also carved into large stone structures in Ireland, Wales and Scotland (e.g. Newgrange in Ireland, Bryn Celli Ddu and Barclodiad y Gawres in Wales, and Templewood in Scotland).

The Grooved Ware pottery found in the south of the British Isles is sometimes known as Rinyo-Clacton ware after the two sites where it was first found, Rinyo on Orkney and on submerged land at Clacton in Essex.[17] It is generally accepted that when the early so-called causewayed camps of the southern downs of England were rebuilt into the henge monuments which survive today, the people who did the work used Grooved Ware pottery. Other sites where Grooved Ware has been found include such well-known megalithic locations as Stonehenge, Avebury, Woodhenge, Mount Pleasant and Amesbury.[18] Until 1975, it was thought that the earliest undisputed sample of Grooved Ware had been found in the primary silts of the ditch surrounding Stonehenge.[19] Since then, radiocarbon dates have shown that shards of identical Grooved Ware found at Skara Brae in Orkney predate the Stonehenge pottery. The shards at Skara Brae were found embedded in layers of midden material which was radiocarbon dated, giving a reliable date for the pottery.

REVISING OUR VIEW

We considered the possibility that the Grooved Ware People who once lived around the Atlantic coast of Europe might have been the origin of the people whom Enoch called Watchers and angels. The idea had certain attractions, but it had one very significant problem for our working hypothesis; whilst these sites are very ancient, they are not old enough to have been in use just before the comet impact in 7640 BC.

Even the very earliest observatories built around the Irish Sea date back about 6,000 years, making them thousands of years too young. The only evidence of astronomical observations that *predate* the Flood comet are a

17 Balfour, M.: *Stonehenge and its Mysteries*, Macdonald and Jane's, 1979
18 North, J.: *Stonehenge, Neolithic Man and the Cosmos*, HarperCollins, 1996
19 Mackie, E.: *The Megalithic Builders*, Phaidon Press, 1977

group of post-holes in what is now the car park at Stonehenge in Wiltshire. Just a few yards from these holes is another group of post-holes that were erected a few hundred years after the Flood, which seems to suggest that there is something rather special about this particular point for observational purposes. (We will discuss this matter more fully in the next chapter.)

The existence of the Stonehenge post-holes did not seem to be enough to connect Enoch with the comet impact, and we rechecked all of the latitude calculations and tried to think of any other explanation. But we soon had to admit defeat; Enoch *had* to have been alive much more recently than the massive comet impact nearly 10,000 years ago.

We sat down and considered all of the facts and possibilities that we had assembled, and the obvious conclusion slowly dawned on us. The data on the magnetic record of the planet had told us that there was a ***second major comet impact*** on the earth, a little over 5,000 years ago: could ***this*** have been Enoch's comet?

This forced a major revision of our working hypethesis, but as a scenario, it seemed sound. The seven-part impact had devastated the world, killing most people on the planet and putting civilization back by centuries. As a result of the *first* impact, the Grooved Ware People had built observatories to recalibrate their calendars so that agriculture could be re-established. When their descendants saw *another* comet heading on an earth trajectory, they must have thought that the world was about to be destroyed all over again, and so took steps to educate friendly neighbours in the science of astronomy. Two cometary impacts must have been inadvertantly interwoven in the verbal traditions.

If these Grooved Ware People were indeed the Watchers, it becomes understandable that they would have taken the leaders of their befriended Middle Eastern tribes to the north for training, in the hope that they might be amongst the survivors. The *Book of Enoch* had preserved the actual story of the 3150 BC comet and the cultural import of the 7640 BC impact.

Our next task was to investigate the places that fitted with Enoch's journey of discovery.

CONCLUSION

The *Book of Enoch* describes three groups of beings: the Watchers, the giants and the angels. The Watchers seem to be an advanced group of beings who were once angels, but who became too closely involved with the local women and bred offspring known as giants. A comparison of these legends across different traditions suggests that they are at least 5,000 years old.

The Bible says that some of these giants survived until the time of King David.

The *Book of Enoch,* which describes where these Watchers came from, gives evidence of certain latitudes within its descriptions. Careful analysis of this data shows that Enoch was taken to places within the range of latitudes 51°- 59° North. This latitude is where a group of people known as the Grooved Ware People lived, on the western edge of Europe over 5,000 years ago.

If these Grooved Ware People were the Watchers, then the comet impact which caused the Flood that Enoch foresaw had to be the one of 3150 BC. This hit in the area of the Mediterranean. Had the Grooved Ware People therefore survived the impacts of 7640 BC, and later, observing the 3150 BC comet, did they decide to warn as many people as possible?

Chapter Seven

THE ENOCH ZONE

THE GEOMETRY OF STONEHENGE

Finding that one of the most ancient characters of Jewish theological legend had gained his instruction in solar astronomy so far north, we asked ourselves the question; is there anything significant about the latitudes, apparently indicated by the eyewitness accounts, described in the *Book of Enoch*? We quickly found that the answer was a resounding yes!

If Enoch is to be dated at the time of the *second* comet (*circa* 3150 BC), the latitudes of 51°N to 59°N, framed between the tiny sliver of longitudes 2°E to 10°W, were a hive of astronomical activity at this precise time, with a level of intensity that the world had not seen before or since.

As we have seen in Chapter Six, the people who lived in this region have been dubbed Grooved Ware People because of the designs that predominantly appear on their ceramic artefacts. The British Isles, particularly in the west, are littered with their prehistoric structures: standing stones and earthworks in fields, or their remains beneath the tarmac of the city streets; moreover, most if not all older churches occupy sites that were held to be sacred thousands of years before Christ was born.

The most famous stone circle, Stonehenge, in the county of Wiltshire, is close to the southern limit of the zone described by Enoch. As we have also seen, at around 8000 BC some unknown group erected two large wooden poles where its car park stands today. They were aligned east-west and could have acted as equinox-sighting markers. This date was well *before* the

Figure 13. *Distribution of some major megalithic observatories.*

cometary impact of 7640 BC, which we knew from the sand layer covering most of Scotland and unfossilized sea shells on top of Snowdon resulted in the swamping of the British Isles. But there is also clear archaeological evidence that just under 1,000 years later, two further posts were erected only 350 metres away, also aligned east-west.[1]

What was so special about this spot that similar structures, capable of being used to fix the solar calendar accurately, were set up at exactly the same place? Particularly given the tiny but widely scattered population of Britain in this era, can it be coincidence that, following the destruction of the earlier equinox observatory (established over 400 years before the Flood) people returned to re-establish it in almost the same spot, 500 years after the comet impact? Very probably there would have been no visible trace of the earlier wooden structure, so we can be pretty sure that the second structure was built according to fresh calculations and not simply on the remains of the first.

There is no evidence of what happened on the site for the next 3,500 years, but at some time around 3020 BC a henge (a circular ditch and raised mound) was constructed with 56 holes dug around its perimeter.[2] The Neolithic builders used deer antlers as picks to dig the henge, which measured about 97 metres in diameter; 6 metres wide and between 1.3 to 2.1 metres deep. They then erected two parallel entry stones on the north-east of the circle. Just inside the circular bank they also dug, and almost immediately refilled, the circle of 56 shallow holes, possibly to hold temporary siting poles. The site appears to have been in regular use until around 2600 BC when it was abandoned. Once deserted, the site quickly reverted to scrub-land.

Around 500 years later, another unidentified group cleared the ground again and radically remodelled the complex using bluestone pillars brought from the Preseli Mountains in south-west Wales. These stones, weighing up to four tons each, were transported on a 380-kilometre journey by raft along the sea coast and up local rivers, until they were finally dragged overland to the site.

The entrance to this earliest setting of bluestones was aligned on the sunrise at the summer solstice and a widened approach was constructed. Around 100 years later, this first bluestone construction was dismantled and

1 http://www.eng-h.gov.uk/stoneh/mes.html
2 http://www.eng-h.gov.uk/stoneh/mes.html

work began on the final phase of the site. The bluestones were moved within the circle, and the gigantic sarsen stones that can be seen today were first erected. These sarsen stones were transported from the Marlborough Downs, 32 kilometres to the north, and set up in a circle of 30 uprights capped by a continuous ring of stone lintels. Within this ring a horseshoe formation of five trilithons was built, each consisting of a pair of large stone uprights supporting a stone lintel. The tapered sarsen stones are of exceptional size, being some 9 metres long and weighing up to 50 tons. It remains a mystery how such huge stones were moved such a distance by these supposedly primitive people.

Early in the 20th century, the English astronomer Sir Norman Lockyer demonstrated that the north-east axis of Stonehenge aligned with the sunrise at the summer solstice, leading other scholars to speculate that the builders must have been simple sun worshippers. In 1963 an American astronomer, Gerald Hawkins, argued that the site was a complicated computer for predicting lunar and solar eclipses[3] but such 'romantic' interpretations were severely criticized by the archaeological establishment, who preferred their own baseless speculation that it was a place of pagan worship.

One would think that an astronomer would have far greater qualifications to assess any possible astronomical qualities for a structure, even if its early dating happens to mean that it is considered the property of archaeologists. Archaeologists are very good at digging and dating, but many of them seem to think that it is somehow illegitimate to try and understand the motivation and mindset of the people whose debris they examine in minute detail.

So, what could have made this site so special that for 10,000 years it was a centre for solar observation? Why did a group of people, more than 5,000 years ago, invest at least 30,000 manhours of labour in digging a circular ditch on Salisbury Plain?[4]

The answer lies in the fact that this southern end of what we have identified as the 'Enoch Zone' has a strange property that would have been of great significance to any ancient sky-watcher.

Wherever an observer is located, on the equinoxes (the days of equal split of day and night that occur around 21 March and 21 September) the rising sun appears exactly due east and the setting sun due west, causing the

[3] Hawkins, G.S.: *Stonehenge Decoded*, Souvenir Press, 1966

[4] Hawkins, G.S.: *Stonehenge Decoded*, Souvenir Press, 1966

morning and evening shadows to align in a straight line. On every other day of the year, the sunset and sunrise will occur either further north or south and will not line up. But at the latitude of Stonehenge a particularly significant alignment happens at the summer solstice (the day of maximum daylight, around 21 June) and the winter solstice (the day of minimum daylight, around 21 December). Historian of science and astronomy Professor John North of Groningen University explained the point:

> *[At the latitude of Stonehenge] A line of sight to the rising midsummer sun is in a direction precisely the reverse of the setting midwinter sun, in both cases . . . a single pair of vertical stones might in principle be used to set the reversible azimuth.*[5]

In simple terms, this means that when the winter solstice is viewed from Stonehenge, the shadow cast by a pole placed to mark the position of the sunrise on the horizon will align perfectly with a shadow cast from a second pole marking the midwinter sunset.

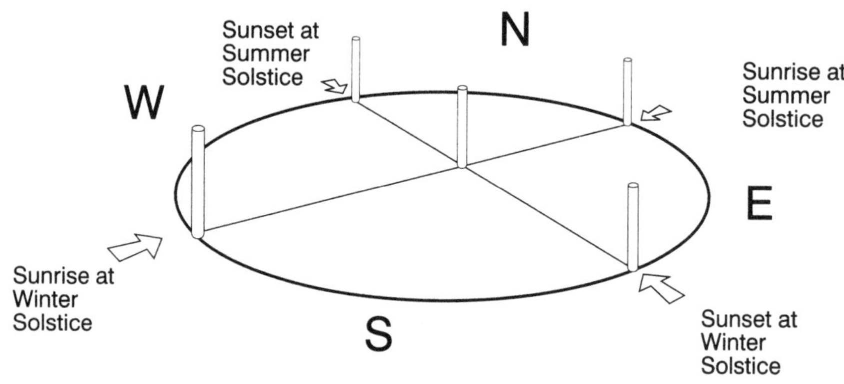

Figure 14. *How the sunrises and sunsets align at the latitude of Stonehenge.*

This effect can be shown in a simple diagram which marks the whole year at the latitude of 51° North as special.

[5] North, J.: *Stonehenge, Neolithic Man and the Cosmos*, HarperCollins, 1996

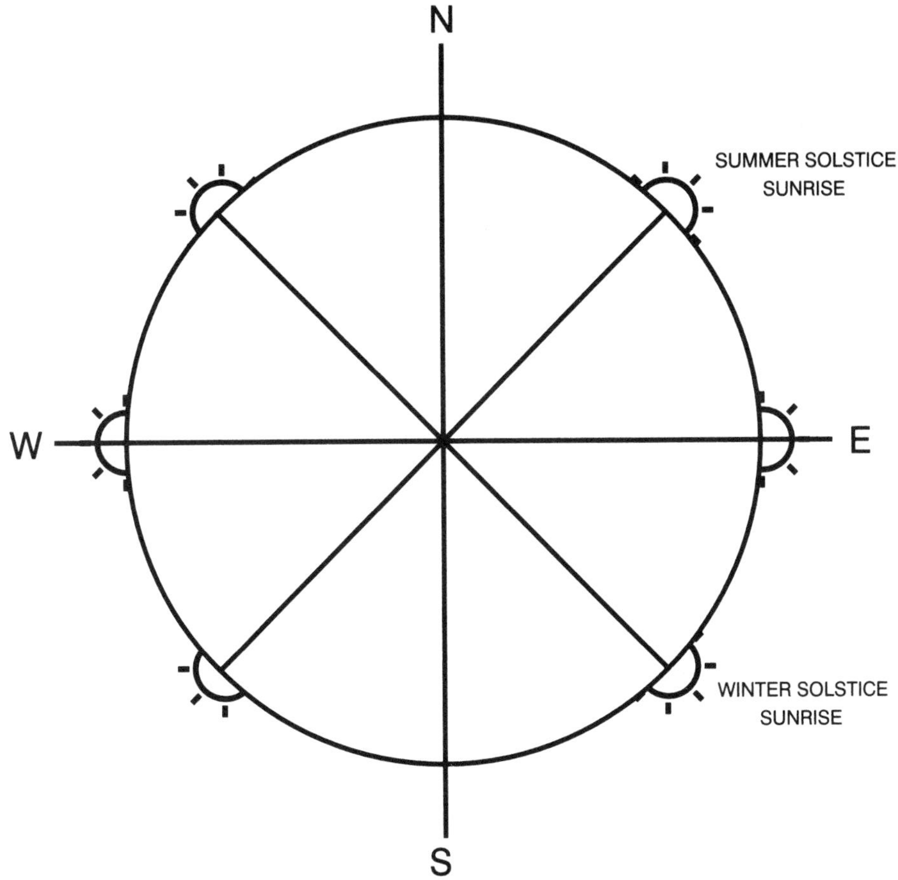

Figure 15. *The movement of the sun's rising and setting points with the changing seasons.*

There are a number of other important sites in the vicinity of Stonehenge that are close enough to share this amazingly neat effect of astro-geometry. These include Avebury, with its huge henge and scores of standing stones that cover over 28 acres, and Woodhenge, a timber-built observatory which is older than the stone structure at Stonehenge and is contemporary with the phase of ditch digging at Stonehenge. It seems probable that longitude was also important to the builders of these sites because Stonehenge, the Avebury ring, Silbury Hill and West Kennett long barrow are all on the 1° 50′ West line of longitude, even though they are spread out across 32 kilometres of countryside.

At a site called Fussell's Lodge on Salisbury Plain, not far from Stonehenge, there is a long barrow with two ditches sited at either end of the structure that have been radiocarbon dated to 4250 BC. John North has shown that at the time they were dug they would have adjusted the horizon and changed the time of rising of first magnitude stars. (First magnitude stars are bright enough to be seen low on the horizon). He makes a strong case that over 6,000 years ago, people living on Salisbury Plain were creating viewing platforms for highly accurate naked-eye astronomy. North has also come to the view that these people had a well-developed geometry which was linked to their astronomy. Discussing the ditches dug by the Neolithic people of West Kennet in Wiltshire, he says:

> *That the plan [of the site] has a definite geometrical rationale can hardly be denied however, and we are certainly not short of independent evidence that Neolithic geometry and stellar astronomy were closely allied.*[6]

North has put forward a very reasoned argument, based on considerable field observation, that the purpose of henges was to provide an artificial horizon for adjusting the viewing conditions when observing the rising and setting of celestial bodies.

It is worth noting that not all henges have stone circles within them, but all the henges which have been excavated have shown evidence of wooden posts erected within the henge. This suggests that the original observations were marked out by posts, and only later were stones used to create a permanent reference point.

LATITUDE 59° NORTH

The Isles of Orkney are off the northern coast of Caithness, which forms the edge of a very flat plateau north of the sweeping mountains of the Highlands. The largest of the group of islands is called Mainland, and it is neatly bisected by the 59° line of latitude, which passes through the principal town of Kirkwall. Although today the area has a sparse population, it has one of the highest densities of megalithic sites in the British Isles.

[6] North, J.: *Stonehenge. Neolithic Man and the Cosmos*, HarperCollins, 1996

The narrow strip of water which separates John o'Groats, in Caithness, from Burwick, on Orkney, is one of the roughest channels in western Europe, but 11,000 years ago it did not exist. At the end of the last Ice Age, the Islands of Orkney were simply mountain peaks on the northern plain which is now covered by the North Sea.

The north of Scotland has experienced dramatic changes since the end of that last Ice Age. During the Weichselian glaciation (the final cold period of the last Ice Age in Scotland), which reached its peak about 18,000 years ago, the whole of Scotland was buried under a layer of ice one kilometre thick. The ice drew water from the sea, making sea levels fall, and the weight of the ice pushed up the surrounding seabed. Nobody could have lived in Scotland at this time, since it was as hostile an environment as the Arctic is today. By 13,000 BC the Milankovitch cycle, which effects the heat the Earth absorbs from the sun, was warming up, and the ice was starting to melt; the mammoth, woolly rhinoceros and reindeer arrived in Scotland around 11,000 BC, but were then wiped out by the tsunami waves from the comet impact which left a layer of sand across much of the country.

A later, beneficial aspect of the comet impact for Scotland was global warming, and by 6500 BC the region had a very pleasant climate. Archaeologist Dr Wickham-Jones notes that: '*the environment had opened up to a climatic optimum. From then on, Scotland has offered an attractive base for year-round human occupation.*'[7]

The evidence for early settlement in Scotland is very patchy. Dr Wickham-Jones complains there is a general lack of detailed archaeological information, with few of the key sites subjected to modern techniques of analysis and very little recent excavation. Most of the material collected has come from farming activity, and this means that artefacts from different periods have been churned together by the plough.

During the period of rapid climatic changes from 10,000 BC the sea level had been rising and falling. As the ice melted the sea rose, but then, as the land was freed of the weight of the ice, it sprang back and the sea bed sank, resulting in changes in level of over 120 metres in the last 10,000 years. These movements left stranded beaches far from the sea in some parts of Scotland, whilst other parts have sunk beneath the waves. We know that people lived in the area of the North Sea to the north-east of Shetland, because one of the ocean-bed core samples taken by a British Geological

[7] Wickham-Jones, C.: *Scotland's First Settlers*, Historic Scotland, 1994

Survey ship contained a flint scraper. This core was taken 145 kilometres off Shetland from 140 metres of water.[8] These North Sea glacial plains were not totally reclaimed by the sea until around 6000 BC, when the land-bridge between southern Britain and continental Europe finally disappeared beneath the waves.

The part of Scotland which would have been the most hospitable for any refugees from the steadily rising North Sea would have been the areas of Caithness, Grampian and Orkney. There is no archaeological evidence for early settlement, but again Dr Wickham-Jones comments:

> *If they settled on the coast [of Caithness, Grampian or Orkney] as it was then, their sites now lie beneath several metres of water. If they settled further inland in most areas their sites would now lie beneath a thick covering of peat.*[9]

The earliest known human settlement in Scotland is on the island of Rum and dates from about 7000 BC, being contemporary with the earliest-known Irish sites at Mount Sandal on the River Bann. By 6000 BC, populations were well established on Islay, Jura, Arran, Oban, at Redkirk Point and around Loch Doon.

Historian Richard Oram comments on the considerable skills that these hardy post-glacial settlers must have possessed.

> *Settlements in the Hebrides speak of navigational skills and seamanship for which no physical evidence remains. It points to an ability to construct craft capable of withstanding quite lengthy sea-voyages, which in turn would suggest a capability to exploit marine resources in deep waters rather than just the shallow inshore fishings.*[10]

SKARA BRAE

One of the most fascinating prehistoric sites in Scotland is the ancient village of Skara Brae on the western-facing, Atlantic coast of Orkney. Its remains

[8] Long, D., Wickham-Jones, C., and Ruckley, N.A.: *Studies in the Upper Palaeothic of Britain and Northwest Europe*, pp.55-62, S296, 1986

[9] Wickham-Jones, C.: *Scotland's First Settlers*, Historic Scotland, 1994

[10] Oram, R.: *Scottish Prehistory*, Birlinn, 1997

were discovered in 1850 when a particularly bad storm ripped turf away from the sand dunes on the edge of Skaill Bay to reveal the remains of a group of stone-built houses. This was the first time in almost 5,000 years that Skara Brae had been exposed to the light of day. The site was taken over by the Ministry of Works in 1924 when a sea wall was built to prevent further erosion of the shoreline, and four years later Gordon Childe, the Professor of Archaeology from Glasgow University, excavated the site and helped to conserve these important buildings.

We found that nobody is sure when Skara Brae was first inhabited, since the earliest of the surviving buildings (radiocarbon-dated to 3215 BC) are known to have replaced earlier ones, but it is certain that it was abandoned very suddenly. A small pile of bone beads was found strewn along the main passageway, suggesting that the owner of the necklace had snapped its cord whilst rushing from apartment seven, and had no time to collect the dropped beads.[11] In one of the wall cupboards was a horde of 2,400 inscribed beads and pendants that must have had great value, yet they were left behind. The date put on this abandonment is *circa* 2655 BC.

Now, this is an interesting date! We have seen that the builders of the henge at Stonehenge had abandoned the site around 2600 BC, and that it had remained unused for the next 500 years. Given that all of these dates have a margin of error greater than 55 years, it appears that Skara Brae and Stonehenge could have been abandoned at pretty much the same time. Could there be a connection?

Dr Anna Ritchie, an archaeologist who is particularly expert on the megalithic sites of Orkney, has confirmed that the earliest radiocarbon dates and pollen diagrams suggest that food-producing communities were fully established in the islands by about 3500 BC. She also believes that it is inherently unlikely that developed settlements such as Skara Brae represent the homes of the first pioneering colonists. In her opinion these sites are the products of a mature, confident, farming society and she is certain that changes in sea level and coastal erosion have destroyed some of the evidence of the earliest inhabitants.[12]

At first sight, the eight best preserved of the dozen or so apartments at Skara Brae look like a set from the *Flintstones* movie. They appear to be a

[11] Mackie, E.: *The Megalithic Builders*, Phaidon Press, 1977

[12] Ritchie, A.: *The First Settlers in The Prehistory of Orkney*, ed. Renfrew, C., Edinburgh University Press, 1985

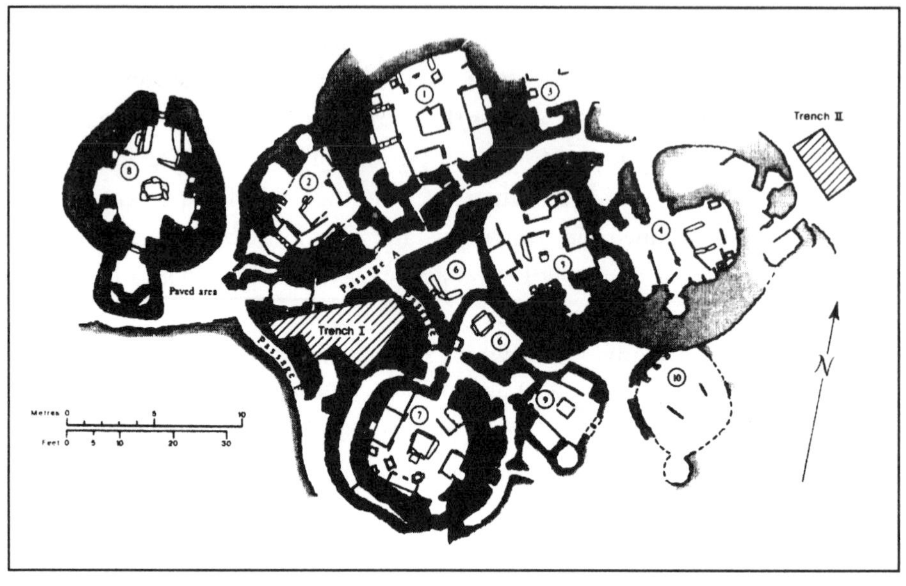

Figure 16. *Plan of Skara Brae, courtesy of Historic Scotland.*

Stone Age version of a modern housing estate, with a formalized regularity of layout. Some prehistoric architect appears to have planned the whole development so that stone versions of modern conveniences were provided inside each apartment. They all have standardized stone cupboards, fireplaces, bedsteads, water tanks and seats. Of the eight apartments, six are linked by a main corridor but the seventh is reached by a separate tunnel running at right angles off the main corridor. There is also a separate house which stands on the far side of a paved open-air courtyard.

The linked seventh and eighth dwellings obviously had some different purpose from the first six. The overall impression is that this was a place designed to accommodate visitors. This notion was further borne out by the evidence of what Americans today call 'trash-can analysis', whereby it is possible to deduce a great deal about a person's lifestyle from what they throw away.

One of the strange features of Skara Brae, which has contributed to its preservation, is the layer of rubbish which has accumulated outside the walls as high as the roof level. Referred to by archaeologists by the euphemism of 'midden material', it consists of all the debris of the inhabitants for 600 years, thrown outside to rot. Once rotted it greatly enhanced the insulation and longevity of the buildings, but how it must have stunk in high summer, when first deposited.

However, allowing your rubbish to build up around your house gives archaeologists a chance to come along thousands of years later and find out what you had for dinner. The layers of midden in Skara Brae have been extensively analysed and have revealed that the inhabitants mainly ate sheep and cattle, topped up with fish, oysters and a very occasional side of pork.

One of the features of the diet of the inhabitants of Skara Brae which interested archaeologist Euan Mackie was the lack of wild game. Looking at other middens across Orkney, he commented that the common sources of meat seemed to include about 50 per cent game along with 50 per cent farmed meat such as sheep or cow. The midden at Skara Brae was unusual in this respect, in that while its inhabitants ate a lot of farmed meat, they did not seem to have facilities for looking after flocks and herds over the winter. When Euan Mackie also noticed that there were far more carcass bones than there were skulls to go with them, it led him to suggest that the village might have been a prehistoric combination of monastery and a college in which a highly organized community lived. He believed that the inhabitants would have divided into specialized groups with a staff of cooks, craftsmen and so on.[13] Certainly the shortage of animal skulls does seem to indicate that the people here imported pre-butchered carcasses, which in turn confirms the impression that these buildings were used for some specialized purpose.

There is another puzzling feature. It is difficult at first glance to see where they got the fuel for their fires, because Orkney at the time was open grassland with hardly any trees.[14] There was no local supply of wood to burn on the many fireplaces of Skara Brae. Yet, from Childe's excavations, we know they had sufficient fuel to heat volcanic rock to high enough temperatures to cause it to heat-craze, and they must have been able to heat the houses to keep them warm enough to live there for so long.[15] The suggested alternative fuels of cattle dung or seaweed do not have a high enough calorific value to

[13] Mackie, E.: *The Megalithic Builders*, Phaidon Press, 1977
[14] Davidson, D.A. and Jones, R.L.: 'The Environment of Orkney' in *The Prehistory of Orkney*, ed. Renfrew, C., *Edinburgh University Press*, 1985
[15] Ritchie, A.: *Prehistoric Orkney*, Historic Scotland, 1995

achieve the temperatures needed to heat-craze volcanic rock, or to fire the pottery the inhabitants made. What's more, the peat burnt on Orkney today was not laid down until nearly 1,000 years *after* Skara Brae was abandoned. It would appear, then, that the village of Skara Brae either relied on driftwood from across the Atlantic to keep its eight fires and workshop furnace burning, or it imported wood from Caithness or Scandinavia.

Surely, there had to be a very good reason indeed to choose to live on this island when food and fuel had to be brought in? Both the thoroughness of the design and the quality of building at this site are simply breathtaking. It is often reported in history books that when the Romans arrived, the ancient inhabitants of Britain were barbarians who painted their naked bodies blue, but the city of Rome was 2,500 years in the future when Skara Brae was built complete with an underground sewage disposal system. When one of the Skara Brae guides pointed out to a modern metal sewage cover and asked Robert to lift it if he wanted to see the sewers, he did wonder if he was about to become the subject of an Orcadian practical joke. But this modern cap was protecting a 5,000-year-old, stone-built drainage channel which connected the houses to an outfall at the sea edge. The drains were made of stone and had originally been lined with tree bark to make them watertight. It was indeed a remarkably sophisticated system for its time.

Each of the houses has a large room with a single entrance fitted with a bolt-securing hole cut in the stone to lock a door from the inside – except for house seven which, rather curiously, has a door that is designed to be bolted from the *outside*. The rooms were at least three metres high with approximately 36 square metres of floor space and, like the *Flintstone* residence, all were equipped with the following set of desirable 'mod cons':

- A central stone hearth with a kerb to retain the fire

- A large stone dresser with two shelves supported on three large stone legs

- A rectangular stone chair

- Two stone bedsteads, with large end stones which Professor Childe has suggested would have supported a canopy. A Stone Age four-poster bed, no less!

- A stone water tank with its seams packed with clay

- Storage space consisting of small stone boxes and cells let into the floor and walls

Many of the houses are also equipped with a small adjoining chamber connected to the drainage system which may well have been lavatories; when the contents of the drains were examined they were found to contain high levels of ancient human excrement.[16]

The houses were arranged so that anyone entering would have to stoop low to go through the doorway and as they straightened up the first thing they would see would be the massive stone dresser with its display shelves. It has been argued that this was a deliberate design feature, and one wonders what objects were on display that required incomers to bow low.[17]

Anna Ritchie assessed the commonality of design and construction between the houses of Skara Brae and other houses uncovered at Rinyo, in the Isle of Rousay and at Barnhouse. She reasoned that the idea of identical houses built to a common plan is a modern idea normally associated with saving costs, but that this could not be accepted as an explanation of the similarity between the houses at Skara Brae, Rinyo and Barnhouse – although she did conclude that there may have been a specialist class of masons.[18]

Apartment seven at Skara Brae was not only unusual in having a door which locked from the outside, it was also the only one with a large stone block in the living area, and beneath one of the beds the bodies of two adult females had been buried. The intact skeletons showed signs of having been interred before the building had been erected, and the bed under which they had been inhumed was the only one in the village to be inscribed – or perhaps labelled.

Apartments seven and eight both seem to be special as they are the only buildings to be embellished by carved patterns on their stonework.[19]

Skara Brae has some of the earliest inscribed marks in the world and, given the careful planning and technical skill exhibited at the site, we considered it

[16] Clarke, D.V. and Sharples, N.: 'Settlements and Subsistence in the 3rd Millennium BC', in *The Prehistory of Orkney*, ed. Renfrew, C., Edinburgh University Press, 1985
[17] Clarke, D.V. and Sharples, N.: 'Settlements and Subsistence in the 3rd Millennium BC', in *The Prehistory of Orkney*, ed. Renfrew, C., Edinburgh University Press, 1985
[18] Ritchie, A.: *Prehistoric Orkney*, Historic Scotland, 1995
[19] Ritchie, A.: *Prehistoric Orkney*, Historic Scotland, 199

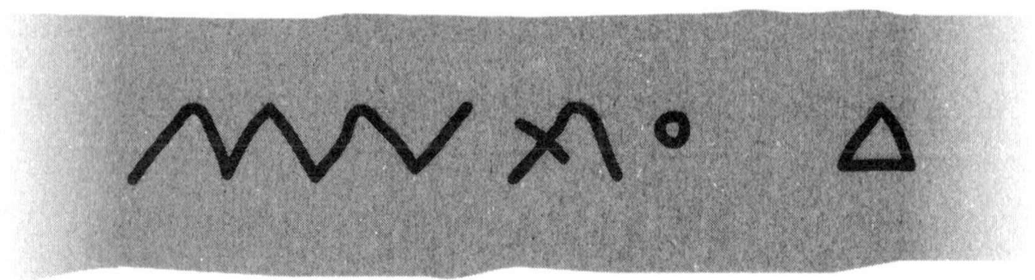

Figure 17. *The inscription on the side of the bed at Skara Brae.*

likely that these images are rather more than idle doodles. People who make marks on pottery may be doing so to make the item look pretty, but people who carve selectively into rock are usually trying to record something that is meaningful to them. Early cave-dwellers left hand-prints and images of the animals they hunted, for example, while the Ancient Egyptians priests inscribed images of people and objects arranged in such a manner that they recorded a coded message (we call them hieroglyphics); but anybody of the

Figure 18. *The Skara Brae motif.*

time who could not read, believed that it was magic for marks on stone to 'speak' stories.

It is a small step to move from a literal drawing of an object to create an abstract symbol. For example, the letter 'A' is believed to be derived from the image of a bull's head, which was progressively inverted over time. So surely it is possible for these megalithic people to have created abstract marks that carried meaning that we have not as yet understood. Not all archaeologists accept that the early pictograms can be understood, but we felt that the marks left by these people must have had a meaning for them, and they were therefore some kind of proto-writing.

One motif in particular, consisting of two lozenges and two spirals, was later to prove to be very important in linking Skara Brae to other sites. There are two major inscriptions on the fabric of the village – apart from a number of single decorated stones built into the walls, the main ones are on the side of the bed structure in apartment seven, and the side of the passageway leading to the same apartment.

Euan Mackie had also considered the inscriptions at Skara Brae, and he linked both the symbolism used and the style of pottery produced with the sites in southern England and the great megalithic tombs of the Boyne Valley of eastern Ireland. There are several symbols which connect these sites, particularly the 'spiral and lozenge' motif found on the Skara Brae potsherds which appear on stones at Newgrange in Ireland and at Barclodiad y Grawes in Anglesey, as well as at locations on the Iberian Peninsula.

STONE THINGS

As we have seen, Grooved Ware pottery is to be found at major sites in the south of England including Avebury, Woodhenge, Mount Pleasant, and Amesbury.[20] So another question that we pondered was, how did Grooved Ware come to be so widespread throughout the south of England *and* Orkney, when it is generally assumed that populations were fairly static? How could a remote village on the west coast of the Orkney island of Mainland be linked to these major sites in the south of England?

Until 1975, the earliest undisputed sample of Grooved Ware had been that found in the primary silts of the ditch surrounding Stonehenge.[21] Since then,

[20] North, J.: *Neolithic Man and the Cosmos*, HarperCollins, 1996
[21] Mackie, E.: *The Megalithic Builders*, Phaidon Press, 1977

radiocarbon dating has shown the shards of identical Grooved Ware found at Skara Brae predate that pottery.

Besides the Groove Ware remains, some beautifully crafted stone objects have been found at Skara Brae which have no obvious purpose of any kind. They are very strange, but archaeologists feel like failures unless they can put a label on an exhibit, and they have resorted to describing them as 'ceremonial cult objects'. From this type of approach, we have to assume that future archaeologists will some day sift through the remains of our age and describe garden gnomes and power-station cooling towers as cultic statues and temples!

The two most intricate objects are stone balls: one 6.2 cm (2.5 inches) in diameter, has been carved all over with that lozenge pattern so common on objects made at Skara Brae; the other, a slightly larger ball of 7.7 cms (3 inches) diameter, has been carved with grooves and knobs. Viewed closely, in their display case at Skara Brae, one can see that they were highly polished as if they had been handled a great deal. In fact, they appeared to have been handled far more than the inscribed 'Skaill' knives which were also on display and which as tools might have been expected to show much greater polish from usage.

Around 400 similar, but less ornate, stone balls have been found in other parts of Scotland between the River Tay and the Moray Firth. Their re-creation using stone tools is relatively easy, but the more elaborate balls of Skara Brae however are difficult to explain. Attempts to recreate them using Stone Age tools by engineer James Macauley failed, as it proved impossible to carve the difficult angles without using strong metal tools. For those other balls it had been suggested that the more intricate patterns had been carved during the Bronze and Iron ages. However, the stone balls of Skara Brae were found beneath the layer of wind-blown sand which was laid down when the village was abandoned in 2655 BC – long before any metal objects reached this part of the world. This poses the question, did the engineers of Skara Brae know something about the technology of working stone that we have forgotten?

It brought to mind three strange facts concerning stonemasonry without metal.

Firstly, at the time that Skara Brae was suddenly abandoned, the town of Giza in Egypt was founded and the Great Pyramid was built for King Khufu, whose reign is thought to have begun in 2638 BC. It is recorded that Hemon, the master mason in charge of the project, had his workmen use a tool that was not metal, and made no sound when it shaped the giant stones of the pyramid.

Secondly, over 1,600 years later, King Solomon had his temple built at Jerusalem, again without any metal being allowed to come in contact with the stones, despite the fact that metals had been used in the region since the fifth millennium BC.

And thirdly, today, in Masonic ritual the candidate, for the entry degree of the Entered Apprentice, the Freemason has to be 'devested' of all metal objects before he is admitted into the lodge and the ritual conducted.

In the light of these facts, perhaps there was once a more advanced stone technology that has been forgotten over the millennia. With this in mind, we turned to Robert Temples' translation of the *Epic of Gilgamesh*, which makes mention of some stone 'things' which have no obvious purpose.

> *He [Gilgamesh] laid himself down and then awoke from a dream. There in the dream he had seen the stone things, rejoicing in life they were. In his hand he raised his axe, he drew his dagger from his belt, he descended upon them like an arrow, he struck at them, smashed them to pieces.*[22]

Gilgamesh had been frightened by stone things, and had seen them as objects of power. Later in the poem, he seems to suggest they are used by travellers.

> *And when you arrive at the Waters of Death, what would you do? Ziusudra's boatman is there, Gilgamesh, his name is Urshanabi, with him are the stone things.*[23]

Perhaps Anna Ritchie is right when she suggests that these stone things were 'objects of power': '*Stone balls and T-shaped objects seem best interpreted as symbols of status and prestige, akin to ceremonial regalia still in use in the modern world.*'[24] After all, we still use similar regalia today. When a monarch of England is crowned, the king-making ritual involves sitting the king (or, of course, queen) on a rough-hewn stone that came from Israel to

[22] Temple, R.: *He Who Saw Everything*, Century, 1991
[23] Temple, R.: *He Who Saw Everything*, Century, 1991
[24] Ritchie, A.: *Prehistoric Orkney*, Historic Scotland, 1995

Ireland thousands of years ago as a king-making stone. In one hand they hold a rod (called a sceptre) and in the other, a decorated sphere (called an orb). Where did the use of this regalia of stately authority start? The current monarchy of the United Kingdom can still trace its ancestry back to Thorofinn, the first Norse ruler of Orkney. Could it be that these king-making rituals have a direct connection with rituals that were once used at Skara Brae?

THE RING OF BRODGAR

It is only an eighth kilometre drive from Skara Brae to the Ring of Brodgar. The road runs down between the two lochs of Harray and Stenness, passing through the middle of a bowl of surrounding hills to where the Ring stands, with its four and half metre high lumps of granite planted vertically across the landscape. This immense circle has 27 standing stones still intact, but it is thought that there were originally 60 of them. The stones of Brodgar are on a heather-covered plateau that is inclined towards the rising sun and, impressively, they are surrounded by a henge cut into the living bedrock.

Henges are unique to the British Isles, where they are sprinkled over the landscape in their thousands. Even by today's standards, the Brodgar henge is a serious piece of civil engineering, being 110 metrest (340 fee) in diameter, 10 metres (30 feet) wide and 3.4 metres (10 feet) deep. When Professor Colin Renfrew excavated sections of it, he estimated that the labour needed to cut this ditch into the bedrock was at least 100,000 man hours.[25] This seems an enormous investment of time for what was a small population of people with an expected average lifespan of little more than 25 years.[26]

Renfrew's calculation is a minimum estimate, but assuming that 40 men could work 50 hours every week through all of the seasons, it would still take them a year to cut the henge alone. Those men would have needed a great deal of support infrastructure, to provide raw food, import fuel, cook the food, make clothes and prepare a continual supply of new cutting tools. In short, this work must have been very important to a community, consuming almost its entire productive output for a long period of time.

[25] Renfrew, C.: 'Investigations in Orkney', *Report Research Comm., Soc. Antiq.*, London, No.38, 1979

[26] Hedges, J.W.: *Tomb of the Eagles*, Tempvs Reparavm, 1992

There are two entrance banks across the ditch into the ring, in the north-west and the south-east, which, at first sight, seem to marry with the general direction of the summer-setting sun and the winter-rising sun. On the farthest point from the road, to the north-east, is a later flat-topped mound which provides a panoramic viewpoint of the whole ring. Engineer and archaeo-astronomer Professor Alexander Thom believed this mound was built to provide an accurate foresight for the rising moon, and he estimated from astronomical observations that the platform was probably built about 1,000 years later than the henge.[27]

In the 1960s, Thom, a retired professor of engineering from Oxford University, established that the Ring of Brodgar and most other megalithic sites in western Europe were built using a standard unit of measure which he dubbed the 'Megalithic Yard'. He also suggested that the reason for digging the henge at this spot was because it provides four major foresights to observe movements of the moon – known as the major and minor standstills – which are important to the prediction of its cycles. In his view, the purpose of the outer bank to the henge would have been to provide a controlled artificial horizon for viewing these major and minor standstills in the moon's orbit.[28] This means that the henge was part of a scientific instrument on the scale of, and as purposeful as, a radiotelescope of today. For its ancient users it provided an horizon that was perfectly flat in all directions and allowed the heavens to be viewed as an exact hemisphere.

At the time of Thom's work, his talk of an international standard of measurement and the construction of astronomical observatories over 5,000 years ago was thought to be laughable. According to the ruling clan of archaeologists the population of the British Isles had been savages, not scientists – so, *de facto*, Thom must be wrong. He has since been proven to be entirely correct, thanks to independent statistical analysis.

Just down the road from the henge structure of the Ring of Brodgar is the smaller circle of more massive stones known as the Stones of Stenness, which also has its henge.

[27] Thom, A. and A.S.: 'Megalithic Rings', *BAR British Series 81*, 1980
[28] Thom, A. and A.S.: 'Megalithic Rings', *BAR British Series 81*, 1980

STENNESS AND BARNHOUSE

At the end of the isthmus separating the lochs of Harray and Stenness is a narrow reed-choked channel, nowadays bridged by a minor road that joins the main road at the village of Barnhouse, which is dominated by the enormous Stones of Stenness. There are four stones standing today, but when it was excavated by Grahame Ritchie in 1973 he found the sockets for 12 massive stones. In the centre of the circle there was a square stone structure, flush with the ground, at the entrance of which Ritchie found the remains of a pair of standing stones. Radiocarbon testing of associated animal bones that were used during the digging of the henge has revealed a build date of 3040 BC.

The Stones of Stenness are remarkable because of the deep-cut ditch which surrounds them. It has been cut two metres down into a single giant rock. To build it required the careful removal of 18,000 cubic metres of solid rock – apparently all done using tools made of flint, wood and bone. Whoever cut through that lot really wanted a ditch in that exact spot! Why did they go to so much trouble to build it?

It is such an unusual structure that Anna Ritchie said of it:

> *The early date for the Stones of Stenness came as a surprise, because is it earlier than many henges in mainland Britain. But this is perhaps confirmation that Orkney was not slow to adopt new ideas and may even have had a hand in the development of innovations usually attributed to an origin in southern England.*[29]

Perhaps there was something special about the site at Orkney which attracted people interested in astronomy? Could this be where Uriel brought Enoch to have his lessons in astronomy?

We decided that it would be instructive to draw up the shape of the solar year over a range of latitudes from the Equator to 65°N.

We found it very interesting that the rising points of the sun at the summer and winter solstices form a perfect right-angle at the latitude of 55° North, forming a 'square year'. This must have been seen as significant to the people

[29] Ritchie, A.: *Prehistoric Orkney*, Historic Scotland, 1995

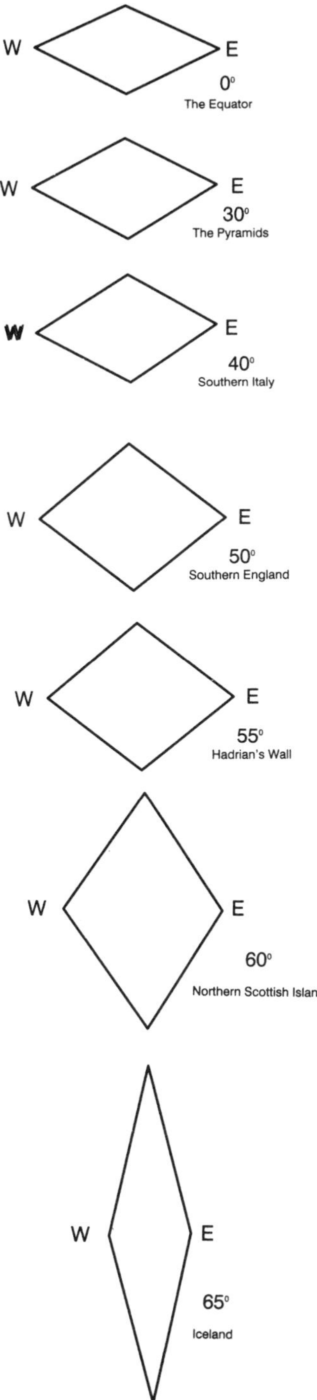

Figure 19. *How the lozenge shape created by sunrise and sunset through the year changes with latitude.*

of the third millennium BC, as we were to discover later. We also noted that they would have been able to achieve this effect at other latitudes if they had built a henge to create a controlled horizon.

Furthermore, we found it curious that the Romans built a structure known as Hadrian's Wall, right along the length of the line of 55° North. This massive structure straddles the full width of the island of Britain. We had already decided that the standard explanation of it being a natural line on which to build a defensive barrier did not hold up. The wall would have been better placed along the River Tweed if designed to keep the Scots and the Picts at bay, although it is hard to imagine how such a lengthy wall could possibly contain enough troops, on a permanent basis, to withstand even a small attack at any one point. The Great Wall of China was designed to keep mounted warriors from sweeping at will across the country, and it succeeded because it was impossible for horses to be lifted over the wall. The tribes north of Hadrian's Wall fought on foot and they would have scaled this barrier with ease. It seems far more likely that the Druids were occupying old megalithic sites on this important line of solar observation, and the Romans wanted to demonstrate power over the Druids by taking control of these sites.

Standing in the ditch would be one way of using the henge as an artificial horizon but there is also another possible way, and that is to fill the ditch with water. A person could then look down onto the reflection which would throw an image of the viewpoint from the bottom of the ditch to the eye of an observer standing in the centre of the circular ditch. It occurred to us that cutting a henge out of solid rock would certainly provide a suitable water container, and we wondered if there was any existing awareness of the use of water in henges. A search provided a report of water-filled henges in Ireland, such as the one just east of the town of Tralee in Ballingowan townland where there is a 19-metre-diameter henge that is flooded to a depth of one to two metres, dependent on the time of the year.[30] Unfortunately, the deliberate use of water has inevitably led the archaeologists concerned to dub the originators a 'water cult', as though they had put water in their ditch because they worshipped the liquid. It is true that modern man is often driven by irrational beliefs (we call our own beliefs 'religion' and those of

[30] Connolly, M. and Condit, T.: Ritual Enclosures in the Lee Valley, Co. Kerry', *Archaeology Ireland,* vol.12, no.6, issue 46, Winter, 1998

others 'superstition'), but these experts do not conceive that the structures may have been built for a practical purpose!

In fact, there is indirect evidence that suggests a water-filled henge at Stenness. Anna Ritchie's book about prehistoric Orkney has an illustration showing an excavation problem which had been encountered digging out a section of the Stenness ditch. When the infill was cleared, the henge kept filling with water and had to be continually pumped dry to allow excavation.[31]

This suggests that the henge at Stenness may have been intended to be filled with water to be used as a reflector disk, to gain the advantage of an artificial horizon without needing to stand in the ditch.

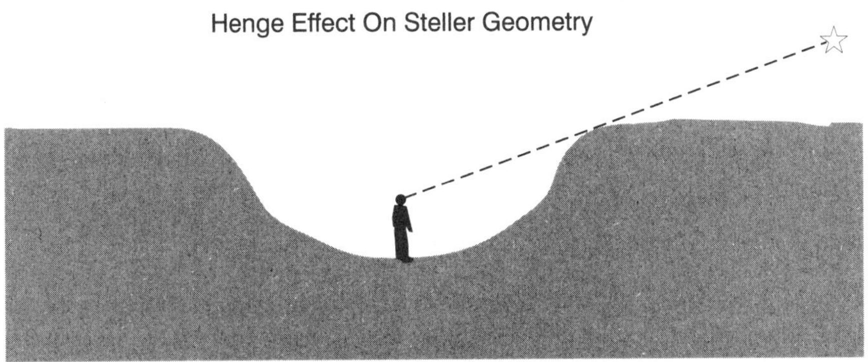

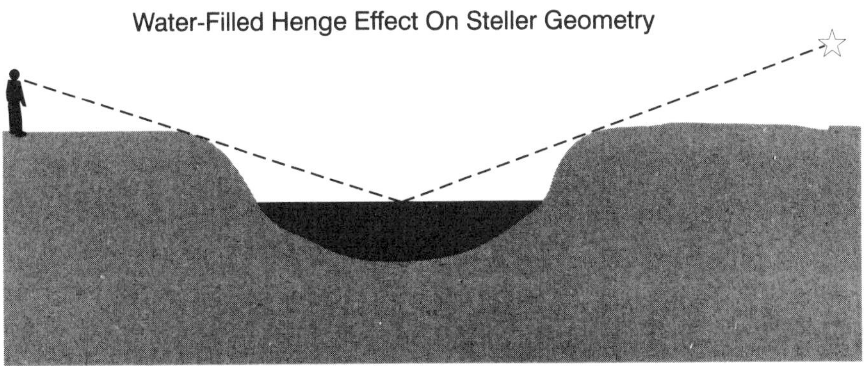

Figure 20. *How henges effect observer's viewpoint.*

[31] Ritchie, A.: *Prehistoric Orkney*, Historic Scotland, 1995

Another structure which the Grooved Ware People built in the area is found at Barnhouse, just 150 metres north of the Stones of Stenness. In 1986, when Colin Richards excavated this area of smooth green fields, he found a series of structures which showed a long period of settlement. The site was extremely rich in finds of Grooved Ware pottery, which we had already seen at many other sites on Orkney and which was identical to the fragments Ritchie had found at the Stones of Stenness. This suggested the complex was contemporary to, and linked with the nearby henge. The remains of about 12 buildings were investigated, and some had made use of imported stone. The floors of houses six and ten used Arran pitchstone, brought from the Western Isles. It had been a sophisticated village, like Skara Brae, and the houses had been equipped with drainage and the same sort of standard interior stone furnishing as Skara Brae. But the village of Barnhouse was not a subterranean village; its houses had stood separately on the surface. The centre of the village seems to have been dominated by two houses which are different from all the other structures in that they are rectangular, not circular. Richards thought these structures may have been temples and that they indicated the existence of a hierarchical social order exercising a high degree of authority over other social groups.[32]

MAES HOWE

Maes Howe, located in the centre of the island of Mainland, is one of the finest preserved Neolithic tunnel mounds in western Europe. It is of the type categorized as a chambered tomb, despite the fact that there were no bodies found in the chamber. The mound is placed centrally within a circular ditch and bank about 150 metres in diameter. This bank does not seem to be a true henge, and Colin Renfrew has suggested it may be the remnants of the construction of the flat, circular, clay platform on which the mound now stands.[33]

Radiocarbon dating for the bank and flat platform show it to be far older than the tunnel mound, dating from 3930 BC, whilst the structure itself dates from around 2820 BC. The view from this artificial plain is spectacular. The site seems to be sitting within a bowl of surrounding high ground. There

[32] Richards, C.: 'The Later Neolithic Settlement Complex at Barnhouse Farm, Stenness', in *The Prehistory of Orkney*, Edinburgh University Press, 1993

[33] Renfrew, C.: 'Investigations in Orkney', *Rep. Research Comm. Soc.Antiq.*, London, 1979

would have been no need to build an artificial horizon because all the surrounding high ground forms a natural horizon, rich in landmark-siting points. The attraction of the site for naked-eye astronomy is obvious.

The quality of the building techniques used in the construction of the chamber is outstanding. Archaeologist Audrey Henshall says of it: '*The excellence of the masonry at Maes Howe goes far beyond that of any other tomb . . . it is one of the supreme achievements of Neolithic Europe.*'[34] The blocks used fit together with a fine precision, surfaces have been chiselled to achieve a flat surface or to round off the edge of the corbelling, and, unlike at other sites, the slabs are accurately plumbed to the vertical. The way massive rectangular slabs have been used is also unique to this site, some being over 5 metres long and weighing three tons.

At the time of sunset at the winter solstice, the sun shines down the main passage and illuminates the wall below the entrance to the north-eastern chamber. This main passage had a large triangular stone block which could be used to seal the passage, although it was not large enough to fill the gap and would have required additional stones to block out the light completely. The chamber was entered from the top by Vikings in the ninth or tenth century AD, who inscribed the walls saying that the chamber was empty when they broke into it.

There is a strangeness about the winter-solstice alignment of this tunnel. Looking out along the tunnel towards the south-west, the entrance frames the high peak of Ward Hill that stands on the island of Hoy across the Clestrain Sound. All the other aligned tunnel mounds we know of have their mouths pointing to flat horizons, and to build a tunnel pointing towards such an obvious obstruction for the sunlight could seem a little careless. But we knew these people did not make mistakes like this.

Anna Ritchie is not convinced that the orientation is deliberate, as she explains:

> *The passage at Maes Howe faces Southwest, and the setting sun at midwinter shines along the passage and into the chamber, illuminating the rear wall. Aubrey Burl has suggested that the reason why the blocking stone does not fill the height of the passage may be that the gap was deliberately designed to allow the sun's rays to penetrate the*

[34] Henshall, A.S.: 'The Chambered Cairns', in *The Prehistory of Orkney*, Edinburgh University Press, 1993

> *tomb. Most Orcadian chambered tombs were built in such a position, however, that the entrance passage faced between east-north-east and south. This is likely to have some general connection with the midwinter sunrise in the south-east, the time of the year at which the brief winter days begin to lengthen and the hope of spring grows stronger.*

No human remains have every been found inside Maes Howe, apart from a fragment of a human skull. Indeed, there are many structures on Orkney labelled as tombs which have fewer bodies interred inside them than the 'village' of Skara Brae.

Anna Ritchie says of one such structure, called the Dwarfie Staine, where no evidence of bodies has been found:

> *In the Island of Hoy is an extraordinary rock-cut chamber which is thought probably to have been a Neolithic tomb. The great block of sandstone, into which the chamber had been cut, lies in a most inhospitable valley at the south-east foot of Ward Hill, the highest hill in Orkney.*[35]

The question remained: given the obtrusive element of the hill, what were the Grooved Ware People particularly interested in observing from the area around Maes Howe? The answer to this was provided by Dutch astronomer Victor Reijs, who has studied the winter solstice orientation of Maes Howe, when the setting sun shines along the tunnel and illuminates the chamber. In August 1996 he was allowed by Historic Scotland (the authority that regulates ancient monuments) to survey the structure and its surrounding horizon. Using his measurements he built a computer model of the aperture of the building with which he predicted every occasion on which the sun would shine into the chamber. He was surprised to find that 20 days before the solstice and 20 days after the solstice, the sun shines into the chamber twice in the same day. The sun appears to set behind Ward Hill on Hoy, which is framed by the tunnel entrance, and then to rise again in the gap between Ward Hill and Brunt Hill on Mainland:

[35] Ritchie, A.: *Prehistoric Orkney*, Historic Scotland, 1995

> *[On the day which is] around 20 days before and after the winter solstice the sun will reappear from behind Ward Hill (this reappearance is a not feature of Maes Howe itself, but rather of the local landscape). The reappearance can be viewed on the back wall of the chamber . . . . The reappearing of the sun behind Ward Hill has been seen by the custodians of Maes Howe on Dec. 2nd 1997.*[36]

So now we knew the attraction of the plain between the lochs of Harray and Stenness, an area known locally as the Bay of Angels. From the level clay platform which was the first structure these people built on the site around 3930 BC – over 1,000 years before the construction of the tunnel mound – they would have been ideally placed to witness the sun setting and rising again on two special midwinter days. What a source of power for any astronomer-priest whose magic could force the sun to set and immediately rise again, and so impress his people! Small wonder these ancient astronomers were able to persuade the short-lived people to work themselves to an even earlier death cutting henges into solid rock using only stone, bone and wooden tools.

The lighting effects around Ward Hill have been part of Scottish legend for many years. Even Sir Walter Scott followed in the tradition of the Grooved Ware astronomers when he used Orkney as a setting for his novel *The Pirate*, playing on the folk memory of magical lighting effects of the area to set the scene for his story.

> *At the west of the Dwarfie Staine stands an exceeding high mountain of a steep ascent, called the Ward Hill of Hoy, near the top of which in the month of May, June and July, about midnight, is seen something which shines and sparkles admirably, and which is often seen a long way off. It has shined more brightly before than it does now, and though many have climbed the hill, and attempted to search for it, yet they could find nothing.*[37]

The artefact referred to as the Dwarfie Staine is one of the most curious structures we have come across. It lies on the island of Hoy, at the base of

[36] Reijs, V.M.M.: 'Maes Howe's Megalithic Month Alignment', *Third Stone*, October-December, 1998, pp.18-20
[37] Scott, W.: *The Pirate*, T. Nelson & Sons Ltd

Ward Hill, and it is an oblong block of stone measuring 8.6 m (28 feet) long, 4m (13 feet) wide and 2m (6.5 feet) high. A square doorway has been cut and inside it has been carved out to produce a short tunnel leading to two separate cells or chambers. Outside, leaning against the hollowed-out rock rests a sandstone block which had been designed to seal the aperture.[38]

It struck us that if one were expecting a comet impact and a subsequent tsunami wave, a good way to survive would be to put yourself into a solid object that could be sealed and was strong enough to withstand the pressure of a massive body of water passing overhead – a sort of Stone-Age bathysphere.

THE PUZZLE OF ORKNEY

All the astronomical sites on Orkney are believed to have been created by a group of people known for their distinctive Grooved Ware decorated pottery who built the artificial viewing platform at Maes Howe nearly 6,000 years ago.

Colin Renfrew had attempted a work out the amount of labour needed to build the chambered tombs of Orkney and had put together data on the time taken to carry out traditional Orcadian quarrying and drystone building work.[38] He calculated the following:

1. In an eight-hour working day, a man could possibly quarry about 7.8 cubic metres of stone.

2. A single cubic metre of living rock will become 4.5 cubic metres of compact rubble, suitable for drystone building. Using a wheelbarrow, a man could load 9.88 cubic metres into the barrow in an eight-hour working day and could be expected to move 14.44 cubic metres a distance of about 25 metres in an eight hour day.

3. Levelling the site could be done at the rate of 28.88 cubic metres per man day.

[38] Ritchie, A.: *Prehistoric Orkney*, Historic Scotland, 1995
[39] Renfrew, C.: *Investigations in Orkney*, Penguin, 1979

4. A mason could build around 3.04 cubic metres of drystone walling in an eight-hour day.

Archaeologist John Hedges suggested that as these figure represented the use of metal tools and wheelbarrows, which were not available, the time estimates should be doubled when considering the working hours needed for using stone tools and sleds or baskets to move the rock. Gerald Hawkins produced some estimates of the time needed to quarry, carry the stone about half a mile and erect it as a standing stone as 1,600 man-hours per stone.[40]

John Hedges found that a large proportion of the structures took less than 10,000 man hours to build, but a significant number (Maes Howe, for example) took much longer. The smaller structures he likened to the building of a modern-day small church or community centre. He commented that this analogy was drawn not because he saw any direct equivalence but to give some measure of the scale of commitment of the enterprise.[41]

The Grooved Ware People built intricate and complex structures all over the Orkneys before abandoning forever the site of their most advanced living quarters. Their observatories fell into disuse, their burial practices were replaced by those of the physically different Beaker People, whose skulls are distinctly rounder than the elongated skulls of the Grooved Ware People, and their advanced stone technology disappeared.

Perhaps they had been invaded and driven away. But we were still puzzled by how they had developed their astronomical sites, which needed generations of work to build and tens of generations to accumulate the information to align the structures accurately. This advanced group of people had developed the sciences of agriculture, building and astronomy to a very sophisticated level. Their sway had lasted for nearly 13 centuries and they showed every evidence of developing their science over this period, moving from the simple artificial horizon of the first Maes Howe platform, through the monumental architecture of the Maes Howe chamber and its associated Barnhouse temples, to the sophisticated alignments and incredibly labour-intensive henges of Brodgar and Stenness.

How, we wondered, had they set about controlling their environment?

[40] Hawkins, G.S.: *Stonehenge Decoded*, Souvenir Press, 1966

[41] Hedges, J.W.: *Tomb of the Eagles*, Tempvs Reparatvm, 1984

How had they developed their science? Modern scientific development relies completely on the use of literature and libraries. Anyone starting out on a new piece of research begins by reading the literature on the subject to find out what is already known. To do this we use writing as a means of recording the results of previous workers. How, we wondered, could a society without writing advance its science?

This northernmost latitude of the 'Enoch Zone' was our most likely candidate for the place where Uriel provided his lesson in astronomy. Now we needed to find out more about these people who were as advanced as anyone else on the planet. The one point that continued to intrigue and puzzle us was their apparently simultaneous exit from leading sites in the Enoch Zone around 4,600 years ago.

CONCLUSION

The area described in the *Book of Enoch*, which we have named the Enoch Zone, is bounded by particular features of observational astronomy. At the *southern* limit of Stonehenge and Avebury, the winter and summer solstice shadows of rising and setting align exactly, whereas at the *northern* limit of the Hebrides the moon's wobble can be seen, and at Orkney the sun can be seen to rise, set and rise again at certain times of the year. The extreme limits of the Grooved Ware People's lands seem to be bounded by observable astronomical effects.

The Grooved Ware People were sophisticated builders. They produced villages such as Skara Brae with modern drainage and standardized ranges of interior fittings, and created artificial horizons, called henges, in the most difficult terrain in order to facilitate their astronomical observations. They also built magnificent underground stone chambers, with aligned tunnels to allow the sunlight inside at particular times of year. These people created a range of symbols which can be found throughout their territory. They also made intricately crafted stone objects which modern engineers have found impossible to reproduce without the use of metal tools – which the Grooved Ware People apparently did not have.

Despite developing an advanced culture, sufficiently skilled to organize and direct massive civil-engineering projects which took many generations to complete, these people vanished without trace around 2655 BC.

Chapter Eight

THE SCIENCE OF PREHISTORY

STORING KNOWLEDGE

From everything we can see inside the zone of Enoch's astronomical instruction, these long-forgotten people had been advanced in certain aspects of science. As far as we knew they did not have any written language and therefore had to pass on all of their knowledge verbally. The average lifespan of little more than 25 years,[1] would not have made it easy to build up a bank of knowledge within their society, and they would have needed to develop sophisticated methods of transferring their knowledge through the development of specialized memory skills.

It is known that the far later Druids used memory techniques that took an individual 20 years to accumulate a basic level of stored facts.[2] We feel sure that the Grooved Ware People, who lived on the western fringes of Europe and particularly around the Irish Sea 5,000 years ago, were led by scientist-priests who advised their people on every aspect of life, from medicine to livestock breeding. For them, science and theology must surely have been synonymous. They left us no written records, but many well-respected Celtic scholars believed that it was these megalithic Grooved Ware People who established the basic beliefs of the later Druids.

Celtic scholar T. W. Rolleston, long-time editor of *The Dublin University Review*, wrote of the links between the Celts and megalithic people:

[1] Hedges, J.W.: *Tomb of the Eagles*, Tempvs Reparatvm, 1992
[2] Caesar, J.: *The Conquest of Gaul*, translated by Handford, S.A., Penguin, 1951

> *The inferences, as I read the facts, seem to be that Druidism in its essential features was imposed upon the imaginative and sensitive nature of the Celt by the earlier population of Western Europe, the Megalithic People . . . The Megalithic people have been brought a step or two out of the atmosphere of uncanny mystery which has surrounded them and they are shown to have played a very important part in the religious development of the Western Europe and in preparing that part of the world for the rapid extension of the special type of Christianity which took place in it . . . very soon after the conversion of Ireland to Christianity, we find the country covered with monasteries, whose complete organisation seems to indicate that they were really Druidic colleges transformed en masse.*[3]

Indeed, speaking of the Druids, Dr Nora Chadwick said of them in her landmark study:

> *No study of the Celts can be complete without taking into account the nature and role of the famous erudite class, the Druids, men who combined the roles of priest, philosopher, angur and teacher.*[4]

One of the most spectacular elements of man's environment is the sky; in the ancient world survival and success may well have depended on understanding its relationship to the seasons and hence to the availability of food supplies. To improve their chances of survival in Palaeolithic times, people would have needed to understand the changing patterns of the sky and to know how to react to the signs they observed. We have seen from the choice of sites for building their observatories that the Grooved Ware People did master many details of observational astronomy.

Gerald Hawkins, the astronomer, commented about this when he said:

> *The times of planting were of most vital concern to primitive men. Those times are hard to detect. One can't count backward from the fine warm days, one must use some other means. And what better means could there be for following seasons than observation of those*

[3] Rolleston, T.W.: *Myths and Legends of the Celtic Race*, G.G. Harrap and Co., 1911
[4] Chadwick, N.K.: *The Druids*, University of Wales Press, 1966

> *most regular and predictable recurring objects, the heavenly bodies. Even in classic times there were still elaborate sets of instructions to help farmers to time their planting by celestial phenomena.*[5]

Any group which had become accomplished enough in controlling its environment to the extent of successfully managing agriculture had to have a knowledge of astronomy. But how would they have achieved this?

If a team of modern engineers were faced with such a challenge, they would use a process that we label 'system control theory' – a good example of this today being the study of tornadoes, which have to be understood so that they can be predicted and their damaging effects mitigated.

For the Grooved Ware People, living in their community all around the Irish Sea, the entire environment was a potentially hostile 'system' which was a permanent threat unless they could find a way to control it. There are three steps necessary before any system can be controlled.

1. Observation and recording

There are two obvious and easy ways for a primitive people to record events: memory or tally marks. In the case of the Grooved Ware People, the most powerful system would be to develop a written language which could then be independent of the mortality of the observer. The Grooved Ware People probably used both a verbal tradition and, as we shall see, simple tally marks, but, as we shall also see, the so-called 'decoration' at Skara Brae and other sites suggests that they may also have been moving beyond simple tally marks towards a system of writing before they suddenly disappeared from history.

That they knew about tally marks is demonstrated by the archaeological record, which shows that the creation of tally bones to record astronomical events started in western Europe about 200 generations after the earliest recorded uses of symbolism such as the Venus figurines and the cave paintings of France.

In 1965, Alexander Marshack studied a number of bones which until that time had been thought to be simple hunting tallies. He was aware of a particular inscribed bone which had been found in near Lake Edward in central Africa. It was dated to 6500 BC and seemed to show a pattern of 168

[5] Hawkins, G.S.: *Stonehenge Decoded*, Souvenir Press, 1966

marks grouped into 16 sets. Marshack identified the marks as recording the phases of the moon over a period of five-and-a-half months.[6]

He assumed that if this really was an example of early astronomical recording, then other examples should be found. He went on to find a number of earlier examples from western Europe, ranging from Kulna in Slovakia to Blanchard in the Dordorgne district of France. One 30,000-year-old bone Marshack found to show a tally of the moon's phases over a period of just over two months. In the same archaeological collection he found a number of sceptre-like rods which came to be called *batons de commandement*; these had been found at a place called Le Placard, in southern France, and were dated to about 20,000 BC. Marshack was able to show, by studying the period from 30,000 BC to 17,000 BC that a conventional tally system had developed along the western seaboard of Europe before the end of the last Ice Age.[7]

Distinguished archaeo-astronomer Edwin C. Krupp, reviewing Marshack's work, commented:

> *The records are not always astronomically exact and the pattern from one month is not duplicated in the next. They are, however, cumulatively correct . . . Perhaps, at least in some respects Marshack is right. . . . Marshack has also analysed the content of the representational cave art from Europe's Ice Age and found that much of it can be interpreted in terms of seasonal indicators drawn from the environment of the Upper Palaeolithic hunters.*[8]

Megalithic art historian Martin Brennan has also found similar tallies recorded in stones within the Grooved Ware Boyne Valley complex. For example, stone SW22 from the Knowth tunnel mound shows a recording system which relates the lunar phases within the solar year.[9]

A database of observations would have enabled the Grooved Ware People to start trying to link together cause and effect, and build a theoretical model to explain the observations they had recorded. This leads to the next step.

[6] Krupp, E.C.: *Echoes of the Ancient Skies*, Oxford University Press, 1983
[7] Marshack, A.: *The Roots of Civilisation*, McGraw-Hill, 1972
[8] Krupp E.C.: *Echoes of the Ancient Skies*, Oxford University Press, 1983
[9] Brennan, M.: *The Stones of Time*, Inner Traditions International, 1994

2. Prediction of Future Events

Before a person has any chance at all of controlling a system, they have to be able to predict its behaviour under as many conditions as possible. This is usually done by building a model of the interactions of the subject in question, and then building up a pattern of causes and effects.

To build a model today we use mathematical reasoning, which is a convention of symbols that allow us mentally to model and manipulate issues in a repeatable and testable manner. At first, we could find no evidence for a system of written mathematics amongst the remains of the Grooved Ware People.

However, archaeologist Dr Caroline Wickham-Jones recognized that sailing and navigational skills had been shown by the very earliest settlers in Scotland around 6500 BC:

> *The landscape through which these Mesolithic communities moved was predominantly wooded and undulating . . . It is much easier to make your way by boat than to struggle through uncleared forests . . . Waterways must have been vitally important to the early post-glacial inhabitants of Scotland as they moved from place to place.*[10]

The Grooved Ware People had established settlements throughout the British Isles, yet they managed to stay in contact. We know this because innovations in pottery and symbolism were shared among them. As we have already mentioned in Chapter Seven, historian Richard Oram had seen this wide spread of communicating settlements as clear proof of their considerable navigational skills: '*Settlements in the Hebrides speak of navigational skills and seamanship.*'[11] They would have needed a common unit of length if they were to be able to navigate accurately and predict journey times. As they show every evidence of being skilful sailors, it is reasonable to deduce that they had solved the problem of navigation.

So how did they measure time and distance? How did they define a unit of length and how did they carry out the calculations to build their aligned structures?

[10] Wickham Jones, C.R.: *Scotland's First Settlers*, Historic Scotland, 1994
[11] Oram, R.: *Scottish Prehistory*, Birlinn, 1997

As we have seen, it is beyond dispute that the astronomers of the Grooved Ware People were able to predict the setting and in fact the re-rising of the sun and the moon, and in fact they could predict rising and setting alignments of the sun half a year ahead. It is a small step to being able to predict eclipses, which we knew from the writings of James Bruce (see Chapter Two for the tale of how he used his knowledge of a forthcoming eclipse of the moon to get himself out of a spot of trouble) and this ability confers great power amongst less astronomically aware people. The demonstrable ability to predict heavenly events leads to the final step of 'system control theory'.

3. Control

Once a person understands the interactions of a system and can predict the effects of any changes to the inputs, they are theoretically in a position to control that system. Being able to make the sun and moon apparently obey their commands must have invested the priests of the Grooved Ware People with considerable social power. However, full control of their environment mighty still have been difficult for a number of reasons. There might have been a lack of technical ability, making it beyond their available skills to achieve the desired intervention. An example would be that our ability to know that a comet is on a collision course with the earth is not yet matched by an ability to deflect it away from our planet.

Some of these factors may present obstacles to developing a totally effective control system, but knowledge of astronomy remains a source of considerable social power.

So, the evidence of the building works and the extensive spread of their influence showed that the Grooved Ware People had mastered the control skills for agriculture and for navigation without seeming to have progressed to written records. We were, however, aware from Skara Brae that they seemed to have become masters of what has been taken to be abstract art. The extent of this art had impressed archaeologist Dr Anna Ritchie:

> *Art seems to have been more important to the inhabitants of Skara Brae than to people living anywhere else. Not only are the buildings decorated but also some of the artefacts.*[12]

[12] Ritchie, A.: *Prehistoric Orkney*, Historic Scotland, 1995

Perhaps, we mused, this 'art' is a key to understanding their technology. Our curiosity regarding the 'art' of the Grooved Ware People caused us to reflect on a number of significant points:

i) The development of civilization accelerated after about 5,000 years ago when writing first appeared in Sumer.

ii) The Grooved Ware People had the same mental capacity as we have today.

iii) The key to our rapid modern scientific progress is our ability to record, access and use information.

iv) Only a tiny proportion of the people in the world really understands the science that makes our society work, and this elite often uses its knowledge to control those who do not have it.

It follows that the Grooved Ware People were, in principle, as capable of some sort of intellectual development and innovation as we are today, and it is quite likely that then, as now, only a small proportion of the population would have understood the science which underpinned their society. Their short lifespans meant that they would have been forced to address the shortcomings of verbal learning and tally mark systems, eventually leading to the development of written language.

Writing seemed to be a key factor in making possible more rapid scientific progress: each generation can read the thoughts of its predecessors without having to learn them by rote before continuing the work.

THE DEVELOPMENT OF WRITING

The development of writing is seen by all historians as a watershed marking the boundary between history and prehistory.

The traditional view of the history of writing says that the earliest way of recording ideas is to draw a picture of the event you want to record. Cave paintings in Europe, dating back to at least 32,000 BC, show this type of recording. The next step is to use a tally system by making a series of similar marks to count a number of events. As we have seen, Marshack has shown this method of recording was in common use in western Europe from

30,000 BC. The Grooved Ware People used a tally system in the Boyne Valley of Ireland, where they also created 'abstract art'. Although writing is not generally thought to have developed until about 5,000 years ago in Sumer, Professor Thom believed that this abstract art, which was found at all the Grooved Ware Sites, represents an early form of writing. .

First Writing?

The earliest form of Sumerian writing, which is pictographic, is called Elamite and dates from about 3100 BC. Archaeologist John Hackwell says of it:

> *The symbols consisted of abstract and picture-like signs cut into tiny pillow-shaped clay tablets and linked together in linear fashion. . . . these abstract forms are similar in appearance to pictures and designs to be found on preliterate pottery.*[13]

The ancient Sumerian city of Uruk was where the early type of stylized pictographic writing developed. These picture characters or 'logograms' soon began to be associated with spoken syllables, which means a much smaller symbol set can be used to convey very complex messages. The main drawback with this way of writing was that the scribes had to learn almost 2,000 independent symbols. This is still true of modern Japanese and Chinese pictogram writing, forcing these people to develop a limited sub-set in order to make use of keyboards.

Cuneiform script, as used to write the Sumerian language, seems to have developed from the need for a book-keeping system for the growing trade in manufactured goods. Archaeologist Denise Schmandt-Besserat was the first person to appreciate the significance of a strange category of clay artefacts. These were tiny spheres, discs, cones, cylinders, tetrahedrons and assorted geometric shapes. She noted that these 'tokens', as she named them, were widespread throughout Israel, Iran, Iraq, Turkey and Syria, and were some of the oldest clay objects to have been fired in order to make them more durable. She reported that she sensed that the tokens were part of a system because she had repeatedly found small and large cones, thin and thick discs,

[13] Hackwell W.J.: *Signs, Letters, Words, Archaeology Discovers Writing*, Macmillan, 1987

small and large spheres and even fractions of spheres, such as half and three-quarter spheres.[14]

She studied more than 10,000 tokens and was able to show that this Sumerian accounting system made use of a methodology that had been developing since about 8000 BC in the Near East. With the arrival of the Sumerians it had flowered into a written numerical system. The development of city life meant that the accounting needs of society increased and eventually the system could not cope, so a better system had been devised. The need to produce an ever-increasing number of token types eventually led to the development of a new system of handling data, which was to be the final step towards the emergence of the Sumerian script.[15] Elamite developed into a type of logogram writing known as cuneiform.

Because this earliest writing uses word symbols rather than an alphabet, it can be read only in vague terms. It does not reproduce speech but a series of word images. Because a single sign can be read in several different ways, according to the reader's subjective perceptions a line of text could have a number of diverse meanings depending on what images he or she perceived. This can be a particular problem when trying to represent collective objects. Hackwell comments that the ancient Egyptians tried to solve this problem by using a class of identifier signs or ideograms to show the exact intention of a word. He gives the example of a drawing of a man followed by five vertical strokes to suggest five men. Symbolic language makes it more difficult to refer to specific, concrete instances because symbols naturally have multiple meanings.

Solutions to these problems seem to have driven the development of writing forward because very shortly afterwards two other forms of writing appeared in Egypt and in the Kingdom of Elam, which was to the east of Sumer in what is today Khuzistan.

Egyptian hieroglyphic writing is thought to have been developed as a result of the Sumerian innovation. The so-called Proto-Elamite writing that developed in Elam has not yet been deciphered, and nothing can be said of its nature at the present time except that, from the number of signs used, it is a form of logogram writing. This type of word pictogram writing also developed, at a later date, in the Aegean, in Anatolia, in the Indus Valley of India and, of course, in China where they still use this system.

[14] Schmandt-Besserat, D.: *Before Writing, Volume One: From Counting to Cuneiform*, University of Texas Press, 1992
[15] Rudgley, R.: *Lost Civilizations of the Stone Age*, Century, 1998

The next major step forward was the alphabet, where each individual sound of a language is coded into a symbol and the symbols are then linked into groups which form the sounds of words. This is a very powerful method of recording because it can record anything that can be voiced, but does not need many different symbols to do it unambiguously. Hackwell summed up the development process;

> *The earliest pictographic writing systems used logograms, then added ideograms, then developed to a stage where many signs stood for spoken sounds. This is called phonetization. Once signs represent sounds there is no need to depict them as physical objects, thus we have a writing system that is abstract.*[16]

It is the general academic view that the first alphabets were developed independently by two different peoples: the Mesopotamians in the east and the Phoenicians in the west. The Phoenicians were a small nation, famous as sailors and navigators, whose land was a narrow strip of territory on the eastern coast of the Mediterranean which is now northern Israel and Lebanon. The southern boundary was Mount Carmel; the place where the remains of the oldest known *Homo sapiens* were found, and one of the most holy locations referred to in the Old Testament. The Phoenicians were Semites, related to the Canaanites of ancient Palestine, and research has indicated that they founded their first settlements in the area about 2500 BC. They became the most successful traders and sailors of the ancient world, travelling throughout the Mediterranean and as far as the British Isles.

It is interesting to note that King Solomon's Temple, built at the end of the first millennium BC, seems to have been constructed by Phoenicians, who clearly had some knowledge or skills that the Jews of Jerusalem lacked. It is the construction of this building that is central to the rituals of Freemasonry.[17]

While other nations required several hundred signs with which to express their thoughts and give visible form to human speech, somewhere between 1700 and 1500 BC the Phoenicians invented 22 simple signs that perfectly matched every sound in their language.

Writing is thought to have arrived in the British Isles only in Roman times,

[16] Hackwell, W.J : *Signs, Letters, Words, Archaeology Discovers Writing*, Macmillan, 1987
[17] *Peake's Commentary on the Bible*

but in June 1996 a newspaper article suggested that it might have been much earlier than previously thought:

> *Archaeologists have unearthed a writing system that could make historians revise long-accepted theories about the birth of civilization in western Europe. The 89 symbol script is preserved in scores of pottery fragments used 3,500 years ago in settlements reaching from the Orkneys to Majorca. It is more complex than any previously known in western Europe and suggests that a bronze age civilization dominated Britain, Spain and France around 1500 BC.*[18]

The article went on to say how this early civilization was crushed by the overwhelming power of Roman military might and lost the battle of the alphabets to the Latin-based script we use today. Dr William Waldren, an archaeologist from Oxford University, was quoted as saying:

> *These finds suggest that some part of western Europe, previously regarded as illiterate may have been as advanced as the ancient Greeks and Romans. Historians may no longer be able to regard the eastern Mediterranean as the only spiritual home of modern culture.*[19]

The climax of the article was a quote from Professor N. Purcell, who lectures in ancient history at Oxford University:

> *It would be sensational if this civilization had developed its own script. It would show they had developed for themselves the complex concept of using symbols to represent sounds and so moved towards developing a rudimentary alphabet.*[20]

What was extremely interesting was the type of symbols used. They were described as 'incisions of vertical, horizontal and diagonal lines, circles and patterns of dots similar to the 'Linear A' script', which had been used at a later date by the Minoan culture on the island of Crete. This newly found script was about 500 years later than 'Linear A', but it seemed to be

[18] Leake, J. and Howard, S.: 'Bronze-Age Script?: *The Sunday Times*, 16 June 1996, p.17
[19] Waldren, W.: quoted in *The Sunday Times*, 16 June 1996
[20] Purcell, N.: quoted in *The Sunday Times*, 16 June 1996

suggesting that there was some sort of common link between western Europe and the Minoan civilization of Crete. Even more interesting were the illustrations of the script which showed symbols that were highly reminiscent of the markings found in many megalithic sites on the western fringes of Britain.

WHERE DID THE FIRST SYMBOLS OF WRITING ORIGINATE?

We increasingly felt that there had to be more to this story than just a simple progression from an accounting system into an alphabetic writing system. Looking at the very earliest examples of the pictographic symbols which developed into the cuneiform script of Uruk, we were struck by the resemblance to megalithic symbols found in the western British Isles. The later cuneiform script is highly stylized and complex, but the inscription on an illustration of a very early Palaeo-Elamite vase from Marudasht, near Persepolis, looks megalithic in nature.

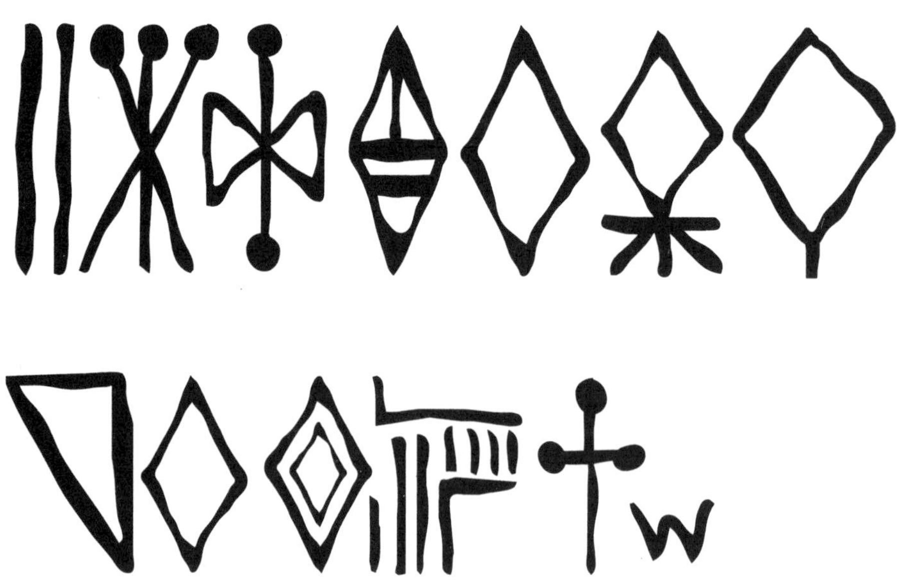

Figure 21. *Elamite inscription.*

In 1983, Martin Brennan published a study of 360 megalithic carved stones of Ireland showing the main symbols used on them, the frequency of occurrence of each symbol type and the way in which the symbols were linked together.[22] All the symbols in the Elamite inscription, dating from about 3000 BC, were occurring regularly in megalithic carved stones dated in a range between 4000-2500 BC.

The story gets more complicated once stone carvings from Tartaria, near Turdas in Transylvania, are taken into account. These carved clay tablets date from 4000 BC and, again, they depict symbols that use the same design as megalithic elements identified by Brennan. Their inscriptions have been the subject of a great deal of archaeological debate as they were found before carbon dating had been fully perfected. In 1961 they were thought to date from about 2900 and 2600 BC, and archaeologist Sinclair Hood, Director of the British School of Archaeology in Athens, wrote in 1962 in the journal *Antiquity*:

> *The signs on the Tartaria tablets, especially those on the roundel No. 2 are so comparable with those on the early tablets from Uruk . . . as to make it virtually certain that they are somehow connected with them. Several of the signs appear to be derived from Mesopotamian signs for numerals. The only difference is that on the Mesopotamian tablets the whole shape of the sign in the case of numerals was sunk in the clay with a round ended stylus, while at Tartaria the equivalent signs were incised in outline.*[23]

Hood added that some of the signs in the Tartaria tablets were also similar to those found in the Minoan scripts of Crete, although they were clearly not Cretan.[24]

Understandably, Sinclair Hood assumed that the Tartaria tablets had to post-date the Elamite script from Sumer, and he put forward an hypothesis to try and substantiate this view. He speculated that Sumerian gold hunters must have travelled to Transylvania to set up mines and trading links and whilst doing so, they had taught the local people the use of writing symbols

[21] Hackwell, W.J.: *Signs, Letters, Words, Archaeology Discovers Writing*, Macmillan, 1987
[22] Brennan, M.: *The Stones of Time*, Inner Traditions International, 1994
[23] Rudgley, R.: *Lost Civilisations of the Stone Age*, Century, 1998
[24] Rudgley, R.: *Lost Civilisations of the Stone Age*, Century, 1998

as part of their accounting system. He did not consider the distance involved a difficulty because he was already aware of the accepted academic view that the early proto-Sanskrit of the Indus valley of India had also been influenced by Sumer.

However, when reliable carbon-dating tests were eventually carried out on the strata surrounding the artefacts, they revealed that the Tartaria tablets were much older than the earliest use of the symbols in Sumer. Since that bombshell, the whole matter appears to have been ignored by the archaeological establishment as just a coincidence. But however much these experts want to cling to their preferred paradigm, it is inescapable that if there was a connection between these two writing methods, it must have been the Sumerians who learnt from the Transylvanians.

Another possibility is that perhaps both peoples were heir to a different common tradition. Indeed, we found evidence supporting the idea that the Sumerians *and* the megalithic people of Europe may have both been influenced by a common earlier source of symbolic recording. The 'Gradesnica Plaque' found at Vratsa in Transylvania also shows distinct similarities between megalithic inscriptions and Elamite symbols, and is dated at between 6,000 and 7,000 years old. A 5,500-year-old seal, found at Karanovo, also bears engravings which are similar to both megalithic markings and Sumerian script.[25]

Rudgley summed up the position well:

> *The idea that the invention of writing could be assigned to Europe rather than Asia is too far-fetched for most scholars to countenance. With the acceptance of the new radiocarbon chronology there was only one other explanation available. Since the Tartaria tablets were earlier than Sumerian writing, they could not be real writing and their apparent resemblance was simply coincidental. It was on that note that . . . the Vinca sign system faded into comparative obscurity, at least as far as mainstream archaeologists were concerned.*[26]

However, one archaeologist continued to work on the classification of these Transylvanian marks, which are known as Vinca signs after the area in

[25] Rudgley, R.: *Lost Civilisations of the Stone Age*, Century, 1998
[26] Rudgley, R.: *Lost Civilisations of the Stone Age*, Century, 1998

which they were found. In 1981 Shan Winn published a classification of hundreds of these signs which he had studied and analysed. He found the signs broke down into five basic elemental symbols:[27]

1. A straight line
2. Two lines that intersect at a centre
3. Two lines that intersect at one end
4. A dot
5. A curved line

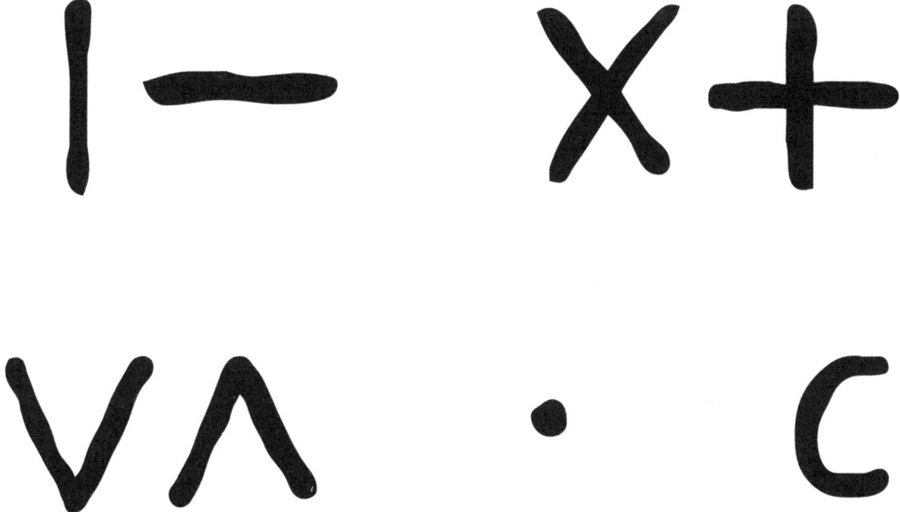

Figure 22. *Vinca symbols.*

Winn realized that these five basic elements could be combined in 18 different ways, and he argued that internal analysis of the Vinca signs supports the conclusion that the signs are conventionalized and standardized, and that

[27] Winn, S.M.M.: *Pre-Writing in Southeastern Europe: The Sign System of the Vinca Culture circa 4000 BC*, Western Publishers, 1981

they represent a corpus of signs known and used over a wide area for many centuries.[28]

The similarities between the Vinca system, the megalithic system and Elamite system began to seem too close to ignore. Some people, such as Professor Thom, kept the battle front open. Writing to his old friend Mr Stan Beckensall in 1978, he said:

> *There cannot be the slightest doubt about the connection between the stones [of Temple Wood Kilmartin] and cup and ring markings [characteristic of the megalithic monuments]. The geometry is identical in the two. If we are ever going to decipher the cup and ring markings every one left should be reported so that they can all be brought together and an attack made on the problem. The ones near backsights for lunar observation or solar observation are of first-rate importance at the moment because we suspect that these tell us what the backsight was for. I realize that to get all the information together is an enormous task, perhaps a lifelong work.*[29]

Starting in 1969, the BBC produced a series of documentaries featuring the work of Professor Thom. One included a long interview between Thom and Magnus Magnusson during which Thom put forward an interesting theory about the 'ring and cup' markings which occur on so many of the megalithic sites.

> *Thom: I have an idea that is entirely nebulous at the moment that the cup and ring markings were a method of recording, of writing, and that they may indicate, once we can read them, what a particular stone was for.*
>
> *Magnussun: Your theories about Stone-Age Einsteins have got up the back of some archaeologists. The idea that the cup and ring marks were used as writing has got up the backs of a lot more. Does it worry you?*

[28] Winn, S.M.M.: *Pre-Writing in Southeastern Europe: The Sign System of the Vinca Culture circa 4000 BC*, Western Publishers, 1981
[29] Thom, A.S.: *Walking in All of the Squares*, Argyll Publishing, 1995

Thom: Not in the slightest, I just go right on recording what I find.[30]

The cup and ring markings that Thom is referring to are found in many Neolithic sites. The purpose of these markings has puzzled many archaeologists. As we have mentioned, Martin Brennan made a major study of the megalithic art of the Boyne Valley in Ireland. He was puzzled as to why megalithic art, which he commented 'represents the first major western European art tradition since the Ice Age', has attracted so little academic attention. All the inscriptions he studied could be broken down to nine basic symbols and combined in many different ways. Brennan analysed 340 different stones in Ireland and found the following frequencies of occurrence for each of the symbolic elements:[31]

1.	The dot or cupmark	20%
2.	The line	34%
3.	The circle	53%
4.	The quadrangle	22%
5.	The arc or crescent	39%
6.	The zigzag	25%
7.	The wavy line	28%
8.	The spiral	27%
9.	The oval or ellipse	17%

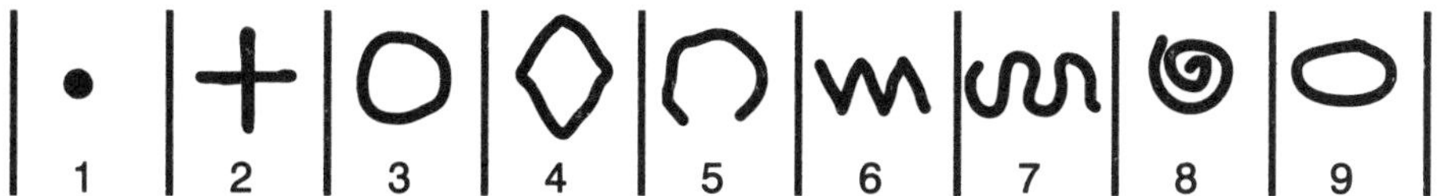

Figure 23. *The main Grooved Ware symbols, after Brennan.*

[30] Thom, A.S.: *Walking in All of the Squares*, Argyll Publishing, 1995
[31] Brennan, M.: *The Stones of Time*, Inner Traditions International, 1994

He also commented that at least half the stones he studied express a relationship between the circle and the arc or crescent:

> *There are about 390 stones in Ireland known to be engraved with megalithic art. They are all found in passage mounds and, when these are assessable or intact, they have all been shown to be astronomically orientated, which reveals the context in which the art appears. The relationship between the art and astronomy is further reinforced by the presence of engraved sundials, calendars and explicit solar-lunar imagery.*[32]

We could now understand what Thom had been suggesting in his interview. The back sight markings could be some form of primitive instructions, describing how the stone could be used for astronomical purposes. Brennan's study of the Irish inscriptions seems to confirm this idea. He went on to propose meanings for some of the basic symbols which he deduced from the context in which they were sited.

Figure 24. *Examples of the combination of Grooved Ware symbols into motifs.*

[32] Brennan M.: *The Stones of Time*, Inner Traditions International, 1994

Not surprisingly, he found that the circle is used to depict the sun and the crescent symbolizes the moon. He reasoned that the wavy line shows how the moon's point of rising and setting moves periodically about the sky, deducing this from a stone found at Knowth (Number SW22)[33] which links the solar and lunar months using circles, crescents and wavy lines to show the relationship.

The widespread systematic use of the same basic symbols by the megalithic people, the Vinca culture and the Sumerians now definitely seemed too much of a coincidence. Is there a common heritage behind these similarities? It would appear that the symbols used by the Grooved Ware People might have had a meaning for them – but would we ever be able to read what they had carved into their tablets of stone?

Was it possible for a megalithic civilization to develop a high level of science, and indeed a system of advanced mathematics, without a written language? We were not sure about that, but shortly we were to meet a man who had studied this question in great detail.

THE MEGALITHIC CULTURE

The megalithic people who inhabited Spain, France, England, Wales, Scotland and Ireland built the earliest structures known to man. We knew this from the work of Lord Renfrew, which we discussed in Chapter One. Today, people go about their daily business in the these countries without a thought for the unknown people who once owned the land. England alone still has over 40,000 known megalithic sites that have survived for thousands of years. Will as much of our own civilization survive for thousands of years?

The name megalith comes from the Greek words for big stones (*megas* – big; and *lithos* – stone).

The earliest known buildings in the world are the megalithic structures of Europe. They are 1,000 years older than the cities of Sumer. This new chronology poses questions about the people who built the structures. As archaeologist Euan Mackie comments:

[33] Eogan, G.: *Knowth and the Passage-Tombs of Ireland*, Thames and Hudson, 1986

If the European megaliths, and even the Maltese temples, are older than the oldest towns then it is difficult to see how urban societies could have played any significant part in the great social processes which were under way in Atlantic Europe between 4500 and 2500 BC . . . there must have been specialised, proto-urban or urban stratified societies in existence before the earliest megaliths appeared.[34]

The structures we were interested in are of four main types:

1. Standing stones, stone alignments and stone circles

2. Tunnel and gallery mounds.

3. Earth mounds and ditches, which may or may not contain stones.

4. Dolmens without mounds which may or may not be the remains of type 2, or could be a separate class of structure.

These structures extend all the way along the coasts of Europe from southern Spain up as far as Denmark, and also appear on the northern Mediterranean coast as well as in southern Italy and Malta. There is even evidence that they were built in parts of North Africa, including Egypt. The whole of the British Isles is covered with them. By contrast, the circular ditch or henge is unique to Britain. We knew from the work of Professor John North that its purpose was largely astronomical.

However, Colin Renfrew points out that the extent of these structures doesn't necessarily imply that there was ever a single megalithic culture. He says:

To define a 'megalithic province' risks removing the tombs from their parent cultures and the communities which built them and used them.[35]

The tunnel graves are a very early type of structure which often lend themselves to carbon dating and we know that the megalithic mounds of

[34] Mackie, E.: *The Megalithic Builders*, Phaidon Press, 1977
[35] Renfrew, C.: *Before Civilisation*, Jonathan Cape, 1973

Brittany predate 4000 BC.[36] There have always been stories about the effects of light in these tunnel mounds but only recently has a new branch of archaeology appeared known as archaeo-astronomy, which sets out to study the astronomical alignments of these monuments. In 1901 Sir Norman Lockyer, who was at that time the editor of *Nature*, studied the temples of Ancient Egypt and made what was then the revolutionary observation that many of them were built in such a way as to allow the sun to shine on important parts of the interior on special days of the year. He surveyed a number of sites in Britain including Stonehenge and arrived at the conclusion that some of the alignments formed part of a calendar which was based on the solstices and the equinoxes.[37] After some considerable time studying British monuments, Lockyer published the suggestion that megalithic tombs were built primarily as observatories or even as houses for astronomer-priests, and burials were later inserted by new immigrants who imitated them and built round barrows, exclusively for the dead.[38]

THE MEGALITHIC YARD

The man who really made archaeo-astronomy an accepted science was Professor Alexander Thom, whom we have already mentioned. He spent 30 years retirement from Oxford University surveying and studying megalithic sites. After examining some 600 sites and conducting a highly detailed survey of half of them, he produced a conclusion that upset the archaeological applecart. In his own words, he made some surprising claims for the genius of these previously unsung prehistoric architects:

> *A statistical analysis of the sites shows that they were so carefully erected that we can from them deduce:*
>
> *(1) the inclination of the ecliptic*
>
> *(2) the inclination of the lunar orbit*

[36] Renfrew C.: *Before Civilisation*, Jonathan Cape, 1973

[37] Lockyer, N.: *Stonehenge and Other British Stone Monuments Astronomically Considered*, Macmillan, 1909

[38] Lockyer, N.: 'Some Questions for Archaeologists', *Nature*, Vol. 73, 1906, p.280

(3) the mean amplitude of the lunar perturbation and

(4) the mean lunar parallax

with an accuracy better than one arc minute.

I have shown elsewhere that megalithic man had a highly developed knowledge of geometry. It now appears that his knowledge of how to apply it put him intellectually in line with the greatest civilizations of antiquity.[39]

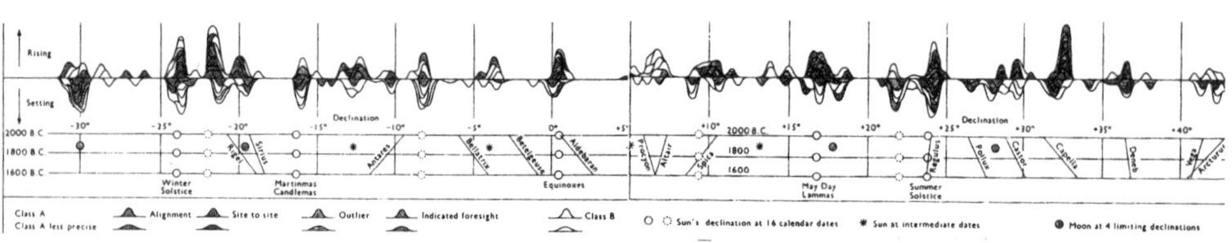

Figure 25. *Histogram of Alignments of Stone Circles after Thom.*

He proved that the more important rings of megaliths were designed using geometric rules and the principles that we now call Pythagorean, although these sites predate Pythagoras by thousands of years. Using statistical analysis, Thom produced evidence to show that a standard unit of length was used throughout the megalithic structures of much of western Europe. Thom dubbed this universal unit of two feet 8.64 inches (82.966 centimetres) the 'Megalithic Yard'. This apparently crazy claim was one of the principal reasons why his work was initially ignored by archaeologists, who thought it ridiculous to believe that these ancient people could have had anything as sophisticated as an international standard of measurement.

[39] Thom, A.: *Walking in All of the Squares*, Argyll Publishing, 1995

Thanks to an objective study by statisticians, the 'megalithic yard' has now become fully accepted as a system of measurement that was in use over, what appears to be an impossibly large geographical area, at a time when people had been previously considered to be little better than cavemen.

The megalithic measure had been employed in the building of structures in Scotland, Wales, England and Brittany; an area of some 150,000 square miles! Thom felt that they were far too consistent to have been delineated by the use of measuring rods, created, copied and distributed across this huge area, as the very act of duplication would have introduced a greater level of error than was evident in the structures. He concluded that there must be some long-forgotten physical reality behind its creation – but neither he nor anyone else has been able to explain how it was derived.

When reviewing Thom's work, Colin Renfrew observed that these megalithic stone circles and other arrangements of stones are laid out in exact halves or full integer numbers of a unit of length Thom called the megalithic yard.[40] This means that the unit that Thom described as the megalithic yard could also have been a double unit which he adopted because it was conveniently close to the modern yard.

The existence of an ancient civil engineering unit is truly remarkable, but things became even more exciting when we learnt that this was the granddaddy of all measurements! It has also been very seriously suggested that the evidence indicates that there was a class of highly trained builders, rather than just scattered bands of primitive shamans and medicine men.[41]

Archaeologist Euan Mackie observed how fundamental the megalithic yard appears to be:

> *. . . a traditional unit of length known as the gaz was in use as late as the nineteenth century in north-west India when it was standardised at exactly 33 inches (0.838 metres) by the British Government. In the 1930's excavations at Mohenjo-daro, one of the oldest city mounds in India and a part of the Bronze Age Indus civilization, radiocarbon dates for which show that it must have been contemporary with Early Dynastic Sumeria and Old Kingdom Egypt, revealed a small piece of shell, part of a longer piece and with nine exactly equal divisions still*

[40] Renfrew, C.: *Before Civilisation*, Jonathan Cape, 1973
[41] Mackie, E.: *The Megalith Builders*, Phaidon Press, 1977

> *remaining which had been cut into it with a fine saw. Five of these small divisions evidently made up a larger unit the boundaries of which were marked with a dot on the line. A. E. Berriman has pointed out that 25 of the major division, now called 'Indus inches', totalled exactly 33 inches, the same length as the traditional gaz. It is difficult not to believe that the metrology of these Bronze Age cities was handed down intact over 45 centuries.*
>
> *Berriman also worked out the length of some small Sumerian length units from scales cut into stone statues of Governor Gudea of Lagash in Mesopotamia who lived in about 2200 BC. These units which he thought were probably the 'shusu' mentioned in the cuneiform texts, were on average exactly half the 'Indus inch'. Thus there were 50 Suneruab shusi in the traditional Indian Gaz . . . Both the shusi and the [Sumerian] units of weight were perpetuated in Greek, Roman and Saxon metrology.*[42]

A similar 'short yard' of about 32.5 inches, known as the *vara*, was in use in Iberia and also seemed to have been taken to Mexico and Peru by the Spanish conquerors, while the traditional measuring rod of the mine overseers of the Austrian Tyrol are also the same length. These measuring rods are claimed to have been used in mining activities since the Early Bronze Age.[43]

So the ancient Indian 'gaz' was the same as a megalithic yard to an accuracy of one per cent and the Iberian 'vara' was less than half a per cent different. There also seems to be a tradition of a 'local' cubit, recorded in the Egyptian Third Dynasty tomb of Hesy. It is said that the ancient Egyptians adjusted their values for units of length according to latitude, to compensate for variations in the length of degrees at different latitudes, because the earth is not a perfect sphere.[44]

There are only two possible ways in which the megalithic yard could have become so widespread.

The first possibility is that it had to be organized by a central bureaucracy that issued measuring rods from one location. However, this is very unlikely, because Thom has argued that the amount of variation he found in the unit

[42] Mackie, E.: *The Megalith Builders*, Phaidon Press, 1977
[43] Mackie, E.: *The Megalith Builders*, Phaidon Press, 1977
[44] Lamy, L.: *Egyptian Mysteries*, Thames and Hudson, 1981

is too small for measuring rods to have been copied sequentially. The cumulative copying error would have been much greater than the actual error which has been observed.

The alternative to the 'ruler' theory is that there must have been a physical reality behind the unit which would enable it to be recreated by any individual who understood the underlying science. This is how the metre is currently defined – in terms of a number of wavelengths of a particular frequency of light. As a result, any national standards office can check the length of a metre without being worried about the changes in length of a metal measuring rod caused by variations in temperature.

We agreed with Thom that the possibility of a central megalithic standards office, issuing measuring rods to most of western Europe, seemed very unlikely in an age when travel must have been very difficult. Consequently, we came to the conclusion that this unit of measurement could not be abstract; it must have some sort of physical basis.

MEGALITHIC MATHEMATICS

When we wrote our first book, *The Hiram Key*, we received many hundreds of letters from all over the world; but one in particular proved to be the start of a very interesting and fruitful relationship. It was a short but intriguing letter suggesting that the writer's own research was running parallel to our own, and that he knew something of great importance that he obviously did not want to discuss in the letter. With the piles of letters we were trying to answer, it took a few months to get around to contacting the writer, but when we did, it proved to be most worthwhile.

Alan Butler lives about three hours drive north of our homes in West Yorkshire, but he was keen to drive down and meet us for a drink one evening in a local pub. Alan arrived with his partner Kate and after a short time he was telling us how he had spent many years studying the Minoan culture of Crete. In particular, he had been looking at the Minoan system of measurement and a 3,500-year-old artefact known as the Phaistos Disc.

Alan Butler is an engineer by background and everything we heard from him seemed to have been carefully thought through. However, initially we remained sceptical about some of his claims and we checked his theories out in great detail over the next few weeks. We tried to find alternative explanations for what he had found, but eventually we were happy to tell him that we believed his conclusions to be plausible.

The bottom line of his research was that nearly 4,000 years ago the Minoans had used a system of mathematics based on a 366° circle, that appears to be directly connected to the mathematics of the megalithic people who lived in western Europe 5,000 years ago.

Butler believed that the megalithic people even knew the polar and equatorial circumference of the Earth to an accuracy of a few metres; more accurate even than our own measurements until satellite calculations during the last ten years. He also suggested that the system of mathematics in use more than 5,000 years ago totally unified space and time, based on the natural geometry of the Earth as a slightly distorted sphere. We decided to investigate his claim that the details of the megalithic system of geo-mathematics leave our own modern mathematics looking very clumsy and unsophisticated.

Butler had started by studying the mathematical structure of the Phaistos Disc. It is engraved on both sides with a series of pictograms laid out inside spirals. Although no one understands the writing system, Butler found that the symbols on the disc are compatible with a 366-day calendar, which was so accurate that over a period of 40 years it would be out by only three days. He also noted that there seemed to be an indication on the disc that would allow even this small error to be corrected.[45]

Butler also made the connection that the precision of measurement of the astronomical movement inherent in the Phaistos Disc was far higher than was necessary simply to create an accurate calendar. The Minoans seemed to be using a circle of 366 degrees with each degree subdivided into 60 minutes, and each minute further divided into 6 seconds. To understand what this means, hold your hand at arms length with your thumb upright and direct it towards the horizon. The area covered by your thumb nail is approximately one megalithic degree (one 366th of a full circle).

This seemed a useful measure – but why, Alan Butler asked himself, did the Minoans need a system that split this already small visual measure down into 360 sub units? Why could they need such accuracy? He decided to see if this small measure of angle represented a useful distance on the Earth's circumference, and his first calculation showed it to be a little over 300 metres. This rang bells, because the Minoans used a unit of length called the Minoan Foot, which archaeologist have observed from their buildings was equal to 30.36 cm.

[45] Butler, A.: *The Bronze Age Computer Disc*, W. Foulsham and Co, 1999

Butler made some quick calculations and realized that 1,000 Minoan feet was equal to 366 megalithic yards. Not approximately . . . *exactly*! He also noted that one megalithic second of arc was equal to 366 megalithic yards, or 1000 Minoan feet, on the Earth's surface.

When viewed as a whole, the system was phenomenal.

In the Minoan and the preceding megalithic system of geo-measurement, the circumference of the Earth is split into 366 degrees and each degree is further split into 60 minutes, with each minute divided again into six seconds. Each megalithic second of arc represents a distance of 366 megalithic yards on the Earth's surface and six of these comprise the distance a megalithic minute of arc covers on the Earth's surface – and is equal to 2,196 megalithic yards (a unit that Butler has called a megalithic mile).

There are 60 megalithic minutes of arc to the megalithic degree, and therefore also 60 megalithic miles. Since there are 366 megalithic degrees to the circle, it follows that the circumference of the earth should be 60 × 366 megalithic miles, which comes out at 21,960 megalithic miles. Convert this number into kilometres and the result is 40,009.98 kilometres.

The polar circumference of the earth is presently estimated to be 40,010 kilometres, so the megalithic people agreed with modern measurements to the last 20 metres! Such a precise match is unlikely to be mere coincidence.

The smallest unit of geometric measurement of the Earth's polar circumference that Butler identified was the megalithic second of arc, which was 366 megalithic yards in length (303.657 metres). Meanwhile, 1,000 Minoan feet equals 303.60 metres – a variance of less than 0.02 per cent. The astoundingly small difference bears testimony to the meticulous surveying of both Professor Thom and archaeologist Professor Graham, who independently first identified the Minoan foot. In fact, if we take Thom's work as being definitive (since he had so many more examples with which to work), then the Minoans' metricated version of the megalithic yard was actually 30.365 centimetres in length. If so, Professor Graham was out by just five 1,000ths of a centimetre in his estimation of the Minoan Foot!

So, it seems that some 4,000 years ago the Minoans of Crete had inherited a system from the megalithic peoples of western Europe, whereby one second of arc was the same as one second of time, and this could be expressed as a distance of 366 megalithic yards on the surface of the Earth. If one were to measure this distance accurately and mark it on the ground in an east-west direction, it actually represents the amount by which the Earth turns (at any given spot) in one megalithic second of time. In this way these prehistoric people reconciled time and distance into one form of measurement.

Butler felt that it was also reasonable to assume that the megalithic peoples had 12 hours in a day, to match the 12 months of the year. In fact everything in the system seemed to sing the same song, from lowest to highest, micro and macro.

From his studies of the Phaistos Disc, then, Alan Butler had rediscovered a verbal system of mathematics which integrated Thom's megalithic yard with an incredibly accurate Minoan calendar. The whole system was a logical way of linking the speed of rotation of the earth on its own axis with the rate of movement of the seasons.

The purpose of the Phaistos Disc was to enable the user to predict the position of the sun against the background stars to an accuracy of one part in 366. But as Alan's expertise developed in the use of this ancient system, he realized it was more subtle than he had first thought. The geometry of the measuring system also had a latitudinal correction built into it.

Because the Earth is almost a sphere, trigonometry can be used to work out its circumference at any latitude, using the angle of latitude. This can be easily measured by sighting on the apparent height of either the pole star or any other convenient circumpolar stars using a navigator's cross staff. The system of megalithic geometry had a built-in means of carrying out this calculation with ease because one of its trignometrical ratios of the angle of latitude (the cosine) is exactly the same numerical value as the number of megalithic miles across one megalithic degree of arc at any given latitude. The observed cosine of latitude can be turned into 1/366 part of the polar circumference in megalithic yards, by multiplying by 6 and then 366. This relationship greatly simplifies calculations, and if the megalithic people had a means of measuring time, then this was the basis of a complete navigation system.

The work conducted by Alan Butler was indeed parallel to our own studies; moreover, it powerfully demonstrated why Enoch would have been brought to the British Isles 5,200 years ago to receive instruction in astronomy (as outlined in Chapter Seven). The written word, astronomy and geometry have long been thought to have arisen in the Middle East, but we now had competing evidence that these sophisticated skills were in use in Europe long before they arrived in Sumer or Egypt.

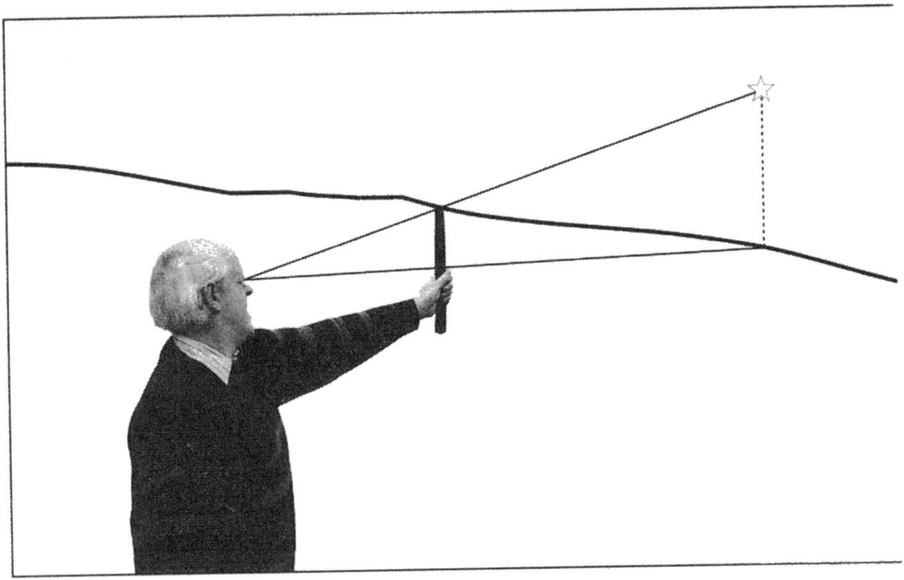

Figure 26. *Using a navigator's cross staff to measure the altitude of a star.*

CONCLUSION

Science can develop only by building knowledge. As the Grooved Ware People did not seem to have writing, they must have developed a verbal system of storing and passing on the detail of their observations, particularly in the field of astronomy. They also developed a tally marking system and adorned their structures with megalithic art, which could be an early attempt at writing.

The very earliest forms of writing display a high degree of similarity with the inscriptions of the Grooved Ware People, and the earliest form of Elamite (a Sumerian script) uses common megalithic symbols.

An even earlier form of writing, 1,000 years older than the earliest Sumerian writing, has been found in Transylvania. This script was similar to later developments in writing found in Minoan Crete. Therefore, the earliest writing seems to have developed out of megalithic symbols in western Europe, well before it started in Sumer.

The people who used these early proto-writing symbols built many stone structures, which are accurately aligned on the rising and setting positions of heavenly bodies. They all lie along the fringes of western Europe and share a common standard of length called the megalithic yard. The only practical explanation for this unit is that it must have had a physical definition which has been lost.

There is a system of mathematics which uses the megalithic yard, based on the number of sunrises in a year. In a remarkable way, megalithic mathematics integrates the speed of rotation of the earth with distances measured on the surface, so providing an ideal tool for navigation as well as a standard unit for building.

The written word, astronomy and geometry did not begin in the Middle East, but in Europe.

Chapter Nine

THE LIGHT OF VENUS

THE HILL OF THE BLACK GROVE

A people we know very little about carpeted Western Europe with prehistoric architecture. There are more megalithic stone structures in the British Isles than there are modern towns and villages, yet few busy citizens today are aware that these structures still sit silently in woodland, on farms and even in town centres.

As we now knew, the people who built them were talented engineers. They left behind structures fabricated from enormous stones, some weighing many tons, built in such an enduring fashion that they are still impressive more than 5,000 years after their builders turned to dust. These ancient sites have entered into the folklore of the largely rural Celtic areas, but are generally forgotten in the high population areas of England. Chris heard from his Irish mother stories of how she had been taught to be wary of the 'fairy' mounds that had to be left untouched, and Robert was told the traditional Welsh stories of the great stones by his grandmother:

> *Never destroy a standing stone or ill luck will befall you for six generations.*
>
> *The stones are giants, turned to stone, but on New Year's Eve (Nos Galon) the spell is lifted to let the giants walk down to the nearest river and drink.*
>
> *Sleep a night with your head against one of these ancient stones and you will wake up either a great poet or mad!*

The island of Anglesey, where Robert and his family have had a home for many years, retains a great number of these standing stones. The local population has always treated the stones with superstitious respect. Ynys Mon (Anglesey) was a last stronghold of the Druids before they were massacred by the Romans, and their legacy has added to the store of folklore attached to the sites.

Robert has been interested in megalithic structures for many years and he was studying some of the sites in Anglesey long before the subject became relevant to our joint research. It came as quite a surprise when we realized that there was a possible link between the *Book of Enoch* and the megalithic structures of western Europe, but by chance his studies of tunnel mounds and twinned menhirs suddenly proved to be central to our current studies.

The site that absorbed him most is known as Bryn Celli Ddu – pronounced 'Brin-kethlee-thee', the name means 'hill of the black grove'.

Bryn Celli Ddu is an earth-covered passage mound situated on Ynys Mon, which is in the middle of a field, and it has to be approached on foot along an unmade farm track. The structure has a passage 27 feet long and three feet wide that faces north-east and leads into an irregular chamber made up of five large side stones surmounted by two capstones. Inside the chamber is a shaped pillar which reaches almost up to the capstones of the roof, which is now supported by two cast concrete beams.

The tunnel and chamber have been built upon an earlier structure which consisted of a roughly circular ditch with some small standing stones around its inner perimeter. In the forecourt to the passage, the remains of a hearth and a platform of white quartz pebbles were found. Bryn Celli Ddu was first explored in 1865 and it was excavated in 1928-9. As well as some ox bones, human bones both burnt and unburnt were found in the chamber and the passage, leading to the interpretation that the structure is a burial mound. There were few other finds apart from two flint arrow-heads, a pierced stone bead and some limpet and mussel shells. When Professor Lynch investigated the site in 1972, he commented on a slot on the south-west side of the chamber (which he likened to the roof box structure), which allowed the midwinter sunlight to enter the chamber, as at Newgrange, in eastern Ireland. However, he was unable to discover any specific purpose or particular astronomical alignments for this slot. When the circular ditch with standing stones on its perimeter had been built, in the earliest phase of construction a decorated stone featuring a series of intricate carvings had been set up in the centre. Some time prior to 3500 BC this stone was taken down and buried, lying flat over the socket it had occupied. There it remained for almost 5,500 years until it was taken away from its traditional home to be hidden away in a Cardiff museum, and a hideous concrete replica was erected in its place.

Another feature of the stone circle is a pit. There was evidence that a fire had been lit in the pit and afterwards a human ear-bone was deposited in the ashes, the whole thing being covered with a flat stone. Unfortunately, the excavation was carried out well before the discovery of radiocarbon dating, so the opportunity of accurately dating the fire was lost for ever.

Dating the structure is not easy and Dr Julian Thomas of Southampton University, who has excavated extensively on Anglesey, confirmed that there are no carbon dates from the site, but he drew parallels with the Irish sites, which suggest a date for Bryn Celli Ddu of around 3500-3050 BC. From his knowledge of the stratified layers of the site he confirmed that the stone circle was abandoned and the decorated stone buried before the passage chamber was constructed.[1]

Dr Thomas commented that the ditch, circle and carved stone are much harder to date. The structure has been described as a 'henge', but he is unconvinced because the ditch is not as deep as a typical henge of the Grooved Ware period. Although its form has much to do with henge monuments, it may be be earlier than any true henge. We think he is correct in this, because the ditch is not deep enough to provide the artificial horizon which seems to have been the purpose of the henge. Probably the ring ditch and standing stones did surround the carved stone – if so, then the best parallel might be in Brittany, and the date could be quite early; almost certainly before 4000 BC. Julian Thomas also thinks it possible that the pillar may well be part of the original structure, and that the mound was erected around it. (See Plates 10, 11 and 12)

The decorated stone and the carving within the structure have parallels with the tombs of the Boyne Valley and also with sites in Brittany. The pillar in the chamber is also a feature of the chamber at Carrowkeel F, an Irish structure.[2]

We were aware of certain comments made by Alexander Thom about the purpose of early pictogram markings on megaliths:

[1] Thomas, J: Private Communication, 1997
[2] Twohig, E.S.: *Irish Megalithic Tombs*, Shire Archaeology, 1990

> *I have an idea that . . . the cup and ring markings were a method of recording, of writing, and that they may indicate . . . what a particular stone was for. We have seen the cup and ring markings on the stone at Temple Wood [in Argyll] and that's on the main stone but we can't interpret them yet.*[3]

As we discussed the possibility that these decorations had meaning, we wondered if the reason that they had not been understood was because this sequence was the key – and yet there seemed to be no obvious pattern with a starting and finishing point. The question he had been testing was whether the passage of the sun's rays highlights a sequence of carvings as it moves around the site. It seemed that if Thom was right, and the carvings could be interpreted, perhaps they could be supposed to be read in the order in which the sunlight falls on them on significant days of the year.

To test this possibility, we observed a number of the Anglesey sites at various times of the day and year, to see if there are any obvious patterns. So far, it is Bryn Celli Ddu that has yielded the most interesting results.

The key days to observe were the solstices, which occur when the sun is at its extreme positions either north (summer) or south (winter), and the equinoxes, when the sun is over the equator, giving days and nights of equal length.

Standing in the centre of the original stone circle there is, as we have said, a re-erected copy of the carved stone, from where the contours of the hills provide clear gaps for possible alignments with the rising moon. The position of the site has been chosen so that the extremes of the moon's rising could easily be plotted against the clear landmarks formed by the dips and peaks of the mountains to the east.

SUNLIGHT WRITING

The first observation of what appeared to be a deliberate lighting effect happened one spring equinox. The first burst of sunlight shone into the tunnel and on to its northern wall, where a series of small indentations called cup markings had been cut into the stonework. As the sun climbed into the sky over a period of about 40 minutes, it lit up a sequence of these markings,

[3] Thom, A.: *Walking in All of the Squares*, Argyll Publishing, 1995

causing them to sparkle like a series of tiny stars in the darkness of the ancient passage. The sun seemed to be skipping from cup to cup as it traced a curve along the wall of the tunnel before climbing so high its light was no longer entering the portal.

Prior to their illumination by the rising sun, these markings had seemed insignificant – it had not been obvious that sunlight would ever reach them, situated as they were along the northern wall of the passage. But now the quartz-veined rock used in the construction of the walls caught the incident light of the rays of the rising sun, focusing it towards an observer in the chamber.

At about 10 o'clock, one of the portal stones casts a shadow onto a stone in the entrance which had a series of grooves cut into the side, where the shadow coincided with one of the more prominent grooves. At first sight the marks had looked as if they might be an Ogham inscription (Ogham is a form of writing developed by the Druids consisting of lines and cups), but they had defied translation. Seeing where the shadow fell and from the geometry of the stones, it became clear that these two rocks could be used as a shadow gauge to tell when the equinox was approaching. The lines above and below would indicate how close to the equinox the sun was, and the height of the shadow on the receiving stone would give any watcher a guide as to when the equinoctial lighting effects were about to happen.

At the time of the equinox, the sun is moving very rapidly across the sky, so the correct angle of illumination to observe the equinox lighting phenomena happens for only about three days. At the spring equinox the sun is moving in a northerly direction, and so its rising rays would start to illuminate further into the tunnel. From compass calculations it seemed that at the summer solstice the first rays of the rising sun might shine right into the chamber, but it was to take two years to test this assumption. Typical of British weather, for the next two summer solstices the sky remained stubbornly overcast.

After seeing how the cup marks in the tunnel had 'spoken' in the sunlight, Robert made a careful examination of the chamber with a powerful torch, which revealed many more small indentations cut into the stones of the chamber. Strangely, they all seemed to be in positions where the sun would *not* be able to shine directly onto them; perhaps, then, they were not all intended to work in the same way? The large number of such cuts could mean that it is just coincidence that the tunnel marks had been lit up in what seemed a deliberate way. The only way to find out if they had been positioned in a deliberate manner was to observe the site on as many bright sunlit days as possible, to see what arbitrary lighting effects might be present.

One sunny afternoon in late March an unexpected but very interesting phenomenon occurred. It was not long after the equinox, but the sun moves very quickly across the sky at that time and it's declination was about 4°. At approximately 20 minutes after one o'clock, a shaft of sunlight, coming from a gap in the north-west, was moving across the floor of the chamber towards the base of the pillar. After about three-quarters of an hour, the sun moved around far enough for the light to form a bar across the pillar.

There are a number of grooves cut into the side of the pillar, and it seemed probable that the light would fall on the grooves, but when it hit the pillar it was much further down. What was clear was that if the sun was further south and therefore lower in the sky, the dagger of light on the pillar would climb higher up. In March the bar of light reached the pillar at 2.10 p.m., which seemed strange if this effect was deliberate. Why was it not designed to occur at noon, when the sun was at its highest point in the sky? (See Plates 16 and 17)

Observations taken for a few hours either side of midday on a range of dates showed that during the summer months the light never reached as far as the marked pillar, only appearing on the floor of the chamber. It was a particularly disappointing summer as for a couple of weeks either side of the solstice the morning sky was overcast, so it was impossible to see where the rays of the rising sun fell within the tunnel and chamber. Nonetheless, despite the absence of direct sunlight, it appeared to be probable that the sun would shine along the full length of the tunnel and into the chamber, but prediction is always difficult with such complex structures.

The builders of Bryn Celli Ddu appeared to have chosen a very odd time of day to set up the stones to cause the bar of light to fall on the pillar. Perhaps they had a reason, but if so, it was elusive. Maybe, after 5,000 years it would be impossible to work out why they did things, and the possibility remained that the light falling on the pillar was just an accident, without any significance to its builders at all.

The only way forward was to keep making as many observations as possible.

When the sun was lower in the sky, around the September equinox, the dagger of light was again falling on the pillar – but at the slightly earlier time of 1.45 p.m. The dagger of light was now clearly defined and would surely climb up the pillar as the sun moved south during the winter. As the light came off the pillar it shone on to a large slab of quartz rock behind it, which forms the north-eastern wall of the chamber. This apparently tooled rock acted as a double parabolic reflector and split the ray of sunlight into two separate beams, which illuminated the opposite walls of the chamber. Slowly both the north and south walls of the chamber were slowly bathed in the full glow of the reflected sunlight.

As the bright sunlight hit them, the carved cup markings on these walls sprang to life, glowing like stars. It had previously seemed impossible for the sunlight to reach these indentations, but the reflective quality of the cut stone had not been obvious at all before the event occurred. The whole chamber was quickly flooded with light in a spectacular manner, but more important still, this reflected image of the sun's disc, thrown on to the side walls of the chamber, illuminated two *other* sets of cup markings, which now glowed like a constellation of small stars. This effect happened at between about 2.30 and 3.15, with the peak illumination of the cup marks around 2.50 p.m.

Looking more closely at the rear stone slab, it was apparent that it had been deliberately shaped to provide two curved surfaces to split and reflect the sun's beam, which was focused on to it by the slot, which Lynch had noticed but not been able to explain. For a group of Stone-Age 'savages' who were not supposed to understand telescopes, it looked suspiciously like a early form of a Newtonian telescope. In the late 17th century, scientist Sir Isaac Newton invented a telescope which used a curved mirror, to magnify images of the stars. His Newtonian telescope had a tube to channel the light on to a concave mirror, which then focused the images of the stars onto an eyepiece for the observer to view. This megalithic structure works on exactly the same principle. Bryn Celli Ddu channels the light of the sun through the slot of the chamber, onto a reflective stone which has been hollowed out in the shape of two back-to-back concave mirrors. When the sun is in the right position in the sky (at the equinoxes) its image is projected by the carved stone onto the shaded sides of the chamber for the observer to view.

By late October the sun is fairly low in the sky, its declination is about -12°, so it is half-way between the equinox and its most southerly position in the sky. At this time the light was now falling on the pillar at a much higher level and, when moving off the pillar, was no longer hitting the worked rock behind it. So once again, it was becoming obvious that these carefully engineered lighting effects only lasted for short periods of the year, and were completely dependent on the declination of the sun.

There were now enough points at different dates to understand the pillar in terms of the marks cut into it and dates they represented, and it was also possible to plot the times that the sunlight hit the pillar against the position of the sun in the sky (its azimuth). This calculation produced a constant reading of 209° (approximately SSW). Why that angle of azimuth had been chosen was not immediately clear but later in the year the amazing answer would present itself.

THE VENUS EFFECT

Venus is the third brightest astronomical object in the sky after the sun and moon, and it can cast a shadow. By early December, Venus was so bright that it could be seen in the sky even whilst the sun was still above the horizon. This brilliant planet has been extremely important to our researches from the very beginning because it is the 'morning star' that is associated with the resurrection rite of Freemasonry's Master Mason degree.[4] In its sunset position it is also known as the 'evening star'.

Watching Venus follow the sun down one day, it occurred to Robert that it was at a slightly higher angle than the sun, and as the days progressed it was moving out from the sun. A quick calculation indicated that the azimuth and declination of Venus placed it in a position where it might project a dagger of light on to the pillar at Bryn Celli Ddu.

We discussed the possibility with Alan Butler, who besides being an engineer is also interested in astrology as an ancient 'science', and is highly informed about the movements of the heavens. Alan made many helpful points, including that Venus can only become an evening star after a superior conjunction (when the sun passes in front of Venus), which would not be visible from earth because the planet would be masked by the sun. The period between this conjunction and its first appearance in the evening sky is between 36 and 40 days, when it will be 10° away from the sun and will disappear below the horizon about 40 minutes after sunset.

From this point onwards Venus gets progressively further away from the sun, setting later and later. Months later Venus can still be seen hours after sunset.

[4] Knight, C. and Lomas, R.: *The Hiram Key,* Century, 1996

The greatest elongation for the 'evening star' in autumn is always to the south of west, and maximum brilliance is achieved exactly 36 days later, at which time Venus is rapidly dropping back towards the sun once more. During this half of the Venus cycle, it is visible for over four months and probably more, so Alan Butler agreed that Bryn Celli Ddu could easily have a Venus effect across many winter nights.

Using his knowledge of astronomy, Alan e-mailed us to say:

> *Towards the end of December Venus appears as an evening star, following the sun down for four years out of every eight, although the pattern is more complicated than just every other year, but it repeats every eight years with a very high degree of accuracy.*
>
> *When Venus is at maximum brilliance this time around the angular distance between the sun and Venus is 38 degrees. The sun sets at 15.51 and Venus sets 2.5 hours later. That means that it will reach the sun's 14.30 position at about 17.00, long after the sun has set. Under these conditions, and with no moon in the sky, you could probably read the Times in that chamber by the light of Venus.*
>
> *I agree your best chance to see it will be on 13 December. There are possible viewing windows on that afternoon and the following afternoon, Saturday and Sunday.*

On the afternoon of 13 December 1997 Robert, accompanied by his son Geraint, returned to Bryn Celli Ddu to see if Venus would shine its light on the pillar. It was a dark and slightly overcast night with Venus very bright in the western sky – it was circled by a shining halo of haze as it burned through the light veil of cirrus cloud to follow the sun down. About an hour after sunset, a slight ground mist was developing, but Venus was still bright enough to produce a remarkably bright dagger of light that slowly crawled across the floor of the ancient chamber.

The line of Venus light was slightly lower down the pillar than that of the sun, which had appeared earlier in the afternoon, but was plain to see on the pillar. It was now certain that whoever built Bryn Celli Ddu was well aware that they would be able to measure the declination of Venus using the light that fell on the pillar by comparing the light from the sun two-and-a-half hours earlier. Why else would they position the slot where they did so that the dagger of light fell on the pillar not at noon, but much later at 14.20 hours, when the sun was well past its zenith? The only reason would have been to take advantage of the relative positions of Venus and the sun.

The careful positioning of the slot in Bryn Celli Ddu is unlikely to be chance. We decided to work out the odds of it being a random choice that the slot is placed at an angle which accommodates both the sun's seasonal rise and fall in the sky and the position of Venus in the same slot.

Any compass direction when the sun is high enough above the horizon to shine into the chamber would have achieved the seasonal sundial effect on the pillar. So the compass azimuth of the slot could have been anywhere between 140° and 260°, a range of 120°. As the slot is just 2° wide, that gives a chance of one in 60 that it could have been in any random direction. The slot also points far enough away from the setting sun for three of the four possible occasions during the eight-year Venus cycle when Venus is an evening star for its light to shine on the pillar after sunset. This event has only three chances in eight of being random, but when combined with the sun's position there are only six chances in a thousand that a position to match both events was accidental. We could be sure, then, that if the builders of Bryn Celli Ddu had just happened to leave a slot in the wall there are only six chances in a thousand it would be in the right place to align with both Venus and with the Sun. This is a low enough probability for any statistician to reject the idea that the direction and height of the slot were unintentional: it was *meant* to happen this way.

Venus throws a dagger of light onto the pillar at 17.04, which was one hour and five minutes after sunset. By marking the position of the sun and of the Venus light pointer, the pillar could be used to work out the difference in altitude of Venus and the sun, and hence the separation between the two. Venus repeats its exact position on the pillar only every eight years, so this observatory is capable of correcting any drift in solar and lunar calendars.

The reason for the choice of angle was now clear. The aperture had been carefully designed to an accuracy of just two degrees. If the slot had been more than 209° (azimuth), Venus would have been too low in the sky for its light to fall on the pillar, and if it had been less than 209° the sun would have still been in the sky when Venus reached the slot.

It was a sobering thought to realize that Robert and Geraint were probably the first people in thousands of years to see Bryn Celli Ddu working as the Venus observatory its makers had built it to be.

THE WINTER SOLSTICE

At the winter solstice, the dagger of sunlight reached right to the top of the pillar – or rather, it would have done if sunlight had not been blocked by the concrete beam which had been put in to secure the roof. The dagger was fully directed on the pillar at 2.22 p.m.

These differing times for the effect are fully explained once it is understood that the effect occurs when the sun is at an azimuth of exactly 209°N. The time of day this occurs will vary slightly with the season and the sun's declination.

The position of the dagger of light on the pillar gives a direct measure of the altitude of the sun, and the gauge works over the period from September to April throughout the winter months. The marks on the side of the pillar indicate dates in early November and late January. When Robert gave a seminar about these findings to members of the Archaeological Sciences Department of Bradford University, he was asked if any of these solar marks could coincide with important agricultural events. Certainly, Anglesey has always supported a large population of sheep and has traditionally lambed around the Easter period. The November mark matched the gestation period of the sheep with an Easter lambing. So if these people had wanted to have their lambs born when the worst of the spring gales were over and the grass is starting to grow strongly, then the sunlight reaching the mark on the side of the pillar would mark the time to put the ram to the ewes

Perhaps these markings went further than guiding animal breeding programmes. Rudolf Steiner, writing about Christmas, has made the following comment:

> *In the third millennium before Christ, in certain northern tribes, only those people were regarded as worthy citizens of the earth who were born in certain weeks of the winter season. The reason for this was as follows: on the Jutland peninsula – whose tribes were called the Ingaevones, or at least were so called by Tacitus – the temple priests of the Mystery sites encouraged sexual union to take place only at a certain time in the first quarter of the year at the time of the full moon after the spring equinox.*[5]

[5] Steiner, R.: *The Festivals and Their Meaning*, Rudolf Steiner Press, 1981

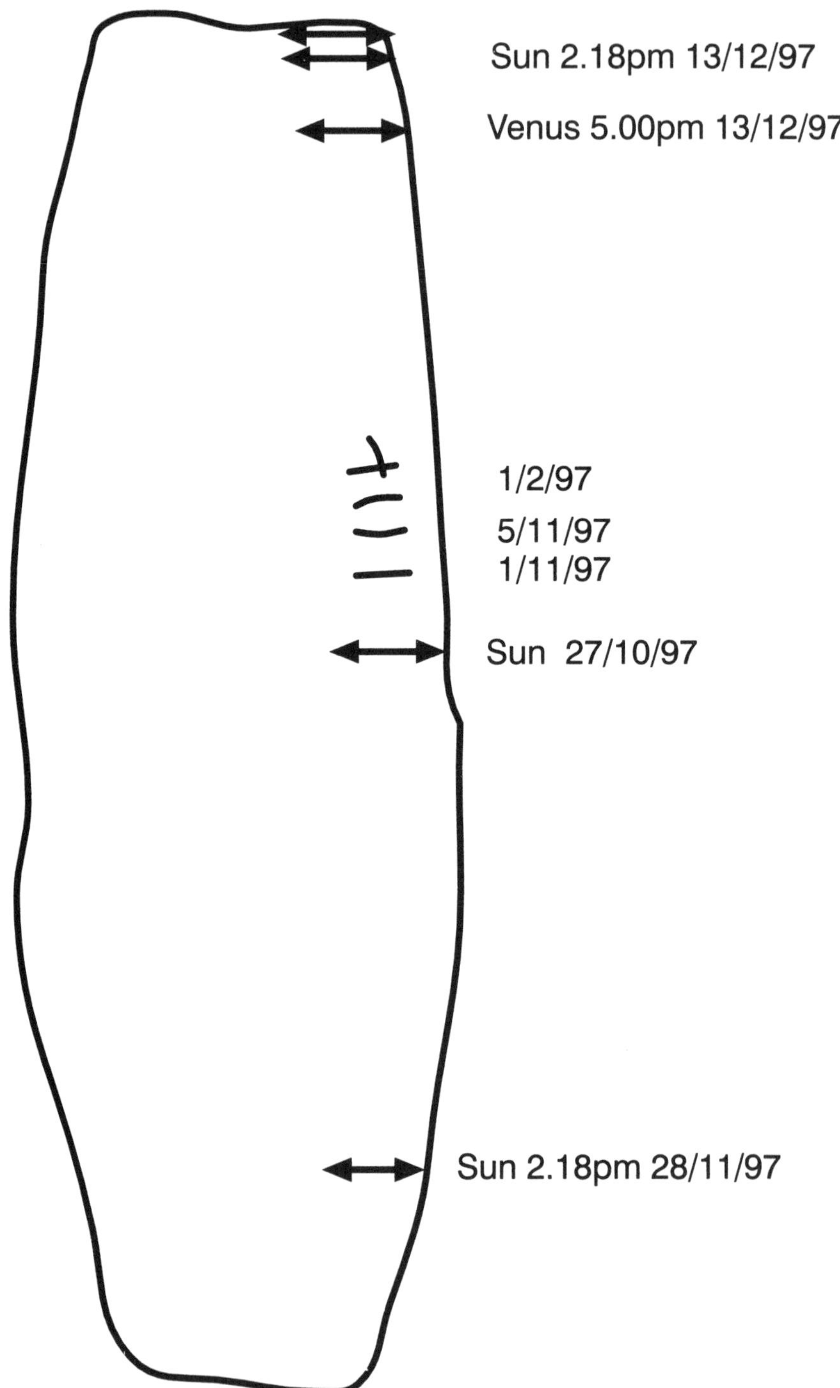

Figure 27. *Where the dagger of sunlight falls at Bryn Celli Ddu on special days.*

The Christian calendar is known to have adopted ancient festivals, and even today Easter Sunday is defined as the first Sunday after the full moon following the spring equinox.

So, as we have seen, the site at Bryn Celli Ddu certainly marked the spring and autumn equinoxes in a most spectacular manner. This was the period when the sunlight, after illuminating the pillar, would move onto the carved rock behind and be split to light up the sides of the chamber with its patterns of cup markings.

In Steiner's next observation about how the matter of conception had been arranged, he again quoted the Roman historian, Tacitus (from *Germania*, 40):

> *On an island of the ocean is a sacred grove and in it there is a consecrated chariot covered with a veil. Only the priest may approach it. He knows when the goddess appears in the sacred chariot. He becomes aware of the presence of the goddess in her holy place, and in deep reverence accompanies her chariot drawn by cows. Then there are days of joy and feasting in all places which the goddess honours with a visit. Then there are joyous days and wedding feasts. At those times no war is waged, no weapons are handled, the sword is sheathed. Only peace and quiet are at those times known or desired, until the goddess, tired of her sojourn among mortals, is led back into the shrine by the same priest.*[6]

Was Bryn Celli Ddu one of these consecrated chariots covered by a veil, a veil of stone? Did the priests at the time of Tacitus interpret the filling of the chamber with light as the presence of the goddess? Was this why, 2,000 years after the chamber had been built, a cow had been buried in the forecourt of the site?

Steiner had more to say about this, as he went on to quote Tacitus' account of what happened next.

> *Then the chariot, the veil and the goddess herself are bathed in a hidden lake. Slaves perform the cult, slaves who are at once swallowed up as forfeit by the lake, so that all knowledge of these things sinks*

[6] Steiner, R.: *The Festivals and Their Meaning*, Rudolf Steiner Press, 1981

into the night of unconsciousness. A secret horror and a sacred darkness hold sway over a being who is able to behold only the sacrifice of death.[7]

Not very far from Bryn Celli Ddu, when the Ministry of Defence were extending the runway of the RAF station at Valley (Fali), a lake was drained prior to infilling. In that lake were found many offerings, dating from at least 3,000 years ago, including bodies of people who may have been thrown in to drown with the valuable offerings. Were these the slaves Tacitus describes as sacrificed after the ritual of the appearance of the goddess in the chariot in 'the hill of the black grove', Bryn Celli Ddu?

THE SOLSTICE SUNRISE

Bryn Celli Ddu had not yet finished revealing its secrets. In 1998, for the first time in three years, the morning of the summer solstice was clear and bright, and as the sun lifted above the horizon the first rays shone down the tunnel and illuminated the base of the south-westerly stone slab. It formed a small red point on the very base of the stone, and as the sun climbed slowly into the sky, the passage was flooded with light, forming a golden path along the floor of the tunnel into the chamber. But as the sunlight strengthened, more lighting effects started to happen. The sunlight was reflected back by the reflective quartz stone, to strike the stone slab to the left of the entrance, where it illuminated a small and very roughly carved spiral, on the stone surface. Within a few minutes the sun had moved far enough to the south for the light to have moved off the reflector and off the spiral.

The origin of the double spiral was discovered by an American artist called Charles Ross. He set up an experiment where he arranged a lens in front of a wooden plank, so that it focused the sun's rays on the plank and burned a track on the wood. Each day he put a new piece of wood in the plank-holder and after 366 consecutive days he plotted out the pattern the sun's rays had burned into the planks. He found that the resulting shape was a perfect double spiral. During the summer the track formed a tight clockwise spiral, whilst in the winter it formed a widely spaced anti-clockwise spiral. At the equinox the track began to straighten out as the loose winter spiral stopped and was transformed into a tight spiral moving in the opposite sense.[8]

[7] Steiner, R.: *The Festivals and Their Meaning*, Rudolf Steiner Press, 1981
[8] Brennan, M.: *The Stones of Time*, Inner Traditions International, 1994

1. The White Wall of Newgrange on the River Boyne. First built before 3200 BC. Excavated and reconstructed in 1968 by Professor Michael O'Kelly and his team.

2. Comet Hale-Bopp photographed in 1997 in the northern skies of Anglesey.

3. The mound of Maes Howe on Orkney with Ward Hill – where the sun rises, sets and rises again – in the background.

4. The great observatory of the Ring of Brodgar on Orkney.

5. The 'stone things' from Skara Brae.

6. A grooved ware pot from Alness in Ross-shire, now in Inverness Museum.

7. The Hill of Many Staines in Caithness. The fan of stone lines acts as a stellar chronometer.

8. A typical apartment of Skara Brae.

9. The workshop of Skara Brae.

10. Bryn Celli Ddu with the replica Stone of Enigmas.

11. The entrance to the tunnel of Bryn Celli Ddu.

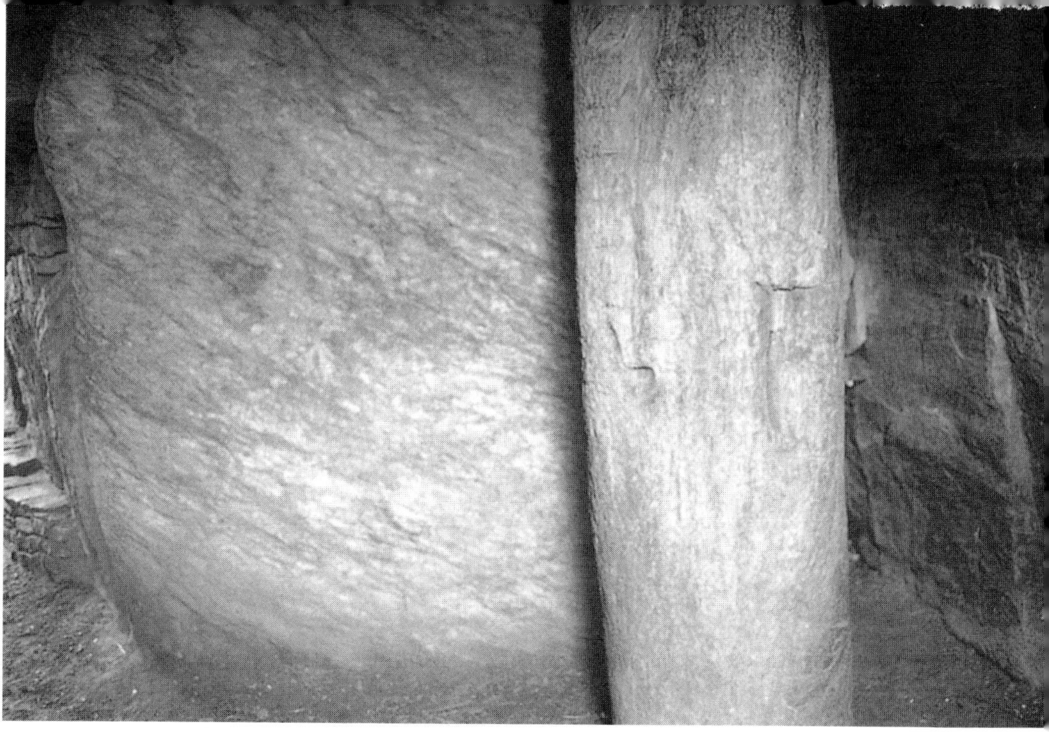

12. The pillar inside the chamber of Bryn Celli Ddu.

13. The spiral on the side wall of Bryn Celli Ddu.

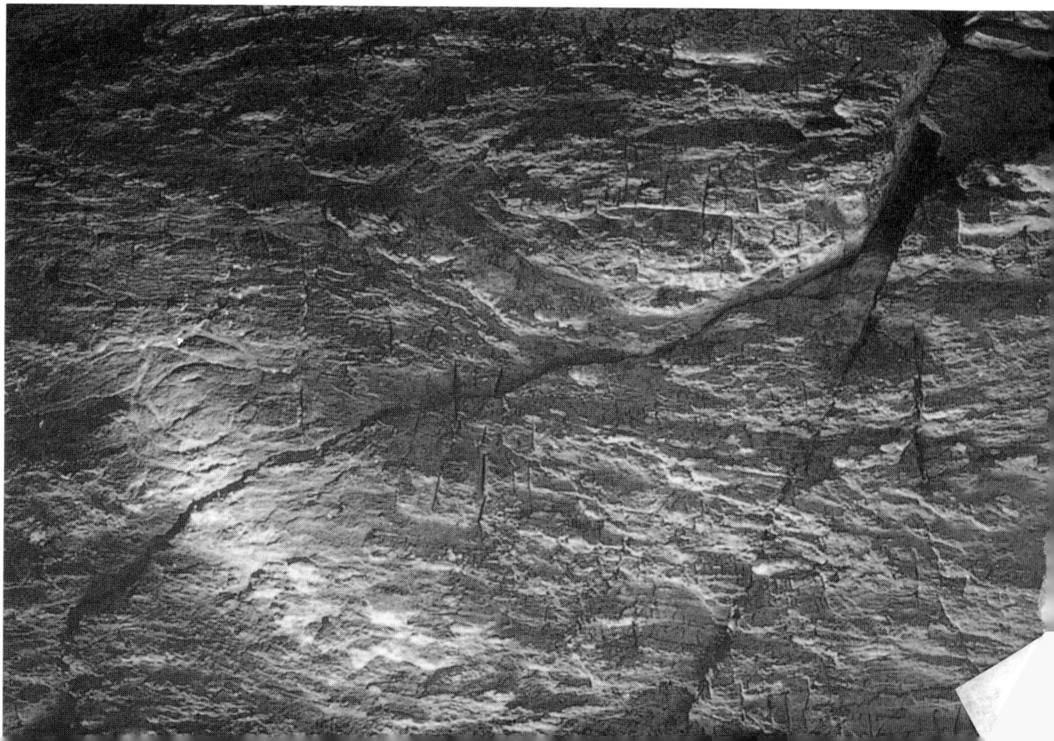

14. The sunlight of the summer solstice sunrise shining down the tunnel into the chamber at Bryn Celli Ddu.

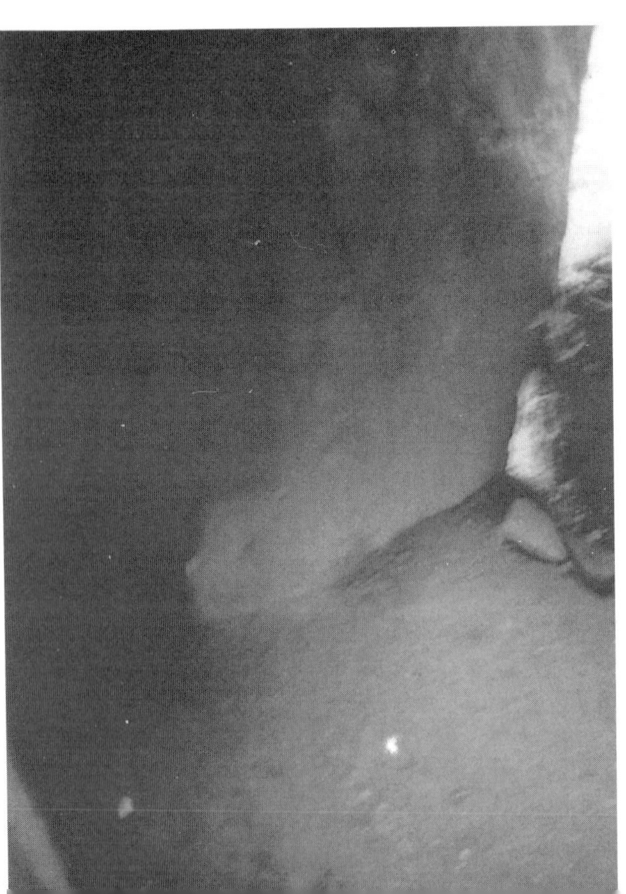

15. The light of the rising sun reflecting off the base of the chamber wall to light up the spiral carving at Bryn Celli Ddu.

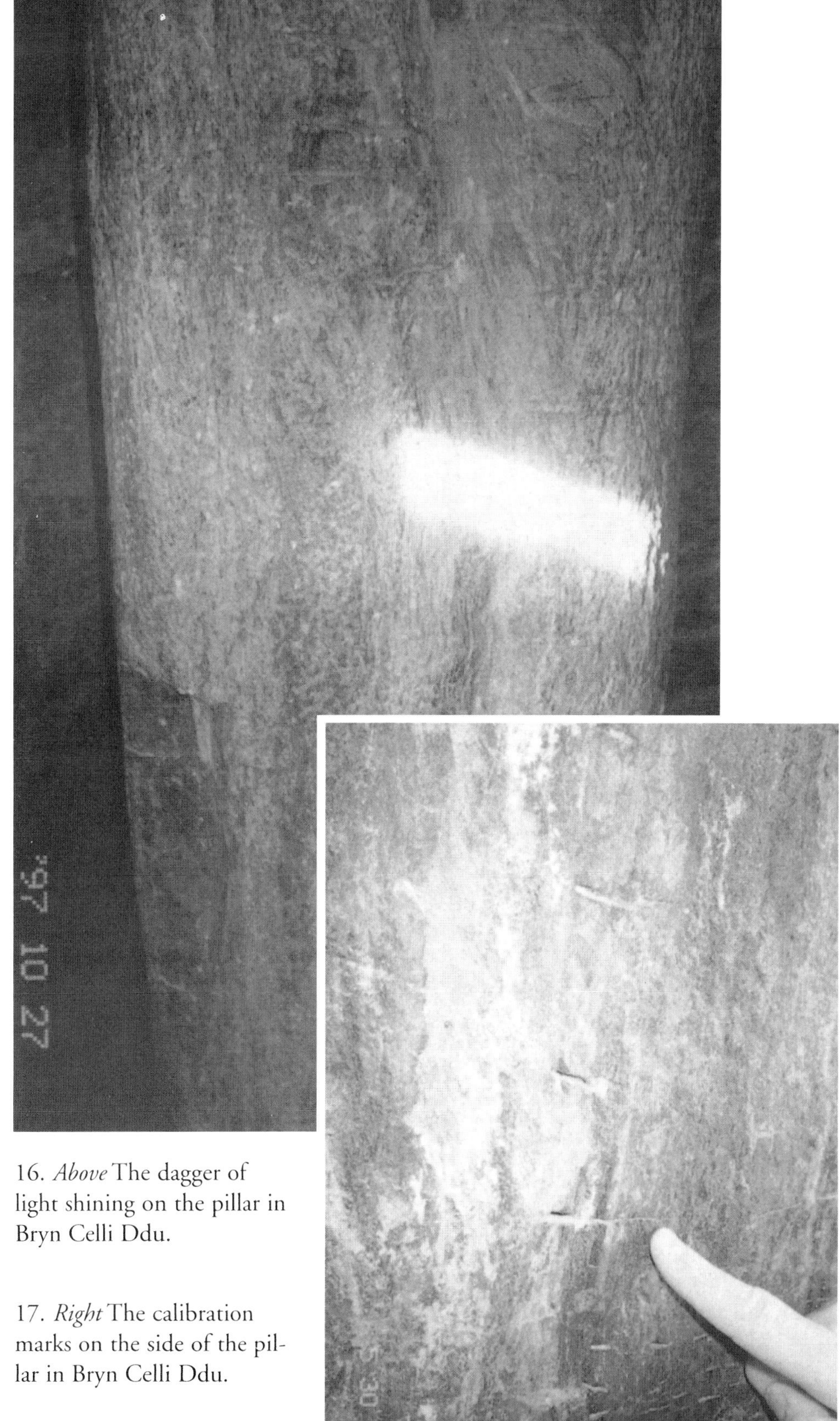

16. *Above* The dagger of light shining on the pillar in Bryn Celli Ddu.

17. *Right* The calibration marks on the side of the pillar in Bryn Celli Ddu.

18. Setting a post in the reconstruction of Uriel's Machine.

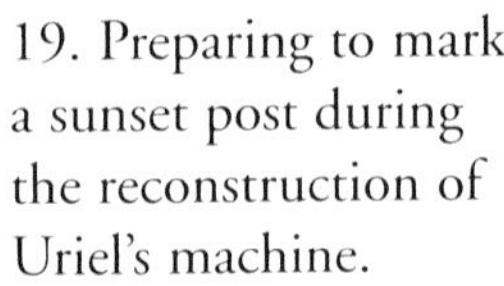

19. Preparing to mark a sunset post during the reconstruction of Uriel's machine.

20. The stone phallus found at Knowth by Professor George Eogan.

21. The mummy of a 6ft 6in tall Cherchen Man. One of the ancient giants of west European origin

22. The inscribed backstone at Newgrange.

23. The standing stone on the Hill of Tara.

24. The entrance to Newgrange.

25. The lightbox above the entrance to Newgrange with a lintel showing eight, one year symbols.

26. Detail of the white wall at Newgrange showing the packed quartz construction.

27. Light reflecting of the white wall of Newgrange.

28. One of the few remaining pieces of quartz that once covered the ancient Egyptian pyramids of the Giza Plateau. Note its size and how the dressed front section is identical to the Newgrange stones.

29. The caves at Qumran facing the rising sun, where the Dead Sea Scrolls were discovered.

30. The hanging angel of Rosslyn Chapel representing Shemhazai suspended between heaven and earth.

31. Professor James Charlesworth points out an Herodian architectural feature at Rosslyn Chapel.

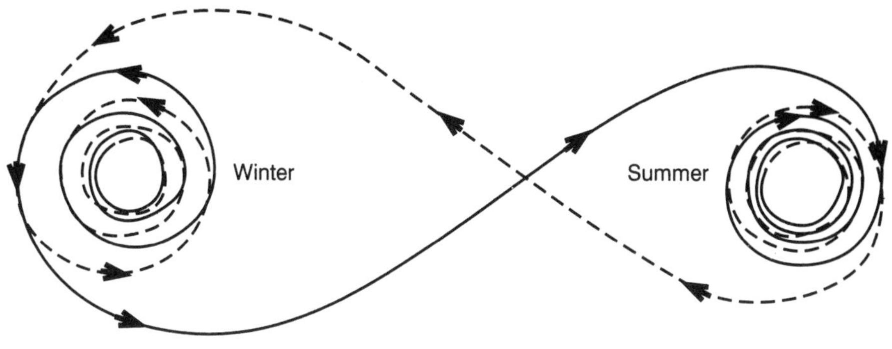

Figure 28. *Path traced by the sun's shadow over a year, after Ross.*

Each spiral therefore represents a quarter of the sun's movement in the sky.

A SCIENTIFIC INSTRUMENT

Before we assess the purpose of Bryn Celli Ddu, it is worthwhile summing up what we now know about it.

The use of Bryn Celli Ddu has varied over the ages. The site started out as a stone circle surrounded by a ditch. In the centre of this stone ring was a standing stone covered in quite magnificent carvings, including spirals and zigzag patterns. Some time before the pillar and its surrounding megaliths were erected, this stone was taken down and buried in the middle of the circle. Along with the stone a human ear-bone was also buried in the middle of the original ring, outside the chamber. This stone has been stolen from its ancient setting to be stored in South Wales and a crude, but accurate, concrete replica casting has been erected in the socket of the original stone.

The alignments of the stones of Bryn Celli Ddu are extremely precise and there are too many to reject them as accidental:

1. The alignment of the passage and its cup mark sequences highlight the equinoxes and the summer solstice.

2. The shadow gauge indicates where in the solar year you are at any time.

3. The pillar and stone edge are positioned to accurately measure the Venus cycle, the winter solstice and the winter agricultural calendar.

The site has gone through many refinements and improvements, but the question remains as to why the carved centre stone was buried in the middle of the ring when the pillar declination gauge was built.

It seems that Bryn Celli Ddu was designed for a very small number of people to enter and observe the solar and Venus cycles with great accuracy. Even the slightest repositioning of the elements of the structure would mean the observatory would not function.

The question then arises as to why these ancient people needed to understand the movements of the sun and Venus so precisely.

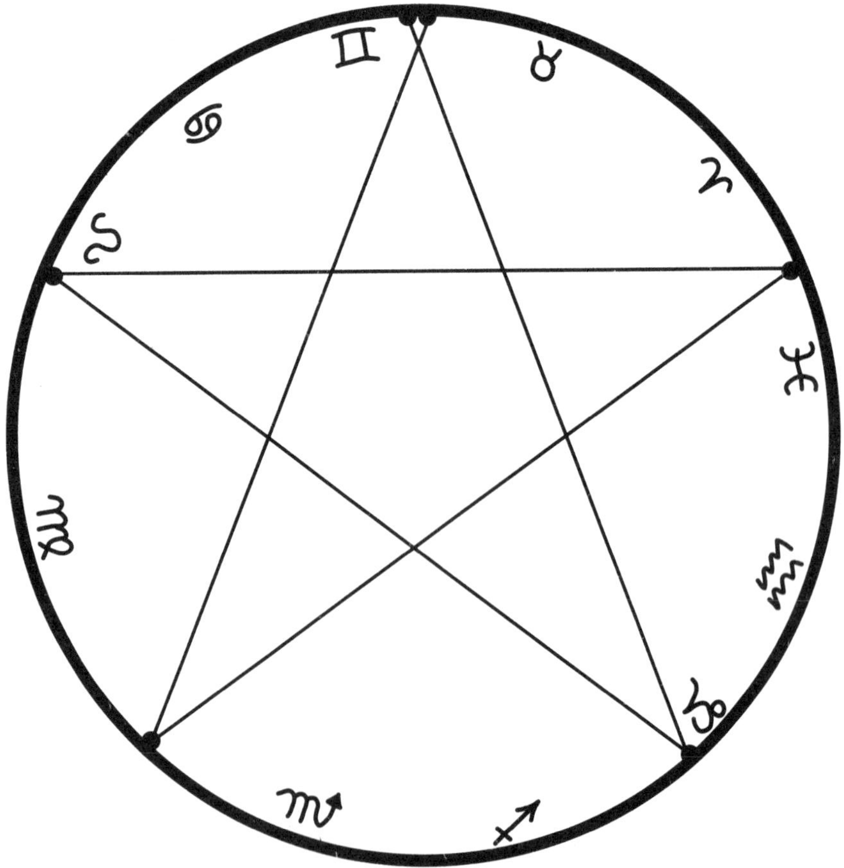

Figure 29. *The path Venus traces out around the circle of the zodiac.*

An obvious answer is that Venus is the most accurate indicator of the time of year available in the solar system. Every eight years it marks a point when the solar calendar, the lunar calendar and the sidereal (position of the stars) calendar all coincide to within a few minutes. Over five Venus cycles – i.e. every 40 years – it synchronizes these calendars to within a few seconds. The eight-year Venus cycle also accurately maps the moon's phases and its sidereal movements to within five hours.

Knowledge of the Venus cycle enables the three main calendars to be regularly realigned and allows detailed predictions of the tides and lunar eclipses to be made. The eighth-century Irish document *Saltair Na Rann*, which records the old oral traditions of the Irish Celts, tells of the knowledge required for leaders of the people in ancient times:

> *For each day five items of knowledge are required of everyone, with no appearance of boasting, who would be a leader.*
>
> *The day of the solar month, the age of the moon, the state of the sea tide, without error, the day of the week, the calendar of the feasts of the deities.*

The sidereal calendar is important for agriculture, the lunar calendar is important to tell the tides, and the solar calendar is needed to know the length of the day and to recognize feast days. Bryn Celli Ddu can do all these things with an extremely high degree of accuracy. Is this simply a coincidence?

The meanings of the symbols used on the centre stone may have been lost, but the spiral seems to be associated with the sun and its movements while the zigzag tally stones may have been used to count the movements of the moon.

Dr Julian Thomas[9] discovered a small flat stone near Bryn Celli Ddu which he described as covered in tally markings, although its age is uncertain because it was found in a disturbed layer of soil. It could have been part of the working notes of the builders or something much later, but it certainly shows that the site has been associated with counting the movements of the heavens over a long period of time. Five thousand years ago the ornately

[9] Thomas, J.: Private Communication, 1997

carved centre stone, whose symbols could also be interpreted as tally marks, was buried in the middle of the circular ditch along with the human ear-bone already mentioned.

These people were using stone to produce rugged and accurate scientific instruments for observing the regular movements of the heavenly luminaries, in a way which must have seemed extremely clever to any unsophisticated observer. We were reminded of the secrets of the heavens given to Enoch by the angel Uriel:

> *This is the book of the courses of the luminaries of the heaven, the relations of each, according to their classes, their dominion and their seasons, according to their names and places of origin, and according to their months, which Uriel, the holy angel, who was with me, who is their guide, showed me; and he showed me all their laws exactly as they are, and how it is with regard to all the years of the world and unto eternity, till the new creation is accomplished which dureth till eternity.*

LEGENDS OF THE SITES

Because the megalithic people did not leave behind any written records for us to inspect, our only means of studying them is by scrutinising their surviving works and listening to legends which are still told about them. We have learnt to treat legends and myths with great respect; whilst they are not history in an exact sense, we had found that often they contain true memories or impressions of actual events. The 19th-century Irish historian Sister Mary Cusack, known as The Nun of Kenmare, said of legends:

> *The history of ancient peoples must have its basis on tradition. The name tradition unfortunately gives an* a priori *impression of untruthfulness, and hence the difficulty of accepting tradition as an element of truth in historic research. But tradition is not necessarily either a pure myth or a falsified account of facts. The traditions of a nation are like an aged man's recollection of his childhood, and should be treated as such. If we would know his early history, we let him tell the tale in his own fashion. It may be he will dwell long upon occurrences interesting to himself, and apart from the object of our inquiries; it may be he will equivocate unintentionally if cross-examined*

in detail; but truth will underlie his garrulous story, and by patient analysis we may sift it out, and obtain the information we desire.[10]

The old Welsh *Triads of the Island of Britain* tell of the stones of Gwydden-Ganhebom on which were written 'the arts and sciences of the world' and of the story of a learned Druid by the name of Gwydion ap Don, who is described as 'a master of the movements of the heavens'. This mythical figure is said to be buried near the Welsh town of Caernarfon under something called 'a Stone of Enigmas'.[11]

Names in yr Cymreag (the Welsh language), like most ancient languages, are never without meaning. Historian and native Welsh speaker Ken Owen told us that the name 'Gwydion' means: man of learning, Druid, magician, philosopher, wise man or possibly scientist, but he also commented that older meanings attached to the name – giant, monster, wizard, sorcerer or woodland deity.

The second and third sections of the name Gwydion ap Don seem to mean something like 'Son of the Talented'. The ap means 'son of' – so he was a son of Don, who was a female figure in an old collection of legends known as the *Mabinogion*. Don was the daughter of an obscure character called Mathonwy and the sister of Math, an extremely powerful Druid about whom many tales of magic are told. The name Math means wealth or power. Don married Beli ap Manogan, whose feast is celebrated by lighting fires at the festival of Beltane which survives today as May Day. Beli is often mentioned as a god of the dead and his feast in the late spring is said to represent life returning to the land after the death of winter.[12]

When using the form 'ap' it is usually the father who is named, not the mother, but here the name is not given as Gwydion ap Beli but as the son of Don. Don is described as mother of the sacred tribe who by her marriage to Beli gave forth an extremely talented group of children who are known in myth as the 'Children (or sometimes Lords) of Light'. Of these children Gwydion was the eldest and was known as an astronomer and a master of light. He is often described as 'one of the men of science'. Amongst his brothers were Ameathon, who is said to have invented agriculture, and Govannan, who knew all the secrets of working metals. He also had a sister called Penardun, who married Lir, King of Ireland.

[10] Cusack, M.F.: *An Illustrated History of Ireland*, Dublin, 1869

[11] Bromwich, R.: *The Triads of the Island of Britain*, University of Wales Press, 1978

[12] Rolleston, T.W.: *Myths and Legends of the Celtic Race*, G.G. Harrap and Co., 1911

Don is considered by Celtic scholars to be a variant on the name Danu, who is the Irish mother of the sacred tribe of the Tuatha de Danann, who were also known as the Sons or Lords of Light.[13]

The Tuatha de Danann were very closely associated with Ireland's Boyne Valley megalithic complex, as we see later, and were believed to be able to control the light of the sun. At the first Battle of Moytura they won by smothering the land in darkness and hiding the light of the sun.[14] As we have seen, Celtic scholar T. W. Rolleston, long-time editor of *The Dublin University Review*, wrote of the links between the Celts and megalithic people:

> *The inferences, as I read the facts, seem to be that Druidism in its essential features was imposed upon the imaginative and sensitive nature of the Celt by the earlier population of Western Europe, the Megalithic People . . . The Megalithic People have been brought a step or two out of the atmosphere of uncanny mystery which has surrounded them and they are shown to have played a very important part in the religious development of Western Europe and in preparing that part of the world for the rapid extension of the special type of Christianity which took place in it . . . very soon after the conversion of Ireland to Christianity, we find the country covered with monasteries, whose complete organisation seems to indicate that they were really Druidic colleges transformed* en masse.[15]

The tales of the *Mabinogion* are drawn mainly from a 14th-century manuscript known as *The Red Book of Hergest* and are generally considered to have been fixed in their present form since the 10th or 11th century.[16] It is important to remember the context in which these tales survived. The object of a bard in telling a story is less to hand down a sacred text than to entertain a prince's court. The story interest is likely to be enhanced as the original myth is changed to improve the telling of the tale. There seemed to be a similarity between a myth about the marriage of foreign princess to an Irish king, who had founded a dynasty of High Kings of Ireland, with the story of the marriage of Don and Beli setting up the line of Tuatha de Danann and founding Druidism.

13 Matthews, J. and C.: *British and Irish Mythology*; The Aquarian Press, 1988
14 Hyde, D.: *A Literary History of Ireland*, T. Fisher Unwin, 1899
15 Rolleston, T.W.: *Myths and Legends of the Celtic Race*, G.G. Harrap and Co., 1911
16 Rolleston, T.W.: *Myths and Legends of the Celtic Race*, G.G. Harrap and Co., 1911

THE JERUSALEM CONNECTION

There is also a remarkable connection between the ancient kings of Jerusalem and the High Kings of Ireland. According to legend, Teamhair was the Israelite princess of the royal line of David, who came to Ireland and married Eochaid, to form the first royal family of Ireland. A few miles to the south of the Boyne Valley complex of megalithic sites is the Hill of Tara, where the ancient High Kings of Ireland were acclaimed by placing their foot on the Lia Fail, the Stone of Destiny. This magical stone, long since lost to Ireland, was said to have been brought from Jerusalem by the Prophet Jeremiah when he took *Teamhair* the daughter of King Zedekiah to the safety of Ireland to escape the wrath of the invading Babylonian King, Nebuchadnezzar.[17]

On 15 and 16 March 597 BC, Nebuchadnezzar seized Jerusalem and took the intellectuals of the city into captivity. A further battle took place and Jerusalem and its temple were destroyed in July 586 BC. King Zedekiah was brought before Nebuchadnezzar at Riblah, where he was forced to watch the killing of his sons before having his eyes torn from their sockets. According to Jewish legends, Zedekiah's daughters escaped because they were taken by Jeremiah to an island in the far north. The Stone of Destiny was said to have belonged to Jacob, the founder of the land of Israel, whose name stems from the Sumerian IA-A-GUB, which meant pillar.

It is said that this stone was taken to Scotland by Columba where it became the king-making Stone of Scone, upon which all kings and queens of England since Edward I (including Queen Elizabeth II) have had to sit when they are crowned.

The Hill of Tara is itself a megalithic mound and is near to two circular earthworks. This hill and the great mound of Newgrange have always been considered to be the homes of the fairy folk, the Tuatha De Danann or Tribe of Dana, who were sometimes called the 'Lords of Light'. The Hill of Tara was where a great foreign bard, Ollam Fodla, settled and established the line of the high kings, founded a Bardic school and set up the earliest Irish Laws, said to be based on the Ten Commandments.

We found it interesting that both Welsh and Irish folklore recalled its distant heroes as scientists, and that the oldest kings of cultural memory sprang from

[17] Looney, T.: Private Communication, 1986

a union between the royal blood of the Irish Sea community and the royal line of David (from which Jesus himself sprang). These two dynasties became interwoven at one of the most important megalithic sites that ever existed.

Could there be truth in the Jewish and Irish legends which independently tell such similar stories? Why did the Jewish princesses head for Ireland when the future of their own kingdom was in such doubt? Could it be that there had been an ancient linkage stemming back to the time of Enoch, when the leader of a Middle-Eastern people was brought to the megalithic sites of western Europe to be taught about astronomy?

In the light of these legends and what we now knew about the astronomical and calendar skills of the community that once lived around the Irish Sea, we decided to revisit the Book of Enoch and its astronomical teachings.

CONCLUSION

Bryn Celli Ddu on Anglesey, built circa 3,500 BC, is a sophisticated calendar machine which can be used to indicate the changing of the seasons. It has been so constructed that during important seasons it reflects light into different parts of its structure and produces dramatic and symbolic lighting effects.

The spiral, which is illuminated by reflected sunlight for a few minutes around dawn at the summer solstice, is a pictogram of the sun's shadow cast over a quarter of a year.

Around the winter solstice, the slot and pillar of the chamber accurately measure the angular distance of Venus from the sun, using the difference between daggers of light cast by the sun and Venus onto the pillar. The positioning of the slot has been carefully designed to make this possible.

Bryn Celli Ddu is thus a scientific instrument for creating and adjusting important calendary elements, including the times of planting, the state of the tides and length of the day. These drift out of synchronization if not regularly corrected, so its builders used Venus to provide the means of correction.

The legends of the site are linked to a mythic astronomer/bard called Gwydion ap Don, who can be shown to be a member of the legendary Irish tribe of gods known as the Tuatha de Danann. The Tuatha de Danann are linked through Irish legend to the line of King David, via the daughter of the biblical Zedekiah, who according to Irish folk tales made her home in exile in one of their old fairy palaces, the Hill of Tara, in the Boyne Valley of Ireland.

Both Welsh and Irish folklore have scientists as distant heroes, and the oldest kings in this cultural memory arose from a union between the royal blood of the Grooved Ware People and the royal line of David. Both groups seem to share the traditions recorded in the *Book of Enoch*.

Chapter Ten

REBUILDING URIEL'S MACHINE

ENOCH'S TUTORIAL

Despite our increased understanding of the 'Book of the Heavenly Luminaries', we remained convinced that there was much more information to be teased out of these ancient observations. Writer and engineer Alan Butler had already helped us immensely by sharing his work on megalithic mathematics, and we invited Alan to read the 'Book of the Heavenly Luminaries' and then spend some time with us to dissect its contents.

Alan arrived for a two-day stay to join us in a brainstorming session where we planned to deconstruct the strange visions of windows and portals described by Enoch. We all met on a sunny Saturday morning and settled round a large table with our notes before starting to discuss the possible meaning of each passage. At first the words 'window' and 'portal' seem to be used interchangably, but slowly things started to become clearer.

We were all agreed that the text specifically states that Enoch had been taken to one or more hilltop observatories by an advanced group of beings:

> *I was transported to another place and Uriel showed me towards the west, a large and lofty mountain of flint hard rock.*

Enoch then goes on to introduce portals and windows.

> *And I saw six portals in which the sun rises, and six portals in which*

the sun sets and the moon rises and sets in these portals, and the leaders of the stars and those whom they lead: six in the east and six in the west, and all following each other in accurately corresponding order: also many windows to the right and left of these portals.

We discussed what Enoch could be talking about and began to think that he was standing inside some sort of structure when Uriel showed him how the year was divided up, which is why he talked of seeing the sun rise and set in 'portals'. (The original word is usually translated as 'portals' although Black and Neugebauer prefer to use the modern word 'gates'.)

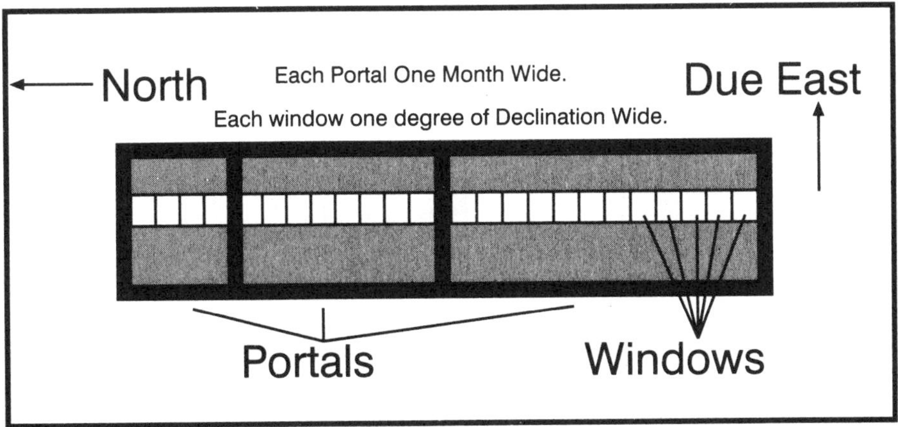

Figure 30. *The windows and portals described by Enoch.*

Perhaps Enoch was taken by Uriel inside some sort of sighting frame, rather than a room. We imagined a structure something like the uprights and trilithons at Stonehenge and decided this fitted quite closely what Enoch was describing. In such an arrangement it would be possible to engineer the gaps between the uprights to designate one month of the sun's movement – north or south of due east and west. The gap for the months immediately either side of east and west would be fairly wide, the next in each case narrower, and the next narrower still. There would be three portals to the north and three portals to the south of due east and west, making six on either side.

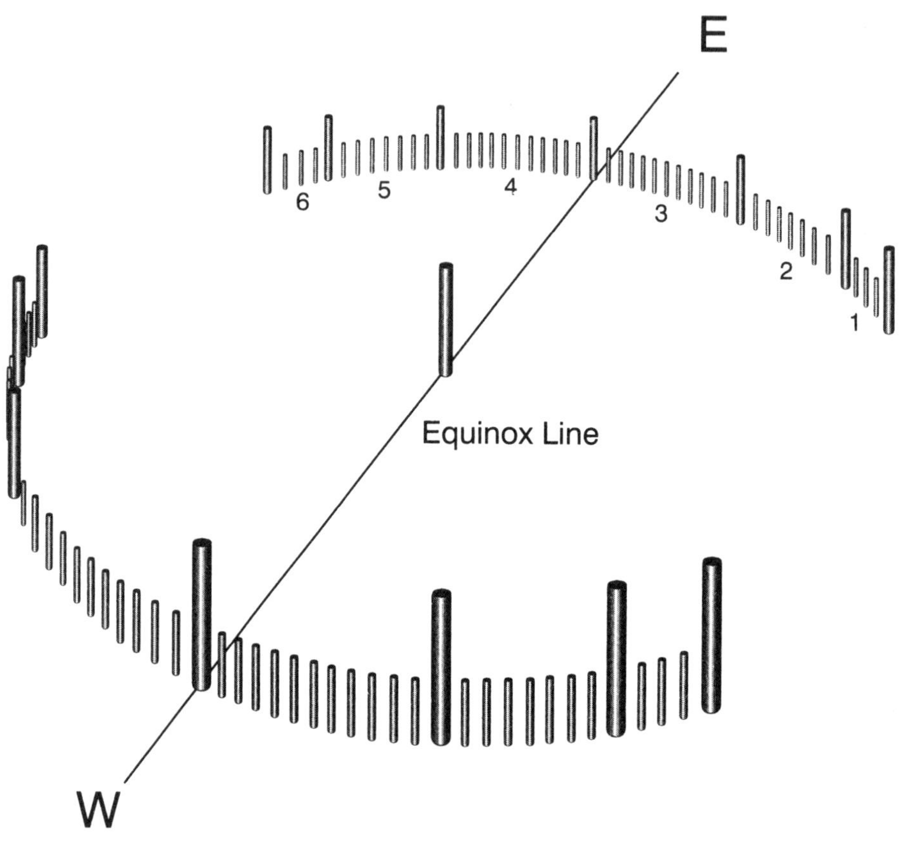

Figure 31. *A complete Uriel machine. The large posts mark the numbered portals and the small posts the windows.*

These portals are divided into smaller sections or windows, but not all portals have the same number of windows. The portals nearest to the east-west line have 12 windows, the next pair of portals outwards have eight, whilst the extreme outer portals have only four, making a total of 24 windows spread over three portals.

Enoch states that there are 12 windows in the portal that he calls 'The Great Portal' which is portal number four. This would be, together with portal number three, the largest of the portals, simply because the sun moves faster along the horizon either side of the equinox.

At this point in the story, it is important to be clear about why the sun seems to move along the horizon as the year progresses. The length of daylight varies though out the year, but there are two days in the year when the day and night are exactly the same length. These days are called an equinox, meaning equal day and night. The dates of these two days are around 21 March and 23 September, and on thesm the sun rises due east and sets due west. On all the other days of the year, the sun sets and rises somewhere else on the horizon. Both the rising and setting points move in the same way, so we will describe a sequence of setting points to illustrate how the sun moves.

If you watch the points where the sun sets throughout the year, starting from the spring equinox, you will notice that each night the sun sets slightly further to the north. Around the time of the equinox it is moving very rapidly, in fact at the latitude of Britain it sets about one-and-half-times its own diameter, further north each day. As the days lengthen, the sun's setting

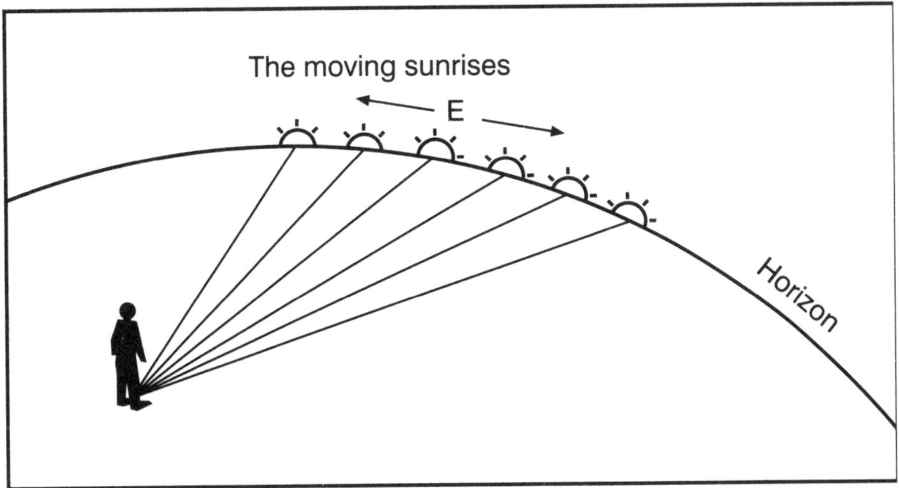

Figure 32. *How the horizon can be used to mark the sun's position.*

point slows down in its apparent movement north until eventually it stops and then starts to slowly return back towards the south. For a day or so, the movement of its setting points is so slight it seems to have stopped moving. At this time of year we get the longest days and shortest nights. This turning point where the sun's setting point stops, before returning back towards the south, is called the solstice (solstice literally means 'the sun coming to a stop'). After the solstice, which is about 21 June, the setting point will start to move slowly back south, increasing in speed along the horizon as the autumn equinox draws near around 23 September.

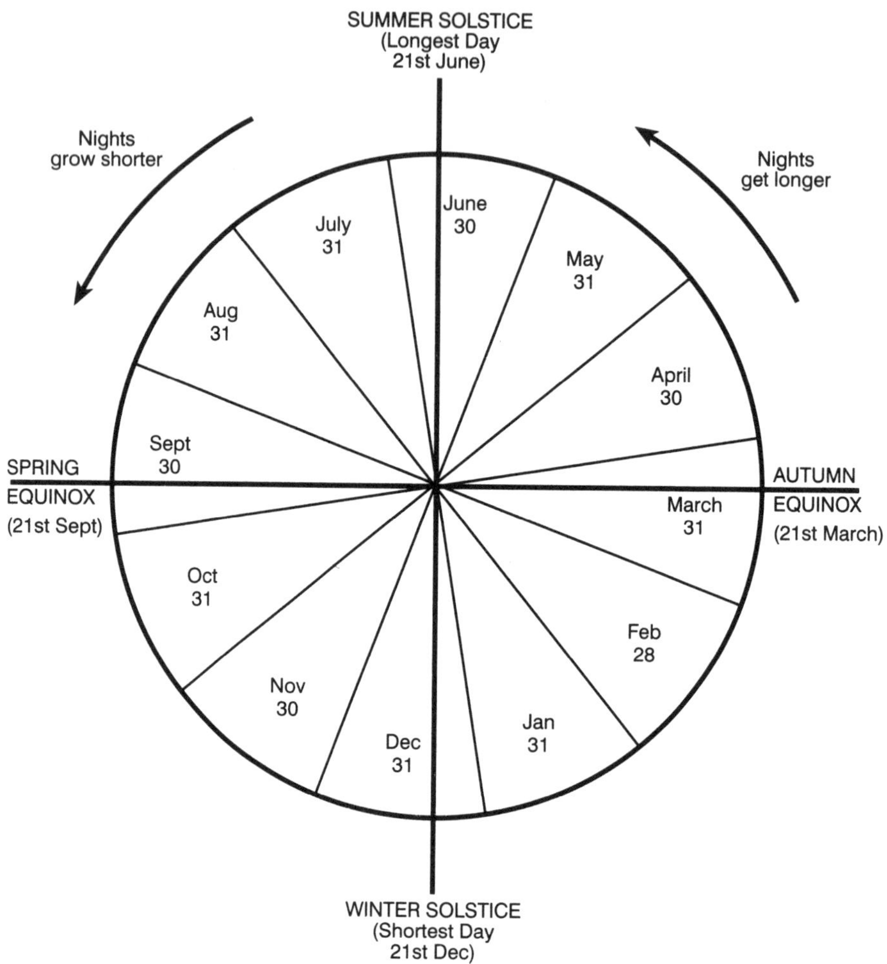

Figure 33. *How the length of day changes with the seasons.*

Now the same cycle will repeat, with the sun's setting point moving rapidly south from its due west setting point of the equinox. At first the sun moves very quickly, but as the days grow shorter the setting point will slow down in its movement south until at the winter solstice, around 21 December. Then it will again stop, reverse and start to move north again back towards its equinox position. You can imagine it rather like the swinging of a giant pendulum along the horizon, moving quickly at the bottom of its swing (the equinoxes), and slowing to a stop, then reversing at the extremes of its swing (the solstices).

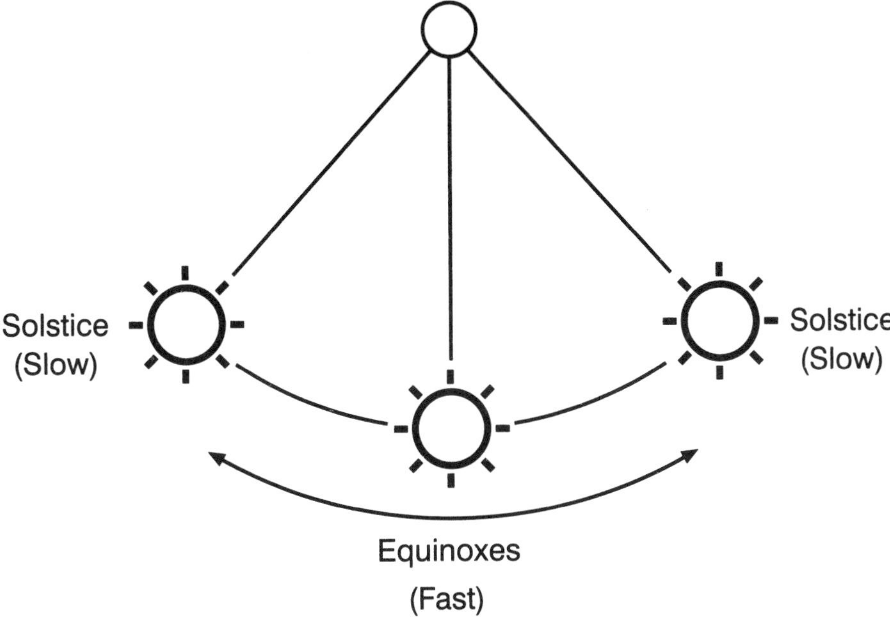

Figure 34. *The sun speeds up and slows down in its apparent movement along the horizon. This is similar to the movement of a pendulum.*

It is this movement north and south of the sun's rising and setting points which Enoch is evidently describing when he refers to the sun moving into different portals, and to the way the length of the night and the day changes.

As we thought about the implications of this, we realized that the windows seemed to represent some sort of measurement system. Certainly, Enoch states that measurements were made:

> *And I saw in those days how long cords were given to two angels and they took to themselves wings and flew, and they went towards the north. And I asked the angel who was with me, saying to him: 'Why have they taken those cords and gone off?' And he said to me, 'They have gone to measure.*

What were these angels measuring? Enoch seems to be describing an observatory which had an uninterrupted view of both the eastern and western horizons. He is suggesting that the windows are described as marking the sun's movement, and its track from one window to the next, shows the changes of its rising and setting points across the horizon.

Could he be measuring the azimuth of the sun's rising and setting point? we wondered. The azimuth is the angle between true north and the direction on the horizon where the sun rises. But this angle varies according to the observer's latitude, the height of the local horizon and the degree of refraction caused by local weather conditions. How could this possibly translate into a single machine? The size of the portals and windows would be different for every site.

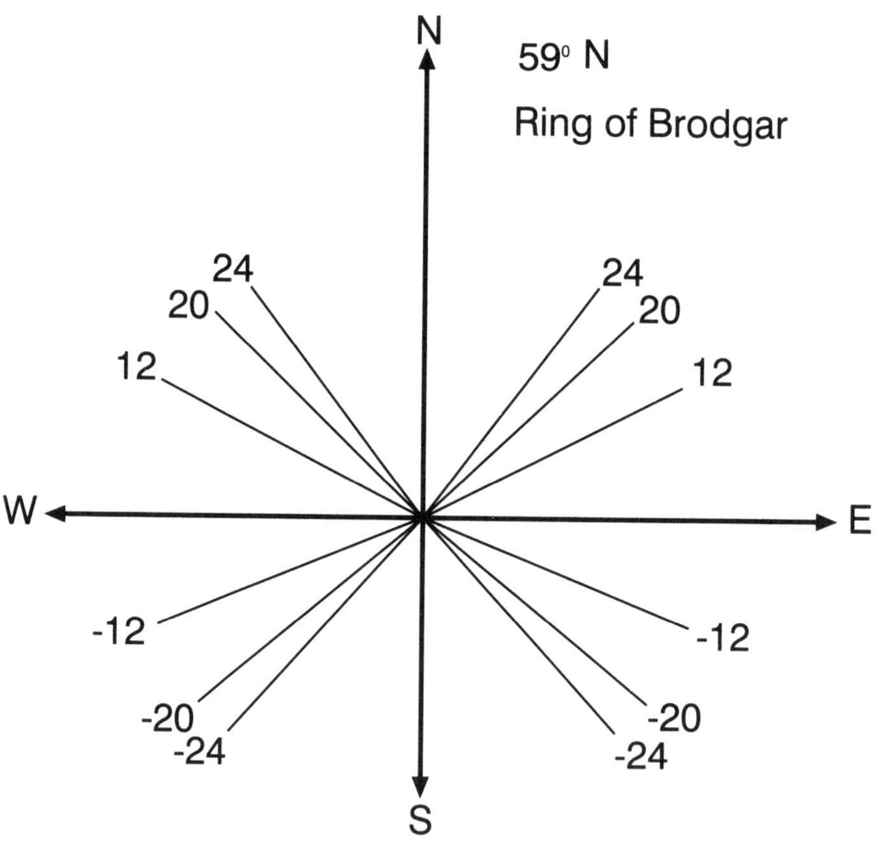

Figure 35. *The layout of an Uriel machine at the latitude of the Ring of Brodgar.*

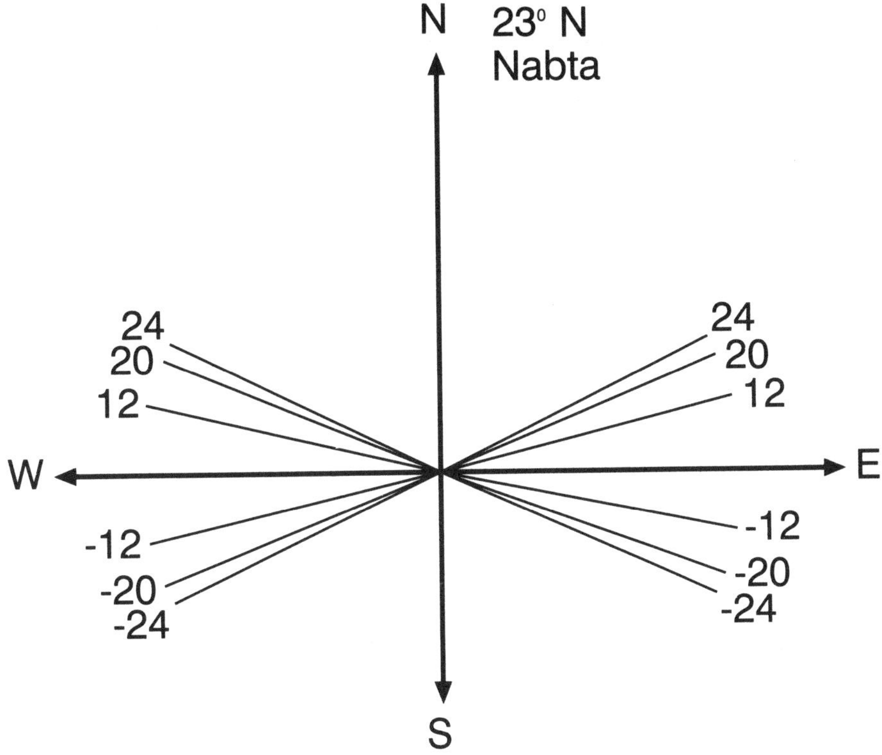

Figure 36. *The layout of an Uriel machine at the latitude of Nabta in southern Egypt.*

As we talked about the 'Book of the Heavenly Luminaries', it dawned on us that it seems to contain a description of a calendar machine which would work at any latitude, because its dimensions are given in terms of time of the sun's transit.

> *The sun goes down from the heaven and returns through the north in order to reach the east, and is so guided that he comes to the appropriate portal and shines in the face of the heaven. In this way he rises in the first month in the great portal, which is the fourth [those six portals in the east]. And in that fourth portal from which the sun rises in the first month are twelve window-openings, from which proceed a flame when they are opened in their season. When the sun*

rises in the heaven, he comes forth through that fourth portal thirty mornings in succession, and sets accurately in the fourth portal in the west of the heaven.

Defining the size of the windows in this way could take account of the problems of location. We drew diagrams and scribbled amendments as we worked out what being described by Enoch. The way the story is related makes it sound as though he was having trouble understanding a complex set of instructions being given to him in a tutorial by the angel Uriel. Our knowledge that Enoch had almost certainly had these experiences in the British Isles caused us to consider how the instructions received might connect in some way with megalithic structures we knew. Steadily, the sophistication of the device began to dawn upon us.

We knew from Thom's work[1] that the megalithic people had built orientated circles, of the type Enoch seemed to be describing, over many latitudes. We realized that once they had developed a uniform standard of measurement (the megalithic yard) they would have understood that the azimuth of the sun varied with geographical position. (For example, assuming a flat horizon, the calculated width of portal four is 20° at Stonehenge and 23° at Maes Howe, portal six is 5° at Stonehenge and 9° at Maes Howe). Yet they would have also seen that the sun is moving in a predictable and reproducible manner. Modern astronomers use a measure of location called declination to explain this difference between the position of the sun and the observed azimuth of its point of rising. If you look up at the sky, particularly at night, all the bright points of light look as if they are on an enormous rotating sphere which surrounds the earth. We call this trick of light the celestial sphere, and use it to orientate ourselves when describing the positions of stars independently of the position of the observer. The earth rotates on its own axis once every 23 hours and 56 minutes, so any star will reappear at the same point in the sky 23 hours and 56 minutes later (this is called the sidereal day). Only the sun takes 24 hours (the solar day) because the Earth is also moving in orbit around it. Astronomers draw up a set of latitude and longitude lines on this imaginary celestial sphere. The longitude is called the Right Ascension, and is measured in time from an arbitrarily chosen star (situated at the point known as the First Point of Aries, where the celestial equator and the plane

[1] Thom, A.: *Megalithic Sites in Britain*, Oxford University Press, 1968

of the ecliptic intersect) whilst the latitude is known as declination and measured in degrees, like terrestrial latitude.

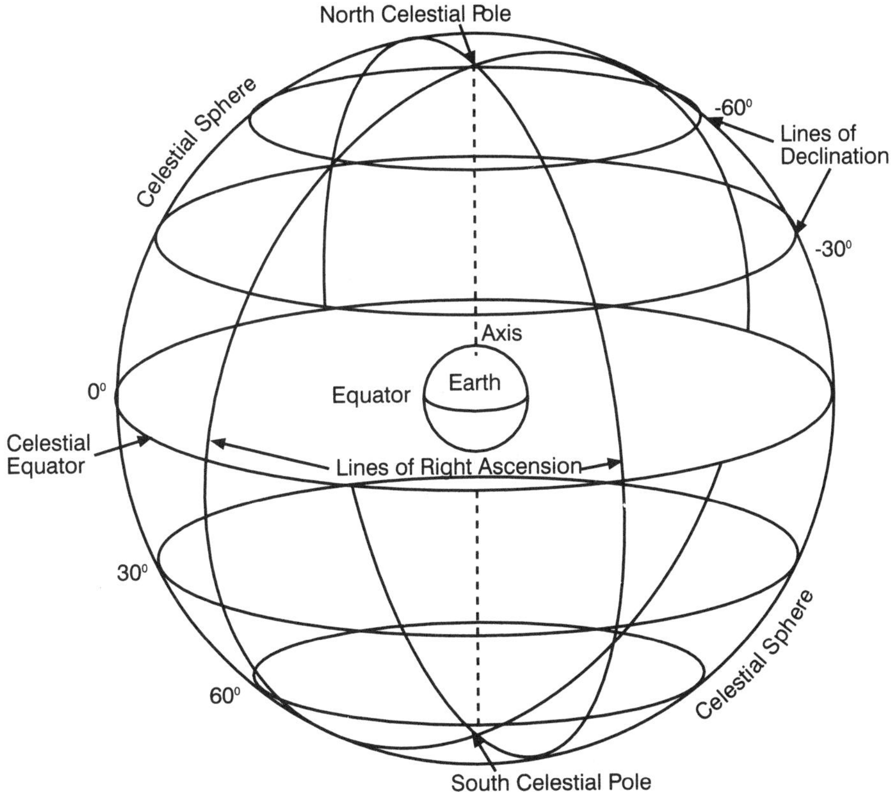

Figure 37. *How declination and right ascension are calculated.*

The ecliptic is the plane of the Earth's orbit around the sun, but because the earth is tilted on its axis by about 23.5°, the sun's declination varies from zero degrees at the equinox to plus 23.5° at the northern summer solstice and minus 23.5° at the northern winter solstice.

As we discussed the mechanism of declination and the choice of 12 windows in the great portal, then checking the sun's declination 30 days after the spring equinox. It worked out to be 11° and 55', as close as practically possible to 12. Now the choice of 12 windows was clear. Each window represented the degree of declination of whatever heavenly object

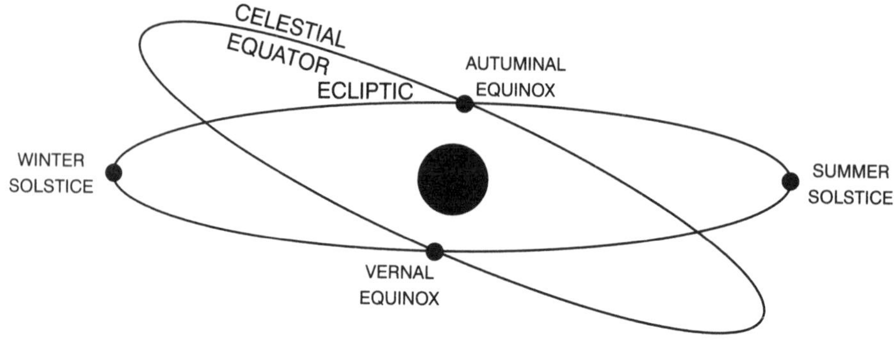

Figure 38. *Orbit of the earth around the sun.*

rose or set in it. The sun has a known variation of declination at particular times and so Uriel used it to standardize the positions of the measuring windows. We now knew why portal five needed eight windows to record the declination and portal six needed four, making a total of 24 windows in each quarter of Uriel's machine. The sophistication of the engineering was breathtaking. Uriel's machine created an extremely accurate horizon declinometer anywhere on the earth's surface by using the known position of the sun as a setting-up tool.

The 'Book of the Heavenly Luminaries' contains nothing less than a prehistoric blueprint to construct a calendar machine. The directions are as follows:

Step 1. Start on the spring equinox. This is the time when the morning and evening shadows on a standing stone form a straight line, and when the shadows of a pair of east-west aligned posts coincide both morning and evening. Set up a central viewing point and take a sighting on the position of the sunrise, and a sighting stone to mark the rising sun. In the evening set up a sighting stone where the sun sets (declination 0°).

Step 2. Count 30 sunrises and then fix another sighting stone at the points where the sun rises and a second one where it sets (declination plus 12°).

Step 3. Divide the distance between the each pair of markers into 12 equal segments, using smaller markers.

Step 4. Count another 30 sunrises and set another marker stone for the sunrise and the sun set (declination plus 20°).

Step 5. Divide the space between these two new pairs into eight equal segments, using smaller stones.

Step 6. Count another 30 sunrises and then mark the sunrise and sunset with a large stone marker (declination plus 24°).

Step 7. Divide the space between these last two stones into four equal segments with smaller stones.

Now to build the other half of the machine, wait until the autumn equinox, when the sun will again rise and set over the first markers. Carry out the same seven steps as the sun moves southwards, this time using the sun's negative declinations. After nine months you will have built a calendar machine which is also an accurate horizon-declinometer.

Although these instructions are very simple, they are obviously based on a thorough understanding of the science of astronomy. To put it another way, this blueprint was easy to follow, but Uriel and his fellow scientists must have had an encyclopaedic knowledge of the solar system in order to create it.

This revelation demonstrated that the machine that Uriel had revealed to Enoch was a simple but highly accurate means of measuring the declination (its apparent height in the sky above the celestrial horizon) of any heavenly object. All that a person had to do was observe in which window the star or planet they were interested in rose or set, and they would immediately know the declination of that object to an accuracy of one degree.

In essence, the markers of Uriel's machine provide a scale in degrees which uses the earth's horizon as a sight line – like aiming down a giant gun barrel to target any object around the plane of the ecliptic. The machine Uriel had described was a method of measuring the declination of any celestial object which falls within plus or minus 24° of the ecliptic. It was also an inspired

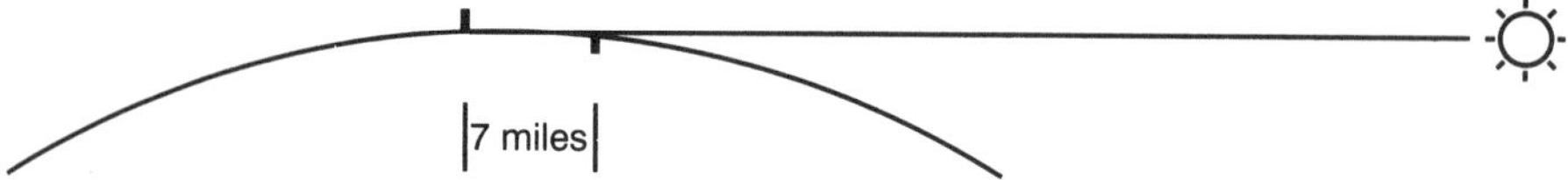

Figure 39. *How the horizon declinometer achieves great accuracy.*

machine which would work at any latitude and with any sort of horizon features, because it used the angle at which the sun became visible to set up the sighting angle.

Because Uriel's machine was constructed from direct observation at a given site, it would automatically take account of any variations in the local horizon. This means that each site would be different and the dimensions of the machine would certainly not be transportable to any other location.

As we considered this ingenious machine further, the range of possible uses began to unfold. The movements of the moon at its extreme positions can go to declinations of plus and minus 30°, six degrees outside the range of the machine, but all the heads of the stars within the plane of the zodiac and all the planets can be plotted. This makes a very useful observational tool which would have enabled Uriel to plot orbits and to predict eclipses (which can only occur when the moon has a declination of zero and is in the same plane as the sun and the earth).

Amazingly, Uriel's machine is also capable of predicting the orbits of comets, and it is clear that the angel Raguel described a major comet to Enoch:

> *[Chapter 23 v 1-4]*
> *From thence I was transported to another place, to the west, right to the ends of the earth. And I saw a blazing fire which ran without resting and did not flag in its course, holding to it equally by day and by night. And I asked, saying, 'What is this that has no rest?' Then Raguel, one of the holy angels who was with me, answered me and said to me; 'This fiery sign follows the luminaries.*[2]

[2] The *Book of Enoch*

We believe that this is a reference to the comet which was the cause of Uriel's concern and the reason why he was trying to educate unsophisticated people such as Enoch, so that they could rebuild civilization if they survived the expected impact. We had already found, from geological and magneto-stratigraphical evidence, that there have been at least two cometary impacts within the last 10,000 years. The first major impact had caused world-wide tidal waves and swamped the British Isles in 7640 BC. But we had also found evidence of a smaller impact (discussed in Chapter Three), confirmed during a conversation with Professor Liritzis of Rhodes University, which was localized to the Mediterranean region around 3150 BC.[3] Although we believe Uriel's people were skilled enough in astronomy to predict an impact, they would not be able to forecast exactly where it would hit. They would only know that any comet has a greatly increased probability of hitting the earth if it is travelling around the sun in the plane of the ecliptic.

Thinking about the dilemma facing Uriel's people when the observatory described in the 'Book of the Heavenly Luminaries' observed this comet within the plane of the ecliptic and on a possible collision course, we tried to think what we would do if we had the responsibility of trying to save our civilization.

Uriel's people knew about the major disaster that had unfolded when the last cometary impacts had occurred over 4,000 years previously (i.e. 7640 BC), and they understood the effects the impacts would have on any survivors. They must have realized that any survivors would need to recreate their calendar if they were to have a good chance of re-establishing agriculture. Once the tidal waves had receded there would be a prolonged 'nuclear winter', during which time nobody would have any idea of the passage of the seasons. If any stored seeds were to have a chance of providing a harvest, they would need to have the best possible opportunity of germination by being planted during the correct season. The gift Uriel gave to the survivors was a chance to re-establish an agricultural civilization in the shortest possible time.

The comet-measuring facility of the Uriel machine would have told its users that this particular comet was directly on course for an Earth impact. They would have known this because the closer the rising of the comet is to the centre of the junction of portals number three and four (see Figure 31), the more probable an impact is. Again, the principle was to use the plane of

[3] Professor Ioannis Liritzis, University of Rhodes, Private Communication

the land to give a perfect sighting line along the plane of the ecliptic.

This ancient machine is nothing less than a celestial computer.

To create a simple machine which allows accurate measurement of the angle of declination of any visible heavenly body implies a high degree of skill in observational astronomy. To be able to translate this knowledge into a simple set of instructions, which would enable someone without any technical knowledge to build an accurate calendar machine from the simplest of readily available materials, is a work of engineering genius.

If civilization was to have any chance of survival after the expected cometary impact then it would be important that the specialized calendars of agriculture, tides and ritual were re-calibrated. But the astronomer-priests who had controlled the function of this calendar could not be sure that they would be amongst the survivers. So they must have known that if their knowledge was to survive, then it would need to be spread as widely as possible and in a form that was simple to understand.

It struck us that this situation is rather like the recent invention of the clockwork radio, designed for use in remote places such as the African bush where spare batteries are not readily available. This radio is technically simple but the science behind it is considerable. We may imagine that Uriel's people, rather than trying to teach Enoch higher mathematics, would have decided instead to give him just enough knowledge to draw practical benefit from their technology.

THE INSTRUCTIONS

As far as we know, the 'Book of the Heavenly Luminaries' was first written down with the rest of the *Book of Enoch* by the people of the Qumran Community around 200 BC. By that time it had survived as an oral tradition for around 3,000 years (that is, from just before the cometary impact of 3150 BC) and not surprisingly, the instructions on how to build and use a horizon declinometer had become a little garbled. Uriel was obviously a good teacher because he concluded with a summary of what he had taught Enoch. Because these instructions are fundamental to understanding Uriel's machine, the following is taken from Charles' 1912 translation of the *Book of Enoch*, as Charles' use of 'portals' and 'windows' is more helpful than Black's usage in understanding the text.[4]

[4] Charles, R.H.: The *Book of Enoch*, Oxford University Press, 1912

Chapter 72
The book of the courses of the luminaries of the heaven, the relations of each, according to their classes, their dominion and their seasons, according to their names and places of origin, and according to their months, which Uriel, the holy angel, who was with me, who is their guide, showed me; and he showed me all their laws exactly as they are, and how it is with regard to all the years of the world and unto eternity, till the new creation is accomplished which dureth till eternity.

And this is the first law of the luminaries: the luminary the Sun has its rising in the eastern portals of the heaven, and its setting in the western portals of the heaven. And I saw six portals in which the sun rises, and six portals in which the sun sets and the moon rises and sets in these portals, and the leaders of the stars and those whom they lead: six in the east and six in the west, and all following each other in accurately corresponding order: also many windows to the right and left of these portals. And first there goes forth the great luminary, named the Sun, and his circumference is like the circumference of the heaven, and he is quite filled with illuminating and heating fire. The chariot on which he ascends, the wind drives, and the sun goes down from the heaven and returns through the north in order to reach the east, and is so guided that he comes to the appropriate (lit. 'that') portal and shines in the face of the heaven.

In this way he rises in the first month in the great portal, which is the fourth [of those six portals in the east]. And in that fourth portal from which the sun rises in the first month are twelve window-openings, from which proceed a flame when they are opened in their season. When the sun rises in the heaven, he comes forth through that fourth portal thirty mornings in succession, and sets accurately in the fourth portal in the west of the heaven. And during this period the day becomes daily longer and the night nightly shorter to the thirtieth morning. On that day the day is longer than the night by a ninth part, and the day amounts exactly to ten parts and the night to eight parts.

And the sun rises from that fourth portal, and sets in the fourth and returns to the fifth portal of the east thirty mornings, and rises from it and sets in the fifth portal. And then the day becomes longer by two parts and amounts to eleven parts, and the night becomes shorter and amounts to seven parts.

And it returns to the east and enters into the sixth portal, and rises and sets in the sixth portal one-and-thirty mornings on account of its sign. On that day the day becomes longer than the night, and the day becomes double the night, and the day becomes twelve parts, and the night is shortened and becomes six parts.

This is one of the sections where Enoch records the relative length of the day and night at the time the observation is made. He does not at any time imply a linear rate of change leading to a zigzag pattern of daylight as suggested by Neugebauer.[5] Enoch is clearly a novice doing his best to describe the relative length of day and night at the time the observation is made, but he may not even have been at the same latitude when he made the different observations.

And the sun mounts up to make the day shorter and the night longer, and the sun returns to the east and enters into the sixth portal, and rises from it and sets thirty mornings.

And when thirty mornings are accomplished, the day decreases by exactly one part, and becomes eleven parts, and the night seven. And the sun goes forth from that sixth portal in the west, and goes to the east and rises in the fifth portal for thirty mornings, and sets in the west again in the fifth western portal. On that day the day decreases by two parts, and amounts to ten parts and the night to eight parts.

And the sun goes forth from that fifth portal and sets in the fifth portal of the west, and rises in the fourth portal for one and-thirty mornings on account of its sign, and sets in the west. On that day the day is equalised with the night, [and becomes of equal length], and the night amounts to nine parts and the day to nine parts.

And the sun rises from that portal and sets in the west, and returns to the east and rises thirty mornings in the third portal and sets in the west in the third portal. And on that day the night becomes longer than the day, and night becomes longer than night, and day shorter than day till the thirtieth morning, and the night amounts exactly to ten parts and the day to eight parts.

And the sun rises from that third portal and sets in the third portal in the west and returns to the east, and for thirty mornings rises in the

[5] Neugebauer, Otto, Appendix A, in Black, Matthew: *The Book of Enoch or I Enoch, A New English Edition*, Leiden, E.J. Brill, 1985

second portal in the east, and in like manner sets in the second portal in the west of the heaven. And on that day the night amounts to eleven parts and the day to seven parts.

And the sun rises on that day from that second portal and sets in the west in the second portal, and returns to the east into the first portal for one-and-thirty mornings, and sets in the first portal in the west of the heaven. And on that day the night becomes longer and amounts to the double of the day: and the night amounts exactly to twelve parts and the day to six.

And the sun has (therewith) traversed the divisions of his orbit and turns again on those divisions of his orbit, and enters that portal thirty mornings and sets also in the west opposite to it. And on that night has the night decreased in length by a ninth part, and the night has become eleven parts and the day seven parts. And the sun has returned and entered into the second portal in the east, and returns on those his divisions of his orbit for thirty mornings, rising and setting. And on that day the night decreases in length, and the night amounts to ten parts and the day to eight.

And on that day the sun rises from that portal, and sets in the west, and returns to the east, and rises in the third portal for one-and-thirty mornings, and sets in the west of the heaven. On that day the night decreases and amounts to nine parts, and the day to nine parts, and the night is equal to the day and the year is exactly as to its days three hundred and sixty-four.

And the length of the day and of the night, and the shortness of the day and of the night arise-through the course of the sun these distinctions are made (lit. ' they are separated'). So it comes that its course becomes daily longer, and its course nightly shorter.

And this is the law and the course of the sun, and his return as often as he returns sixty times and rises, i.e. the great luminary which is named the sun, for ever and ever. And that which (thus) rises is the great luminary, and is so named according to its appearance, according as the Lord commanded. As he rises, so he sets and decreases not, and rests not, but runs day and night, and his light is sevenfold brighter than that of the moon; but as regards size they are both equal.

The next few chapters describe how to use the machine to measure the orbit of the moon; the body with the most complex celestial movements. Then the section on the observational machine closes with these comments in Chapter 74; 1-3:

> *And I saw another course, a law for her [the moon], (and) how according to that law she performs her monthly revolution. And all these Uriel, the holy angel who is the leader of them all, showed to me, and their positions, and I wrote down their positions as he showed them to me, and I wrote down their months as they were, and the appearance of their lights till fifteen days were accomplished.*

The skill of Uriel in designing the machine for use by unskilled people shows in the way that the positioning of the sighting windows, or sighting poles, is described in terms of the time at which the alignment should be sighted and set up. This technique takes care of the difference in angle which occurs at different latitudes. For an Uriel machine to work, the viewing angles are entirely dependent on the latitude it lies on. (See Figures 35 and 36.)

This is very difficult concept to explain to anybody who does not have a basic knowledge of astronomy and an appreciation of the tilt of the Earth's axis. By describing the machine in terms of elapsed time from a known orientation, i.e. the equinox, the machine is designed in such a way that it will automatically adjust for different latitudes.

Although the description of the machine in the Book of Enoch quoted above is elaborate, it can be summarized as a seven-step algorithm, which we gave earlier in this chapter (pp 246-247.)

RESURRECTING URIEL'S MACHINE

We decided the best way to understand the workings of this machine was to build our own.

Fortunately, there was a perfect site close to where we both live in West Yorkshire. On a lonely hilltop with breath-taking panoramas stands a ruined megalithic stone circle, and although none of the standing stones is left in place, the area of the original circle is still clearly visible. This observatory was built by the people of a large ancient settlement known as Meg's Dyke, the remains of which are less than a mile away. We therefore decided to build the machine on this original site using slender wooden staves to mark the positions of the sun.

We received the permission of Mr Clarkson, the farmer who owns the site to visit it regularly and to leave marker pegs in place. He warned us that he couldn't promise that his sheep and cows wouldn't disturb our sticks, and we soon learned to make sure they were well planted, as the sheep in particular seemed to consider each new stick a delightful personal scratching post.

At the times prescribed by Enoch's instructions, we went to the circle to take sightings from the centre of the ring towards the horizon, and then place a stick on the sight line. We started at the autumn equinox, taking a sighting from the centre towards the rising sun to mark the point and then in the evening taking another sighting on the setting sun. We confirmed the alignment's accuracy by sighting along the two outer markers and the centre point to see they all lined up. We continued to take regular sightings and built up the machine slowly. Not every dawn or sunset was clear, but if it was clear the day before we took a provisional sighting in case of bad weather and were lucky enough not to get more than three successive days of overcast dawns and sunsets.

One of the first things we believed about building the machine was that we needed at least two people to take a sighting. One stood with an eye-level sighting stick in the centre of the circle (a sighting stick was used to make sure all the horizon sightings were done at the same azimuth), whilst the other moved the horizon-marking post on the perimeter of the circle until it aligned with the sun's disc. (See Plates 18 and 19.)

We used this method on all the early sightings until November, when we had a run of bad weather in the evenings, and were struggling to get a marker for the boundary between portal 8 and portal 7. As Robert was coming home from work, the sky suddenly cleared to a beautiful sunset – so he rushed to the Ringstone, arriving as the sun was brushing the horizon – but he had no-one to hold the sighting stick. Forced to consider a single-handed method of marking, he realized that his shadow formed a perfect sighting line. By standing outside the circle, holding the marking stave, he moved until the long shadow thrown by his staff touched the centre marker of the circle. The point where the staff shadow crossed the circle perimeter was where the marker post needed to go. His shadow was well over 100 feet long as the sun set, and provided an extremely accurate marker. The horizon markers could be placed very accurately by a single individual, and what is perhaps more important, the shadow of a staff could be used to take a very accurate reading of the position of the sun within the portal.

We conducted a number of random measurements of the sun's declination using this method and then checked the reading with astronomical tables. It soon became obvious that our resurrected Uriel machine was accurate to within half a degree, even with an extremely quick measurement. The only thing to watch out for was the time the measurement was taken, as it had to be done when the sun was grazing the horizon.

The site of this ancient stone circle is a round, flat-topped hill, sloping slightly to the south, within a circle of large hills. This afforded many horizon features to mark the sun's position, and gave uninterrupted access for the sun's light from every direction when it rises or sets. The flat top of the hill makes for very long shadows when the sun is grazing the horizon, and seems to be a deliberate feature in the choice of the site. Certainly there are few places which provide such ideal conditions, and the topology of the ground near Meg's Dyke is nowhere near as good for shadow casting. If its ancient inhabitants had wanted a site for accurate calendar measurement, there would have been nowhere better for many miles in any direction. It therefore seemed probable that the megalithic settlement had been constructed at Meg's Dyke because it was near to the observatory, rather than the other way around.

One important point that we learned from building the machine was the oddness of the year. We know that it takes the Earth approximately 365.25 days to complete an orbit of the sun. Because it is impossible to have a quarter day we take a year as being 365 days and have leap years every fourth year, when we add an extra day to the month of February. This more-or-less harmonizes our normal calendar with the movements of the sun. Building an Uriel machine forced us to strip away our preconceptions of what a year is, and think simply as its creators had. Counting the days from one winter solstice to the next, there were 366 sunrises between the two alignments, and we believe that the megalithic mathematician decided that there were 366 days in the year.

Our normal year of 365 days does not split up into the equal four parts which the solstices and equinoxes seem at first glance to suggest. Counting the year in sunrises, as these megalithic people did, we noticed that the year is actually asymmetrical due to the eccentricity of the earth's orbit. This is so because there are 182 sunrises from the winter solstice to summer solstice, whereas there are 183 sunrises from summer solstice back to winter solstice. The same asymmetry occurs if you count from the spring equinox to the autumn equinox, which gives 183 days, while autumn back to spring gives 182 days. Only in a leap year are both halves equal.

A MEGALITHIC STANDARD

Once rediscovered, Uriel's machine turned out to be the key that would lead us to solve the problem (as we saw in Chapter Eight) Professor Thom had found so elusive – the secret of the megalithic yard. Thom had very skilfully demonstrated that this 2-foot-8.64-inch-long 'megalithic yard' was in evidence throughout the structures of much of western Europe, but he could not identify how it had been arrived at, nor could he fathom how it had been replicated so accurately over such a huge area.

After surveying more than 600 sites throughout Britain, Thom commented on the accuracy of the unit of length saying:

> *This unit was in use from one end of Britain to the other. It is not possible to detect by statistical examination any differences between the values determined in the English and Scottish circles. There must have been a headquarters from which standard rods were sent out . . . The length of rods in Scotland cannot have differed from that in England by more than 0.03 inch or the difference would have shown up. If each small community had obtained the length by copying the rod of its neighbour to the south the accumulated error would have been much greater than this.*[6]

Like Professor Thom, we suspected that this standard unit had to have some physical reality. It seemed impossible for it to be arbitrary, because the minds of the megalithic peoples had already proved to be fully orientated to the observable movements of the solar system. From Alan Butler's work we knew that megalithic geometry had linked together time and distance as a coherent whole. Surely, we thought, these people had to have derived this unit from their observations.

This notion was simple to arrive at; the proof took rather longer.

We drew Alan Butler into the discussion because his mind was so well attuned to megalithic mathematics, and his detailed knowledge of astrology

[6] Thom, A.: *Megalithic Sites in Britain*, Oxford University Press, 1968

gave him an insight into the human relationship with the movement of the heavens.

The discussion about what might lie at the heart of the megalithic yard continued for some time, covering everything from harmonics to geo-trigonometry. Strange questions were debated, such as: if we created an organ pipe one megalithic yard long, what note would it produce when blown? We seemed to be getting nowhere, then, slowly but surely, the discussions came around to another question: how could the Grooved Ware People have developed a concept of time?

Time, we decided, had to be the key. But how could they accurately measure the passing of time without a clock?

One idea which seemed possible was that the movement of the moon relative to the fixed stars could be used to calculate the time during the night – but the calculations seemed extremely complicated and too clumsy for people who had developed such an elegant and simple system of geometry. Next we moved on to consider timing the movements of fixed stars, remembering that this was how 18th-century inventor John Harrison had checked the time-keeping of his early sea clocks.

Any pair of separated posts will produce a fixed time if the passage of a bright star from one post to the next is observed, because once the posts are fixed, any major star can be chosen to produce a period of time that will always be the same to an accuracy of a second or so. This is because the movement measured has nothing to do with the star, but everything to do with the rotation of the Earth. Put simply, observing a star move from one fixed point to another gives a reading of the planet's rotation that will never vary, and we already knew that this was how the Grooved Ware People solved the problem of translating the sun's declination to an horizon-azimuth measurement.

The idea of watching a star's path between two points was fairly straightforward, yet we needed to know what distance apart the poles might have been set. We also needed to consider how the Grooved Ware People might have translated this time period into a form that they could use at any part of the night. We knew that these People had divided the circle into 366 parts (discussed in Chapter Eight) because there are that number of sunrises in one orbit of the sun, so it seemed reasonable to assume that they would have used one 366th part of the horizon (one megalithic degree) as the basic measure of a star's path. If so, they would have simply divided a large circle into 366 parts (easily done by trial and error) and watched a bright star traverse between two of the posts.

The only way we could think of to record the time interval, in a manner that could be recorded and reproduced in daylight, was to do what all traditional clocks do – swing a pendulum. We had many false starts, but eventually Alan Butler suggested the idea of swinging a weight and shortening its length to speed it up and lengthening it to slow it down. We knew that the number 366 was central – and almost magical – to these megalithic builders, so we adjusted the line until it gave exactly 366 beats for the full appearance of a star between two posts placed a megalithic degree apart.

As a 366th part of one revolution of the Earth, a megalithic degree is equal to just over 236 seconds, or 3.93 minutes of time. Through trial and error we found the length of line (between fulcrum and the centre of the weight) that produces exactly 366 pulses (a pulse being a full swing from one extremity to the other). We then measured this line and found it to be 16.32 inches in length.

For a brief moment it seemed to be far too short to be of any interest, then we remembered that Thom had doubled up the basic unit he had found to make his megalithic yard appear close to a modern yard. He had observed the smaller unit but chose to call it a 'half megalithic yard'. So we doubled our length, and it came out to exactly 32.64 inches – a precise megalithic yard!

So here was the answer to one of the greatest puzzles of prehistory.

What these ancient engineers had done was to mark out a circle of substantial diameter using a cord and centre pin, and then divide the circumference into exactly 366 equal cords by trial and error. They had then erected two posts to mark out one 366th part of the circle, and swung an adjustable pendulum until it produced exactly 366 beats during the transit of a convenient bright star between the two posts. The length of the pendulum is now exactly one half of a megalithic yard, a basic unit of construction discovered by Professor Thom when he surveyed hundreds of ancient sites in Scotland, England, Wales and western France.[8]

The thought of these prehistoric people measuring out the circles with lines suddenly made complete sense out of one of the passages from the *Book of Enoch* that we had just looked at:

[7] Sobel, D.: *Longitude*, Fourth Estate, 1996
[8] Thom, A.: *Megalithic Sites in Britain*, Oxford University Press, 1968

And I saw in those days how long cords were given to two angels and they took to themselves wings and flew, and they went towards the north. And I asked the angel who was with me, saying to him: 'Why have they taken those cords and gone off?' And he said to me, 'They have gone to measure.'

Once understood, anyone could use this principle to find the 'sacred' length without reference to anyone else. It would work every time, everywhere, and it would be totally accurate. This explains the consistency that so amazed the eminent professor.

A classic example of the use of this megalithic principle came to light when Robert later visited a site known as 'The Hill of Many Staines' at Caithness in northern Scotland. At first glance the rows of equally spaced standing stones seemed to form a rectangular grid which was aligned due north-south and east-west, but when looked at more closely, the fan shape previously recorded by Thom could be seen. The work required to set up so many stones must have been immense, and when Thom had surveyed them he had found that the fan-shaped structure had the narrow part of the fan pointing north. He had observed that the spokes of the fan were each separated by the same angle of 1.28°, which we knew was exactly the angle which a fixed star will move on successive nights.

In this way, then, the lines of the stone fan were separated by exactly the same angle as the zodiac moves each successive night. The site was, and still is, an accurate chronometer. Any of the 12 first-magnitude stars (that is, those bright enough to be seen whilst rising, in contrast to less-bright stars, which have to be high in the sky to be observed) would be visible as it moved over the first line of the fan. Then, for the next 18 nights, the exact same time would be observed when the chosen star arrived over the next line of the fan. Additionally, when the moon was full and due south, as shown by the north-south centre line of the fan, the sun would be exactly opposite the moon and its position relative to the earth would be known. Combining this knowledge with an position of a known first-magnitude star also gives a means of calculating longitude!

The megalithic unit of measurement used at 'The Hill of Many Staines', and other sites up to 1300 kilometres away, is a truly staggering concept of measurement. Professor Thom's megalithic yard was based on pure geometrics, derived from three absolutely fundamental values:

1. The orbit of the Earth around the sun

2. The rotation of the Earth on its own axis

3. The mass of the Earth

The Earth's orbit gave the 366 split of the horizon, the rotation of the Earth gave the timespan, and the mass of the planet (gravity) dictated the length of the line to give 366 beats.

Simply brilliant!

CONCLUSION

The portals and windows described in a section of the *Book of Enoch* called the 'Book of the Heavenly Luminaries', are part of a description of how to build a sophisticated horizon declinometer for measuring the position of any bright object in the sky. The device is calibrated using the known position of the sun by timing its rising and setting from the equinoxes, which are easy to determine accurately.

We decided to rebuild an Uriel machine on the site of a ruined stone circle in West Yorkshire, following the instructions from the Book of Enoch. As we built it and came to understand the celestial geometry used in its design, it was clear that it could be used as an highly accurate timing device.

By experiment, the physical principle behind the megalithic yard is shown to be related to the principles of the Uriel machine, and, as a result, the lost physical principle behind the megalithic yard is rediscovered.

[9] Thom, A.: *Megalithic Sites in Britain*, Oxford University Press, 1968

Chapter Eleven

THE VENUS CHAMBER

THE WHITE WALL

The megalithic yard was found by Professor Thom throughout most of the 'Enoch Zone' (as defined in Chapter Seven), which was once home to the Grooved Ware People. The major exceptions were the megalithic sites of Ireland, which apparently showed no correspondence with this unit of measurement. We decided that we needed to try and understand why this western side of the zone was different, and so we booked a flight to Dublin and a hired a car to drive north to the Boyne Valley, where some of the most splendid megalithic sites in the world are to be found. The world's oldest stone-lined chambers, known as tunnel mounds, were built here well over 5,000 years ago.

We arrived on St Brigit's Day (1st February), a Christian festival adopted from the half quarter day which is the old Celtic Feast of Brigid. St Brigit is celebrated in Roman Catholic myth as the midwife to Mary, mother of Jesus and wet-nurse to Jesus himself. The date of the Celtic Brigid's festival originally marked the halfway point between the winter solstice and the spring equinox and the time when the first sheep's milk of the year became available, but like Christmas, Easter and scores of other ancient festival days, it is now just one meaningless day on the Roman Catholic calendar.

It was a beautiful cloudless day as we headed north out through the Dublin suburb of Swords and up the N1 to the market town of Drogheda. The scenery of the eastern seaboard of Ireland is spectacular, with the broad sweeps of the bays and headlands giving a long string of safe havens for small boats. The currachs of the ancient Britons gave way to the fleets of small fishing boats and have in their turn been replaced by the leisure craft of today, but the sea is still the convenient means of transport it always has been for the lands surrounding the Irish Sea.

At Drogheda we turned left up the Boyne Valley, in the general direction of the Hill of Tara where the ancient High Kings of Ireland had been acclaimed by placing their foot on the Lia Fail, the Stone of Destiny. The road became little more than a country lane as it followed the southern side of the River Boyne. Then through the trees, across the river, we suddenly saw the great white wall of Newgrange on the skyline. We stopped the car and admired the dramatic hemispherical wall of white quartz as it sparkled in the sharp winter sunshine.

It took us nearly an hour, and a full circumnavigation of the area, before we realized that things had changed considerably since Robert's last visit several years before. It turned out that we had stopped the car to admire Newgrange almost in front of the new £5 million visitor centre, but it was so well-blended into the landscape we had missed it completely. Once inside, we found it superbly equipped to introduce visitors to the history of the region before they are taken by bus to the actual structure known as Newgrange.

This imposing site is one of the best examples of a type that archaeologists inevitably describe as a passage tomb. It was built nearly 1,000 years before the pyramids of Egypt, using 280,000 tons of river rolled stones, and its eastern section is faced with quartz on top of a ring of dressed granite stones. As we stood in front of the huge, white-crystal wall of Newgrange, we were both powerfully reminded of the words of Enoch, who was almost certainly a nomadic tent dweller:

> *And I went in till I drew nigh to a wall which is built of crystals and surrounded by tongues of fire: and it began to affright me. And I went into the tongues of fire and drew nigh to a large house which was built of crystals: and the walls of the house were like a tessellated floor of crystals, and its groundwork was of crystal. Its ceiling was like the path of the stars and the lightnings, and between them were fiery cherubim, and their heaven was (as clear as) water. A flaming fire surrounded the walls, and its portals blazed with fire. And I entered into that house, and it was hot as fire and cold as ice: there were no*

> *delights of life therein: fear covered me, and trembling got hold upon me. And as I quaked and trembled, I fell upon my face.*

We have dated Enoch's journey of instruction as happening shortly before the comet impact of *circa* 3150 BC (see Chapter Six), and we also know that he was in the British Isles because of his latitude and because of the instruction he received in astronomical matters. So he could have been describing Newgrange itself, which was built less than 50 years earlier than his visit to the cold north.

Indeed, what else could Enoch have been describing? As far as archaeology knows, there were no other buildings on this scale anywhere in the world at this early date. And certainly none known to have been built of crystals!

Could anyone doubt it? Enoch describes the building to which he was taken as 'a large house built of crystals' and 'the walls of the house were like a tessellated floor of crystals'. We had never seen a building dressed with white quartz crystal before, let alone one that is in the right place and at the right time for Enoch's visit. Furthermore, the description of the wall looking like a tessellated floor is accurate for Newgrange because the quartz is regularly interspersed with water-rounded black rocks that form diamond shapes across the entire surface. Enoch's description of fire surrounding the walls could be either a description of the building's brilliance in sunlight, or of it surrounded by torches at night. Perhaps the ring of torches is more likely because Enoch describes hail and snow, so perhaps his visit took place near, or even on, the winter solstice.

We continued to inspect the site in a state of awe. Could this really be the place described by one of the ancient heroes of Jewish legend, who lived nearly 2,000 years before even Moses was born?

THE STRUCTURE

We noted that the mound is not a perfect circle but is made up of a series of sections of parabolas, which make a slightly heart-shaped plan. There are a number of very carefully and beautifully worked stones within the mound, but around it is an outer circle of 12 rough standing stones which, in the opinion of Professor Michael O'Kelly who excavated the site, were probably set up well before the main structure was erected.

Inside Newgrange there is a single vaulted chamber entered through a passage that faces the sunrise on the winter solstice. In front of the mouth of the tunnel is an enormous stone carved with interlacing spirals, jagged V-shaped series of lines, and many diamond figures.

It is now accepted that the tunnel alignment was designed to allow the rising sun at the winter solstice to shine right down into the far end of the chamber. That has to be a deliberate design feature of the building, because a special slot was cut about the entrance to let the light in for a short and very precise period of time.

It is fortunate that this lightbox survived, because when the tunnel was found in the last century the people who excavated it tried to prise the lintel stone out. Thankfully they didn't succeed, or the astronomical alignment of the structure would never have been discovered. When the site was fully investigated and finally restored by Professor O'Kelly, he was extremely careful to ensure that any disturbed stones were put back as close to their original positions as possible.

We had to stoop down to walk up the narrow tunnel which was lined with enormous slabs of solid rock. The plan view of the chamber is in the form of a cross, and in each of the arms there is a beautifully worked stone basin – except for the right-hand alcove, which has an extra smaller basin standing inside the larger one, with two depressions. The basin in the back alcove was broken a few hundred years ago by a treasure hunter.

We counted 21 stones on the right-hand side of the passage and 22 on the left as we came out, and wondered whether this asymmetry was deliberate. Walking around the outside of the building, we saw that only three of the 93 base stones had engravings on them, including the stone that was directly in line with the passage. On this stone there was a carving similar to one at Skara Brae: the double spiral interlaced with the two lozenges. (See Plate 22 Figure 18 on p166.)

Professor O'Kelly had reported that from studying the turf used for infill, it was clear that the builders had been farmers. When the mound was restored, some of the turf was tested and it was discovered that it had been taken from fields which had been used to grow the cereal crop known as spelt, but had then been left to revert to a wild state. This suggested that they were efficient enough at farming to understand crop rotation and the principle of allowing fields to lie fallow, rather than cropping them to exhaustion.

So Newgrange was built by a group of people who were good enough farmers to be able to feed the specialist group of builders who engineered this massive structure. O'Kelly said of the builders:

> *As we came to know the monument better and came to discover its complexities, . . . we came to realize that we were not dealing with questions of brute force and mere strength of numbers so much as with intelligent and well-organised method, more on the lines of the organisation and division of labour practised today in any comparable undertaking . . . we have no doubt that the whole undertaking was carefully thought out and planned from first to last and carried out with something like military precision.*[1]

By 2500 BC Newgrange was in a state of decay. The rich farmlands which had fed the builders fell into disuse and the fields that had grown corn quickly reverted to scrub.[2] The magnificent white-quartz wall had collapsed over the entrance, hiding most of the decorated kerb stones, and around 500 years later an incoming group known as the 'beaker folk' came to live around the overgrown mound. (The 'Beaker Folk' are so called because of the distinctive ceramic vessels which they buried with their dead, in individual burials under round mounds. Their culture originated around the Rhine sometime about 2500 BC, and they came to Britain about 2200 BC. They used bronze technology and seem to have been peaceful immigrants to a land left vacant by the disappearance of the Grooved Ware People.)[3]

For more than 4,000 years the grassy mound lay undisturbed. Legend says it was the home of Oengus, son of the Dagda (the good god) and it became known as Brug Oengus (the Mansion of Oengus) and the whole area was called Bru na Boinne or the Mansions of the Boyne. According to Celtic legend, the Dagda and his son Oengus were two of the most important members of the Tuatha de Danann, which placed the mounds under the protection of the fairy folk. So they remained until AD 1699, when the passage entrance was rediscovered by Charles Campbell, who owned the site. It was visited and recorded by Edward Lhwyd, who was then Keeper of the Ashmolean Museum at Oxford. Michael O'Kelly said of this period:

[1] O'Kelly, M.: *Newgrange, Archaeology, Art and Legend*, Thames & Hudson, 1982
[2] O'Kelly, M.: *Newgrange, Archaeology, Art and Legend*, Thames & Hudson, 1982
[3] Hardingham, E.: *Circles and Standing Stones*, Heinemann, 1975

> *We know that after the cairn had started to collapse there was a Beaker-period occupation of around 2000 BC outside the southern part of the mound but no trace of this was found in the tomb so the entrance must by then have been hidden. Nor was there any sign inside the tomb of the gold coins and ornaments of the Romano-British type deposited around the edge of the collapsed mound and on the mound itself during the early centuries of the Christian era. When the tomb was entered in 1699 it is probable that deposits of cremated bone and the grave-goods which had originally been placed in the basins were brushed aside or ignored.*[4]

With the greatest respect to the late Professor O'Kelly, we have to disagree. We do not believe that there are any grounds to invent grave goods that have been mysteriously whisked away without any mention. Newgrange was not built primarily as a tomb.

AN ENGINEERING MASTERPIECE

Whoever built Newgrange was able to organize a large workforce with sufficient skill to construct a corbelled roof chamber, align a 24-metre-long passageway exactly with the line of the rising sun at the winter solstice, and carve the intricate patterns which adorn the structure.

The construction of Newgrange itself is a splendid achievement, but there are two other passage mounds of similar size and magnificence from the same period and in the same part of the Boyne Valley. These two, Dowth and Knowth, are presently being excavated and are not open to the public, although limited tours of Knowth will soon be possible.

We were impressed by the skills that the people of the Boyne Valley must have possessed in the period between 3,700-3,100 BC to create these structures. These include:

1. Agriculture to produce enough supplies of food for people to live in the same place long enough to complete the work.

2. Specialization of job function. They needed food providers, stone

[4] O'Kelly, M.: *Newgrange, Archaeology, Art and Legend*, Thames & Hudson, 1982

transporters, stone carvers and builders. The same people could not have done all of these jobs.

3. Knowledge of the movements of the sun over the year.

4. Building skills.

5. Stone-working skills.

6. Organizational skills which enabled them to complete projects which must have taken more than a single lifetime.

7. A driving vision to give them a motive to create this awe-inspiring structure and a means of motivating workers to carry out the required tasks.

We gave thought to the amount of labour needed to built Newgrange. As we have seen in Chapter Seven, Colin Renfrew had attempted a similar exercise for the chambered tombs of Orkney, and we used his basic figures, as refined by John Hedges.

Using the dimensions from an excellent short guide to Newgrange by Claire O'Kelly (one of the original excavators and restorers of the site in 1962), the absolute minimum amount of labour involved was calculated as:[5]

1. Site clearing and preparation.	12,000 man-hours (unskilled)
2. Erection of the kerbs, tunnel and chamber.	153,000 man-hours (skilled)
3. Construction of the mound.	160,000 man-hours (unskilled)
5. Carrying of materials.	156,000 man-hours (unskilled)
4. Facing with quartz.	10,000 man-hours (skilled)
5. Decoration of the stonework.	200,000 man-hours (skilled)
Total	691,000 man-hours (with 52 per cent of the work required skilled labour)

If we assume that those involved could sustain this heavy work for 50 hours

[5] O'Kelly, C.: *Concise Guide to Newgrange*, C. O'Kelly, Cork, 1984

a week, every week, it would have taken them 266 man-years. So if they had an available labour force of 266, they could theoretically have completed the structure in a year.

However, we must not forget the problems of obtaining materials. The quartz used in the facing had been brought from the Wicklow Mountains, 70 kilometres to the south, whilst the sea-rolled granite which interspersed the quartz had been brought from Dundalk, 48 kilometres to the north. Even the great stones of the kerb and chamber had all been transported over 10 kilometres from Tully Allen, the nearest suitable quarrying site for the greywacke used for the megaliths. At the time Newgrange was built the area was heavily forested, so they must also have felled enough trees to make a roadway along which to drag the great stones.

The reality is that it must have taken a community of many hundreds of people many years to plan and build Newgrange, even assuming that they did nothing else (Professor O'Kelly has estimated 30 years). In fact, there would also be boats to build, clothes to make, children to educate, as well as farming, hunting and cooking.

This structure is undoubtedly a major feat of civil engineering. It even shows evidence from its construction that the builders understood the action of static stress forces in the way they cantilevered the roof structure to ensure its stability.

If you now consider that there are two other similar-sized structures built at about the same time – at Dowth and Knowth – the people who built them invested a staggering two million man-hours in these constructions, around 3500 BC. These people were not just casual hunter-gatherers knocking up a pile of stones, for the structure displays building skills of a high order of refinement. Claire O'Kelly, (the wife of Michael O'Kelly) who worked on the 1962 excavation, commented:

> *A surprising discovery made when the upper surface of the passage roof was exposed was that grooves or channels had been picked (by using a hammer and points, as for the execution of the ornament) on all the slabs so as to carry off the rainwater percolating through the cairn. By means of a most skilful arrangement, water was led away from one slab to another until it passed into the body of the cairn on either side of the passage.*[6]

[6] O'Kelly, C.: *Concise Guide to Newgrange*, C. O'Kelly, Cork, 1984

The roof slabs of the corbelled chamber had been carefully packed with burnt soil, used as a kind of putty, to make sure water was kept out of the chamber. (It was this burnt soil which carbon dated the building works to about 3200–3500 BC.) The builders intended this structure to be weather-tight and to last, and it is still dry and solid today. In addition, the roof of the chamber incorporates a balancing structure which carries the weight of the roof where the passage roof joins the chamber roof and was also constructed to drain off water. Claire O'Kelly comments again: 'That it is the most effective weather proofing is well demonstrated because the chamber remains dry even in prolonged bad weather.'[7]

The amazing amount of human labour that went into making Newgrange is also found at many other sites across the British Isles. Similar calculations have been carried out by Gerald Hawkins for Silbury Hill in England, which he believes required 24,000,000 man-hours.[8] As we saw in Chapter Seven, John Hedges had found for Orkney that while many structures took less than 10,000 man-hours, some took much longer.

KNOWTH AND DOWTH

Knowth lies a little to the east of Newgrange and Dowth is to the west on the same hilltop ridge. From any one of the three sites the other two are clearly visible, forming a triangle on the northern side of a great meandering bend of the River Boyne. There are at least another 40 smaller mounds within this river bend, not all of which have been excavated.

The mound at Dowth was badly damaged by diggings conducted in 1847-48, but it nevertheless remains an impressive structure of about 85 metres in diameter and 13.3 metres in height. It is surrounded by 115 stones, and has two chambers facing westwards. The northern passage is approximately 8 metres long, leading into a cruciform chamber with a corbelled roof. The mound's southern chamber has an 3.3 metre-long passage leading into a circular chamber 5.5 metres in diameter.[9]

There are two tunnels built within the mound at Knowth: one faces due east, the other due west. Unfortunately, the entrances to the tunnels were

[7] O'Kelly, C.: *Concise Guide to Newgrange*, C. O'Kelly, Cork, 1984
[8] Hawkins, G.S.: *Stonehenge Decoded*, Souvenir Press, 1966
[9] Eogan, G.: *Knowth and the Passage-Tombs of Ireland*, Thames & Hudson, 1986

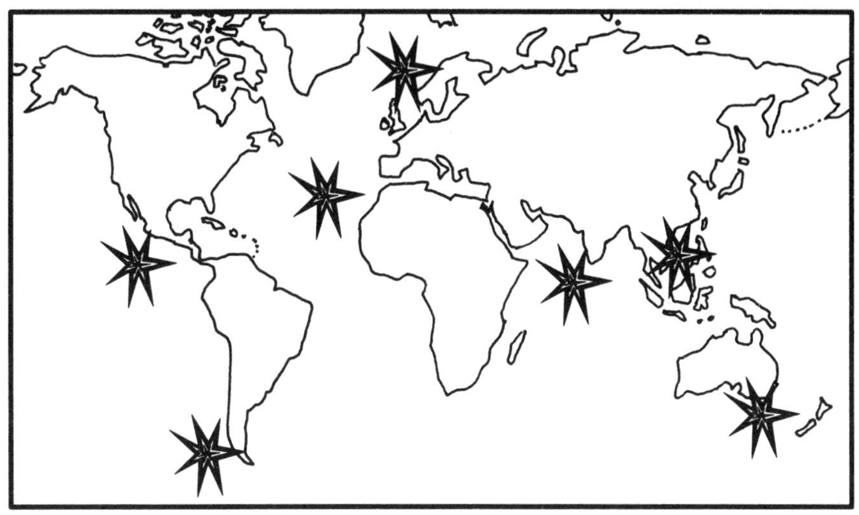

Figure 40. *The Boyne Valley Complex.*

disturbed during the early Christian period when a settlement was built in the mound and the openings to the tunnels were modified and closed off, so today there is no way of knowing if they originally incorporated any kind of roof-box structure such as the one found at Newgrange. The two tunnels were found by Professor George Eogan of University College, Dublin, during 1966, whilst excavating the site.

The mound at Knowth is roughly an oval with its major axis of 95 metres and its minor axis of around 80 metres, covering about 1.5 acres. This structure has been the subject of a considerable number of settlements since it was first built, including ditches dug into the mound during the late Iron Age and in the early Christian period. One of the High Kings of Tara had a palace on the site, and in the Middle Ages the Normans built a keep on top of it. To add insult to injury, a certain Mr Wakeman dug into it in the early 19th century, seeking stone to mend the local roads.

The two tunnels in the mound are arranged back to back, and the one opening towards the east leads down a long passage into a cruciform chamber with a corbelled roof. The cruciform shape of the chamber is formed by an extension of the line of the passage with two alcoves off it, covered by a roof which extends to a height of over 5.7 metres.

There is a passage to the western chamber some 35 metres, which has a long straight section for about three-quarters of its length, and then curves towards the right before ending in a capstone-roofed chamber. Where the passage bends, there is a large stone basin. Professor Eogan believes that this basin originally stood in the floor recess in the chamber and was moved at some time to its present position. Perhaps later people had tried to remove it and had failed to carry it out through the passage.

The site at Knowth is rich in carvings and greatly impressed Colin Renfrew, who said of it:

> *No-one could have predicted that the site would yield so many sculptured stones, and of such variety, a corpus of works actually far larger than that at Newgrange. . . . Back in the summer of 1982 I had the privilege of accompanying Professor Eogan down the long entrance passage into the great eastern chamber of Knowth, and it is an experience which I shall never forget.*[10]

THE ECONOMICS OF THE MEGALITHIC BUILDERS

As we have already noted, the skills required to produce the structures built by the Grooved Ware People all around the Irish Sea demonstrate a degree of maturity in their economic development which is far in advance of their usual image as semi-naked woad-painted savages. They were capable of successfully planning and implementing massive civil-engineering projects which consumed a very large proportion of their available labour force. They were a relatively short-lived people with an extremely high infant-mortality rate, which makes their achievements even more astounding. We could not help remembering the statement Euan Mackie had made about these people: '*there must have been specialised, proto-urban or urban stratified societies in existence before the earliest megaliths appeared.*'[11]

What were these people like who, Professor O'Kelly tells us, were prepared to spend 30 years building a single tunnel mound?[12] Professor Eogan found evidence of a settlement under the various sites which predated the building of the structures.

Population studies of the area around Newgrange in 3200 BC carried out by Dr Frank Mitchell suggest about 1,200 people lived in the Boyne Valley

[10] Eogan, G.: *Knowth and the Passage-Tombs of Ireland*, Thames & Hudson, 1986
[11] Mackie, E.: *The Megalithic Builders*, Phaidon Press, 1977
[12] O'Kelly, M.J.: *Newgrange, Archaeology, Art and Legend*, Thames & Hudson, 1982

Basin.[13] This alone does not give a picture of the available workforce, because the short-life expectancy meant that the bulk of the population was very young by modern standards. John Hedges carried out a detailed mortality study of the Grooved Ware People living in Orkney, and found those under the age of 20 would have outnumbered those over 20 by the ratio of three to one. This mortality profile confirmed previous studies carried out at Carrowkeel in County Sligo in Ireland.[14] It is believed that about one in ten women died in childbirth and that most women died between 15 and 24, with very few surviving into old age.[15] Applying Hedges' mortality figures to Mitchell's population figures gives an estimate of the available male workforce between the ages of 15 and 30 years as about 240. The men who planned it would not live to see it completed. So what inspired them to such efforts?

Over the period of at least 40 generations when the Grooved Ware People lived along Bru na Boinne, they would have accumulated about 48,000 bodies to bury. No more than the remains of a few hundred individuals have been found jumbled with animals bones within their massive 'tombs'. This simple calculation really does pose a difficult question for those who casually label any ancient structure a tomb. If the sole purpose in building these structures was to bury and honour the dead, why have so few bodies been preserved? Did the Grooved Ware People venerate only a few selected bones of 0.4 per cent of their dead, or were their structures built for a purpose other than being store-houses of dead bodies?

Archaeologist Dr Elizabeth Twohig of University College, Cork, also thought about this puzzle.

> *Careful consideration shows that the monuments cannot have been built solely or even primarily for burial. Many have very few burials in them, and while in some instances the paucity of human remains may be due to tomb robbing (for example Newgrange), the overall impression is that only a very small proportion of the population can have been buried in the monuments. Apart from the megalithic tombs, few Neolithic burials are known in Ireland, with the exception of the*

[13] Mitchell, F.: *The Irish Landscape*, Collins, 1976
[14] Macalister, R.A.S., Armstrong, E.C.R, Praeger, R.L.: 'Bronze Age Cairns on Carrowkeel Mountain Co. Sligo', *PRIA*, 29C, 1912, pp.311-347
[15] Hedges, J.W.: *Tomb of the Eagles*, Tempvs Reparatvm, 1984

single grave burials of the south east and the occasional pit burials on the habitation sites such as Lough Gur. The small number of burials demonstrates, therefore, that the function of tombs was not merely as a place for the disposal of the dead. . . . The carvings on the passage tombs provide further evidence of rituals in the tombs; they are clearly not purely decorative but held some symbolic significance for those who executed them and those who saw them . . . The conspicuous siting and huge cairns of many sites point to a need to impress observers, be they outsiders or members of the tribe or band who were to be reminded of the necessity for group solidarity and the power of the leaders.[16]

Professor Eogan also commented on this:

It may well be that the remains were kept until a special day on which they were committed to the tomb. If this was the case some could assume that other ceremonies were part of the burial rite, some perhaps taking place in the open air. Indeed, the recessed area before the tombs at Knowth I with their settings of stones, the spread of exotic rocks, and so on may belong to the material remnants of such ceremonies.[17]

The Grooved Ware People were certainly innovative. Eogan, who excavated Knowth, said of them:

It is possible that they worked out some method of calculating and measuring, especially lengths, although there is no evidence for a megalithic yard as postulated by Alexander Thom. In the corbelled roof, these people had almost achieved a true arch; and at Knowth and Newgrange, the results are so perfect that even an awareness of the effects of stress and the ways of counteracting it must have been acquired. This may presuppose certain powers of understanding; they were undoubtedly a thinking and conscious people, intellectually as well as spiritually motivated, and were developing a body of knowledge which could have laid the foundations of scientific

[16] Twohig, E.: *Irish Megalithic Tombs*, Shire Archaeology, 1990
[17] Eogan, G.: *Knowth and the Passage-Tombs of Ireland*, Thames & Hudson, 1986

> *development. Further confirmation comes from their deliberate selection of a hard rock, like greywacke, as the main building material. An elementary grasp of geology was thus exhibited, whilst the tomb structures clearly demonstrate architectural and engineering abilities. All this suggests a widening of the inhabitants perceptual apparatus, a domestication of the mind was taking place.*[18]

We know from the structures they left behind that a large proportion of the population as not concerned with food production, so it follows that in order to sustain the size of population they had to have been skilful in exploiting both land and sea resources to feed themselves. How had they acquired skills of a type which have previously only been associated with development of the cities of Sumer? Professor Eogan had considered this question when he commented:

> *A knowledge of land management, so as to establish a successful pattern of utilisation, was essential – for an exhausted soil could not have supported and sustained such a large population.*

He has put forward four possible ways in which these people could have acquired their obvious skills.[19]

1. The acquisition of a knowledge of farming by chance, through a source and means of transmission which are unknown.

2. Indigenous development due to local adaptive processes by the Mesolithic people.

3. Irish Mesolithic people travelling abroad, acquiring a knowledge of farming and introducing it at home.

4. The arrival of agricultural foreigners either by accident, such as farmer-fishermen blown off course, or by virtue of a more positive and intentional immigration.

[18] Eogan, G.: *Knowth and the Passage-Tombs of Ireland*, Thames & Hudson, 1986
[19] Eogan, G.: *Knowth and the Passage-Tombs of Ireland*, Thames & Hudson, 1986

It has been suggested that Knowth was built towards the end of the series of Boyne Valley structures and it might have been that the very construction of such a massive public work exhausted this society so much that it finally led to destabilization. But Eogan states that there is no evidence for a fall-off in architectural quality, loss of vigour or any form of decay or weakness in the fabric of society. Indeed, he observes that 'the end of this culture is as enigmatic as its beginning'.[20] [These ideas are investigated more fully in Appendix 3.]

THE LIGHTBOX

It was in 1963 during the course of his excavations that Professor O'Kelly discovered the unusual slot above the entrance to the passage. He described what happened as he came to discover the purpose of the slot on 21 December 1969:

> *At exactly 9:45 am (BST) the top edge of the ball of the sun appeared above the local horizon and at 9:58 am the first pencil of direct sunlight shone through the roof box and right along the passage to reach across the tomb chamber floor as far the front edge of the basin stone in the end-chamber, the tomb was dramatically illuminated and various details of the side and end chambers as well as the corbelled roof could be clearly seen in light reflected from the floor.*[21]

He went on to observe that the angular relationships involved in the construction make it very unlikely that the effect was due to chance. He also commented that the effect only occurred for about a week before and after the winter solstice, and was most dramatic on the day itself.

The passageway is not a simple flat structure. It has been built up a slope which is not the natural level of the site and is curved in an 'S' shape so that the beam of light is very closely collimated (formed into a parallel-sided focused beam) by the stones.

[20] Eogan, G.: *Knowth and the Passage-Tombs of Ireland*, Thames & Hudson, 1986
[21] O'Kelly, C.: *Concise Guide to Newgrange*, C. O'Kelly, Cork, 1984

Archaeologist David Heggie had dismissed the alignment as 'not really significant enough to excite much interest', basing his view on his calculation that any declination of the sun between minus 22° 58' and minus 25° 53' minutes would align with the edges of the slot, giving only one chance in 13 that the alignment was pure chance.[22] This probability is not statistically significant enough to allow the hypothesis that the alignment was accidental, to be rejected with confidence.

The astronomical features of the passage mounds are not unique to Newgrange. Elizabeth Twohig says of them:

> *Less elaborately constructed slots have been claimed at other sites and it seems as if other monuments were also deliberately orientated so as to allow the sun to penetrate the chamber on significant days of the year. At Knowth it appears that the rising sun could shine into the eastern tomb at the equinoxes and the setting sun shone into the western tomb on the same days. At the most elaborate of the Loughcrew tombs, Cairn T, the sunlight enters at the dawn on the equinox days and the panel of light illuminates a series of radial line patterns which are carved on various stones in the tomb.*[23]

Because of the damage caused to the entrances to the passages at Knowth and Dowth by later settlers, it is not possible to be certain what astronomical properties they originally had. Professor Eogan has suggested that the orientations of Knowth imply that there could have been two ceremonies at different times: the vernal equinox on 20 or 21 March, and the autumnal equinox on 22 or 23 September. The spring equinox represents the beginning of the growing season, and the harvest would have been gathered at the autumnal equinox.

He envisaged a morning ceremony at Knowth on the east side, and an evening ceremony on the west side, and says that due to the size of the chambers they could have contained only a small number of people, presumably the priests who performed the ceremonies. No one knows what form these ceremonies would have taken, but various features such as stone settings must have served a related purpose.

Eogan found it of interest that at both Knowth and Newgrange, phallus-

[22] Heggie D.C.: *Megalithic Science*, Thames & Hudson, 1981
[23] Twohig, E.: *Irish Megalithic Tombs*, Shire Archaeology, 1990

shaped stone objects have been found which could indicate that the rites might have concerned fertility, emphasizing the continuity of society.[24]

As we have already mentioned, at both Knowth and Dowth the original entrances to the tunnels have been totally obliterated by later occupation, but the entrance to Newgrange has survived intact. In 1989 Dr Tom Ray of the Dublin Institute for Advanced Studies surveyed the roof box and produced a detailed report which defined the aperture into the chamber in terms of the azimuth and altitude of the sun, in the regions of the sky when it would be able to shine into the chamber. Dr Ray summed up his findings:

> *Newgrange predates the astronomically orientated structures (phase III) of Stonehenge by about 1,000 years. The evidence presented here supports the theory that the orientation of Newgrange was deliberate, which would make it therefore the oldest megalithic structure known for certain to have an astronomical function.*[24]

On the basis of his three-dimensional survey of the site, Dr Ray dismissed Heggie's assessment as over-simplistic. Taking into account the rising path of the tunnel and using a far more accurate survey of the slot, he pointed out the chance of the orientation being random was at very least one in 26, but added that the slot was not a totally precise marker of the winter solstice as its orientation allows sunlight into the chamber a few days before and a few days after the solstice. He assumed this was for a ritualistic reason, saying 'Such low accuracies suggest that ancient man's interest in these bodies may have been ritualistic rather than for the purpose of calendar construction.'[26]

This apparent sloppiness on the part of the designer of Newgrange worried us, because the choice of altitude for the slot did not seem to be quite as casual as Dr Ray seemed to be suggesting. He had noticed that if the top slab of the roof slot had been 20 centimetres lower, or the passage a few metres longer, then no sunlight would have entered the chamber. If the builders' only objective had been a ritualistic one of allowing sunlight into the chamber for a few days around the time of the winter solstice, then they could have simplified their construction problems considerably by merely lifting the roof box by a few centimetres or by building the passage on the

[24] Eogan, G.: *Knowth and the Passage-Tombs of Ireland*, Thames & Hudson, 1986
[25] Ray, T.P.: *Nature*, vol 337, no. 26, January 1989, pp.345-346
[26] Ray, T.P.: *Nature*, vol 337, no. 26, January 1989, pp.345-346

flat. Why had they made such a complicated construction, when a far simpler mound would have achieved exactly the same effects without needing a fraction of the effort to build it? We knew from Eogan's work that these people had build a large number of simpler mounds around the main one at Knowth and had built them on the flat. Both the eastern and western passageways in the Main Mound at Knowth had been built on the flat. There would have been no difficulty in building Newgrange with a passage which was on the level and by doing so they would have achieved exactly the same effect as Dr Ray was suggesting they wanted.

Professor O'Kelly had made a number of comments about the methods of construction, and never suggested that the builders did things without good reason:

> *We came to realize that we were not dealing with questions of brute force and mere strength of numbers so much as with intelligent and well-organised method . . . Let us outline a possible building sequence . . . At this stage of the work, we must assume that axis of the passage and chamber, the centre point of the latter and the position which the roof-slit must occupy relative to it, have already been determined by the expert who had been taking the solar observations. The width and length of the passage and the layout of the chamber with its side and end cells would also have been determined. . . . We have no doubt whatever that the whole undertaking was carefully thought out and planned from first to last and carried out with something like military precision.*[27]

This attention to detail does not square with Dr Ray's suggestion that the builders were only interested in a low accuracy of alignment, which they could have achieved without creating the rising S-shaped curve that they did actually construct. We knew from Knowth that when it suited their purpose they did build similar mounds without bothering to create a curved rising passage. Therefore, they must have had a purpose, but we did not know what it was.

We knew from Robert's observations at Bryn Celli Ddu that these people had been interested in Venus as well as in the movements of the sun. Was there any evidence for a Venus alignment at any of the Boyne Valley sites? we wondered.

[27] O'Kelly, M.J.: *Newgrange, Archaeology, Art and Legend*, Thames & Hudson, 1982

Whilst studying the Anglesey site Robert had developed an analytical procedure, which he called a virtual aperture, whereby he had been able to use observations of the sunlight, combined with accurate timing and knowledge of the latitude and longitude of the site, to calculate an illumination aperture defined in terms of the sun's azimuth and altitude. He had used this method to predict the observation of Venus at Bryn Celli Ddu which had actually occurred, and so he applied the same methodology to Newgrange. The virtual aperture he calculated matched very closely with physical measurements taken by Dr Ray, and indeed, when Ray's temperature and pressure adjustments were taken into consideration, matched almost exactly.

We were now convinced that this 'virtual-aperture' method could take full account of the local conditions and so needed no correction for the local horizon or atmospheric refraction. Applying it to Newgrange produced some amazing results. Taking the size of the lightbox and Professor O'Kelly's date and time measurements of azimuth and altitude, the 'virtual-aperture' method quickly produced a list of which other celestial objects would appear in this lightbox.

READING URIEL'S LINTEL

Venus appears as a morning star around the time of winter solstice four years out of every eight, the other four years it appears as an evening star, following the setting sun down. Some years it is brighter than others and its closeness to the sun varies throughout the cycle. Here is the pattern of the Venus at the time of the winter solstice:

Year	Position	Brightness	Rising time before sun	Declination
1	Morning	99.5%	24 min.	–23:16
2	Morning	36%	254 min.	–13:02
3	Evening	86%	–	–
4	Morning	91%	126 min.	–20:07
5	Evening	17.5%	–	–
6	Evening	97.5%	–	–
7	Morning	72.3%	224 min.	–15:11
8	Evening	63.2%	–	–

This table shows the basic eight-year cycle of Venus. The first column shows the year of the cycle. The next column says if Venus is appearing as the morning or the evening star. In years one, two, four and seven Venus is a morning star rising before the sun. On the other four years of the cycle it is an evening star, following the sun down. Column three describes the brightness of Venus; how bright it appears in the sky depends on where it is relative to the sun, the angle of reflection controlling how much light it can reflect towards the earth. Its brightness is shown as a percentage of the maximum possible brightness it can ever achieve. Column four give the time before sunrise that Venus appears in the eastern sky. Column five gives the declination of Venus at those times when it is a morning star at the winter solstice.

This cycle repeats very closely every eight years and repeats exactly every 40 years. A new cycle started in the year AD 1 and another will begin in the year AD 2001.

So, we now knew that there were four possible occasions throughout the eight-year cycle when the light of Venus rose before the sun during the winter solstice at Newgrange. However, it would not be at the same distance from the sun in each of the morning star phases, as the table of brightness and declination shows.

On only one of these occasions does Venus pass across the aperture of the Newgrange lightbox, and it turns out that this is the occasion when it is at its very brightest. On this morning, exactly 24 minutes before sunlight enters the chamber, light bounces off the surface of the planet Venus and enters the chamber at Newgrange as a collimated beam through the lightbox. For about 15 minutes the chamber is brightly illuminated by the cold, steely light of a full Venus, the third brightest object in the sky. As the ghostly light of Venus moves off the slot, the warm golden light of the sun fills the chamber before it also moves on and the chamber returns to darkness again. On all other occasions Venus is rising too far to the north for its light to enter the carefully designed lightbox.

Now we knew why the builders of Newgrange had curved the passage-way, sloped it upwards and made such a small aperture in the lightbox. The curve and slope of the chamber stop the brightness of the dawn sky brightening the chamber with ambient scattered light. Even on a bright, sunlit winter's day, the chamber is still almost pitch-black. When we visited Newgrange together, we were alone with the guide on the second day of our visit. She very kindly darkened the chamber and allowed us to stand for a

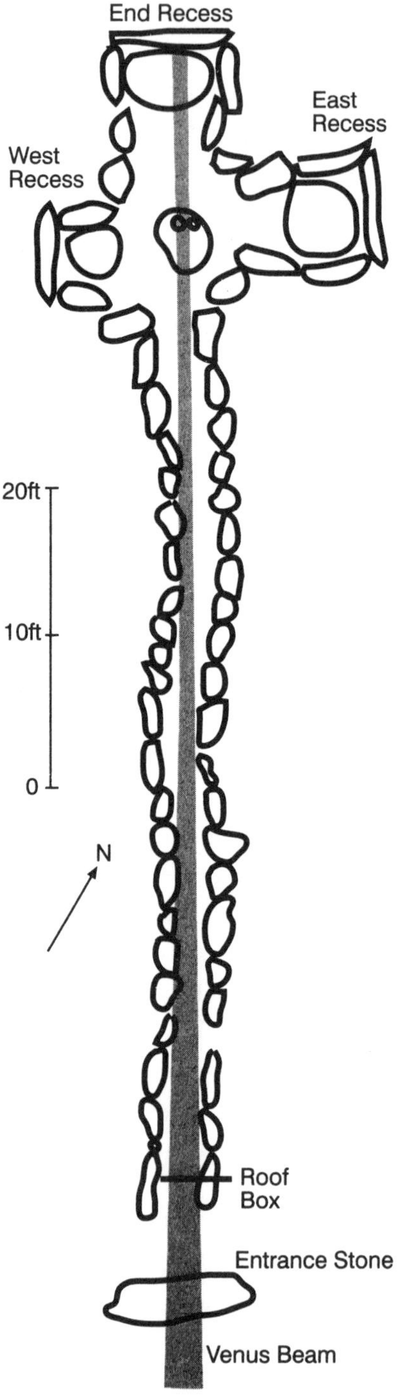

Figure 41. *The path of the light of Venus in Newgrange, once every eight years.*

few minutes while our eyes adjusted to the gloom, and despite the bright sunlight outside very little light penetrated the chamber. The ancient designer had created a perfect light-trap and collimator combined!

Tom Ray had taken Heggie's estimate of one in 13 and showed that to achieve the sunlight alignment, the chances of it being accidental are one in 26. We can now add the information that for the slot to align with only one of the four possible risings of Venus is one in four, and for the one that it aligns with to be the brightest is one in 16. Of the five major tunnels built by these people into mounds of the Boyne Valley, only Newgrange has a light trap to minimize scattered light from the sky. There is thus a one in five chance of that being accidental. Putting all these probabilities together there is just one chance in 2,080 that the designer incorporated every one of these elements at the same time by pure chance. To any statistician, the case would be considered proved. Newgrange is a precision instrument designed for astronomical observations.

Dr Ray was correct when he said, 'I suggest that the width and height of the gap in the floor of the roof box may have been deliberate.'[28] We would go further and say that whoever the designer was, he left clear instructions for the people who came after him. If it was not the man whom Enoch described as Uriel, then it must have been one of his predecessors in the role of the 'guide to the courses of the luminaries of the heavens'.

THE WRITING ON THE WALL

Above the entrance to Newgrange, on the lintel which forms the top of the lightbox, are clearly carved exactly eight rectangular boxes with a line joining each corner to form a cross.

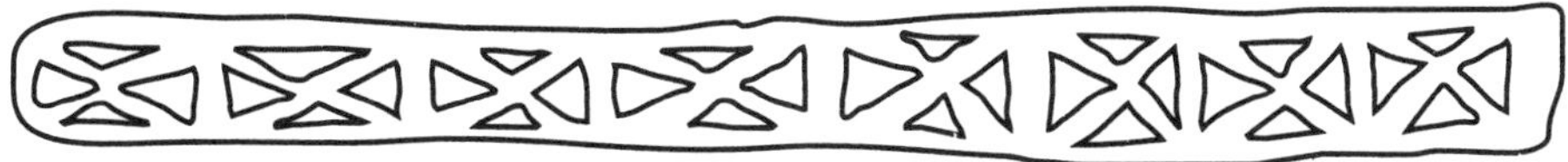

Figure 42. *The carving above the lightbox at Newgrange.*

[28] Ray, T.P.: *Nature*, vol. 337, no. 26, January 1989, pp.345-346

We had often discussed this symbol of the diagonal cross because it seemed to be the way that the megalithic people signified a year. We had noticed while we were reconstructing our own Uriel machine that the pattern of the shadows cast by the markers of the winter and summer solstice sunrises and sunsets formed an X-shaped cross. The exact angle of the X varies according to the location of the particular Uriel Machine.

At Stonehenge, the latitude of 51° North is the only place in the northern hemisphere where the winter solstice sunrise and summer solstice sunset align exactly, whilst the the summer solstice sunrise also aligns with the winter solstice sunset to produce a totally symmetrical image. However at any latitude a distinctive X-cross is produced – the basic pattern is always the same. We realized that this symbol was a short-hand way of representing the movement of the sun over a full year and could well have been used to represent this concept.

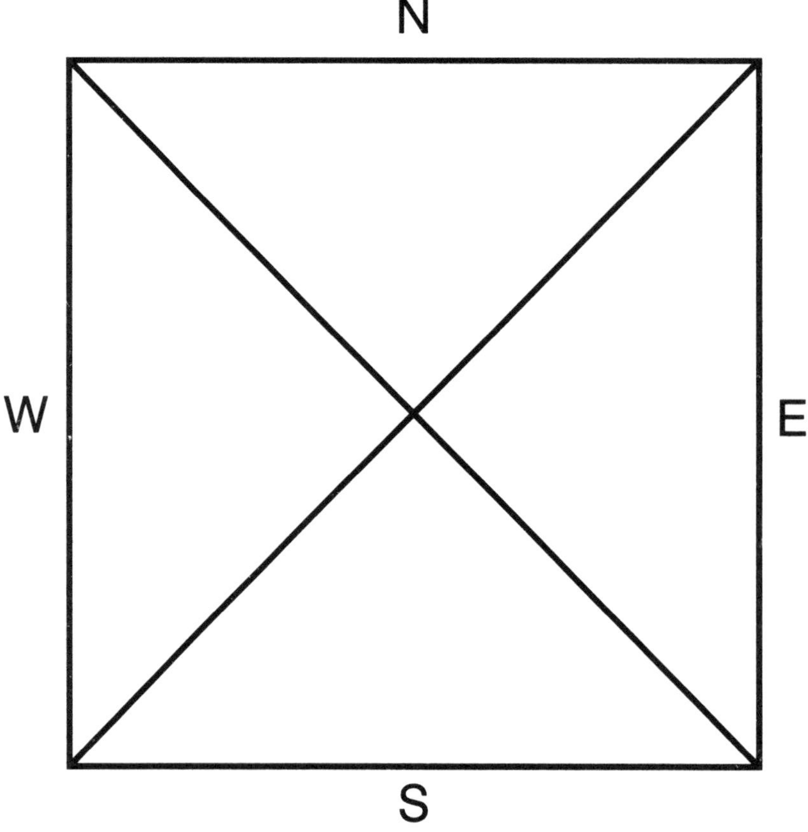

Figure 43. *The cross of the year's turning.*

In all other latitudes – bar one – the angles of the solstice sunrises and sunsets are not symmetrical. The exception is 55° north, where the angles produce a perfect square. (See Figure 19.)

For the users of an Uriel machine there could be no better way of symbolizing a year than to use a X-cross. In fact, we cannot even conceive of a logical alternative – they would almost have had to use this symbol. And here at Newgrange, on the lintel of the lightbox, was a confirmation of this theory regarding a megalithic symbol, because there were eight such symbols, indicating that each did represent a solar year within the eight-year Venus cycle.

The occurrence of eight identical symbols, no matter what they might mean, above the top of a roof box designed to match an eight-year cycle must be deliberate. The highest number of replicated identical symbols on any of the carved stones of Newgrange is ten (occurring on stone Co. 1/C 2, the corbel in the south side of the west recess). This means that if the number of crosses above the lintel is purely random, the people who carved them could have chosen any number between none (a plain lintel) and ten (the highest number of identical symbols they had shown they had the patience to carve). This means the odds of there being eight identical symbols in that place by chance is one in 11. The combination of this probability with the chances of everything else being random is one in 22,880.

We later found that Martin Brennan had come to the same conclusion about this symbol, despite the fact that the Venus significance of the lintel was not known to him: '*The lintel at Newgrange has 8 units, each composed of 4 triangles and each probably making a year sign.*'[29]

Another symbol that is very common at Newgrange, as well as other megalithic sites, is a diamond shape which archaeologists call a 'lozenge'. If we assume that this was also derived from the geometry of the sun's rays, a potential solution to its meaning was quickly apparent thanks to our observations whilst building an Uriel machine.

The diagonal cross of the year symbol has four legs which represent the direction of a solstice sunrise or sunset, but the shadows created by the marker poles on an Uriel machine at a solstice will also provide a diamond shape that will vary in its angles according to latitude. (See Figure 19.)

We knew from our observations that these lozenges vary in proportion according to the latitude at which the reading is taken. At 55° north, a

[29] Brennan, M.: *The Stones of Time*, Inner Traditions International, 1994

regular diamond with four 90° angles is produced. Places south of this geometrically primary latitude produce increasingly wider diamonds, and those further north become progressively taller. It therefore occurred to us that these latitude-specific shapes of the lozenge could be used to identify a location in the way that a post code or a zip code does today. If this interpretation is correct, the different lozenges would have described some major megalithic sites: (See Figure 19.)

This lozenge symbol is often found in conjunction with double spirals. In particular this symbolism is found at Skara Brae, Newgrange, Pierowall (in Orkney), and on a mace-head found at Knowth. John North also reports that the same pattern is found at a 7,000-year-old site in Vrsac (in Serbia) and on a shard of pottery within the ditch at Stonehenge. We found that North had come to a similar conclusion as to the origin of the lozenge:

> *Suppose, for example, that a religious architect were to have marked out two parallel lines towards the rising midwinter sun and then to draw across them to parallel lines (with the same spacing) towards the setting midwinter Sun. A lozenge-shape would result, its angles depending on geographical latitude and local horizon. . . . The fact remains that like the cross of Christianity or the crescent of Islam, the lozenge and chevron could easily have been taken over from an older symbolism and given a precise meaning, before being eventually repeated again and again without much thought of it.*[31]

As we started to make some sense of the proto-writing of the Grooved Ware People, we began to consider the triple spiral found at Newgrange.

We had discussed the appearance of the spiral on ancient artifacts on many occasions. It appears in many cultures, including pre-dynastic ceramics of Egypt as well as on the megalithic structures of western Europe, and Robert had long felt it must represent something important, Chris, however, thought that the shape was too geometrically fundamental to isolate as meaningful. Nonetheless, once we had discovered Uriel's machine, this possibility suddenly became much more real.

Some desk research had shown that the meaning of the spiral had been found by Charles Ross, who had demonstrated it to be the path traced by the

[30] North, J.: *Stonehenge, Neolithic Man and the Cosmos*, HarperCollins, 1996
[31] North, J.: *Stonehenge, Neolithic Man and the Cosmos*, HarperCollins, 1996

shadow of the sun over a quarter of a year.[32] This connected with our observations, because the only essential pieces of equipment for building an Uriel machine are two straight sticks to align the equinoctial shadows and mark out the centre and the sunrise/sunset. If those same two sticks are placed in the ground a few feet apart, the sun will cast some very interesting shadows over the year. As the sun moves outward from the spring equinox to the summer solstice it will trace a spiral on the ground, then it will retrace itself back to the starting point for the autumn equinox. Then it moves out in the opposite direction to create a spiral in the other direction, before winding backwards again to its starting point. (See Figure 28.)

A single spiral therefore equals three months, and a full year is an 'S'-shaped double spiral that has been covered twice over. So perhaps the megalithic builders used this fundamental solar spiral shape to represent the quarter-year identified by Ross.

This simple thought has huge consequences.

Before going to Newgrange, Chris had put to Robert a theory he was almost embarrassed to express because it sounded somewhat bizarre. Looking at the plan of the tunnel and internal chamber at Newgrange, it seemed to him to be highly reminiscent of the female reproductive organs. Unlike later geometric buildings, these earlier megalithic structures have an organic quality to them that appears to be deliberate rather than a consequence of engineering *naïveté*. Certainly, the builders of Newgrange proved that they could build large straight, flat walls with complex curves, but they chose to have internal forms that are almost animal-like in their fluidity. (See Figure 41.)

But it was not mere casual observation based on the possible uterus profile of the chamber and entrance. There were many fragments of the jigsaw which seemed to be coming together.

The light of Venus is associated with resurrection in Freemasonry, because every Master Mason is brought back from a figurative death to the light of this planet rising in the morning just before sunrise in the east. We also knew that the kings and pharaohs of ancient Egypt were considered to be sons of god because they were resurrected to the light of Venus rising from the direction of the 'Way of Horus' over the Sinai.[33] A later 'son of God' who

[32] Brennan, M.: *The Stones of Time*, Inner Traditions International, 1994
[33] Knight, C. and Lomas R.: *The Hiram Key*, Century, 1996

was resurrected, Jesus, and the Jerusalem Church, had the same view of Venus[34] – Jesus was even described as being 'the bright morning star'. The New Testament associates Jesus' birth with the appearance of a bright star, and the Star Prophecy was of great importance to the Jews of Qumran.

In this context, it is useful to remember that according to Eogan, phallus-shaped stone objects have been found at both Newgrange and Knowth which, he says, probably indicates rites of fertility.

We both had considerable reservations about the casual and almost unthinking way that archaeologists label every ancient structure as a simple tomb. On the basis that it contains the remains of many interred humans, Westminster Abbey in London could be dismissed as a stone-tomb monument. But everyone knows that that would be wrong, because this building is also for the worship of God, the weddings of the aristocracy, baptism of children and the place where princes and princesses are made the kings and queens of England. Few major structures in any ancient civilization are given over to a single purpose. Birth, death, marriage, kingship and all other rites of passage have to be marked in some important way. People interlace such concepts, and only archaeologists live in their theoretical world of specialized purpose.

A few human bones and ashes have been found inside Newgrange. It has therefore been called a tunnel grave. Phallus-shaped objects were also found, so we might equally well assume that these megalithic dildos indicated a prehistoric whorehouse!

Many people today think of the Great Pyramid of Kufu, which stands on the Giza Plateau, as being a funerary structure built to house the body of the deceased pharaoh. But this later Egyptian structure was carefully built and exquisitely sealed without a single body or any funerary goods whatsoever. This fact is carefully ignored by popular opinion which seems to want to pigeon-hole everything in a nice easy manner, despite the absence of any evidence or even logic.

This hugely expensive and impressive building of Newgrange must have been multifunctional.

We knew that in early times, birthing of humans was as timed just as much as the production of sheep or crops. Even Jesus was required to fulfill ancient requirements of birth dates. According to tradition his mother Mary

[34] Knight, C. and Lomas R.: *The Hiram Key*, Century, 1996

conceived him precisely on the spring equinox and he was born at the winter solstice (Christmas). He went on to die at the same time of year as his birth – the spring equinox, and was then reborn at the first Sunday of the full moon thereafter (Easter). Furthermore, according to the Bible, Jesus's priestly cousin, John the Baptist, was conceived on the autumn equinox and born at the summer solstice. These astronomical dates for Jesus and John are not coincidental.

On the basis of this and many other fragments of ancient belief, Chris suggested that perhaps women were inseminated at festivals held at certain times of year that reflected the status of the potential offspring – royalty, priesthood, mason or humble drone. The heavily pregnant women of high-status individuals, such as the priesthood, may have been taken into the chamber with the remains of the recent dead to await the coming of the light of Venus, whose ghostly light would have been deemed to reincarnate the spirits of the dead to the birthing infant; minutes later the warm glow of the life-giving sun would celebrate the resurrection of the deceased person in their new form as a child. Perhaps the bowls found in the alcoves of the chamber were to contain the ashes or bones of the dead.

It would have been difficult to ensure that the women gave birth at just the right moment, so they may have remained in the 'womb' chamber for several days until the birth occurred. The remains of the dead could then be taken out and discarded.

In this context, it is intriguing that the Druidic priests and the leading Essenes of the Qumran Community referred to themselves as the 'sons of light'.

Such a process would have provided the community with a flow of reincarnated souls, allowing them to believe that their leaders were transcending their very short lives. Certain key individuals would have been thought to be immortal as a result of this ability to return with their knowledge of science to lead their people through adversity. They would probably have taken the name of the dead person who was thought to be their precursor and their lives would have been structured as a continuation of the previous, person's existence. Such a belief-system could explain the long lives accorded to ancient kings in Sumerian legend and in the Old Testament. Perhaps this honour was given to Enoch, because he was said to have lived for 365 years.

This concept is still used today, in that when the Dalai Lama of Tibet dies, a search is conducted for the infant who is his immediate rebirth. In this way his followers believe that one man has ruled them for many generations. And we were later to find that even this Eastern religion may have a direct historical connection with Newgrange.

Robert had remained as skeptical of Chris's theory of a possible theology of megalithic rebirth as Chris had originally been about Robert's belief that spirals had a single meaning. But suddenly the two ideas came together in a forceful way.

We both looked at the three-spiral motif cut into the great stone at the entrance to Newgrange and then both looked closely at a three-spiral design marked on its own onto the hidden part of the inner chamber, where only the reflected light of Venus could strike.

'You realize what that triple spiral symbol means, don't you?' said Robert.

'No, but it must mean something very important indeed,' Chris replied.

Figure 44. *The triple spiral motif from Newgrange, possibly representing the gestation period of a human female.*

'One spiral is drawn by the sun every three months, so three spirals must equal nine months. And nine months is the human gestation period. So, it looks as though your resurrection theory might be right; this was a birthing chamber.'

It now seemed almost certain that the chamber at Newgrange was not a tomb but a place where the Grooved Ware People believed that the light of Venus transferred the souls of the departed into the bodies of the newborn.

We debated this process of seasonalized birthing and at first concluded that such resurrection rituals may well have been reserved for the families of the priests and kings, because it would be too much of a strain on the resources of the community have all women heavily pregnant at the same time. We further speculated that it could even have been possible that different 'castes' of their society were expected to birth at certain months of the year. Such a practice in ancient times might have given rise to the fact that each of the 12 tribes of Israel was once associated with a different month and therefore a different sign of the zodiac. However, a little further reading told us that the Roman historian Tacitus had recorded that the Celtic tribes of western Europe always tried to ensure that their children were born at the winter solstice (as we mentioned in Chapter Nine), which means they would have had mating rituals at the time of the spring equinox. It seemed probable that this was a relic of a practice inherited from the much-earlier Grooved Ware People. No wonder we still talk of being 'full of the joys of spring, when a young man's fancy lightly turns'! At one time it must have formed an important part of our rituals.

The connection between this birthing ritual and the Grooved Ware People was easy to understand, despite a gap of over 2,000 years between the two cultures. The spring equinox was the time of this ritual; it was also the starting point of the Uriel machine and the commencement of the year in the Qumranian calendar. As we have noted, Jesus also seemed to have had to comply with this time of birth, so what we needed to consider further was how such practices might have been conveyed to the Jewish people. Once again we looked to the *Book of Enoch* for a possible lead.

GOD'S HOUSE

The Jews of the first millennium BC believed that their god, Yahweh, lived inside the Jerusalem Temple. The ancient oral tradition that was eventually written down as the *Book of Enoch* recalls how this prehistoric hero went inside a crystal building to meet a man who he also thought to be God:

> *And I looked and saw therein a lofty throne: its appearance was as crystal, and the wheels thereof as the shining sun, and there was the vision of cherubim. And from underneath the throne came streams of flaming fire so that I could not look thereon. And the Great Glory sat thereon, and His raiment shone more brightly than the sun and was whiter than any snow.*
>
> *None of the angels could enter and could behold His face by reason of the magnificence and glory and no flesh could behold Him. The flaming fire was round about Him, and a great fire stood before Him, and none around could draw nigh Him . . . And until then I had been prostrate on my face, trembling: and the Lord called me with His own mouth, and said to me: ' Come hither, Enoch, and hear my word.' And one of the holy ones came to me and waked me, and He made me rise up and approach the door: and I bowed my face downwards.*

The next section is interesting because the man who he considers to be 'god' is receiving Enoch as a spokesman for the Watchers, who have sent him to plead for mercy now that they stand accused of 'going native' by taking the local women for wives. They are said to have spawned giants as their sons because they have mated with these lesser women.

As we discussed in Chapter Four, section of the *Book of Enoch* known as the Book of Giants, found at Qumran, says that one of the giants, called Mahway, sees a vision of a stone tablet which is treated with water. A preserved fragment of a ceremony tells how the stone is immersed in water and then lifted out again. In this same fragment, the Watchers describe themselves as castaways who are prepared to die together if they have to. Ohya, leader of the Watchers, appeals to them to carry on for the sake of Azazel.

A fragment is preserved of a conversation between Gilgamesh and Ohya, where Gilgamesh complains that the opponents who are persecuting them have taken over the holy places, so that the castaways cannot stand against them. Ohya replies that he has been forced to have a dream. The fragment finishes, 'Now I know that on. . . . Gilgamesh . . .'; what this strange forced dream told him about Gilgamesh has not been preserved.[35]

[35] 4Q531 Frag 1 Wise, M.; Abegg, M.; and Cook, E.: *The Dead Sea Scrolls, a New Translation*, Harper San Francisco, 1996

The next fragment explains how Ohya reports to the misbred monsters that Gilgamesh has cursed the souls of their opponents, whom he calls the 'potentates', and the giants seem to be glad to receive this support.

The Watchers now decide to appeal to Enoch to interpret the dreams which have been forced upon them. The giants believe that Enoch will 'interpret the dreams and tell how long the giants have to live . . .'[36] There then follows a strange description of how Mahway travels to meet Enoch:

He mounted up in the air like strong winds and flew with his hands like eagles, he left behind the inhabited world and passed over Desolation the great desert and Enoch saw him and hailed him and Mahway said to him. . . . The giants await your words and all the monsters of the earth and we would know from you their meaning.[37]

Enoch replies, 'Behold destruction is coming, a great flood and it will destroy all living things.' But where had he discovered this? The *Book of Enoch* says that God told him.

After Uriel had told Enoch to go into the chamber and listen carefully to what he would be told, the Irish god/king, the leader of the Watchers, tells Enoch that Watchers are supposed to speak on behalf of ordinary men, and not the other way around.

He tells Enoch to tell the Watchers that they have sinned.

And He answered and said to me, and I heard His voice: 'Fear not, Enoch, thou righteous man and scribe of righteousness: approach hither and hear my voice. And go, say to the Watchers of heaven, who have sent thee to intercede for them: 'You should intercede for men, and not men for you': Wherefore have ye left the high, holy, and eternal heaven, and lain with women, and defiled yourselves with the daughters of men and taken to yourselves wives, and done like the children of earth, and begotten giants (as your) sons? And though ye were holy, spiritual, living the eternal life, you have defiled yourselves with the blood of women, and have begotten (children) with the blood of flesh, and, as the children of men, have lusted after flesh and blood

36 4Q531 Frag 1 Wise, M.; Abegg, M.; and Cook, E.: *The Dead Sea Scrolls, a New Translation*, Harper San Francisco, 1996

37 4Q531 Frag 1 Wise, M.; Abegg, M.; and Cook, E.: *The Dead Sea Scrolls, a New Translation*, Harper San Francisco, 1996

> *as those also do who die and perish. Therefore have I given them wives also that they might impregnate them, and beget children by them, that thus nothing might be wanting to them on earth.*

This message Enoch is given ends as follows:

> *From the days of the slaughter and destruction and death of the giants, from the souls of whose flesh the spirits, having gone forth, shall destroy without incurring judgement – thus shall they destroy until the day of the consummation, the great judgement in which the age shall be consummated, over the Watchers and the godless, yea, shall be wholly consummated.*
>
> *And now as to the watchers who have sent thee to intercede for them, who had been aforetime in heaven, (say to them): '"You have been in heaven, but all the mysteries had not yet been revealed to you, and you knew worthless ones, and these in the hardness of your hearts you have made known to the women, and through these mysteries women and men work much evil on earth."*
>
> *Say to them therefore: "You have no peace."'*

We read this as meaning that the comet has been seen heading towards earth and a re-run of the 7640 BC flood is expected. At the Watchers 'HQ' in the Boyne Valley of Ireland, the king who is called 'god' has told his Watchers that the coming disaster is due to their sinning with the local women. They are instructed to train some leading local leaders in the science of astronomy by bringing them to the observatories of the British Isles.

The Watchers bring Enoch and Uriel gives him his training, but the watchers then ask Enoch to put in a good word for them when he is taken before 'god' in the chamber at Newgrange. Enoch does his best but 'god' says it is too late – the disaster will strike the earth.

CONCLUSION

Newgrange in Ireland, which fits the description of the House of Crystal found in the *Book of Enoch*, was built by sophisticated engineers who fully understood astronomy. The whole complex of structures along the River Boyne seems to have been built by the Grooved Ware People for carrying out an astronomical ritual, and not for burial of the dead, as is widely assumed.

Investigating the tunnel direction at Newgrange reveals a skilfully designed Venus alignment once every eight years, when Venus is at its brightest. The symbols on the roof box and within the chamber suggest that it was used for a seasonal birthing ritual, similar to that ascribed to the Druids.

The description of Enoch's meeting with 'God' now makes sense in terms of an audience with the leader of the Grooved Ware People at Newgrange. The message 'God' gives to Enoch, to take back to his local Watcher group, in Cancian, is a warning about the coming comet, which dates the conversation to just prior to 3150 BC.

Chapter Twelve

THE SPREAD OF ANCIENT KNOWLEDGE

THE EGYPTIAN OBSERVATORY

Enoch had been taken on his guided sites of astronomical observatories because a comet was on collision course with the earth, and a disaster similar to the one remembered of 7640 BC was expected. We know from the magnetostratigraphical record of the planet that the comet described to Enoch did hit around 3150 BC. We did not know whereabouts this comet had impacted, but we had contact with a man who did.

We had told researcher and author Robert Temple of our conclusions about this second, lesser impact and he put us in touch with Professor Ioannis Liritzis of the University of Rhodes, who had been investigating this same event. Quite independently, Professor Liritzis had found evidence that a comet did hit the Mediterranean Sea around 3150 BC. He had developed his own case from a variety of evidence, but he had not considered the disturbance to the magnetic record of the earth that we had detected. He was as pleased to hear our confirmation of his findings as we were to hear of his.

A comet of this magnitude striking the Mediterranean must have caused huge injury to the people of the area and one would expect it to be detectable in the most ancient records, which were just starting to be collected at this time. The biggest clue that something major occurred is the fact that this date is precisely the point at which the first Ancient Egyptian Dynastic period began. In his book *Chronicle of the Pharaohs*, Egyptologist Peter Clayton gives a starting date of 3150 BC for the Dynasty Zero, and asks:

> *... but why, suddenly, should Egyptian civilization erupt almost like a lotus flower from the primeval waters in one of the old creation legends, and where did it come from? The full answers to these questions have yet to be found.*[1]

The answer seems to be that whatever was there before was destroyed, or weakened so much that a new beginning had to be made. We found it extremely interesting that Clayton also said of the early jubilee or renewal ritual, that the early Egyptian kings at Abydos wore tightly fitting cloaks with a pattern of lozenges. This was a potential connection with the megalithic inscriptions which contain the lozenge as a key part of their design. We were also fascinated to note that the oldest known city of dynastic Egypt is that of Memphis, and the hieroglyphics of its name translated originally as 'White Wall'.

Our immediate thought was that the great quartz structure at Newgrange in Ireland's Boyne Valley might also have been called 'White Wall', because titles were originally always descriptive. If the beliefs of the Watchers had been brought from a headquarters at Newgrange, it would make sense for the new establishment to take this same name.

This was obviously a speculative thought, one which might have been quickly forgotten had it not been for other important connections that presented themselves.

We had already identified in our first book[2], that the Ancient Egyptian hieroglyph for the morning star (Venus' eastern rising) had a literal translation of 'sacred knowledge' – the flag shape representing 'divine' and the five points meaning both star and knowledge. (See Figure 8.)

We now looked more closely at some of the most important hieroglyphs of Ancient Egypt, and we were simply staggered to see how they signified their early priesthood. This pictogram shows a figure kneeling in front of a curved row of four staves in the ground. The left hand is on the hip and the right hand points to a risen, five-pointed star, and just below this star is a rising sun.[3] (See Figure 8.)

We could now see that this is a picture of a priest studying a star above the rising of the sun, from inside a Uriel machine! It could be coincidence,

[1] Clayton, P.: *Chronicle of the Pharaohs*, Thames & Hudson, 1994
[2] Knight, C. and Lomas, R.: *The Hiram Key*, Century, 1996
[3] Wilson, H.: *Understanding Hieroglyphics*, Michael O'Mara Books, 1993

but we could not begin to calculate the extraordinary odds that are stacked against such a thing being purely chance. We already knew that the Egyptians shared the Grooved Ware People's belief that Venus was a symbol of rebirth, but this level of commonality was wholly unexpected.

Then Egypt produced another surprise for us.

In March 1998, a team led by Southern Methodist University Anthropology Professor Fred Wendorf announced that they had found a megalithic site at a remote place called Nabta that lies west of the River Nile in southern Egypt. The site consists of a stone circle, a series of flat, stone structures and five lines of standing and toppled megaliths. Romauld Schild of the Polish Academy of Sciences confirmed that one of the megalith lines was oriented in an east-west direction.

Five megalithic alignments at Nabta radiate outward from a central collection of megalithic structures, and whilst no human remains have been found, the team has excavated several cattle burials including an articulated skeleton buried in a roofed, clay-lined chamber. This was an interesting echo of the bull which (as touched on earlier) was found buried at the entrance to Bryn Celli Ddu in Anglesey.

The small stone circle contains four sets of upright slabs, two of the sets being aligned in a north-south direction while the second pair of slabs provides a line of sight toward the summer solstice horizon. An east-west alignment is also present between one megalithic structure and two stone megaliths, which stand about a mile distant. Furthermore, there are two other geometric lines involving about a dozen additional stone monuments that lead both north-east and south-east from the same megalith.

The team has made an estimate of the site's date by observing that there was a well-attested change in climate around 4,800 BP (uncalibrated), which in calibrated radiocarbon years gives an approximate calendar date of 3300 BC. This is when the monsoon moved south-west and the area again became hyper-arid and effectively uninhabitable.

This dating seems to be based upon an assumption that unknown local inhabitants built the site before the carbon-datable vegetation disappeared. All they have established is that the area became uninhabitable at this point of climate change, and assumed that because no one lived here after that time, the site must predate it.

However, there is another possible explanation. If a group of astronomers wanted fully to understand the workings of the solar system, particularly in relation to the declination of the Earth, they would have wanted to study astronomical effects at certain key points on the planet's surface.

The site at Nabta is not an arbitrary place to find a megalithic site. It is very special. In fact, it is the most likely spot for a megalithic site directly related to the structures established by the Grooved Ware People. Nabta is the only practical place on the planet where people from Europe could have constructed an observatory right on the Tropic of Cancer!

At Nabta, the noon sun is close to its zenith for about three weeks before and three weeks after the summer solstice, but on one day, and one day only, the sun's rays strike the ground absolutely vertically and upright stones will cast no shadow at all for several minutes. Like Skara Brae, Nabta is not an hospitable place but it is of great importance to astronomers.

The people who built Skara Brae and the Ring of Brodgar in Orkney went to a great deal of trouble to be at that particular northern latitude. There was no fuel on the islands, no timber for houses or boats and they had to import much of their meat in a pre-butchered condition. The builders of Newgrange and Stonehenge moved huge stones over immense distances and through difficult terrain to achieve the results they wanted. These astronomer priests knew that the further south they travelled the higher the sun rose in the sky at summer solstice, and they could not help but realize that if they headed far enough towards the equator, they would arrive at a 'holy' latitude where the sun was perfectly in the centre of the heavens.

We know that experts have commented that the Grooved Ware People were great sailors and, with their deep understanding of the stars, they must have been masters of navigation. So there were only two possible ways for them to travel to this very special latitude of 23°27' north: one was down the coast of Europe and Africa along the edges of the western Sahara; the other was down the River Nile. The Atlantic journey would have been very dangerous – it is famous for its storms, and there would have been the difficulty of finding fresh water along the endless expanse of barren coast. Sailing the rivers of France, crossing the Mediterranean and heading down the southern-facing Nile would seem far preferable, with at least a guaranteed supply of drinking water.

The inhospitable nature of the location at Nabta would not have mattered, because they were building a scientific observatory at a critical location, and they would have overcome adverse conditions. If our scenario is correct, the dating of 3300 BC may not be far out, because that is the time that the greater observatories of the British Isles were being planned and built. Additionally (as we discussed earlier), Enoch appears to have been a desert dweller from Egypt or the Levant, and his transportation to the British Isles prior to 3150 BC demonstrates a link between the Grooved Ware People and the upper Nile area.

This early date would also correspond to the pre-dynastic period of Ancient Egypt before the comet strike led to the creation of the unification of the two lands as one. At this time legend records that the people called the Watchers, (who Sitchin had said came from the 'oldest, far-off land') were in Egypt – along with a superior group of people from outside whom they considered to be gods.

Were these 'gods' and Watchers the visiting astronomers from the north? Certainly, their superior technology would have made them seem to be more than mere men. And there is evidence of another journey to the Middle East by remarkable people.

THE SUMERIAN ARRIVAL

Most people are now aware of the Sumerian people as great innovators, yet they remain an enigma. Their dating is remarkably close to the explosion of building amongst the Grooved Ware People. Sometime soon after 3250 BC, they had arrived in the already developed land between the Euphrates and Tigris rivers, and began to intermarry with the native population. These mysterious Sumerians said that they came from an unknown place called Dilmun, and spoke an language unrelated to any other known language.

History records that they soon became rich and powerful. Their art, architecture, crafts, and religious and ethical thought outshone anything in the region and the Sumerian language became the prevailing speech of the land.

Norwegian historian, anthropologist and explorer Thor Heyerdahl said of these people:

> *From them we learned to write . . . From them we got the wheel, the art of forging metals, of building arches, of weaving cloth, of hoisting sail, of sowing our fields and baking our bread. They gave us domesticated animals. They invented units for weight, length, area, volume and instruments to measure it. They initiated real mathematics, made exact astronomical observations, kept track of time, devised a calendar system and recorded genealogies.*'[4]

[4] Heyerdahl, T.: *The Tigris Expedition*, George Allen & Unwin, 1980

Heyerdahl showed that they arrived by boat, almost certainly sailing down the rivers Tigris and Euphrates which flow out of Anatolia across Mesopotania and Sumer before flowing into the Persian Gulf. They show some similarities to the Grooved Ware People in that they invented units of measurement, had true mathematics, and through their astronomical observations, had a calendar system.

However, there are some important differences that need to be explained. Most important was the Sumerians' use of metals. By contrast, the Grooved Ware People must have developed a sophisticated stone technology because (as we have seen), despite their obvious stature as scientists, they did not use metal. Such was their skill that artefacts found at places such as Skara Brae show workmanship that seems impossible to modern stonemasons without the aid of metal tools.

We knew (as we have already mentioned) that according to legend, the Egyptian pyramids and King Solomon's Temple were built without the aid of metals, and candidates for Freemasonry are divested of all metals before being allowed to enter the lodge blindfolded. However, if this was a continuation of an old Stone Age technology, it certainly was not embraced by the Sumerians.

As we have also seen, the Watchers and their giant offspring were told, via Enoch, that they had done many terrible things and that they would be destroyed for their misdeeds. They were taken to task for teaching men 'to make swords, knives, shields and breastplates, and make known to them the metals of the earth and the art of working them'. Chapter Eight of the *Book of Enoch* continues to accuse the Watchers of committing fornication and teaching men the secrets of enchantments and astronomy. We are told that Shemihazai is rejected by God for luring 200 other angels to cohabit with local women, and that the offspring of these unnatural unions are the giants who become wicked leaders of men.

The timing of the arrival of the Sumerians suggests that they could have been a breakaway group of 'observers' from the Newgrange headquarters, who were expelled for interbreeding with the local women. Certainly it is recorded that the Sumerians did interbreed with the indigenous population and they immediately started to teach them about mathematics and astronomy, as well as metals.[5]

[5] Woolley. L.: *Ur of the Chaldees, Seven Years of Excavation*, Pelican, 1929

As we have seen, the principal crimes that God accused the Watchers of were mating with local women, teaching the secrets of the heavens and using metals. Both the crimes and the dates fit. And so does the punishment, with the comet of 3150 BC arriving 100 years after their first arrival in Sumer.

No one knows where these advanced people with a totally alien language came from. There are few candidate locations to consider, and when one realizes how much they knew about astronomy, it seems very reasonable to connect them with the observatories of the British Isles. Similarly, no one knows where the Grooved Ware People went or what their language sounded like, but we do now know that they were highly advanced.

If we are right in this explanation, – i.e. that the Sumerians were an offshoot of the Grooved Ware culture – the later Babylonian achievements in geometry and astronomy must have been firmly based on the achievements of the people who build the observatories around the region of the Irish Sea. The number of degrees in a circle was changed from 366 to 360 to make sub-divisions easier, but the basic divisions of the time of day were maintained. The Sumerians' most important festival was the celebration of the new year which, like that of the Grooved Ware People, began at the spring equinox.

Such evidence as there is, suggests that these people were not particularly tall, but Gilgamesh, the famous Sumerian king, describes himself as a giant in scroll 4Q531 Frag.1 of the 'Book of Giants'.[6] The Sumerian word for 'king' was 'lugal', which literally meant 'big man' – in other words, kings were taken to be giants. The name Gilgamesh seems to translate as something like 'man of the summer stone'. Perhaps, like the later Og of Bashan (discussed in Chapter Six), the giants were so rare that that their strength and their knowledge made them kings.

THE GIANTS WHO WENT EAST

The *Book of Enoch* tells us that Watchers and their giant offspring had asked Enoch to speak out on their behalf; the 'Book of Giants' says:

> *all the giants [and monsters] grew afraid and called Mahway. He came to them and the giants pleaded with him and sent him to Enoch [to speak on their behalf].*

[6] Wise, M.; Abegg, M.; and Cook, E.: *The Dead Sea Scrolls*, Harper San Francisco, 1996

This was so that they might be spared the coming destruction, but their message fell on deaf ears. The words that came back sound as though the 'god' at Newgrange wanted to disown them before the comet struck.

> *'All the mysteries had not yet been revealed to you . . . You have no peace . . . behold, destruction is coming, a great flood, and it will destroy all'*

They believed that a re-run of the previous comet disaster was about to happen, and needed to find safe shelter. They knew that the best chance of survival was to be on high ground, well away from the sea.

If these Grooved Ware People were really smart, they would have known that the safest place on the planet was in central Asia. A perfect location would have been what is now the Xinjiang Uigur Autonomous Region in western China, a plateau encircled by the huge mountains of Tibet and Mongolia. If any place on Earth was going to be spared the great waves of seawater, this would be it.

And that is where some of the giants went, heading eastwards from existing bases in Anatolia.

This may sound like a strange claim, but there is evidence which suggests that the Grooved Ware People *did* produce giants who settled in China.

Since the late 1970s, archaeologists have exhumed scores of desiccated corpses from burials in the salty desert sands around the edges of the Tarim Basin in the Chinese region of Xinjiang. Some were identified as being 4,000 years old and new information suggests that they may be much earlier still. These bodies are extraordinarily well preserved, with intact skin, flesh, hair, and internal organs. Buried individually or in pairs, in undecorated coffins, bottomless coffins or covered by hollowed-out logs, the bodies were quickly dried out in the desert heat and then freeze-dried during the region's bitter winters. These ancient people are dressed in colourful robes, trousers, boots, stockings, coats and hats.

Archaeologist Victor Mair, Professor of Chinese in the Department of Asian and Middle-Eastern Studies at the University of Pennsylvania, was almost lost for words when he saw the evidence for himself in the museum in the provincial capital of Urumchi:

> *'I'd been to the museum several times before but, on this occasion, stepping through a curtain, I came across a new exhibit so beautiful,*

> *so breathtaking, so defying of the imagination, I thought at first that it had to be a hoax'.*[7]

Archaeologist Dr Elizabeth Wayland Barber was equally impressed by these near-perfect remains, but it was their racial characteristics which constituted the puzzle: '*The mummies appeared to be neither Chinese nor Mongoloid in facial type; they looked distinctly Caucasian.*'[8]

It was disturbingly obvious that these people were not part of the indigenous population. They had high-bridged noses, large eye sockets, pronounced jawlines and a dental overbite, blond or red hair, and many men had full beards. There was no doubt – these were Europeans.

We were wide-eyed as we read the report that described some of these European-Chinese people as 'giants of their time'.[9] Cherchin Man (named after the area he was buried in), was an impressive 6' 6" tall and Cherchin woman a statuesque 6' 2", which would make them stand out in a crowd today, let alone thousands of years ago when people were generally shorter.

Profesor Mair was amazed to find that the exhibition displaying these mummies was only a local initiative, and that the Chinese authorities had decided to say little about these extraordinary finds. For them, the fact that Europeans had lived in prehistoric China was perhaps too sensitive a subject for open debate.

As we have just said, the clothing of the mummies was remarkably well preserved. Dr Barber is an expert in ancient textiles, and when she began analysing the styles of weaving and the design of their clothing, it added further confirmation that these people had come from the west. She was particularly impressed by the range and type of hats found in the grave, describing some of them as apparently similar to the headgear of Phrygian archers from the Anatolia region. This observation fell in line with our feeling (discussed earlier) that Anatolia could have been an important centre for the Watchers.

Barber found echoes of myth and memory central to western thinking.

> *Yet another female – her skeleton found beside the remains of a man – still wore a terrifically tall, conical hat, just like those we depict on*

[7] *The Sunday Times*, London, 31 January 1999
[8] Barber, E.W.: *The Mummies of Urumchi*, Macmillan, 1999
[9] *The Sunday Times*. London, 31 January 1999

witches riding broomsticks at Halloween or on medieval wizards intent at their magical spells. And that resemblance, strange to say, may be no accident. Our witches and wizards got their tall, pointy hats from just where we also got the words magician and magic, namely, Persia. The Persian or Iranian word Magus (cognate with the English might, mighty) denoted a priest or sage, of the Zoroastrian religion in particular. Magi distinguished themselves with high hats, they also professed knowledge of astronomy, astrology, and medicine, of how to control the winds and the weather by potent magic and how to contact the spirit world.'[10]

Professor Mair has proven that the old Chinese word for a court magician was 'mag', which is phonetically from the same root as 'magi'. Furthermore, the Chinese written character for 'mag' is a cross with slightly splayed ends, identical to that used by the medieval Order of the Knights Templar, the group of people who we knew were protectors of the ancient sciences and prehistoric rituals. Mair even found a 2,800-year-old Chinese drawing of men with round European eyes and big noses, one of which was carrying this 'magus' symbol.

The myth of the three magi visiting Jesus as he is born beneath a blazing star is a reference to the same ancient belief system, one that has now been found over what seems to be an impossible spread of distance and time.

The textile technology of these people is another problem for the traditionalist historian; it is much more sophisticated than it has any right to be. As well as being able to make felt, these people could weave colourful patterned twill cloth and had excellent skills at weaving tapestry, skills which had previously been assumed to have developed in Egypt about 1500 BC. They also wove a kind of patterned band known mainly in Japan called *kumihimo*. Dr Barber comments:

Did the Japanese receive the method [of weaving kumihimo] from further west long ago or did they invent it on their own? Certainly we have no evidence that any one from so far east had trekked to Central Asia yet. So if any influence in the matter travelled to or from Japan, it was later and headed east.[11]

[10] Barber, E.W.: *The Mummies of Urumchi*, Macmillan, 1999
[11] Barber, E.W.: *The Mummies of Urumchi*, Macmillan, 1999

A newspaper article on these mummies identified their name recorded in ancient Chinese records:

> *According to early Chinese written records, strangely tall, blond-red, hairy people were sufficiently well known hereabouts by the 1st millennium AD to have had their own name, the Tokharians. At Qizil, in the Caves of a Thousand Buddahs, you can see them on wall paintings: blue eyed, bearded, hair characteristically centre-parted.*[12]

The textiles demonstrate that the lozenge symbol was important to these people. Barber was shown a decorated piece of cloth with a simple but elegant pattern of what she described as polychrome lozenges. At first glance it appeared to have an ancient mend, but then she realized that two edges had been carefully joined by the stitching closed selvages (the woven edge of the cloth). Someone had deliberately woven the pattern in such a way that the interiors of the lozenges would match up perfectly when seamed together – a feat Barber acknowledged would take careful planning.

Figure 45. *The lozenge pattern woven into the Cherchen fabrics, after Dr E Wayland Barber.*

Amazingly, the style of weaving and the choice of patterns used on the clothing of the mummies was almost identical to the Scottish tartans and plaids of the Hallstatt and Latene Celtic culture, which developed in Central Europe. Dr Barber comments:

[12] *The Sunday Times*, London, 31 January 1999

> *The dominant weave [of the Urumchi people] proved to be normal diagonal twill and the chief decoration was plaid, as in the woollen twill material of a Scottish kilt . . . .Many historians have assumed that the idea of plaids was relatively new to Scotland in the seventeenth century. Archaeology tells a different story. The Celts have been weaving plaid twills for three thousand years at least.*
>
> *If the Bronze and Iron Age ancestors of the historic Celts wove woollen plaid twills so similar to modern ones, clearly the pre nationalist Scots in the intervening centuries wove this sort of thing too. The historians were thrown off by the problem that European textiles just don't survive well from any period. So we have as little Scottish cloth from 1500 AD as from 100 BC. But the overall similarities between the Hallstatt plaid twills and recent Scottish ones strongly indicate continuity of tradition . . . Not only does this woollen plaid [of Urumchi] look like Scottish tartans but it also has the same weight feel and initial thickness as kilt cloth and Hallstatt materials.*[13]

Barber acknowledges that two unrelated peoples could come up with the same twill weave, plaids and tartans, but when she considered all the factors which had coincided, she was quite firm in her conclusion: 'It rules out coincidence.'

It seems certain, then, that these people had a direct connection with the population of the British Isles who also wove plaid and tartans, the people we now call the Celts. Perhaps they both learned their weaving skills from the Watchers; the Grooved Ware People of western Europe.

These European settlers used a woven-wool textile technology, and Barber comments that woolly sheep with a coat suitable for making woollen yarn did not appear in Europe until 4000 BC. When a first sample of organic material was sent from the graves of the mummies to Nanjing University it was dated to 4500 BC, but then Beijing University dated a sample of carbon to roughly 2000 BC.

Dr Barber doubts both extremes as a guide to when these people arrived in the area. She believes that the language clues to the time of the arrival of

[13] Barber, E.W.: *The Mummies of Urumchi*, Macmillan, 1999

the Urumchi people in China are more telling. This approach produces a date of around 3000 BC:

> *The first of these Eurasian expansions was proto-Indo-European. Since all the daughter languages share words for soft metals, linguists concluded that all the Indo-Europeans already knew how to use them – principally gold, silver, copper. Therefore they must already have entered the first age of metals, the Bronze Age, before splitting up and that would put the Indo-European break-up somewhat after 3000 BC when the use of soft metals became widespread. Recent archaeological finds from Turkey however, show that people back at 7000 BC were already picking up hunks of raw copper and investigating their properties. (Copper sometimes occurs naturally in pure form and Anatolia is one place where it does.) So a somewhat earlier date [for the mummies of Urumchi] is not unthinkable.*[14]

Was it the 3150 BC comet and the quarrel with the Grooved Ware People that drove the giants to trek east to this Asian flood haven?

We were also intrigued by the way in which some of the cemeteries in the Tarim Basin, in particular the Loulan area, were marked. Dr Barber describes them in a way which conjures up images of the enormous Uriel machine of Woodhenge, in Wiltshire, England:

> *The Loulan people may have bestowed few grave goods on their dead before closing the graves, but they made up for it with elaborate formations of wooded 'tombstones' afterwards. Upon filling the pit those early folk all over the Loulan area marked the grave by erecting posts . . . [in one particular grave] the mourners drove dozens of good-sized logs vertically into the ground in tight concentric circles. More wooden posts, farther apart, stand out in the ground in straight lines spreading radically from the circle, like rays around a child's drawing of the sun. The pattern is so striking that the excavators would like to view them as actual sun symbols.*[15]

[14] Barber, E.W.: *The Mummies of Urumchi*, Macmillan, 1999
[15] Barber, E.W.: *The Mummies of Urumchi*, Macmillan, 1999

If these people came from the British Isles 5,000 years ago, they would have brought their astronomical technology, and a study of the alignments of these Chinese sites may well demonstrate that these circles are much more than a pretty design of wooded stakes.

There is also what appears to be a connection with the mating rituals which (as we saw in Chapter Nine) we believe were conducted at such places as Newgrange at the spring equinox in order to provide births at the winter solstice. Rock carvings near Urumchi, where some of the mummies were found, include life-size depictions of men and women with European features engaged in blatantly sexual dancing. The women are generously proportioned and the males are staggering around with unwieldy erections.

There is also evidence that spring rituals (when a young man's fancy lightly turns) involved the use of powerful hallucinogenic drugs. At Merv oasis, a little to the west of Urumchi, there is a religious complex that dates back to the second millennium BC. In its most important room, the 'White Room', are storage vessels which contain traces of poppy and ephedra. Apparently, the poppy derivatives provide such stunning highs that the ephedra had to be used to prevent the shaman from losing consciousness completely.

The world of archaeology has many holes in its knowledge because there is an assumption of discontinuity across space and time. But now that so much new evidence is pointing to major connections between apparently unrelated cultures and myths, we can start to gain a better understanding of what may fill those gaps. We decided to investigate what happened to other strands of the Grooved Ware culture.

THE INHERITANCE OF THE JEWS

At some point a little over 3,000 years ago, a group of tribes in the land that is now Israel began to consider themselves as a discrete group. The nation of the Hebrews – or the Jews, as they came to be called – was created, along with a reconstructed history assembled from a variety of ancient oral myths. According to the Old Testament the Jews arrived from their Egyptian captivity to capture the land that their new god, Yahweh, had promised them despite the fact that it was the home to a people known as the Canaanites.

The reality, though, is that most of Jewish theology was taken directly from the indigenous people of this 'promised land'.

The biblical term Canaanite does not have a particularly precise meaning. It is a generic term for the various people who lived in the land of Israel before the arrival of the Israelites. Generally, archaeologists and biblical scholars use 'Caananite' to mean the Bronze-Age culture of Palestine. Recent archaeological finds indicate that the inhabitants of the region themselves referred to the land as 'ca-na-na-um' from around the mid third millennium BC – the time when all of the sacred megalithic sites of the British Isles were abandoned.

The word entered the Hebrew language as *cana'ani*, meaning 'merchant', because this was the occupation for which the Canaanites were best known. The word also gave rise to the Akkadian term *kinahhu*, which referred to a red-coloured wool that was one of the principal exports of the Canaanites. When the Greeks encountered the Canaanites, it may have been this fact which caused them to rename the Canaanites as Phoenicians, which is derived from a word meaning red or purple, and descriptive of their famous red cloth. However, while both Phoenician and Canaanite refer to approximately the same culture, archaeologists and historians commonly refer to the people *before* the establishment of the Jewish nation as Canaanites and their descendants *thereafter* as Phoenicians.

At a fundamental level, in the tradition of Canaanites deities, El was considered to be the creator and Baal the preserver of creation.[16]

The name El simply means 'god', and Baal meant 'lord'. Each city had a baal and therefore Baal-Sidon was the city god of Sidon who was an entirely different deity from other gods of the same name such as Baal-Hadad. In effect, each city had its god who was referred to as 'lord' – a word which entered the *Torah* and the Bible as a synonym for the single God.

The fundamental difference between Mosaic Judaism and the religion of the Canaanites is that the Canaanite deities were closely associated with astronomical phenomena and with the processes of nature. Their festivals were concerned with annually recurring cycles of the seasons, rather than with the various historical events that underpinned the theology of the followers of Moses.

When the Jews first formalized their religion there was an accommodation of these two approaches, and it was much later that attempts were made to remove Canaanite ideas from their belief system. George Anderson, Professor of Old Testament Literature from Edinburgh University,

[16] Föhrer, G.: *The History of Israelite Religion*, SPCK, 1973

confirmed the divide that opened up between the two schools of Jewish thought.

> *Much that was borrowed from Canaanite religion was later swept away in various Yahwistic reform movements; but much remained as part of the religion of Israel.*[17]

We believe that the earliest form of Judaism was created out of an amalgam of different ideas that came directly from Egyptian and Canaanite beliefs. The ideas from Egypt were, broadly speaking, assembled under a tradition centred on Moses, and those from the Canaanites on ideas that centred on Enoch. As the two traditions quickly combined, the rituals of the Canaanite festivals marking the cycle of the seasons were merged into the celebrations of the historical achievements of the Moses' tradition.

A prime example of this is the Jewish Passover, which is celebrated from sunset on the 14th day of Nisan – which just happens to be the vernal equinox, the time of the birthing festival! The festival commemorates the circumstances of the flight from Egypt under Moses, but its chosen timing is a continuation of a ritual that was, even then, at least 7,000 years old.

The Old Testament tells us (in Judges 2:11-13), just how quickly Canaanite ideas began to be absorbed by the newly arrived Hebrews:

> *And the children of Israel did evil in the sight of the LORD, and served Baalim: And they forsook the LORD God of their fathers, which brought them out of the land of Egypt, and followed other gods, of the gods of the people that were round about them, and bowed themselves unto them, and provoked the LORD to anger. And they forsook the LORD, and served Baal and Ashtaroth.*

The term 'Baalim' used here is the plural of Baal, and simply refers to the fact that there was a different baal, or lord, in each city. When it says that they served Ashtaroth, this suggests an adoption of a spring sexual festival and a recognition of Venus worship.

According to Canaanite legend, El was known as the father of the gods and mankind as well as the creator of creatures. He was viewed as having grey hair and beard, and was thought to be a heavy drinker. As a young god

[17] Anderson, G.W., 'The Religion of Israel', *Peake's Commentary on the Bible*

he came across two women who he took as his wives, and one of those wives was Asherah (also known as Athirat), 'the Lady of the Sea', who later gave birth to the twins Shachar, god of the dawn, and Shalim, the god of dusk.

Interestingly, it was believed that this new family constructed a sanctuary in the desert and lived there for exactly eight years, which is the basic cycle period of Venus. We could not help but see a potential connection with the Newgrange birthing chamber that allows the light of Venus to enter for a few minutes once every eight years. According to Isaiah 14:12, El was the father of Helel or Lucifer, the 'light-bringer', usually taken to mean Venus in its role of the morning star.[18]

It is now known that the Israelites who invaded their promised land appropriated many Cannanite holy places, including Hebron and Beersheba in the south; Bethel, Gilgal, Shechem and Shiloh in the central area; Dan in the far north; and most important of all, the ancient sanctuary of Jerusalem itself. These holy sanctuaries were actually megalithic sites including standing stones, dolmens and stone circles!

Professor Anderson confirms that the normal equipment of these Canaanite sanctuaries included the altar, a standing stone called a *messebhoth* and a wooden pole, called an *asherah*, which was named after Asherah (described above). *The mother of the gods of dawn (Shachar) and dusk (Shalim).*

This is pure megalithic thinking, straight from Stonehenge and Newgrange! As we knew from our own experiments, the only tools required to build an Uriel machine are two wooden poles which have to be used to measure the angle of the sun's shadow at dawn and dusk. An ancient stone image of a man, 70 metres tall, holding an *asherah* in each hand, has been carved out of the hillside in Sussex, on the south coast of England, and is known as the Long Man of Wilmington. We also recalled the two 10,000-year-old equinox aligned poles found near the Stonehenge circle.

Most fascinating of all, it struck us that these early Canaanite beliefs could probably help unlock the lost theology of the Grooved Ware People who built the megalithic sites of western Europe.

The goddess Asherah, mother of dawn and dusk, was, as we have seen, considered to be the consort of the creator god, El, sharing his supreme status. She was worshipped as 'creator of gods' and was usually associated with birth and nursing. In this, her role was directly analogous to Mary, the

[18] Siren, Christopher B.: cbsiren@hopper.unh.edu

Figure 46. *The Long Man of Wilmington in southern England. This 70 m-high figure is holding an Asherah in each hand.*

mother of Jesus in Christian myth. Indeed, we found that the entire structure of the Enochian belief system was very accurately reflected in the Christian story of the resurrection, as well as seeming to tie in with the apparent beliefs of the Grooved Ware People.

The principal god El is almighty, but his son Baal (the Lord) takes up the dominant position and is often referred to as 'Prince Baal' or 'prince, lord of the earth'. Baal has the task of establishing a kingdom on earth, secure it by building a temple and defend it against his enemies, but he nevertheless loses it, only to rise as king once more at the end. Unlike El, he is not a creator; but he is the preserver of creation, the giver of fertility and growth. When he falls into the hands of the god of death, nature languishes until the shout goes up: 'Aliyan Baal lives; the prince, lord of the earth, is here', which announces his resurrection.[19]

Whilst this has obvious similarities to the story of Jesus Christ, it also made us think about our hypothesis (outlined in Chapter Eleven) that the remains of the dead were taken into Newgrange, along with birthing women

[19] Föhrer, G.: *The History of Israelite Religion,* SPCK; 1973

or a recently born child, to continue a cycle of rebirth. We could picture the remains of a dead king being taken into the chamber and as the light of Venus shone in, the new infant would be proclaimed with the cry; 'He lives, the prince, lord of the earth is here.' (The king is dead. Long live the king!)

We could not forget either, that Jesus was very specifically said to have been born in a grotto, under the light of a blazing star at the winter solstice (the time of the Newgrange Venus incursion occurs once every eight years at the winter solstice).

Astarte (also known as Athtart, Ashtoreth or Ashtaroth) was a consort of Baal, and many nude goddess statues have been identified with her as a goddess of fertility and sex. In the city of Sidon she merited royal priests and priestesses; there she served as a goddess of fertility, love, war and sexual vitality, and even had sacred prostitutes who operated in her name.

The association of Venus with sexual acts and birthing has continued into other theologies. Astarte became identified with Aphrodite by the Greeks and simply as Venus by the Romans. The counterpart of Astarte for the Babylonians and the Assyrians was Ishtar, who was viewed by Akkadian theology as being Venus in its role as the morning star. As a goddess, Ishtar was considered to be the Great Mother, the goddess of fertility and the queen of heaven.

The megalithic sites of Canaan that were adopted by the Hebrews included springs, standing stones, mountain tops, caves and stone circles called *gilgal*. We found it odd that biblical scholars have talked for scores of years about stone circles existing in ancient Israel without any surprise that these structures do not appear anywhere else in the world outside western Europe. The recent discovery of a stone circle in southern Egypt has caused many raised eyebrows, yet academia has hardly noticed the strange role of Canaan as a megalithic civilization.

Whilst the term *gilgal* was applied to any stone circle in Canaan, it was also used by the Hebrews to designate the town that housed the most important circle of them all. This Gilgal, thought to be about two kilometres north east of Jericho, was the place were Saul, the first king of the Jews, was crowned. According to Professor Herbert May, there was a place called 'the hill of the foreskins' close to a stone circle, where flint knives were used in rites of circumcision that were conducted in connection with the Gilgal sanctuary.[20]

[20] May, H.: 'Joshua', *Peake's Commentary on the Bible*

Professor Hooke states the great importance of this Canaanite stone circle:

> *An early tradition attributes considerable importance to Gilgal as a religious centre: there the invading Israelites were circumcised, it is the first place where the Ark was installed, and there the first Passover after the entry into Canaan was celebrated.*[21]

It appears that the Jewish custom of circumcision was adopted from an ancient Canaanite practice, (and could therefore be a practice that was inherited from the Grooved Ware People).

The Old Testament tells more about the nature of these stone circles. In 1 Kings 18:30-35 we are told that the prophet Elijah repairs a dilapidated stone circle:

> *And Elijah said unto all the people, Come near unto me. And all the people came near unto him. And he repaired the altar of the LORD that was broken down. And Elijah took twelve stones . . . And with the stones he built an altar in the name of the LORD: and he made a trench about the altar, as great as would contain two measures of seed . . . and he filled the trench also with water.*

In this biblical passage we have a clear description of a henge being dug around the circle of stones, which was then filled with water. This is extremely important because no henges have ever been found or described as existing outside of the British Isles. This also gives some written evidence to further support our belief, (discussed in Chapter 7), that many henges of the British Isles were intended to be flooded.

The word *gilgal* used by the Canaanites for a stone circle is Sumerian, or perhaps it shares a common origin with Sumer. This caused us to look at some other words from this language and we were intrigued to find that *duku* signified a 'holy mound', but literally meant 'birthing determiner'. Once again a strong indicator that these megalithic chambers where connected to birthing rituals.

[21] Hooke, S. H.: 'The Religious Institutions of Israel', *Peake's Commentary on the Bible*

THE ENOCHIAN PRIESTHOOD

By the time of King Solomon (that is, the tenth century BC), the Canaanites occupied little more than a chain of cities along the coast, controlled by the city state of Tyre, which by then had expanded its trade through the Mediterranean and even had colonies as far away as Spain. This Phoenician era saw a shift in Canaanite religion, when a larger pantheon of gods became pushed aside in favour of previously less important, singular deities supported by ruling priest-kings.

The first king of the Jews was Saul, who chose to call his son and successor 'Issh-baal', which was a Canaanite name meaning 'man of baal', indicating an Enochian outlook for the new Jewish state.

When a young man called David killed the giant 'Goliath' he became king of the Israelites and took the ancient city of Jerusalem as his own. It is now generally agreed that the original inhabitants remained in the city and greatly influenced Jewish thinking. David inherited the privileges and obligations of the earlier Canaanite city kings as well as acquiring the priestly functions, rooted in Canaanite tradition, which he inherited from Melchizedek, the king of Jerusalem.

It is surely not a coincidence that there is a Masonic order called 'The Holy Order of the Grand High Priest' that celebrates the Canaanite order of Melchizedek. According to its own history it believes itself to be very ancient, although its earliest extant record dates only from 1780. This branch of Freemasonry states that the Melchizedek priesthood is superior to the Aaronite priesthood associated with Moses (looked at in Chapter Two), which we believe is entirely accurate.

The pre-eminence of the ancient Canaanite priesthood of Melchizedek over the ideas of Moses is born out by the history of the Jews. None of David's sons born at Hebron has a name dedicated to Yahweh. His sons Absalom and Solomon are derived from the divine name 'Shalim' contained in the name 'Jerusalem'. According to Professor Fohrer, there is unmistakable evidence that the Canaanite priestly family of Zadok officiated as priests of the Hebrews' god, Yahweh.

Basically this means that the megalithic or Enochian religion survived to enter into Zadokite Judaism, and its only real threat was from the new ideas attributed to Moses and his brother Aaron.

King Solomon built his famous temple at Jerusalem on a site that was already a Canaanite sacred sanctuary, and according to oral traditions of Freemasonry still in use today, when workmen were sent to clear the ground, they struck a stone that seemed to make a hollow sound. Upon raising this stone, they discovered an vault below which was found to be the remains of an Enochian temple.

A workman is lowered down on a rope by his colleagues and discovers one of the two pillars on which Enoch had engraved all the secrets of civilization that existed before the Flood. This stone must have been the central locking stone of a corbeled megalithic chamber, similar to that found at Newgrange in Ireland (which was also engraved with megalithic symbols). Other workmen follow him down, but they have so weakened the corbeled roof by removing the centre stone, that it collapses upon them.

The layout of this Enochian chamber is still recorded in Freemasonry. (See Figure 1).

The Bible and Masonic legend tell us that Solomon then called in Hiram, King of Tyre, who was head of the Canaanites/Phoenicians, to provide the specialist workmen who could build an appropriate building for Baal-Yahweh, the god of the new kingdom of a united Israel and Judah. We found it extremely revealing that Solomon decided that his people did not have the required talents to design or construct this particular building.

As we have pointed out, the megalithic structures of western Europe were constructed without the aid of metal tools, despite the fact that the Grooved Ware People must have been fully aware of their existence. The Watchers they had sent to other lands must have reported back about the use of metals in Europe and the Middle East. However, we believe that by 3500 BC their own stone technology was so advanced they simply did not need or want such innovations. We can infer that the megalithic builders of Canaan also rejected the use of metals because Deuteronomy 27:5 tells us that the Jews adopted this ban for themselves:

> *And there shalt thou build an altar unto the LORD thy God, an altar of stones: thou shalt not lift up any iron tool upon them.*

This ban of the use of metals was continued for the next two temples on the site (Zerubbabel's and Herod's), and it is still in use by Freemasonry. Before a candidate is brought into a Masonic temple for his ritual of initiation, he is divested of all metals, although in modern English lodges, this ban is often relaxed so that married men can wear their wedding rings. Nonetheless, their finger has to be taped over so that the metal can not be seen or come in direct contact with stone.

According to Masonic legend, the architect of Solomon's temple, who worked with Solomon and Hiram, King of Tyre, was a man called Hiram Abif. He was murdered shortly before the completion of the building by workmen who wanted to extract the secret of the building technique from him. When he refused to tell them what they demanded, these men struck him a series of blows and he was killed. According to Freemasonry, this was the moment when the secrets of a master mason were lost and have never been recovered.

In our first book, *The Hiram Key*, we speculatively linked this Jewish legend with an earlier event in Egypt when king Seqenenre Tao II was murdered in Thebes. We know that Egyptian and Canaanite myths were interwoven to produce a unified account of their disparate history, and we still believe that the legend of Hiram Abif could be an amalgam of two traditions. However, in an attempt to make sense of the name 'Hiram Abif', we made reference to an existing theory that it could be a mixture of Hebrew and old French, meaning 'the king who was lost'.

In March 1999 Chris travelled to visit The Grand Lodge of Scotland with Professor Philip Davies, to seek the Grand Lodge's co-operation in the founding of a professorial chair in Freemasonic Studies at Sheffield University. This was an idea that we had proposed after being somewhat disappointed at the low level of objectivity within Masonry's official attempts at research. The University saw it as being perfectly complementary to existing areas of study, and Freemasonry has given the idea a cautious but warm welcome. We were particularly pleased when the Grand Master of our own Masonic province of Yorkshire – West Riding – committed substantial funds towards the establishment of this academic post.

Whilst at Scottish Grand Lodge in Edinburgh, Philip Davies was particularly keen to look at some of the 2,000 volumes that make up the Morrison Collection, which contains Masonic documents that have not been closely studied for well over 200 years. Whilst looking through a book written by Dr Anderson (the first historian of the Grand Lodge in London from 1717), we came across an explanation of the name of Hiram Abif, by identifying the original spelling of Huram Abhif.

It made reference to the original Hebrew of 2 Chronicles 4:16 where it says; *Shelomoh lammelech Abhif Churam ghafah*, which translates literally as 'did Huram his father make to King Solomon'. As an eminent biblical scholar, Professor Davies quickly confirmed that 'Abhif' did seem to be identifying Huram as Solomon's 'father', and as King David was Solomon's actual father, Davies thought that this probably meant that Hiram Abif was a reference to Solomon's *father-in-law*.

From the Bible we already knew that King Solomon had been accused of marrying into a line of Canaanite, (or Enochian), high priests. This identification of Hiram Abif as Solomon's father-in-law therefore linked the Temple architect with the Canaanite tradition. It is recorded that soon after the temple was completed, Solomon lost interest in the new god Yahweh, and turned back to the old Canaanite gods.

Furthermore, the Temple itself was perfectly Enochian. It faced due east, aligned to the equinoctial sunrise across the Garden of Gethsemane and above the mount of Olives. In front of its eastern-facing entrance were the two free-standing pillars of Boaz and Jachin: Boaz marked the sunrise of the summer solstice and Jachin, the winter solstice. (Similar in concept to the aligned passages of Knowth do – thus underlining the links between the Grooved Ware People and the Canaanites.)

THE RISE AND FALL OF ENOCHIAN JUDAISM

The Babylonian King Nebuchadnezzar chose to capture Jerusalem at the vernal equinox in 597 BC. Sixteen months later, after an attempted fight back, Nebuchadnezzar retook the city and destroyed Solomon's Temple. He took the city's elite into captivity for 58 years, during which time, we believe, these senior Jews first started to write down the oral traditions and sort out all of the contradictory material that they had assembled over the hundreds of years since they first entered the land of Canaan. An Old Testament scholar, Professor Georg Föhrer, explains that this rationalization of disparate material was quite a task, and started with assumed connections for their early heroes:

> *The genealogical linking of the patriarchal traditions represented an important step forward; Abraham, Isaac, and Jacob/Israel were placed in father-son relationships. In addition, the traditions concerning the patriarchs were connected with the Moses tradition. This took place at first without the interpolation of the Joseph novella, so that the narrative apparently progressed directly to the story of how Jacob and his family migrated to Egypt, as Deut. 26:5 still presupposes. Finally the Joshua tradition was appended in an early, simple form, so that it constituted a continuous narrative with the patriarchal and Moses tradition. In this*

> *narrative the patriarchal tradition emphasised the element of promised territory; the Joshua tradition was intended primarily to depict the realisation of the promise. The Moses tradition, supplementing the promise and its realisation, was made to justify Yahweh's claim upon Israel and describe Israel's obligation towards Yahweh.*[22]

Through the years of the captivity, these senior figures from Jerusalem refined their thinking about their relationship with their god Yahweh, and slowly he became God with a capital 'G'. The important aim for them was to return to Yahweh in the hope that He would repair their ill-fortune, which they believed had arisen through their own failure to honour their God.

The Enochian concept of sin being an external factor inflicted on people was replaced by a concept of sin that was the individual's own fault. The leading figure in this period of Jewish rethinking was Ezekiel, who proposed an idea of cleansing away sin that was to become very important. In Ezekiel 36:25 he says:

> *Then will I sprinkle clean water upon you, and ye shall be clean: from all your filthiness, and from all your idols, will I cleanse you.*

The priesthood that returned from the Babylonian captivity was mostly made up of Zadokite priests, although there were some who traced their lineage back to a ceremony held at Ithamar in Egypt where accommodation had been arrived at so that both groups – the Zadokite and the Enochians – now declared a common ancestor in Aaron.

The discovery of the Dead Sea Scrolls has told us that the Zadokite priesthood withdrew from mainstream activities when the Hasmonean kings claimed the office of high priest for themselves in 152 BC. They retreated, in part at least, to Khirbet Qumran – a rocky outcrop overlooking the Dead Sea some eight miles south of Jericho.

The remains of the small settlement in this inhospitable part of the Judaean desert have now been excavated. The buildings are on a small plateau surrounded by a network of caves that face east across the Dead Sea. Looking at this site, it is easy to imagine that it may well have been a Canaanite sanctuary with caves which would be perfect for astronomical

[22] Föhrer, G.: *The History of Israelite Religion*, SPCK, 1973

alignments with the eastern sky from solstice to solstice. It was in these caves that the deliberately damaged scrolls were found.

The small group of buildings were for practical purposes such as a bakery, pottery, workshops and meeting rooms, which suggests to us that the place may well have been a retreat or place of instruction rather than a village with a static community (in the same way that we believe Skara Brae was used thousands of years before). The original group who excavated the site concluded that it was some kind of monastery, and they believed that they had located a scriptorium where the scrolls had been manufactured. However, both of these theories are now generally thought to be wrong, and it is thought that the people using Qumran lived in tents.

It seems extremely possible to us that the caves here were used for birthing purposes and for other rituals of an Enochian nature. The Qumranians were different from all other Jews in that they buried their dead with heads pointing south and feet to the north. They also had a very unusual calendar system.

THE QUMRANIAN CALENDAR

Calendars have been central to the development of early civilizations, and the most important single defining factor of the Qumran Community, writers of the Dead Sea Scrolls, was their obsession with calendars – no less than 80 per cent of the documents found are connected with calendars.

In their new translation of the Dead Sea Scrolls, Michael Wise, Martin Abegg and Edward Cook draw attention to a little appreciated fact about them.

> *Adherence to a particular calendar is the thread that runs through hundreds of the Dead Sea Scrolls. More than any other single element, the calendar binds these works together. It is the calendar that makes the scrolls a collection. The calendar is the intentional element. No matter who wrote the scrolls or put them in caves, the manuscripts do, in some sense, form a library because they all embrace one particular solar calendar and its ancillary developments. Therefore if we want to understand the Dead Sea Scrolls, we must come to terms with their system for measuring sacred time.*[23]

[23] Wise, M., Abegg, M., and Cook, E.: *The Dead Sea Scrolls, a New Translation*, Harper San Francisco, 1996

The calendar Wise *et al.*, are discussing here is a solar calendar with 364 days in its year. The translators observe that scholars have so far been unable to identify any system of intercalation that the Qumranians would have used to align their favoured year with the actual year of 365.25 days. They express their puzzlement at how these calendars could have been used in real life and they link them closely to the *Book of Enoch*, commenting that 'nearly a dozen copies of this work were found among the Scrolls'. They go on to categorize four other main calendar cycles which run through the writings of Qumran.

The first of these was a three-year lunar cycle made up of months either 30 or 29 days long, giving a lunar year of 354 days, and so every three years an extra lunar month is needed to bring the solar and lunar calendars back in line with each other. The others were: a six-year cycle of priestly service in the Temple, a 49-year cycle called a Jubilee, and 294-year cycle made up of six Jubilees.

These cycles seem strange to a modern mind, but they represent a cyclical thinking which we only came to understand when we realized what the 'Book of the Heavenly Luminaries' was describing. Wise *et al.*, sum up their thoughts on the matter of calendars very clearly:

> *The man on the ancient street may not have cared about time or known what year it was, but the Qumran calendar texts shine a light on a different corner of the ancient world. Their priestly authors were perhaps even more obsessed with time than we are.*[24]

These people evidently placed great importance on calendars and it occurred to us that there could be a simple explanation for the adoption of the 364-day year. Supposing that the Zadokite priests who withdrew to the desert sanctuary of Qumran wanted to get back to some of the fundamentals of Canaanite theology, as a group of fundamentalists might do today? The first thing that they would have wanted to do would be to create a *gilgal* using two *asherah*, so that they could measure the year in the old way. They would need to start by marking an equinox, and if that had been the autumn equinox, they might have made an Uriel machine that ran through to the next vernal equinox. If they were in a rush to establish themselves, they

[24] Wise, M., Abegg, M., and Cook, E.: *The Dead Sea Scrolls, a New Translation*, Harper San Francisco, 1996

might have assumed that the gap between these two equinoxes is half a year, but they would be wrong because there are 182 days in this 'half' and 183 in the other 'half' of the year. They might have simply doubled the number of days between the two events and come out with a 364-day year.

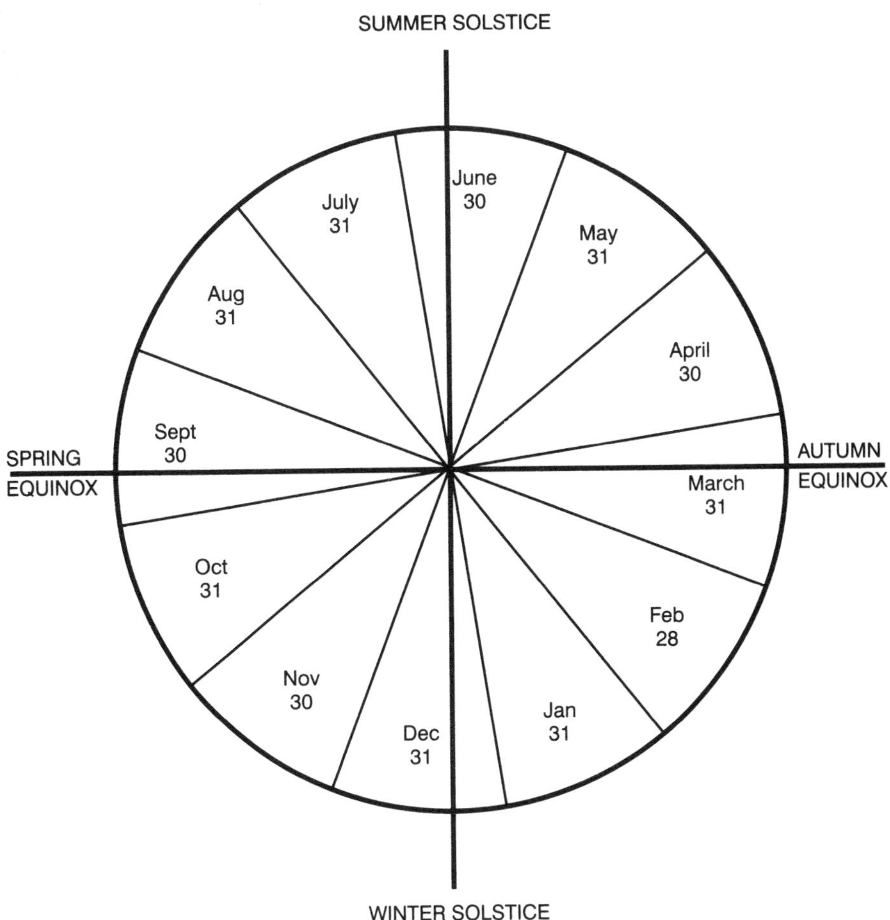

Figure 47. *The calendar and the major points of the solar year.*

Whatever the reason, the Essenes of Qumran kept their solar calendar of 364 days as their ritual year. By the time of Jesus, they had come to believe that God would allow them to make this sacred calendar real, and it seems that they may have used it for all purposes. There was an ancient prophecy that as the 'end of time' came the seasons would be out of their correct place. Naturally, the adoption of the 364-day calendar would take less than 150 years fully to transpose summer and winter. Could this be why we find, for example, stories of Jesus cursing a fig tree for not providing fruit in season?

THE SONS OF LIGHT

The authors of the Dead Sea Scrolls had several ways of describing themselves; the Sons of Zadok, the Poor or Meek, the Perfect, the Holy Ones, the Sons of Light or the Sons of Dawn.[25]

We find it interesting that these priests of the Enochian tradition, who occupied east-facing caves, should choose to call themselves Sons of Light or Sons of the Dawn. From our previous work, we have already concluded that John the Baptist, Jesus, and Jesus' brother James, were all senior members of the Essene group that believed they were leading the way for God to give power to his chosen people.[26]

Associated with Qumran, there is a man called Honi the circle drawer, who is described by Josephus in passing as belonging to a family which has a 'hidden' tradition, connected to Noah, which involves cave-dwelling. Professor Robert Eisenman believes that Honi's grandson, Hanan, is possibly identifiable with John the Baptist, and that he was also called 'Hidden'. He goes further to consider that Jesus and James were also very likely to be descendants of Honi and therefore also party to this 'hidden' tradition. This family was associated with rain-making, which towards during the first century BC, took on a meaning of 'righteousness falling from heaven'.[27]

Robert Eisenman has spent huge amounts of energy over the years analysing the Dead Sea Scrolls in a way that is removed from the standpoint of any religion. Not every scholar agrees with his views, but we have repeatedly found that our findings often coincide with the professor's interpretation. The following words make this point:

A succession of priestly Zaddikes [Zadokitespres] has already been in existence for a century or two before the official appearance of this so-

[25] Eisenman, R.: *James the Brother of Jesus*, Faber & Faber, 1997
[26] Knight, C. and Lomas, R.: *The Hiram Key*, Century, 1996
[27] Eisenman, R.: *The Dead Sea Scrolls and the First Christians*, Element, 1996

> *called 'Zealot' movement: to identify at least four so indicated in the same literature: Onias, Judas, and Honi . . . One should probably include John, Jesus, and James in the list. The all-important rain-making capacity adhering to the Zaddik tradition seems to have been transmitted from Honi to his daughter's son, Hanin or Hanan ha-Nehba (i.e. Hanan the Hidden) . . . Not only does the 'Hidden' tradition attach itself to the person of Honi, Hanin's grandfather, but it persists in clinging in Christian tradition to John (cf. Onias=Honi=Hanin=John, whose mother in Luke 1:24 'hid herself' for five months . . . where Elizabeth 'hides' him in a mountain cave when Herod sought to destroy John (the basis of the similar tradition about Jesus?) and asks Zechariah: 'Where have you hidden your son?', the typical note of cave dwelling.*[28]

We have come to view the Dead Sea Scrolls from an entirely different direction, having found potential ancient links with the megalithic builders of western Europe, and moreover we now find that Eisenman has connected John, Jesus and James with this same tradition in a way that is very much in line with our own researches in *The Hiram Key*.

According to the Bible, Mary conceived at the spring equinox and gave birth to Jesus at the winter solstice. Her much older cousin, Elizabeth, conceived at the autumn equinox and gave birth to John the Baptist at the summer solstice. So, with these two holy figures of the New Testament, we have all four key points of the solar year marked out.

The Gospel of Luke tells us in 1:78-79 that John was born at dawn, when God brought light to 'them that sit in darkness and the shadow of death'. Given that we know from Eisenman that John's mother was in a cave at the time, this really does sound like a description of a megalithic ritual birth.

We have always thought it strange that Herod was said to want so much to kill the baby Jesus that (as we are told in Matthew 2:16, this already unpopular king was prepared to murder every infant boy to ensure success. The Jews were already known as ferocious people who fought one another, and anyone else, at the drop of a hat, so such an action would have guaranteed an immediate uprising of terrible proportions.

In Christian myth it is said that no one recognized the pregnant Mary as

28 Eisenman, R.: *The Dead Sea Scrolls and the First Christians*, Element, 1996

special in any way, making her give birth amongst the animals – yet immediately after the birth King Herod the Great fears for his authority. Herod was a powerful king of Judaea and fully supported by the Romans; what could he fear from this humble child?

It seemed to us that there can only be two rational explanations for this claim. Firstly, it is not true, and the concept is a later invention of Christian writers who desperately wanted their hero to be very important. Alternatively, it is true that Herod feared both Jesus and James, because they were the focus of the rising of an ancient Canaanite cultic tradition which could undermine Herodian authority if they were allowed to become leaders.

We are told in the New Testament (Matthew 2:2) that there was an expectation of a special birth:

> *Where is he that is born King of the Jews? for we have seen his star in the east, and are come to worship him.*

But in the Book of James 21:1-3, which is a part of the Apocrypha, we get more details when Herod asks the wise men about the new-born king:

> *What sign saw ye concerning the king that is born? And the wise men said: We saw a very great star shining among those stars and dimming them so that the stars appeared not: and thereby knew we that a king was born unto Israel, and we came to worship him. And Herod said: Go and seek for him, and if ye find him, tell me, that I also may come and worship him. And the wise men went forth. And lo, the star which they saw in the east went before them until they entered into the cave: and it stood over the head of the cave.*

This is explicit. Jesus was born in a cave to the light of a bright star that shines brighter than any other from the east. And that means Venus!

Was this ritual identical to that performed 3,000 years earlier at Newgrange?

Jesus was proclaimed to come from the royal line of David, a king who (as we saw earlier) adopted the Canaanite religion of the priests of Melchizedek. The legends of the magi tells us only that they were 'wise men', but we know from Dr Elizabeth Barber's previous assessment that the word 'magi' had a specific meaning from China to Arabia:

> *Magi distinguished themselves with high hats, they also professed knowledge of astronomy, astrology, and medicine, of how to control the winds and the weather by potent magic and how to contact the spirit world.*

This was confirmed by Professor Krister Stendahl of Harvard University:

> *The Messianic star became significant in the Qumran community and in the early church . . . The 'magi' were originally a class of priests among the Medes, but in Hellenistic time the word stands for men from the East (or Egypt) who possess astrologic/astronomic wisdom.*[29]

If Jesus was to be the new king of the Jews, the priesthood knew that he would have had to conform to the secret tradition of birthing in a cave to the light of the morning star at dawn on, or around, the winter solstice. This would have had to occur on the brightest of the four possible winter-solstice appearances of Venus over its eight-year cycle – the time when the planet was in the same powerful position, relative to the rising sun – as we identified at Newgrange. The calculation would take a team of astronomers, which explains the presence of the magi.

The fact that the magi were also associated with control of the weather makes a full connection with the rain-making attributed to Honi 'the circle maker'. The Essene priests were widely famous for their medical skills, and it is their symbol of a snake and a staff that is the international mark of medicine today.

It seems, then, that this was a very carefully planned birth and the magi were there from the start. We know that Venus will be in its special position at the winter solstice in the year 2001 (as given in Chapter Eleven), and it therefore was in the same position in the year AD 1 and 7 BC. As Herod the Great died in 4 BC, we can only conclude that Jesus was born in late December in 7 BC.

The special circumstances of the birth of Jesus may have no bearing on the Christian tradition, yet it is very telling once the old Canaanite ideas are considered. We believe that this indicates that the births of John and Jesus were carefully planned and widely known about. They were to be a

[29] Stendahl, K.: 'Matthew', *Peake's Commentary on the Bible*

fulfilment of the 'star prophecy' which is so important to the writers of the Dead Sea Scrolls.

Even the New Testament makes reference to the star imagery, both at the birth of Jesus and in Revelation 22:16 where Jesus says; 'I am the root and the offspring of David, and the bright and morning star.'

Both John, Jesus and his brother James eventually died at the hands of the authorities, so it seems that they each must have been a threat to the establishment. It is said in the Bible and Jewish legend that Salome, the granddaughter of Herod the Great, demanded that John the Baptist's head be brought to her on a plate. This may indicate that John was politically active, since as a ascetic priest operating in the wilderness he was hardly likely to have been known to Salome, let alone to have engender such hatred.

Jesus was tried by Pontius Pilate, the Roman military governor of Judaea, and crucified for representing himself as the 'king of the Jews' – a title which, as we explained in *The Hiram Key*, we believe he was fully entitled to.[30]

In AD 66, war broke out between the Jews and the Romans which, according to Josephus, resulted in the annihilation of 1.3 million Jews. The Roman army was led by Vespasian, who had come to Judaea directly from commanding a legion in Britain. In the spring of AD 68 his army destroyed Qumran and went on to lay siege to Jerusalem. (Intriguingly, according to Robert Eisenman, a grandson of Honi, *also* called Honi 'the circle maker', built circles shortly before the fall of the Temple in AD 70.[31]) The following year Vespasian was named as the new emperor and returned to Rome, leaving the war in Judaea to his son Titus. In AD 70 Titus utterly destroyed Jerusalem, and at the same time conquests in Britain continued under the Roman general Gnaeus Julius Agricola.

At this time, the Zadokite priests were hiding their scrolls at Qumran, and the 'Copper Scroll' found at Qumran lists the treasures and the scrolls that were deposited under the Temple in Jerusalem at the same time. These were the really important scrolls of the Qumran Community.

After the destruction of the Jewish stronghold at Massada in AD 72 Enochian Judaism was all but wiped out. Without the true Zadokite priesthood of Jerusalem to lead them, the Jewish Diaspora of the Roman Empire turned towards rabbinical Judaism, based solidly on Moses rather than Enoch, and many others picked up a new mystery cult from a former

[30] Knight, C. and Lomas, R.: *The Hiram Key*, Century, 1996
[31] Eisenman, R.: *The Dead Sea Scrolls and the First Christians*, Element, 1996

oppressor and now theological opponent of the Jerusalem Church who preached his own gospel of a resurrected Jesus. His name was Paul.

However, there were survivors. Sometime in the next 20 years or so after the fall of Jerusalem, a man called John wrote the Book of Revelation, which is entirely Enochian in its form despite some Christianized overlays.

This book describes in great detail the memory of the first Flood, when seven stars impacted upon the earth, nearly destroying it.

> *And the stars of heaven fell unto the earth, even as a fig tree casteth her untimely figs, when she is shaken of a mighty wind. And the heaven departed as a scroll when it is rolled together; and every mountain and island were moved out of their places . . .*
>
> *And the kings of the earth, and the great men, and the rich men, and the chief captains, and the mighty men, and every bond man, and every free man, hid themselves in the dens and in the rocks of the mountains . . .*
>
> *And the third angel sounded, and there fell a great star from heaven, burning as it were a lamp, and it fell upon the third part of the rivers, and upon the fountains of waters . . .*
>
> *And the fifth angel sounded, and I saw a star fall from heaven unto the earth.*

The *Book of Enoch* became very popular amongst the early Christians – but for some unknown reason it was soon lost. We can only assume that there was an attempt to destroy it by the people who were trying to forge a new religion from misunderstood scraps of earlier ones. Certain elements of these old religions were misinterpreted and others were discarded as being unintelligible or 'pagan' – a term which simply means someone who has a different interpretation to the cult of the resurrected Christ.

In fact, several of the Zadokite priests escaped to Europe, where they formed some of the leading families, who secretly protected their Zadokite genealogy whilst being conventional Christian families on the surface. The descendants of these priests returned as Crusaders in the 11th century AD and the Order of the Knights Templar was formed with the specific task of recovering their sacred scrolls.

Despite the best efforts of the Romans, the 'Sons of Light' lived on.

CONCLUSION

The recent discoveries of stone circles in the desert of Egypt are consistent with what we know of the Grooved Ware People. Futhermore, the timing of the quarrel between the Newgrange group and the Watchers around the Mediterranean fits in with the start of Egyptian building of the city of the 'White Wall'. The unification of the two lands of Egypt occurs immediately after the 3150 BC comet impact.

The Watcher group split up around the time of the impact, some going to Egypt, others to Sumer and some to a high plateau in central Asia in what is now China. However, a major group remained in Canaan, becoming the giants of biblical legend and retaining megalithic beliefs, which continued to influence religious practices.

The astronomical and star myths of the megalithic Canaanites became part of the Enochian tradition of Qumram, and reappeared both in the Dead Sea Scrolls and in the Jerusalem Church of John, Jesus and James.

Chapter Thirteen

THE KNOWLEDGE OF THE DRUIDS

THE SOUL LIVES ON

Many people associate megalithic sites such as Stonehenge with the Druids, despite the fact that there is no evidence that the Druidic priesthood existed at all until the 3rd century BC. However, there is an increasing conviction that there is a genuine connection between the beliefs of these priests and the Grooved Ware People. Celtic scholar Nora Chadwick has observed that:

> *The view is widely held that the institution [of Druidism] is pre-Celtic and was adopted by the Celts of Gaul and Britain from the earlier peoples among whom they settled.*[1]

Professor O'Kelly, the excavator of Newgrange, goes further:

> *Perhaps a lengthening of perspective is overdue in respect of Irish mythology and heroic saga . . . If this were the case it would not only free a great deal of early Irish tradition from the Celtic straitjacket in which it has hitherto been confined, but would also bring it nearer in time to the people who built the Boyne tombs. Can it have been they who planted the first seeds of Irish oral literature and should one*

[1] Chadwick N.K.: *The Druids*, University of Wales Press, 1966

> *begin to think of this not as a window on the Iron Age but as one on the Late Neolithic?*[2]

So, one of the greatest authorities on the subject has concluded that we must look back to the Grooved Ware People really to understand the underlying ideas behind the stories of the Celts and the Druids. We decided to look more closely at some of the important legends of the Celtic people.

THE LEGEND OF TARA

Tara was a foreign princess who was brought to Erin (the ancent name for Ireland) by a knight called Barach, so that she could marry the High King and establish a new royal line of the Ard Ri a Tara; the High Kings of Tara. She was married to Prince Eochaid by Ollamh Fodla, who possibly accompanied her. The term 'Ollamh' is not a name, but a title which means something like great or most wise Druid.

This oral tradition of Ireland was told to Robert some 15 years ago by Tim Looney, the late Irish historian, whilst standing on the windswept heights of the Hill of Tara. Tim was an acknowledged authority on the traditions attaching to the ancient sites of Ireland and after his death his extensive collection of early Irish material was left to the people of Ireland. Today it is housed in the grounds of Cashel Cathedral in the specially built Tim Looney Library, which forms his lasting memorial.

The Hill of Tara is one of the larger Grooved Ware sites in the Boyne Valley and keeps cropping up throughout the history of ancient Ireland. The learned Ollamh Fodla was certainly real, and is credited with establishing the Irish tradition of kingship. Nineteenth-century historian Mary Cusack said of him:

> *Ollamh Fodla distinguished himself by instituting the earliest instance of a national convocation or parliament in any country. Ollamh Fodla constructed a rath [hall] at Tara and died there in the fortieth year of his druidship.*[3]

[2] O'Kelly, C., in O'Kelly, M.: *Newgrange, Archaeology, Art and Legend*, Thames & Hudson, 1982

[3] Cusack, M.: *The Illustrated History of Ireland*, Dublin, 1868

Addressing the question of where Tara, Barach and Ollamh Fodla came from was our next concern. The famous 12th-century '*Book of Invasions*' (*Leabhar Gabhala*) gives a first clue when it states that Ollamh Fodla established a college of Druids, teaching the laws of Moses, at Tara.[4] The obvious question is why and how a man associated with founding an Irish line of kings should want to follow the laws of Moses.

There is also a connection between Ollamh Fodla, Tara and a mysterious object called the 'Lia Fail', meaning the 'Stone of Destiny'. Pat Gerber, who specializes in Celtic history at Glasgow University, starts to make sense of the Moses connection when she says:

> *At the northern edge of the Phoenician's west coast sea route, an old prophet landed in Ulster. He was given the title Ollamh Fodla . . . and he was made King because of his great wisdom ascending the Irish throne in Anno Mundi 3236 (520 BC) remaining there for 40 years . . . He founded a school of prophets and made laws based on the 10 commandments . . . (he) was accompanied by a Princess and a scribe called Simon Brett. The Princess brought with her a harp, once the emblem of David, later the emblem of Ireland, which is said to be buried at Tara, where the great stone, the Lia Fail, was set up.*
>
> *Who exactly were these people? Is it merely the desire to make connections that suggest links where there is nothing more than coincidence? Jeremiah, Princess Tea [Tara] and Barach fled from Egypt around 580 BC and lo and behold an elderly prophet a Princess and a scribe turn up in Ulster in 520 BC.*[5]

As we have seen, in July 586 BC King Nebuchadnezzar destroyed the temple built by Solomon and then had the eyes of Zedekiah, the Jewish king, plucked from their sockets immediately after he had been forced to watch his sons being slaughtered. From the very name of Zedekiah it is clear that he was himself a Zadokite priest, and the Bible says that he sent his daughters to Egypt for safekeeping during the war with the Babylonians. Barach, who as we have just seen, in Irish legend accompanied the foreign princess, was also the name of the scribe to Jeremiah (this too comes from the Bible), who witnessed the destruction of Jerusalem.

Was this biblical Barach, then, actually the same individual who brought

[4] Hyde, D.: *A Literary History of Ireland*, T. Fisher Unwin, 1899
[5] Gerber, P.: Stone of Destiny, Canongate Books, 1997

the daughter of King Zedekiah from Egypt to the 'islands of the north'? If so, did he also bring with him a holy stone of king-making, so that the royal line of David could survive in exile? This would certainly explain how the teachings of Moses arrived in ancient Ireland.

We certainly know that Jewish king-making required the use of a sacred stone. In II Chronicles 23:11-13 it says:

> *Then they brought out the king's son, and put upon him the crown, and gave him the testimony, and made him king. And Jehoiada and his sons anointed him, and said, God save the king.*
>
> *Now when Athaliah heard the noise of the people running and praising the king, she came to the people into the house of the LORD:*
>
> *And she looked, and, behold,* the king stood at his pillar [stone] *at the entering in, and the princes and the trumpets by the king:*

Barach's leader, the prophet Jeremiah, tells in 43:8-10 how he was instructed by God to hide the great stones of Israel in the face of the threat from Nebuchadnezzar:

> *Then came the word of the LORD unto Jeremiah in Tahpanhes, saying,*
>
> *Take the great stones in thine hand, and hide them in the clay in the brick kiln, which is at the entry of Pharaoh's house in Tahpanhes, in the sight of the men of Judah;*
>
> *And say unto them, Thus saith the LORD of hosts, the God of Israel; Behold, I will send and take Nebuchadrezzar the king of Babylon, my servant, and will set his throne upon these stones that I have hid; and he shall spread his royal pavilion over them.*

Jeremiah 46:13-24 says God also told Jeremiah to rescue the daughter of the king who is in Egypt and take her to the people of the north for safety:

> *The word that the LORD spake to Jeremiah the prophet, how Nebuchadrezzar king of Babylon should come and smite the land of Egypt.*

> *O thou daughter dwelling in Egypt, furnish thyself to go into exile: for Noph shall be waste and desolate without an inhabitant.*

> *The daughter in Egypt shall be confounded; she shall be delivered into the hand of the people of the north.*

We had confirmed that the tradition of a holy king-making stone exists in the Bible and we knew that Jeremiah was told to hide one of these important stones and to take the daughter of Zedekiah from Egypt to live in exile in the north. Perhaps he took the stone with him so that he could carry out both of God's instructions at the same time. As we have seen, Ollamh Fodla is said to have accompanied the princess to Erin (Ireland) – could *he*, therefore, actually be the same person as Jeremiah? Certainly the dates for both events are very close, once the different calendar systems are taken into account.

Genealogist of the House of Stewart, Lawrence Gardener, appears to think that the Princess Tara *was* from Judah: 'Eochaid I of Tara married the daughter of King Zedekiah of Judah in about 586 BC'[6]. In addition, the poems of the Welsh bard Taliesin, as we will see, suggest the kings of Tara were descended from Enoch, so the tradition of a princess of the House of David, who came to Ireland with a stone used in the king-making ceremony, is an enduring Celtic story.

THE LIA FIAL

The stories of the legends of Tara were written down by the monks of the Celtic Church, who we know kept a different calendar (with a shorter year) than the Roman Catholic Church, which used the calendar of Julius Caesar at this time. So the difference in dates is within the limits of error of these two ways of dating the past.

The king-making stone, called Lia Fail, was one of the treasures of the 'Tuatha De Danann', which means 'the people of the Goddess Danu'. The legend of these people is directly connected with the Lia Fial:

> *The Tuatha De Danann, people of the Goddess Danu, came from the North [of the world, not just of Ireland]. They were skilled in Druidic lore and magic, and brought major objects of power into Ireland among which was the Stone of Fal. This stone shrieks under the foot of the rightful king. The stone upon which British rulers are crowned, is probably the one carried off from Scotland by Edward I in 1296.*

[6] Gardener, L.: *Bloodline of the Holy Grail*, Element, 1996

This is the original Stone of Scone, used for the installation and crowning of Scottish kings; some writers maintain that this stone was the sacred king stone from Tara in Ireland, brought to Scotland by the Dalraidic kings. Magically it is essential for the royal line of Britain to be installed upon the sacred stone, a tradition still upheld today.[7]

This king-making Stone of Scoon (this is the spelling we prefer), which we discussed in Chapter Nine, is also traditionally said to be the stone that Jacob used as a pillow when he dreamed of the ladder to heaven. As Genesis 28:11-12 says:

And he lighted upon a certain place, and tarried there all night, because the sun was set; and he took of the stones of that place, and put them for his pillows, and lay down in that place to sleep.

And he dreamed, and behold a ladder set up on the earth, and the top of it reached to heaven: and behold the angels of God ascending and descending on it.

The kings and queens of England still have to be crowned whilst sitting above the Stone of Scoon. A historian of heraldry found powerful connections between this stone and the use of Jewish symbols in Celtic heraldry:

The jewel studded regalia takes second place to that piece of rough and apparently valueless stone on which the sovereign sits for the actual crowning. No doubt a desire to perpetuate an ancient custom could account for the continued use of this 'Coronation Stone', but this does not explain the origin of this custom; why this particular stone was chosen or the veneration in which it has always been held by people of the British race. For these things there is no explanation unless we accept the tradition that this is 'the Stone of Israel' which Jacob, father of the Israel people, used for a pillow on the occasion of his prophetic dream.

According to tradition, Jacob's descendants kept this stone as a sacred national treasure until, when the Israel nation fell, its guardians fled with it to Ireland. There for nearly a thousand years, the kings of

[7] Stewart, R.J.: *Celtic Gods, Celtic Goddesses*, Blandford, 1990

> *Ireland were crowned while seated on it. It was then taken to Scotland and used for the same purpose until Edward I took it to Westminster.*[8]

So how did the Lia Fial get to Scotland? Legend says Columba, a prince of the Royal House of Tara, and a Druid trained in the ways of the Celtic Church, took part of it with him to Argyll when he was exiled to Dunadd. However, Pat Gerber isn't sure about this story as she says:

> *Whether or not it is true that Columba brought part of the Lia Fail as a parting gift from Tara, he may well have brought his own altar. These traveling altars were sometimes made of stone, and occasionally of stone imported from the Holy Land.*[9]

Standing outside the Kilmartin Museum near Dunadd, and looking at a reconstruction of the currach Columba sailed from Ireland to Scotland, we couldn't avoid thinking that the very last thing we would want with us on a voyage in that tiny vessel was a large and heavy rock weighing several hundredweight! Perhaps Columba thought differently, or perhaps he brought just the *tradition* with him and consecrated a suitable stone when he arrived in Scotland.

What *is* certain is that the Jews had a tradition of holy stones which were part of their king-making ritual, the Irish Druids had a tradition of holy stones which were part of *their* king-making ritual and the Scots had a tradition of holy stones which were part of *their* king-making rituals. The Welsh too, had a tradition of holy stones containing the knowledge a king needed to rule. But the English, not having such a tradition of their own, stole Scotland's stone. In 1296 Edward I of England, whilst on a pillaging expedition around Perth, stole the Stone of Scoon from its Scottish home at Moot Hill and carried it off to Westminster Abbey, where he had a wooden seat made to hold it. It remained there until Christmas Day 1950 when group of Scottish students liberated it and took it home to Scotland. It was again seized by the English after being placed in Arbroath Abbey, draped with a Scottish Flag, on Easter Monday 1951. The Stone has since been returned to Scotland 'on loan', with clear instructions it must be returned to Westminster if needed for an English coronation.

In fact, the common tradition of a king-making stone is probably more

[8] Bennett, W.H.: *Symbols of Our Celto-Saxon Heritage*, Covenant Books, 1976
[9] Gerber, P.: *Stone of Destiny*, Canongate Books, 1997

important than the question of if there is more than one stone involved in all these stories.

Nonetheless, is the stone now residing in Edinburgh Castle the stone pillow on which Jacob slept? Perhaps not, but it has certainly been *believed* to be that stone for hundreds of years. The very existence and persistence of this belief right down to the coronation of Queen Elizabeth II in 1953 suggests that the tradition of a Jewish link with the kings of Britain may have some truth in it. Perhaps Princess Tara *did* bring the royal line of David to Ireland and established a new line of the High Kings of Tara. The Phoenicians were known to have traded with Ireland since around 600 BC, so it is certainly possible for the daughter of Zedekiah to have fled to the these 'Isles of the North'. Tacitus, writing in the first century AD, made the point that Ireland's harbours were well known to traders and had been for a long time when he talked of Agricola giving sanctuary to an Irish prince.[10] '*Ireland is much like Britain; and its approaches and harbours have become well known from the merchants who trade there.*'

There is another important link between the Jewish and Celtic traditions. The Zadokite priesthood of the Dead Sea Scrolls called themselves the 'Sons of Light' and the Tuatha de Danann were known as the 'Lords of Light'. Interestingly, tradition says that these Lords of Light could make the sun go dark, which seems to suggest that they were accomplished astronomers who possessed the ability to predict eclipses.[11]

What is truly amazing is that this same tradition says that the Tuatha de Danann were believed to have lived in a mound that had once been covered in a white reflective wall that concealed a chamber where strange ceremonies connected with a bright star took place.[12]

Certainly, the Tuatha de Danann are closely associated with the megalithic complex along the Boyne Valley and, as we have already mentioned, from the legend of their arrival in Ireland they were reputed to be able to control the light of the sun. At their first battle to come ashore on Irish soil, fought at Moytura, they won by smothering the land in darkness and hiding the light of the sun.[13] Celtic scholar T.W. Rolleston wrote of what he saw as the links between the Celts and the megalithic people:

[10] Tacitus: *The Agricola*
[11] Ross, A.: *Druids, Gods and Heroes from Celtic Mythology*, Peter Lowe, 1986
[12] Squire, C.: *Celtic Myth and Legend, Poetry and Romance*, Gresham Publishing Co., 1890
[13] Hyde, D.: *A Literary History of Ireland*, T. Fisher Unwin, 1899

> *The inferences, as I read the facts, seem to be that Druidism in its essential features was imposed upon the imaginative and sensitive nature of the Celt by the earlier population of Western Europe, the Megalithic People.*[14]

ANGUS OF NEWGRANGE

Another founding deity of the Tuatha de Danann (the tribe of Danu), was called the Dagda, known as the 'Good god'. He had a cauldron which fed everyone who made claim on his hospitality, and no one was ever turned away unsatisfied, he also had a harp, which as he played, caused the seasons to arrive in the right order. The 11th-century *Book of Leinster* retells the story of the Dagda and his wife.

> *The Dagda had a living harp; as he played upon it, the seasons came in their order – spring following winter, and summer succeeding spring, autumn coming after summer and in its turn, giving place to winter. His wife was called Boann and the River Boyne is named after her because she brought it into existence. Formally it was only a well, shaded by nine magic hazel trees. All people were forbidden to approach the place. Only Boann, with the proverbial woman's curiosity, dared to disobey this fixed law. She came towards the sacred well, but as she did so, its waters rose up at her in a mighty rushing flood. She escaped but when the waters subsided from the land they never quite went back to the well and became the Boyne.*[15]

They were a demonstrative and fertile couple having numerous children, the most important being Brigid, Angus (Aengus) and Ogma.

> *Aengus was an externally youthful exponent of love and beauty. Like his father, he had a harp, but is was of gold not oak, as the Dagda's was and so sweet was its music that no one could hear and not follow it. His kisses became birds which hovered invisibly over the young men and maidens of Erin, whispering thoughts of love into their ears. He is chiefly connected with the banks of the Boyne, where he had Bru or shining fairy palace.*[16]

[14] Rolleston, T.W.: *Myths and Legends of the Celtic Race*, G.G. Harrap and Co., 1911
[15] Squire, C.: *Celtic Myth and Legend, Poetry and Romance*, Gresham Publishing Co., 1890
[16] Squire, C.: *Celtic Myth and Legend, Poetry and Romance*, Gresham Publishing Co., 1890

Could the 'shining fairy palace' on the River Boyne be a memory of Newgrange before its brilliant eastern wall of quartz collapsed around 2600 BC?. Certainly, these sites are still considered to fairy mounds in Irish folk stories repeated to young children.

Indeed, all the stories of the Tuatha de Danann are associated with the complex of mounds around Newgrange, known as the Bru na Boinne; a fact that Dr C. O'Kelly comments on when looking at the legendary context of Newgrange, where she highlights two main traditions from the Irish mythical tradition.

> *With regard to the Bru na Boinne there seem to be two main concepts: the Bru is the abode of the mythological or supernatural beings known as the Tuatha de Danann (peoples of the goddess Danu) and the Bru as the burial place of the pagan kings of Tara. In the Book of Lecan, the Dagda built a great mound for himself and his three sons, Aengus, Aed and Cermait (Ogma).*[17]

She mentioned a strange story concerning Angus/Aengus (Oengus an Broga) and the role he plays in the story of Diarmuid and Grainne, one of the founding myths of ancient Ireland.

> *[Newgrange] was the mansion to which Oengus an Broga brought the body of Diarmuid, one of the great Irish folk-heroes, after his death on Ben Bulben so that he could 'put aerial life into him so that he will talk to me every day.*[18]

The story of Diarmuid and Grainne tells how the beautiful virgin Grainne, daughter of the Irish High King of Tara, is to be married to a powerful and once mighty warrior, who is somewhat passed his prime manhood (Finn mac Cumhal). Instead, she persuades one of his young and attractive warriors to elope with her. They run away and spend an idyllic eight months wandering around the more attractive parts of Ireland until Finn catches up with them but, at that very moment, he is attacked by a wild boar. Dairmuid rescues

[17] O'Kelly, C., in O'Kelly, M.: *Newgrange, Archaeology, Art and Legend*, Thames and Hudson, 1982

[18] O'Kelly, C., in O'Kelly, M.: *Newgrange, Archaeology, Art and Legend*, Thames and Hudson, 1982

Finn from the boar but is mortally wounded. The ungrateful Finn stands over him, preventing anyone from administering first aid until he dies. At this point Angus appears with a host of Tuatha de Danann and takes the heavily pregnant Grainne and the dead body of Dairmuid to the Bru na Boinne (Newgrange). Taking them both into the mound he makes the strange speech: 'I will send the bright light of a soul from the sky into him so that he may talk with me each day.'[19] Grainne then gives birth to a son who is sent to be fostered and 'to learn to become the warrior his father had been'.

Stripped of its romantic trappings, this strange tale appears to date from a time when the tunnel into the Newgrange chamber had not been concealed by the collapse of the wall. (If so, it is at least 4,600 years old.) When the young woman runs off with younger more attractive suitor than her appointed mate, she becomes pregnant, but the young man is killed. The custodian of Newgrange then arrives on the scene, takes the dead body and the pregnant woman into the mound in order to save the soul of the dead man. The son is then born and grows to be the warrior his father had, quite literally, been.

Perhaps this refers to a belief that the light of Venus is the bright light which carried the dead Diarmuid's aerial soul into the new-born son. We wondered if this cruel story contained knowledge about the purpose of the tunnel and chamber at Newgrange.

We found that other stories also had overtones of connections we recognized from the *Book of Enoch*. Discussing Irish myths, Nora Chadwick even refers to a race of giants:

> *The historical tradition taught that Ireland was infested by a race of giants, as well as the Tuatha de Danann, before the coming of the Gael. The former were known as the Formori and they were the enemies of the Tuatha de Danann.*[20]

We couldn't help thinking of the stories in the *Book of Enoch* about the battles between the Watchers and the Giants (outlined in Chapter Six). Dr Chadwick added her view on the meaning of these ancient myths when viewed from the beginning of the Christian era:

[19] Squire, C.: *Celtic Myth and Legend, Poetry and Romance*, Gresham Publishing Co., 1890
[20] Chadwick, N.K.: *The Celts*, Penguin, 1971

> *The gods were no longer all-powerful, they took their places in the far past, as an ancient race, before the 'present Ireland'. But they moved about on the soil of Ireland sometimes as a race apart, sometimes having intercourse with normal human beings. They were known as the Tuatha de Danann.*[23]

These are the ancient people who call themselves the Sons, or the Lords of Light, who were godlike but interbred with ordinary men and women. This is a carbon-copy of the Enochian story, from the very land that we believe was at the heart of the whole Watcher mystery. Were Uriel and his fellow 'angels' the Tuatha de Danann – the Lords of Light who maintained their immortality through a cycle of rebirths under the light of the morning star? Did some of their members break away and mate with ordinary people to produce extremely tall offspring?

The time had come to look more closely at the Druids, from whom these stories had come.

THE DRUIDS

Most people probably think of Druids as white-bearded and wearing long white robes, cutting mistletoe with a golden sickle at the time of the full moon or perhaps making bonfires of human beings shut up in gigantic figures of wicker-men. But what is *really* known of these priests who were so powerful in the British Isles when the Romans arrived?

We certainly know from Adamnan's account of St Columba, written soon after Columba's death, that this most important early saint of the Celtic Church was considered to be a Druid and a prince of the royal line of the kings of Tara. Columba is reported to have won a battle of magic with Broichan, Druid to King Brude Maelchon, king of the Picts. This tells us that a lot of the Druidic beliefs survived until the mid fifth century, sitting comfortably alongside the Celtic version of Christianity, which was very different from that of the Roman Church.[22]

Until the early part of the first century BC, the Druids were the guardians of some of the best preserved megalithic sites in western Europe. In the year

[21] Chadwick, N.K.: *The Celts*, Penguin, 1971
[22] Marsden, J.: *The Illustrated Life of Columba*, Macmillan, 1991

AD 60 the Emperor Claudius dispatched General Suetonius Paulinus to destroy the Druids, causing them to retreat to their stronghold of Ynys Mon, now called the Isle of Anglesey. Why did these Celtic priests pose such a threat to the Romans that a systematic campaign of genocide was pursued against them?

Julius Caesar wrote of the these priests:

The Druids officiate at the worship of the gods and regulate public and private sacrifice and give rulings on all religious questions. Large numbers of young men flock to them for instruction, and they are held in great honour by the people. They act as judges in practically all disputes, whether between the tribes or between individuals; when any crime is committed or a murder takes place or a dispute arises about an inheritance or a boundary, it is they who adjudicate the matter and appoint the compensation to be paid and received by the parties concerned. Any individual or tribe failing to accept their award is banned form taking part in sacrifice, the heaviest punishment that can be inflicted. Those who are laid under such a ban are regarded as impious criminals. Everyone shuns them and avoids going near or speaking to them for fear of some harm by contact with what is unclean, if they appear as plaintiffs, justice is denied them and they are excluded from a share of any honour.

The Druidic doctrine is believed to have been found existing in Britain and thence imported into Gaul, even today those who want to make a profound study of it generally go to Britain for the purpose.

The Druids are exempt from military service and do not pay taxes like other citizens. These important privileges are naturally attractive, many present themselves of their own accord to become students of Druidism and others are sent by their parents or relatives. It is said that these pupils have to memorise a great number of verses, so many that some of them spend twenty years at their studies. The Druids believe that their religion forbids them to commit their teachings to writing, although for most other purposes, such as public and private accounts, they use the Greek alphabet. But I imagine that this rule was originally established for other reasons, because they did not want their doctrine to become public property and in order to prevent their pupils from relying on the written word and neglecting to train their memories.

This description of the Druids not committing their teachings to writing exactly reflects the view of Freemasonry, which requires its members to memorize huge amounts of ritual to a word-perfect standard. Only in relatively recent years has Masonic ritual been written down, and even so, it is not permitted to read it during ceremonies.

Julius Caesar's next comments once again confirmed the role of a cycle of controlled rebirth:

> *A lesson which they take particular pains to inculcate is that the soul does not perish, but after death passes from one body to another, they think that this is the best incentive to bravery, because it teaches men to disregard the terrors of death. They also hold long discussions about the heavenly bodies and their movements, the size of the universe and of the earth and the physical constitution of the world and the power and properties of the gods and they instruct young men in all these subjects. Unless the life of a man was repaid for the life of a man, the will of the immortal gods could not be appeased.*
>
> *The Celts all claim to be descended from the god of the underworld who they call Father Dis. For this reason they measure time not by day but by nights and in celebrating birthdays, the first of the month and new year's day, they go on the principle that the day begins at night.*[23]

Julius Caesar, born in 100 BC, was co-opted into the college of priests in 73 BC. In 59 BC he was elected consul for Gaul when he wrote this account of the Druids, and in 55 BC he mounted an exploratory expedition against Britain.

Caesar very clearly describes the Druids as priests, judges and astronomers. They practised the art of memory and had developed a verbal tradition for recording their rituals and secrets, and were as obsessed with their genealogies as any Jewish priest. They believed in rebirth of the soul, and we found that a modern sect of Druids still practises a resurrection ritual which involves the initiate in being reborn anew from a grave of stones. These modern Druids claim to have inherited this ritual from their ancient forebears, and it is more than interesting that their movement was founded

[23] Caesar, *The Conquest of Gall*, Penguin Classics, 1964

in the week of the summer solstice in 1717, at the Apple Tree Tavern in London, which was home to one of the four lodges of Freemasons who established the Grand Lodge of London, also at the summer solstice in 1717.[24]

It must have been a busy week for this little pub.

This practice aligns with the third degree in Freemasonry, where the candidate is figuratively murdered and then resurrected in pitch blackness as the light of Venus slowly brightens in the east. This is now usually achieved with the assistance of a bulb on a dimmer switch and a cut-out aperture in the shape of a five-pointed star!

In Gaul, Caesar wrote a book on astronomy which unfortunately has not survived, but it is known that he learned about the movements of the heavens from the Druids, who were knowledgeable about calendars. It can be no coincidence that Caesar's major achievement was reforming the Roman calendar system, which had been a confused mess. Writer David Duncan comments:

> *From the beginning the Roman calendar was a powerful political tool that governed religious holidays, festivals, market days and a constantly changing schedule of days when it was legal to conduct judicial and official business in the courts and governments . . . [the inaccurate calendar] played havoc not only with farmers and sailors but also with a population becoming more dependent than ever on trade, commerce, law and civil administration in a rapidly growing empire that desperately needed a standard system for measuring time.*[25]

The Druids had an advanced and accurate calendar system and archaeological evidence of this, in the form of a engraved brass plate, was found in Brittany. Archaeologist Evan Hadingham says of it:

> *The interest in a calendar recorded by both Caesar and Pliny was confirmed when the remains of an actual Celtic Calendar were discovered at Coligny, in the Ain district of France, at the turn of the century. This calendar was once a large bronze plate, nearly five feet*

[24] Private Communication: The Order of Bards, Ovates and Druids
[25] Duncan, D.E.: *The Calendar*, Fourth Estate, 1998

square, and was found close to a Roman road and the pieces of a bronze statue dated to the first century AD. Although the names of the months are written in Gaulish, the lettering and numerals are Roman. The calendar reckons by nights (which is how Caesar say the Celts counted time) and by lunar months.[26]

This calendar had been attributed to the god Managan, whose name appears twice at the top of the list of days and is a Welsh name for the Dagda – the good god whose harp playing made the seasons change. We believe that this reference to Managan shows that the Julian calendar was a solar system of day reckoning which came from the Tuatha de Danann via the Druids.

Once Julius Caesar learned of the teachings of the Druids in matters of astronomy and the immortality of souls, the Romans started to take an unhealthy interest in the British Isles. From 55 BC onwards, Rome became obsessed with controlling the islands of Britain. Caesar mounted two expeditions into southern Britain but England was not taken until the reign of Claudius in AD 43. This determination to conquer Britain puzzled Roman historian Harold Mattingly:

Britain, though apparently in a disturbed condition, could hardly be regarded as dangerous to Rome; and if great mineral wealth was expected from it the hope was certainly disappointed.[27]

Why then, did mighty Rome want to conquer an obscure island off the west coast of Europe? Tacitus relates:

Julius Caesar, the first Roman to enter Britain with an army, did indeed intimidate the natives by a victory and secure a grip on the coast. But he may fairly be said to have merely drawn attention to the island it was not his to bequeath. After him came the civil wars with the leading men of Rome fighting against their country. Even when peace returned Britain was long neglected. Augustus spoke of this as policy, Tiberius called it an injunction. The emperor Gaius unquestionably planned an invasion of Britain but his impulsive ideas shifted like a weathercock. It was the late emperor Claudius who

[26] Hadingham, E.: *Circles and Standing Stones*, William Heinemann, 1975
[27] Mattingly, H.: *Roman Imperial Civilisation*, Oxford University Press, 1956

> *initiated the great undertaking. He sent over legions and auxiliaries and chose Vespasian to share in the enterprise, the first step towards his future greatness. Tribes were subdued and kings captured and the finger of destiny began to point to Vespasian.*[28]

Certainly, it is a curious fact of history that Julius Caesar made it a requirement for any candidate for Roman citizenship that they must first publicly renounce Druidism.[29]

DESTRUCTION OF THE DRUIDS

It appears, then, that Rome was determined to wipe out the Druids. After reviewing the classic sources, Nora Chadwick is quite clear about the Roman attitude towards the Druids when she writes:

> *The occupation of Britain by the Romans was largely resolved on in order to destroy Druidism at its roots. This is a bold assumption; but strangely enough it was accepted by the German scholar Ihm in what is one of our most authoritative modern studies of the Druids and it has been endorsed by Sir Ronald Syme and R.G. Collingwood.*[30]

Celtic legend lists three primary meeting places of the Druids of the Isle of Britain. One was called Bryn Gwyddon (The Hill of Science) and it was somewhere on Ynys Mon (Anglesey). Another was in the kingdom of the Gwyr Gogledd, the men of the North, somewhere around Perth. The third was in what is now the south of England.

The Druids fought a mighty battle against the determined onslaught of the Romans on Ynys Mon. This had been the main Druid stronghold until it was finally invaded by Suetonius Paulinus in AD 60 in the reign of Nero.[31] It took Paulinus's men a year before they captured Castell Ior, where the Druids made a last stand. The Romans landed at Wylfa Bay and circling round Llanfechell, entrenched themselves on Morawydd, a hill outside Cemaes. Initially they were repulsed and thousands of Romans died in what has since been known as Lon Hyd y Corffau (Lane of the Corpses), but finally Roman

[28] Tacitus: *The Agricola*
[29] Squire, C.: *Celtic Myth and Legend, Poetry and Romance*, Gresham Publishing Co., 1870
[30] Chadwick, N.K.: *The Druids*, University of Wales Press, 1966
[31] Chadwick, N.K.: *The Celts*, Penguin, 1971

might prevailed and Castell Ior was razed to the ground and all its defenders put to the sword.[32]

This battle ensured the Druids a place in Celtic myth. But the sequel to these events is even stranger.

Suetonius Paulinus had mounted his attack from the fort of Chester and was operating with very long supply lines. He over-reached himself, for no sooner had he taken Castell Ior than he was forced to abandon Anglesey. Tacitus criticized him, saying:

> *Suetonius Paulinus enjoyed two years of success, conquering fresh tribes and strengthening forts. Emboldened thereby to attack the island of Anglesey, which was feeding the native resistance, he exposed himself to attack in the rear.*[33]

The attack was mounted *well* to his rear, to be precise, it was a general rising of the south of Britain lead by Queen Boudicca of the Iceni tribe. She quickly over ran London, Colchester and Verulamium, and in the process retook the southern meeting site of the Druids. Paulinus was in trouble and had to march against the victorious Boudicca. He defeated her somewhere around the area where Birmingham now stands, but in victory he treated her and her followers so badly that it looked as if he would provoke a new rebellion from the rest of the inhabitants.

Tacitus recalled what happened:

> *The whole island [of Britain] rose under the leadership of Boudicca, a lady of royal descent for Britons make no distinction of sex in their appointment of commanders. Had Paulinus on hearing of the revolt, not made speed to help, Britain would have been lost. But many of the rebels did not lay down their arms, conscious of their guilt and of the special reasons they had for dreading what the governor might do. Excellent officer though he was, it was feared that he would abuse their surrender and punish every offence with undue severity. The government therefore replaced him.*[34]

[32] Edwards, G.T.: *A Short History of the Churches and Neighbourhood of Llanbadrig, Llanfechell, Llanfflewin and Bodewryd*, Oriel Cemaes, 1997

[33] Tacitus: *The Agricola*

[34] Tacitus: *The Agricola*

Throughout these adventures, Paulinus was accompanied by a young officer called Julius Agricola. Tacitus said of him:

> *Neither before nor since has Britain ever been in a more disturbed and perilous state. Veterans had been massacred, colonies burned to the ground, armies cut off. They had to fight for their lives before they could think of victory. Everything combined to give the young Agricola fresh skill, experience and ambition; and his spirit was possessed by a passion for military glory.*[35]

Agricola returned to Rome with Paulinus to be appointed a member of the college of priests. After the death of Nero, the new emperor, Galba, put him in charge of recovering treasures stolen from the temples during Nero's reign. Rome now went through a very troubled period of instability, having three emperors in 12 months. Agricola had been befriended by the general Vespasian, who had been to Britain on the AD 43. When Nero committed suicide, Vespasian was busy destroying the Temple of Jerusalem and killing as many Jews as possible.

Realizing that in AD 69 Rome was ripe for the taking, Vespasian returned with sufficient forces to ensure he became emperor. Agricola supported him and was rewarded by being made commander of the 20th legion in Britain. He served Vespasian well and was again promoted, this time to governor of Aquitania. Then in AD 78, Vespasian sent him back to Britain on a special mission. He was instructed to capture all the Druid sites and kill as many of the Druids as possible.

Remarkably, this was just five years after the Romans had completed their destruction of the Zadokite priesthood by the taking of the stronghold of Masada, whose population of 1,000 had committed suicide after holding out for two years.

Agricola returned as governor of a British province which controlled the Druid's southern meeting place but had not succeeded in holding Anglesey or taking Scotland. Agricola was certainly thorough. He first established control of North Wales, subduing the Ordovice tribe and re-establishing the fort of Segontium just outside Caernarfon. His supply chain guaranteed, he then set about training a troop of horsemen to swim the perilous Menai Straits. Tacitus explains why:

[35] Tacitus: *The Agricola*

He carefully picked out from his auxiliaries men who had experience of shallow waters and been trained to swim carrying their arms and keeping their horse under control and made them discard all their equipment. He then launched them on a surprise attack and the enemy, who had been thinking in terms of a fleet of ships and naval operations were completely nonplussed. Who could embarrass or defeat a foe who attacked like this?[36]

Agricola chose to attack at a time usually devoted to pageantry and ceremonial visits.[37] Tacitus describes these regular meetings of Druidism.

On an island of the ocean is a sacred grove and in it there is a consecrated chariot covered with a veil. Only the priest may approach it. He knows when the goddess appears in the sacred chariot. He becomes aware of the presence of the goddess in her holy place, and in deep reverence accompanies her chariot drawn by cows. Then there are days of joy and feasting in all places which the goddess honours with a visit. Then there are joyous days and wedding feasts. At those time no war is waged, no weapons are handled, the sword is sheathed. Only peace and quiet are at those times is known or desired, until the goddess, tired of her sojourn among mortals, is led back into the shrine by the same priest.[38]

The festival described can only have been the spring equinox rite. We knew Bryn Celli Ddu is subject to brilliant lighting effects at the spring equinox (see Chapter Nine), which could easily be interpreted as a visit by the goddess. The sanctuary of Bryn Celli Ddu is close to the Straits, just opposite the fort of Segontium. We also suspected from Tacitus's comments that the tribes who wanted their children born at the winter solstice would need to impregnate their women at this time. Agricola's swimming horsemen literally caught them with their pants down and took advantage of the spring meeting at Bryn Celli Ddu to overwhelm the remaining Druids of Ynys Mon.

Agricola never released Ynys Mon again building a fort at Holyhead to control the island. But the Druids still had a stronghold left, in Scotland. We

[36] Tacitus: *The Agricola*
[37] Tacitus: *The Agricola*
[38] Tacitus: *Germania*, 40

know this from the evidence of Columba who went to Inverness in AD 564 to confront the last vestiges of the ancient Druidical power which still survived. So despite Agricola's best efforts to destroy the Druidic priesthood, some survived for 300 years at least.

By AD 80 Agricola had taken all of northern England as far the River Tay. He built his only east-west road along the line of latitude 55° north, to enable him to subdue the Druids – who, we believe were occupying the old megalithic sites at this latitude where the solstice sunrise and sunset angles produce a perfect square, as we discussed in Chapter Seven. Indeed, Agricola was very systematic in building roads to supply his troops. During his whole campaign, every other road he built ran north-south. He must have faced a logistics problem in supplying the large number of troops he needed to suppress the high density of Druid sites at this latitude, a problem he solved by building this particular road, which was later to provide the line for Hadrian's Wall, the route of which had so puzzled us.[39] The following year he built a line of forts from the Firth of Forth to the Firth of Clyde, and by AD 82 controlled the Scottish lowlands and was considering an invasion of Ireland.

Tacitus records:

> *The side of Britain facing Ireland was lined with his forces. In its soil and climate, and in the character and civilization of its inhabitants, it is much like Britain and its approaches and harbours have now become better known from merchants who trade there. An Irish prince, expelled from his home by a rebellion, was welcomed by Agricola who detained him, nominally as a friend, in the hope of being able to make use of him. I have often heard Agricola say that Ireland could be reduced and held by a single legion with a fair-sized force of auxiliaries; and that it would be easier to hold Britain if it were completely surrounded by Roman armies, so that liberty was banished from its sight.*[40]

This was not idle speculation on the part of Agricola, for he actually succeeded in establishing his bridgehead in Ireland. Nevertheless, it has always been believed that the Romans never got to Ireland and the Irish

[39] Margary, I.D.: *Roman Roads in Britain*, John Barker, 1973
[40] Tacitus: *The Agricola*

Celtic culture remained untainted. In accordance with this view, Roman coins found in the Boyne valley had always been explained away as imports – until an article appeared in the London *Sunday Times* on 21 January 1996.

> *A nondescript patch of land 15 miles north of Dublin has shattered one of Ireland's strongest myths. It indicates that the country was, after all, invaded by the Romans. . . . From beneath the soil at Drumanagh, clear evidence has emerged of a Roman coastal fort of up to 40 acres . . .*
>
> *The fort has been identified as a significant Roman beachhead, built to support military campaigns in the 1st and 2nd century AD. It was heavily defended and is believed to have developed into a big trading town. Coins found at the site show that Roman involvement in Ireland extended at least from 79 AD to 138 AD.*
>
> *Experts on the Roman period hailed the find this weekend. Barry Cunliffe, professor of European archaeology at Oxford University, described as 'staggering'. 'It is one of the most important sites in Europe and fits in exactly with what Rome was doing along all the frontiers of its empire. Drumanagh is absolutely critical as it may explain the scatter of Roman material which has been turning up in Ireland' . . .*
>
> *Barry Raferty, professor of archaeology at University College, Dublin, said it was the most important find in Ireland. He believes hundreds of people populated the fort in houses densely packed into the enclosure . . . A full excavation of the Drumanagh site will provide the answers to a mystery that has endured for nearly 2,000 years.'*[41]

This site was established in the early years of Agricola's governership and puts the comments of Tacitus into a firm context. Tellingly, this location was only a few miles away from Newgrange itself! Agricola was surely trying to ensure that he gained control of every important Druidic site – and these were all located on the megalithic sanctuaries of the Grooved Ware People.

Little is known of Agricola's expedition to Ireland, beyond the fact he seemed to have made very good use of his captured Irish prince's local knowledge to enable him to set up the Roman settlement near the mouth of

[41] Byrne, Ciaran, and Mass, John, in *The Sunday Times*, 21 January 1996.

the Boyne. By contrast, we know a lot about his expedition to Inverness, because Tacitus recorded it in great detail. By AD 84 Agricola had reached the Moray Firth, driving the Druids and their followers before him towards a final sacred site, which Tacitus calls Mount Grampius. Agricola's fleet patrolled the seas between the mainland and the Isles of Hebrides and Orkney. As the cornered Druids turned to fight, Tacitus reports a speech made by their leader, identified as a man called Calgacus:

> *When I consider the motives we have for fighting and the critical position we are in, I have a strong feeling that the united front you are showing today will mean the dawn of liberty for the whole of Britain. You have mustered to a man and all of you are free. There are no lands behind us and even on the sea we are menaced by the Roman fleet. We, the choicest flower of Britain's manhood, were hidden away in her most secret places. We, the most distant dwellers upon earth, the last of the free, have been shielded till today by our very remoteness and by the obscurity in which it has shrouded our name. On, then, into action and as you go think of those that went before you and of those that shall come after.*[42]

Tacitus reports that during the battle 30,000 Britons were killed and the last Druid stronghold was destroyed:

> *An awful silence reigned on every hand, the hills were deserted, houses smoking in the distance, and our scouts did not meet a soul. These were sent out in all directions and made sure the enemy had fled at random and were not massing at any point.*[43]

Agricola's mentor, Vespasian, died in AD 79, to be briefly replaced by Titus, who lasted for little over a year before being replaced by the tyrant Domitian. This new emperor did not like Agricola, and Tacitus reports that Domitian ignored Agricola when he returned to Rome, and then, becoming afraid that Agricola might be too popular with the Army and might form a focus for rebellion, had him poisoned.

[42] Tacitus: *The Agricola*
[43] Tacitus: *The Agricola*

In sum, Agricola had been closely involved with Rome's ongoing attempts to wipe out the Jews and Druids, the two groups of people who are linked by the knowledge in the *Book of Enoch*. There must be a strong suspicion that both were of the royal line of David and were considered to be a threat to the 'Divine rule of Rome' – so they had to be destroyed.

We now knew that Agricola had stretched his resources to the limit to make sure he controlled every sacred site of the Grooved Ware People. Salisbury Plain, Anglesey, the Boyne Valley, Caithness and Sutherland and the Northern Isles. Just as Vespasian had destroyed the Jews of Jerusalem and Massada, so his supporter Agricola had applied Rome's final solution to the Druids.

However, as we have said above, Columba's battle of magic with a Druid at Inverness, in AD 564, suggested that Agricola had *not* been completely successful in his attempted genocide. Could we pick up the trail again? The answer to this question lay in the riddles of a sixth-century Welsh bard.

THE FIRST EISTEDDFOD CHAIR

According to Welsh tradition, King Maelgwn of Gwynedd was one of the earliest patrons of the arts. He is believed to have founded the Eisteddfod, competitive meetings of poets and musicians, still conducted in Wales today.[44] The winners once became the official bards to the court of the king of Gwynedd, taking a chair at his table.

According to the *The Oxford Book of Welsh Verse*, the traditional role of the bard was to express the tribe's tribute to the skill and personal bravery of the chieftain, on whose goodwill their future depended, and it states that it is believed that this tradition of chosen court poets existed long before the coming of the Romans.

This poetry is some of the earliest in the Welsh language (Y Cymreag). Composed by a group known as the Cynferidd (the first poets) it is associated with the sixth-century kingdom of Gwynedd and survived in verbal tradition until at was written down in the *Red Book of Hergest* and the *Book of Taliesin*, in the eleventh century. The Cynferidd wrote the first poems in language that a modern speaker of Welsh would understand.[45]

[44] Edwards, H.T.: *The Eisteddfod*, University of Wales Press,1990
[45] Parry, T.: *The Oxford Book of Welsh Verse*, Clarendon Press, 1962

As historian of the Welsh language Kenneth Jackson said, on the subject of dating the beginnings of the modern Welsh:

> *The Welsh is as old as the middle of the sixth century. This is a point of great importance to literature, because on it there depends the question of whether the historical poems attributed to the late sixth century poets Taliesin and Aneirin were the first poetry to be written in what is now the Welsh language.*
>
> *The Bard Taliesin was the first winner of this competition and he won his chair with a poem which we can still read today, a poem called Hanes Taliesin, or the Tale of Taliesin. Taliesin is the pseudonym taken by one Gwion ap Gwreang when he competed at Conwy Eisteddfod.*[46]

This raises an important question. Why did Gwion choose Taliesin as his bardic name?

The legends of Taliesin say he stole the heritage of the Goddess Cerridwen by drinking from a special cauldron of knowledge that she had prepared for her own son. Cerridwen chases him and using his new found knowledge he takes on many different forms; but despite changing shape many times is finally eaten by Cerridwen, in the shape of a hen, when he turns into a grain of corn. When Cerridwen changes back to her own shape she is pregnant and gives new birth to Taliesin as a boy child. Not wanting the child but unwilling to kill him, Cerridwen casts him into the sea in a skin bag. He floats ashore near a castle, where he is imprisoned by its owner, the king of the giants,Ysbaddaden.

Mabon (the name the gaint gives to the boy Taliesin) is brought up as prisoner by Ysbaddaden, but falls in love with Ysbaddaden's daughter Olwen. When the king of the giants and his household are taken prisoner by the king's uncle, the boy is freed. However, he then goes to the court of this victorious uncle and takes part in a poetry competition, which has as its prize the freedom of the captured king of giants. His poetry is so fine he makes all the competing bards sound like the burbling of children, and as a result, he wins the freedom of his ex-captor Ysbaddaden – and the hand of his daughter Olwen in marriage. On 25 March, Taliesin (the name means

[46] Jackson, K.: *The Dawn of the Welsh Language, Wales through the Ages,* vol. 1, Christopher Davies, 1959

Bringer of Light[47]) marries Olwen (literal meaning White Track, the Welsh name for Venus[48]), daughter of the king of the giants.

Robert Graves, who analysed the poetry of Gwion in detail, commented:

Little Gwion, son of Gwreang of Caereinion, was a person of no importance who accidentally lighted on certain ancient mysteries and becoming an adept, began to despise the professional bards of his time . . . he was a paganistic cleric with Irish connections. Proclaiming himself a master-poet Gwion took the name Taliesin, as an ambitious Hellenistic Greek poet might have taken the name of Homer.[49]

THE WHITE AND HOLY STONE

Having considered the puzzle of Gwion, we addressed another. Who was this Maelgwn Gwynedd, apparent founder of the Elsteddfod, who was seeking a poet for his court?

What we know of Maelgwn today comes from the contemporary writings of Gildas, a monk from the west of Britain. Professor Gwyn Williams, of University College Cardiff said of Gildas.

At the time Gildas wrote the Britons were governed by kings. Gildas's work alone is one long denunciation of them for abandoning Latin, romanitas and Christianity and lapsing into what he saw as barbarity. Almost in passing he names a few of them: at least two ruled in what was becoming Wales. There was Vortipor, 'tyrant' of the Demetae in the south-west, there was Gwrthefyr, king of Dyfed, placed precisely in the mid-sixth century on a memorial stone raised in what is today Carmarthenshire and inscribed in both Latin and the ogham script of the Irish. And there was Maelgwn Gwynedd, ruling Gwynedd in lavish, magnificent and Celtic style from a court at Deganwy on the North Wales coast, but who had been trained in the monastery at Llanilltud Fawr (Llantwit Major) in the Vale of Glamorgan in the south east; according to both Britons and Saxons, he was the most powerful of the kings of the Britons.[50]

[47] Spence, L.: *Mysteries of Celtic Britain*, Nelson & Sons, 1890
[48] Spence, L.: *Mysteries of Celtic Britain*, Nelson & Sons, 1890
[49] Graves, R.: *The White Goddess*, Faber & Faber, 1948
[50] Williams, G.A.: *When Was Wales?*, Penguin, 1985

So Maelgwn was an ex-monk from a monastery of the Celtic Church in South Wales.

There is an old tradition that Christianity was brought to South Wales as early as AD 58 by King Bran of Glamorgan. King Bran is described in medieval Welsh documents, known as the *Triads of the Island of Britain*, as the head of one of the three holy families of Britain:

> *The first, [holy family] the family of Bran the Blessed, son of Llyr Llediath, that Bran brought the faith of Christ first into this island from Rome where he had been imprisoned . . .*[51]

The monastery where Maelgwn had trained was run by a matrilineal descendant of Bran known as St Illtud: his mother was a royal princess of line of Bran[52] and his father a warrior called Bicanus. When Illtud was educated, he showed such a wonderful memory that he was said to remember every sentence that was ever spoken to him.[53] When he first settled in Glamorgan, he made his cell in a deep cave which contained an important stone, now lost. Illtud was said to sleep with his head on this stone, 'he lay all night upon the cold stone'. There is an identical legend about him reported from Brittany from a completely independent source.[54]

Illtud also had strong links with Ireland, there is an old tradition, from the Gower peninsular of South Wales, that St Patrick was the son of a local man called Mawon and trained as a priest at the monastery of St Illtud. When he was ordained, he took the name Padriag Maenwyn (Patrick of the White Stone) before he was abducted by the Irish.[55] These two traditions suggested that Maenwyn (or its variant Maelgwn) was a title given to successful students of Illtud, perhaps those who learned the tradition of the white stones. Pertinently, holy water in y Cymreag is dwr swyn, so perhaps the title meant not so much white stone, as holy stone.

Maelgwn ap Cadwallon was born on Anglesey, where his father Cadwallon Lawhir the son of Cunedda, the leader of the Gwyr yr Gogledd (Men of the North) and king of Strath Clyde – had driven Irish invaders out

[51] Blackett, A.T. and Wilson, A.: *Arthur and the Charters of the Kings*, M.T. Byrd and Co., 1980
[52] Bowen, E.G.: *The Settlements of the Celtic Saints of Wales*, University of Wales Press, 1956
[53] Doble, G.H.: *Lives of the Welsh Saints*, University of Wales Press, 1971
[54] Doble, G.H.: *Lives of the Welsh Saints*, University of Wales Press, 1971
[55] Newell, E.J.: *A History of the Welsh Church*, Elliot Stock, 1895

of the island at the battle of Cerrig y Gwyddwl early in the sixth century.[56] (This battle was fought around Agricola's old fort at Holyhead). Prior to the sixth century, the island of Anglesey had been a popular destination for Irish clerics and settlers, and these incomers built on the site of previous megalithic monuments.[57] Maelgwn's father had fought a long battle to drive out these Irish invaders and secure the ancient sites of the Grooved Ware People for his own people, the Cymru.

Maelgwn later commemorated the site of the battle of Cerrig y Gwyddwl, by giving the fort to St Cybi to build the church which still stands there.[58]

Legend says Maelgwn was chosen by a Pictish princess to father her son, Brude macMaelchon, High King of the Picts, who held court at Inverness around AD 564. (This is the same Brude whose Druid lost a battle of wits with the Irish Columba.) The kingship of the Pictish kingdom, which at the time extended from Orkney down to the Firth of Forth, was by matrilinear decent, and the Pictish princesses had the right to choose the noblest men available to father their children. As Maelgwn was, as we have just seen, a direct descendant of Cundedda, and was himself king of the richest and most cultured kingdom of west Britain at the time, it would certainly have been a good political alliance. We do not know Brude's mother's name, but certainly his father's name, Maelchon, could be a Pictish form of Maelgwn. Historian R.B. Hale says of Brude:

> *Brude macMaelchon's mother almost certainly chose king Maelgwn of Gwynedd in north Wales to be the father of her son. A cultivated man who encouraged poetry and art at his Court in Deganwy, he had been in his youth a monk, a fact pointed out by St Gildas. However, Brude macMaelchon, child of this union, was brought up and educated with his mother's people in the land of the Picts and may never have met his father.*[59]

So, were battles to control specific areas and dynastic marriages both taking place to ensure that the ruling families, descended from Cunedda, controlled as many of the Grooved Ware sacred sites as possible?

[56] Bromwich, R.: *Trioedd Ynys Prydein*, University of Wales Press, 1961
[57] Bowen, E.G.: *The Settlements of the Celtic Saints of Wales*, University of Wales Press, 1956
[58] Bowen, E.G.: *The Settlements of the Celtic Saints of Wales*, University of Wales Press, 1956
[59] Hale, R.B.: *The Magnificent Gael*, MOM, Ottawa, 1976

This, then, was the political situation when Gwion stood up to recite a poem to flatter and intrigue the powerful Maelgwn, in the hope of winning a permanent chair at the king's table.

We are well aware that the ritual of modern Freemasonry teaches certain ways of speaking and a number of unusual concepts which, if used in normal speech, stand out to any other Mason. There is no need for secret handshakes and passwords. Any Mason knows enough ritual to recognize its use by any other Mason, and as the whole ritual is based on question and answer, it is impossible to impersonate a Freemason without learning the ritual in its entirety. In a similar way, did Gwion knew a secret tradition which he knew Maelgwn was also aware of?

Certainly Robert Graves was convinced that Gwion, whilst studying in Ireland, had learned a religious secret, which he alluded to in his poetry:

> *Gwion was no irresponsible rhapsodist, but a true poet, whilst other bards knew only Latin, French, Welsh and English, he was well read also in the Irish classics and in Greek and Hebrew literature. I realized that he was hiding an ancient religious mystery – a blasphemous one from the Church's point of view.*[60]

Graves in fact took the view that Gwion was following a belief in Goddess worship, but we believe Gwion knew the myths of Enochian Judaism and decided to advertise this fact to Maelgwn who, as a student of Illtud, was heir to the same tradition. His competition work appealed to the common language and symbolism he shared with Maelgwn, and he did it by telling riddles that only the king would know the answer to.

His poem '*Hanes Taliesin*' definitely poses many riddles. Learned critics of Taliesin's poetry have said it is connected with a secret Druidical doctrine of the transmigration of souls.[61] Be that as it may, the answers to some of Gwion's riddles were now clear to us from our studies of the Grooved Ware People.

The poem starts with the statement: 'I am the chief bard to Elphin, and my original country is the region of the summer stars.' He then lists a number of riddles saying that he has been a number of different people; not saying who these people were, but what they did. Although we cannot answer all Gwion

[60] Graves, R.: *The White Goddess*, Faber and Faber, 1948

[61] Graves, R.: *The White Goddess*, Faber and Faber, 1948

Taliesin's riddles, some stand out. Here we have extracted certain riddles, the answers to which are to be found in the *Book of Enoch*.

Riddle: I was the instructor of Enoch.

Answer: The *Book of Enoch* says: 'And in those days the angel Uriel answered and said to me: "Behold, I have shown thee everything, Enoch, and I have revealed everything to thee that thou shouldst see this sun and this moon, and the leaders of the stars of the heaven and all those who turn them, their tasks and times and departures."'

Riddle: I am able to instruct the whole universe.

Answer: The *Book of Enoch* says: 'Such is the picture and sketch of every luminary which Uriel the archangel, who is their leader, showed unto me.'

Riddle: I have been in Asia with Noah in the Ark.

Answer: The *Book of Enoch* says: 'Then said the Most High, the Holy and Great One spake, and sent Uriel to the son of Lamech, and said to him: 'Go to Noah and tell him in my name, 'Hide thyself!' and reveal to him the end that is approaching: that the whole earth will be destroyed, and a deluge is about to come upon the whole earth, and will destroy all that is on it. And now instruct him that he may escape and his seed may be preserved for all the generations of the world."'

Riddle: I know the names of the stars from North to South.

Answer: The *Book of Enoch* says: 'And I saw how the stars of heaven come forth, and I counted the portals out of which they proceed, and wrote down all their outlets, of each individual star by itself, according to their number and their names, their courses and their positions, and their times and their months, as Uriel the holy angel who was with me showed me. He showed all things to me and wrote them down for me: also their names he wrote for me, and their laws and their companies.'

Riddle: I was with my Lord in the Highest sphere.

Answer: The *Book of Enoch* says: 'And from underneath the throne came streams of flaming fire so that I could not look thereon. And the Great Glory sat thereon, and His raiment shone more brightly than the sun and was whiter than any snow. None of the angels could enter and could behold His face by reason of the magnificence and glory and no flesh could behold Him. The flaming fire was round about Him, and a great fire stood before Him, and none around could draw nigh Him: ten thousand times ten thousand (stood) before Him, yet He needed no counsellor. And the most holy ones who were nigh to Him did not leave by night nor depart from Him. And until then I had been prostrate on my face, trembling: and the Lord called me with His own mouth, and said to me: ' Come hither, Enoch, and hear my word.' And one of the holy ones came to me and waked me, and He made me rise up and approach the door: and I bowed my face downwards.'

So the answers to five of Gwion Taliesin's riddles are contained in the *Book of Enoch* which, as we discussed in Chapter Two, had been thought to have been lost in the first century AD. This poem was written mid sixth century, so does this mean that the traditions of the *Book of Enoch* had been secretly preserved? Gwion was certainly showing off secret knowledge, but he was doing it with the intention of impressing Maelgwn. The riddle undoubtedly impressed Maelgwn, because Gwion won the bard's chair at the Eisteddfod, and henceforth sat at the table of Maelgwn to compose poems in his praise.

In the same way that a modern Mason might say, 'Do you bring anything with you?', expecting a very specific answer from a Brother Mason, Gwion was posing questions that only a fellow initiate would know the answers to. Maelgwn was initiated into the same tradition of knowledge, and so responded to the unanswered questions and awarded Gwion the chair, making him his Court Bard.

A MASONIC PUZZLE

Our studies of Enochian Judaism had helped us answer some of Gwion's riddles. Strangely, from our Masonic background, we could also answer another.

Riddle: I have been chief director of the work of the tower of Nimrod.

The answer to this riddle is Peleg, and it is contained in the Ritual of the

Degree of the Noahites (or Prussian Knights) and also contained in the Ancient Charges of Freemasonry, which had attracted us because of their references to the content of the lost *Book of Enoch.*

The traditional history of this degree says how Peleg was stricken dumb by God for attempting to build a tower to heaven, whilst working as chief architect to Nimrod. Peleg is said to be a descendant of Noah.

Nimrod was the character in the Book of Genesis, described as 'the first potentate on earth', and as the grandson of Noah. He is said to have been an empire-builder whose lands included large areas of southern Mesopotamia. Some scholars identify Nimrod as being the same person as Gilgamesh.[62]

The ritual story is delivered in this degree by an officer of the lodge who is called the Knight of Eloquence:

> *To every mason let it be known notwithstanding the recent vengeance which the Deity had taken upon mankind for their iniquities, by causing a universal deluge – notwithstanding the Deity had given the rainbow as a sign of reconciliation, vouchsafing that favour declared that the world should not again be destroyed by waters, the descendants of Noah, from their want of faith in the divine prediction, being apprehensive of a second deluge said – Let us build a city whose top may reach the heavens and let us make a name lest we be scattered abroad upon the face of the earth. To accomplish their designs, they began to erect a high tower in the plain of Shinar; but this enterprise being displeasing in the eyes of their Maker, as tending to frustrate or delay the execution of his design, that mankind should not always continue together, he obliged them to discontinue the project, by confounding their language, so that one could not understand another. From this circumstance the city took its name of Babel, which signifies confusion; and a dispersion of the people and a planting of nations ensued.*
>
> *It was on the night of the full moon that the Lord worked this wonder, in remembrance of the which, the Noahites hold their lodges at this season. The architect was named Peleg; at least, it was he who gave the idea of this building. As a punishment for his contumacy, and the presumption of his brethren, he was deprived of his speech; and to avoid the outrages of his companions, who considered him the cause*

[62] Genesis, *Peake's Commentary on the Bible*

of the failure of their design, he travelled into countries remote from Shinar, and from thence only by moonlight, as he was fearful of massacre if his person were recognized. His place of retirement was Prussia, where having erected a triangular dwelling, he, by humiliation, and contrition for the part he had taken in the plain of Shinar, obtained remission of his sins, and had his speech restored to him. This dwelling of Peleg's was discovered fifteen cubits deep from the surface of the earth, in the year 553 BC.

Archaeological evidence associates the Celts with the Hallstatt culture (touched on in Chapter Twelve) which existed in western Germany between 700 to 500 BC. The date given here therefore ties in with a Celtic origin, especially as it is believed that they began to settle in the British Isles during this period.

In it was found a stone of white marble, on which was inscribed the particulars I have related in the Hebrew tongue and adjacent was the following epitaph:- Here repose the ashes of the grand architect of the tower of Babel, director of works for Prince Nimrod. The Lord had pity on him because he became humble.[63]

Not only was the answer to the riddle 'Peleg', but the legend that Gwion alludes to was recorded on a White Stone – no wonder Maelgwn was flattered!

The preamble to the ritual of this degree says that the members of this degree are called Knights or Prussian Masons. It goes on to say that the mysteries of the initiation can only be celebrated when the moon is full and that at the time of the Crusades the Knights of the various nations were confederated in Palestine, and mutually communicated their secrets in Masonry. The Prussian Knights were claimed to have initiated the Christian Princes and their attendants who also became Masons.[64]

The introduction to this ritual book also give a brief introduction to Freemasonry and makes the following interesting statement:

The proper business of a Mason is astronomical, chemical, geological

[63] *Ritual of the Degree of the Noahites or Prussian Knights*, Reeves and Turner, 1812
[64] *Ritual of the Degree of the Noahites or Prussian Knights*, Reeves and Turner, 1812

and moral science, and more particularly that of the ancients, with all the mysteries and fables founded upon it.

Let us endeavour to turn the stream; to go from priest-craft to science, from mystery to knowledge, from allegory to real history. But for the planetary motion, there could have been no division of time. The relations of the sun to the planets and fixed stars make up all the natural divisions of time; such as the day, the month, the year, and the corresponding seasons. The day is marked by the motion of the earth on its own axis. The month (lunar) by the appearances of the moon; and (solar or calendar) by the grouping of stars into twelve divisions which are called the Zodiac, pictorially marked by signs and seen opposite to the solar side of the earth, in the successive months. The year is complete when the sun appears to return to a given spot from which it is said to start. There is no plain historical truth, no revelation, about God, in existence, other than those of the relations of the sun to the planets and stars, in physics, and the cultivation of the human mind in morals. All other such pretensions to history may be historically disproved. The emblems of the most ancient temples of which we have ruins are emblems of time, of planetary bodies, their motions and relations.

Next, the ritual of this degree spells out how this degree, and all Freemasonry, is built upon the astronomical knowledge that was so important to the ancient Grooved Ware People. Remarkably, the information that comes from the use of an Uriel machine is described, including the study of the course of comets:

The true meaning then of the building of Solomon's Temple in Freemasonry is, and the practice of the lodges should be, to the effect that the grand secret of all religion is this allegorical typification of the solar relations and plantary motions with mental and moral cultivation, and that such, in truth, is the great lost secret of Freemasonry

The Key, then to the mysteries of Freemasonry, as well as the mysteries of the Christian and Jewish religions, is the Eleusinian mysteries of the Pagan religion; and the further Key to all those mysteries, is the worship of the Sun as God, under a variety of personifications, in all its Zodiacal transits, in the personification of the year, of the seasons, of the months, of time generally, and of all the divisions of time, and the source of all physical and all moral phenomena. The Masonic building of Solomon's temple is the getting of a knowledge of the celestial globe, knowing the mysteries of all the figures and groupings of stars on that globe; knowing further, that this globe is the foundation of all religion, knowing how to calculate the precession of equinoxes, the return of comets and eclipses, and all the planetary motions and astronomical relations of time. Such is not the knowledge now gained in Masonic Lodges; I will present the reader with that knowledge; but such should be the knowledge; for such would be real and useful knowledge. The ancient priests thought that knowledge should be concealed from the multitude, or found profitable that it should be so; and hence our sacred and mysterious [Masonic] writings. But now, we do not think that knowledge should be kept from the multitude, and hence our infidelity and our revealings.[65]

Here we must mention the importance of the fact that this Masonic degree is named as being for 'Noahites', which can also be spelled 'Noachide'. It refers to the secret tradition of Noah, one that was held by Honi the circle maker (commented on in Chapter Twelve) and his descendants who included John the Baptist, Jesus and James.

For the first Book of Constitutions produced by the Grand Lodge of London on 25 March 1722, authored by Dr Anderson, the following statement was ordered to be printed on the cover:

A Mason is obliged by his Tenure to observe the moral Law as a true Noachide.

In the editions printed in 1723 and 1738 it stated:

The first Name of Masons was Noachide.

Intriguingly, on the day preceding the spring equinox in 1990, George Bush, President of the United States of America (and a senior Freemason), signed into law the historic Joint Resolution of both Houses of Congress

[65] *Ritual of the Degree of the Noahites or Prussian Knights*, Reeves and Turner, 1812

recognizing the seven Noachide laws as the 'bedrock of society from the dawn of civilization' and urged his country to 'return the world to the moral and ethical values contained in the Seven Noachide Laws.'[66]

To sum up, Gwion's riddles were certainly leading us to believe that he had tapped an ancient source of knowledge, which included the main myths of Enochian Judaism; but he also gave a riddle which suggested his source was *not* the same one as we had happened upon whilst searching for the truth about Freemasonry.

However, he gave us one extra clue about where he might have gained this knowledge. To understand this riddle, one needs a background in Celtic myth and the genealogies of the Tuatha de Danann of Ireland. Here is that riddle.

Riddle: I was in the Court of Don before the birth of Gwydion

The answer is: I was Beli (nee Managan), father of Gwydion, at Bru na Boinne the Court of Dana (Don). Now his opening reference in the poem 'Hanes Taliesin' to having his original country in 'the region of the summer stars' makes sense. The summer stars are the stars in the north. He is actually telling us he knows the meaning of the movements of the stars and his knowledge has come from the north. The Lia Fial (the king-making stone, discussed earlier in this chapter) was brought to Ireland by the Tuatha de Danann from the north, and he is also telling us he knows the secrets of the stones which tell of the movement of the stars. Gwydion is the master of the knowledge of the stars and is buried in the kingdom of Gwynedd beneath the Stone of Enigmas [as we discussed in Chapter Nine], which contains all the knowledge of the stars, traditionally a white or holy stone.

In essence, then, the answer to this riddle tells us that Gwion has been to Ireland and learned the stories of the Bru na Boinne, but he is linking them to the Kingdom of Gwynedd and the court of Maelgwn (the White Stone).

In another of his poems, Gwion tells how he obtained his wisdom: The song is rendered into Saesneg (English), prose which in no way captures the charm and elegance of Taliesin's original, but tries to remain true to his meaning.

66 House Joint Resolution 104, Public Law 102-4, (R. Bobowik: private correspondence).

'I have been in many shapes before I obtained a congenial form. I have been the narrow silver strip of a sword blade. I have been a point in the air. I have been a shining star. I have been the written word. I have been the first book. I have been the light in a lantern of three year quarters. I have been a bridge for crossing sixty rivers. I am the eagle. I have crossed the sea in boats. I have ordered battles. I have been both sword and shield. I have been the string of the harp. I have been enchanted for a year under the waters. There is nothing I have not been'[67]

The theme of the poem draws on all the many features of the megalithic sites. The ideas of the narrow beams of silver light characterize the intense point source of Venus light, which we knew floods the chamber at Newgrange every eight years. Gwion Taliesin says he has been a narrow strip of silver, a point in the air and shinning star. The description could hardly be more evocative of the Venus light which regularly shines inside Bryn Cellu Ddu, one of the important sites of the Druids within Maelgwn's kingdom of Gwynedd, whose mysticism Gwion Taliesin claimed to be heir to. Had he, therefore, also witnessed the 'sword' of silver light climbing the pillar of Bryn Celli Ddu? Certainly he had every opportunity to do so. Is *this* where Gwion Taliesin married Olwen – the 'white track' – at the spring equinox?

Gwion is clearly showing off his knowledge of the mysteries of Ireland, but in doing so, he tells us that the sixth-century Irish and Welsh knew material from Enochian Judaism, which had been lost to both Jews and Roman Christians of the time. (It is significant that it nevertheless still existed in Freemasonry in the 17th century.) As we have already pointed out, Gwion flatters Maelgwn by playing up to his knowledge and his title of White Stone, setting riddles to which only a student of Illtud would know the answers. Examining the sources of this secret knowledge has left us clues to its survival from the Grooved Ware astronomer priests, down to the kings and bards of sixth-century Wales.

[67] Williams, I.: *Canu Taliesin*, Caerdydd, 1960

CONCLUSION

The line of David which Irish legend says married into the line of the High Kings of Tara, established the tradition of a king-making stone which survives to this day. The Irish legends also tell of resurrection beliefs associated with Newgrange. The Druids collected and retold these stories, absorbing the Enochian Jewish beliefs.

In the first century AD, the Romans, otherwise tolerant of subject nations' religious beliefs, devoted considerable effort to destroying both the Enochian Jews and the Druids. We conclude that this was because, as the royal line of the true kings, they represented a threat to the divine status of the Roman Emperors. Despite their best efforts the Roman overlords did not quite succeed, because an Enochian tradition survived and resurfaced in Celtic Christianity during the sixth century.

The evidence for this survival is found in the poems of Gwion, who took the Barchic name Taliesin when he told riddles from the Book of Enoch to King Maelgwn of Gwynydd.

Chapter Fourteen

THE ONE RELIGION

THE LAST SON OF THE STAR

By AD 73 the Romans under Vespasian's son, Titus, had all but the destroyed the last members of the Enochian-Zadokite Jewish priesthood that we remember as the Jerusalem Church. Next, the Emperor Vespasian sent Agricola back to Britain with the instructions that he was to capture all the Druid sites and take no prisoners.

The two living strains of Enochian Judaism were to be snuffed out on the orders of the Roman Empire.

However, genocide is rarely 100 per cent successful, and there were some survivors from both of these ancient groups. In Israel, some descendants of the smitten priesthood made a bold attempt at regaining their lost power some 62 years after Titus had left Jerusalem in ruins. The leader of the Jews in their rising against the Romans was, almost certainly, from the same family as John the Baptist, Jesus, and James. We deduce this from the fact that John, Jesus and James, members of the same family, each headed the movement known as the Jerusalem Church: John, then Jesus, then James. Following the death of James, leadership transferred to a nephew of Jesus and James, indicating the continuing importance of this family. Like Jesus, Simon was a Galilean who was known as the messiah and 'the star that was rising out of Jacob'. The name he was given on assuming the leadership was Simon bar Kochba, which means 'son of the star'. Certainly, it seems unlikely that this 'holy' position would go to an outsider.

The revolt led by this 'son of the star' was the direct result of a proclamation by the Emperor Hadrian that Jews were to be banned from entering Jerusalem except for one day a year, and that the Jewish rite of circumcision was to be made illegal. Bar Kochba organized the war with the support of Akiba ben Joseph, one of the most influential rabbis of the period. Akiba proclaimed bar Kochba to be the messiah, saying of him: 'That is the king Messiah.' Akiba immediately applied the Star Prophecy to this leader, with the authenticating text: 'There shall come a Star out of Jacob to rule the world.'

As with the previous Jewish war of AD 66, bar Kochba had many early successes, retaking Jerusalem and at least 50 other towns in Judaea. Hadrian sent in another army, but it was also defeated. Inevitably, though, the Romans gained the upper hand and finally crushed the Jewish army at Bethar near Jerusalem in August AD 135. Bar Kochba either died or fled.

Once again the price had been high. Half a million Jews are said to have been killed and thousands of Jewish women and children were sold into slavery. Jerusalem suffered almost complete destruction before being rebuilt by the Emperor Hadrian under its new name of Aelia Capitolina.

Professor Robert Eisenman has observed that that during the Bar Kochba war, the followers of this 'son of the star' returned to the caves of Qumran, and that this presence of Bar Kochba's forces at the site needs to be explained. He also notes that the scrolls found in Cave IV were placed there by these people after AD 132, rather than in AD 68, when the other scrolls were deposited.[2] This cave contained many scrolls included 'The Book of Giants', the story of 'Enoch and the Watchers' and a 'Vision of the Son of God'.

The Bar Kochba war was the end of the Jewish struggle to fulfil the Star Prophecy, and ideas of a messiah arising to lead the nation of the Jews faded away. But the descendants of the high priesthood who had escaped in AD 70 were prospering in Europe, emerging as some of the most prominent families of northern France in particular.[3]

The Romans had tried hard to destroy the old religions that threatened their claim to be divine rulers. The patriarch of Constantinople at the end of

[1] Eisenman, R.: *The Dead Sea Scrolls and the First Christians*, Element, 1996
[2] Eisenman, R.: *The Dead Sea Scrolls and the First Christians*, Element, 1996
[3] Knight, C., and Lomas, R.: *The Second Messiah*, Century, 1997

the fourth century, St John Chrysostom, thought that the battle had been won, saying:

> *Every trace of the old philosophy and literature of the ancient world has vanished from the face of the earth.*[4]

He was wrong. Even as he spoke, the Scottish line of Cunedda, which, ruled Scotland, Wales and the North of England, was being converted to Celtic Christianity by St Ninian. And Celtic Christianity was closer to Enochian Judaism than it was to the rebranded Mithraism that passed for Christianity in Rome.

CELTIC CHRISTIANITY

The oldest written records in Wales were collected by monks of the Church of Wales from around the sixth century onwards, although the majority of the surviving copies of the manuscripts date from the 11th century. These accounts are known as the '*Triads of the Isle of Britain*' and the stories in them cover periods back as far as 450 BC, but the information contained in them has been largely ignored, because they stem from verbal traditions and were written down long after the events they purported to describe, as well as the fact that they were originally written in Yr Cymraeg (Welsh) rather than Latin.

The accounts of history contained in these stories are in the form of many elaborate saga-cycles in which prose was the medium of narrative. It is noted that Welsh storytellers yielded to none in volume of their material, but as their tales were delivered orally, many centuries sometimes passed before they were committed to writing.[5]

Triad No. 35 says that Christianity came to South Wales in AD 58 when King Bran of Glamorgan brought the new faith to the land.

> *In 51 AD king Caradoc was defeated in a major battle with the Romans . . . and Ostorius Scapula took Caradoc to Rome along with his father king Bran and the rest of the [royal] family. The Romans made Bran a citizen and they stayed until 58 AD. 'Bran the Blessed.*

[4] Doane T.W.: *Bible Myths and Their Parallels in Other Religions*
[5] Jones, G. and Jones, T.: *The Mabinogion*, Dent, 1949

son of Llyr Llediath, that Bran brought the faith of Christ first into this island from Rome where he had been seven years as a hostage . . . As a Bard himself, King Bran would have had to submit the new [religious] ideas to a convention or Gorsedd of Bards, for whilst in 57 AD the main body of the North Wales Bards of the Ordovices were murdered on Anglesey by Suetonius Paulinus [the battle of Castell Ior, see Chapter Thirteen] no such massacre of the South Wales Bards occurred. In the South, the Druid order of the Bards simply now became the ministers of the new religion as they incorporated Christianity into their total function. There was no great massacre and no break in the continuity of the nation's heritage and customs.[6]

If the claim that Christianity reached Wales in AD 58 is true, it speaks volumes for the form it must have taken. As the Bible tells us, at this time James the brother of Jesus was the leader of the Jerusalem Church. He took the title of 'Mebakker' (meaning bishop) of Jerusalem, and wore a mitre and a jewelled breastplate as signs of his authority. Paul, on the other hand, was a virtual loner, hated by the followers of James and often jeered at, attacked and even imprisoned when he spoke to Jews everywhere from Ephesus to Jerusalem. The story which Paul taught had little to do with the beliefs of the Jerusalem Church; as he wrote in Galatians 1:15-16:

It was the good pleasure of God . . . to reveal his son to me, that I might preach it to the gentiles.

This is an admission that what he was teaching to non-Jews was to be distinguished from the beliefs of the Zadokite priesthood in Jerusalem and Qumran. And this unauthorized evangelism eventually brought Paul into a physical conflict with hostile Jews which, we are told in chapter 21 of Acts, resulted in Roman troops having to save Paul from being lynched.

It was only after the murder of James in AD 62 and the destruction of the Jerusalem Church over the following ten years that the ideas of Paul started to be taken seriously, by those who knew nothing of the original story. It therefore follows that the form of Christianity that reached Wales in AD 58, would have been from James (in Hebrew Jacob, hence the expression Jacobite Church for that led by James, the brother of Jesus). Quite simply,

[6] Blackett, A.T. and Wilson, A.: *Arthur and the Charters of the Kings*, M.T. Byrd and Co., 1980

Welsh Christianity must have followed the teachings of the Jacobite Church *not* the Pauline Church.

Given the evidence that the High Kings of Tara had adopted Jewish ideas 600 years earlier (as demonstrated in Chapter Thirteen), and the Druidic priesthood had absorbed Enochian ideas from both the Jewish Zadokite tradition and the old Grooved Ware traditions of Britain, it seems logical that only these 'Jacobite' ideas would have been acceptable.

From what we already knew about stone and cave legends connected with Illtud – teacher of Maelgwn and St Patrick, and son of a princess of the line of Bran – it seems that the Gorsedd of Bards decided to keep the best of both traditions. They kept the megalithic interest in stones and calendars and added to it the concept of Jesus as the prime example of the all that is best in the Druid's relationship with God. In doing so, they adopted a version of Christianity which was extremely acceptable to the Celtic nations of Britain, who were comfortable with the ideas which the Druids had inherited from the Grooved Ware People and the Enochian Jews.

We knew from the riddles of Taliesin that knowledge of Enoch had survived in the teachings of Illtud. Bran and his Druids may have had little difficulty in merging the Jacobite Christian religion with their own tradition, including its own calendar and its own Druidic tonsure, where they shaved the front part of their heads but allowed the hair at the back to grow long.

It is said that St Patrick came from South Wales to take the message of Christianity to Ireland, and that he met a Gorsedd of Bards at Tara and converted them to his new faith with little difficulty.[7]

> *He had much success in converting Irish chiefs and secured the attention of the Irish King Laoghaire at Tara by miraculously overcoming the Druids.*[8]

It has recently been discovered that the places that Patrick visited to preach his new religion were Druidic sites that had themselves been built upon ancient Grooved Ware sites. For example, a pre-Christian fort and hut sites have been found on the summit of Croagh Patrick – Ireland's 'holy

[7] Hanson, R.P.C.: *Saint Patrick, His Origins and Career*, Oxford University Press, 1968
[8] Jones, A.: *Chambers Enclyopaedic Guide to the Saints*, Chambers, 1992

mountain' in County Mayo, with spectacular views over Westport Bay – which is where St Patrick is said to have fasted for 40 days and 40 nights.

In 1992, Neolithic decorated art was discovered on St Patrick's Chair, a natural rock outcrop along the pilgrimage route, towards the mountain top. Mayo people used to gather on the mountain before St Patrick's fast to honour the Celtic god Lug at the Festival of Lughnasa. Patrick seems to have spent a lot of time with Druids on Neolithic sites to achieve a very rapid conversion to Christianity.[9] Perhaps he was arguing his case that Jesus – the new example of perfect Druidism – should be brought into the ancient teachings.

Douglas Hyde records that the *Colloquy of the Ancients*, a medieval account of Patrick, shows how well-versed and interested in recorded ancient Druidic lore Patrick was:

> *St Patrick began to feel a little uneasy at the delight with which he listened to the stories of the ancient Fenians, and in his over-scrupulous sanctity he feared it might be wrong to extract such pleasure from merely mundane narrations. Accordingly he consulted his two guardian angels on the matter, not only to the effect that there was no harm in listening to the stories themselves, but actually desiring him to get them written down in poet's tamhlorgs and in the words of the Olluna, for it will be a rejoicing to numbers and to the good people to the end of time, to listen to these stories.*[10]

This interpretation made sense of Rolleston's comments about the rapid spread of Celtic Christianity in Ireland.

> *Very soon after the conversion of Ireland to Christianity, we find the country covered with monasteries, whose complete organisation seems to indicate that they were really Druidic colleges transformed en masse.*[11]

In the mid-sixth century St Finnian, the abbot of one of these converted Druidic colleges in the Boyne Valley, took on a young pupil called Colomba, who was the son of Prince Fedilmith of the Ur-Neill kings of Tara.

[9] Hanson, R.P.C.: *Saint Patrick, His Origins and Career*, Oxford University Press, 1968

[10] Hyde, D.: *A Literary History of Ireland*, T. Fisher Unwin, 1899

[11] Rolleston, T.W.: *Myths and Legends of the Celtic Race*, G.G. Harrap and Co., 1911

Columba grew to be an extremely influential figure in the history of both Celtic Christianity and the line of the Stewart kings of Scotland. In 563 he left Ireland and sailed to Scotland where he became an important political influence on the establishment of the kingdom of Dalriada, the kingdom that encompassed much of Ireland as well as western Scotland. So important was he that he was able to change the line of succession from a weak king called Eogan to a younger and much stronger man called Aidan. His justification for this change he gave as divine intervention: God told him to do it in a dream.

Historian Ian Findley comments: '*This tale reveals Columba as an unscrupulous manipulator of the credulous, making an unpopular decision and blaming it on divine intervention.*'[12]

Columba's whole purpose for his mission to Scotland seems to be connected with an urge on the part of the High Kings of Tara to spread their domains into the lands which the Grooved Ware People had once owned. Historian Ian Bradley says of Columba's motives:

> *As abbot of Iona, Columba was to be instrumental in building up the power of the rulers of this new Scottish kingdom [of Dalriada] and in forging a close alliance between them and his own northern Ur-Neill kinsmen in Ulster. It is conceivable that he went there initially either at the behest of the king of Scots Dalriada or of his own royal relatives for largely political reasons.*[13]

Like Bran and St Patrick (Maengwyn: 'White Stone') before him, Columba attended a Gorsedd of Bards where he pleaded the case for the new prime example of Druidism – Jesus Christ. He held this meeting with the Druids of Brude MacMaelchon at Teilte, where he declared: '*Christ is my Druid, he is my true miracle worker.*'[14]

Having made this statement of the new faith to the Pictish Druids, Columba then went on to send a white stone (this was a freshly consecrated

[12] Findley, I.: *Columba*, Victor Gollancz, 1979

[13] Bradley I.: *Columba, Pilgrim and Penitent*, Wild Goose Publications, 1996

[14] Spence, L.: *Mysteries of Celtic Britain*, Nelson and Sons, 1890

stone, *not* the king-making stone, the Lia Fial, discussed in Chapter Thirteen) to King Brude with instructions that water should be poured on it to make the water holy and give it healing properties. (As we also saw in Chapter Thirteen, Brude was known as MacMaelchon, which is the Pictish for son of Maelgwm, meaning Son of the White Stone). Columba was clearly aware of this link with his careful choice of present to the king and he would also have been aware of how this title linked Brude with the Cymru of southern Scotland and North Wales. His political skill won the day, and this first alliance led eventually to the establishment of the line of his family's descendants as kings of the Scots.

Columba created an ark to keep his holy writings, known as the Monymusk Reliquary, which carried no Christian symbolism whatsoever. (It can still be seen in the Museum of Scotland in Edinburgh). In battles as late as the Battle of Bannockburn in 1314, Scottish warriors carried Columba's Ark before them into battle, just as the Ancient Israelites had done with the Ark of Moses. The symbol of his religion was not the Christian Cross, but the Wheel or Celtic Cross, which incorporates the megalithic symbols of the aligned tunnels and chambers of the solstice markers. Historian Derek Bryce, who has made a detailed study of the Celtic Cross, says of it:

Figure 48. *St Illtud's Celtic Cross.*

> *The basic symbolism of these crosses, like the ancient pillar stones, is the world axis, the link between heaven and earth, the point about which the heavens revolve.*[15]

Columba went on to set up a monastery on Iona, which in time became the main burial ground of the High Kings of Tara and later their successors in Scotland, the MacAlpin kings of Scots. (It is interesting to note that the last famous burial there was of the late leader of the British Labour Party, John Smith.) From the establishment of Iona it became the regular practice of the High Kings of Tara to retire when they were too old to lead their warriors into battle and become monks there.[16]

This merging of Druidism with the Enochian elements of Christianity had developed into a strong religion which did not have many of the supernatural overtones of Mithraism (a popular Roman mystery cult) that Paul's concept of a man being God had incorporated into Roman Christianity. As a result, the Roman Church, successor to the decaying Empire of Rome, was disturbed by both the teaching and practices of this new faith, which did not require that Jesus was a god.

The Roman Church accordingly sent Augustine across to Canterbury, in order that he might regularize the practices of the Church in these troublesome islands to the west of Europe. In 603, when Augustine summoned the British Church leaders from the dioceses in Wales, the Celtic bishops decided in advance that only if the Roman emissary rose and greeted them as a brother would they co-operate with him. When the British Church leaders came into him at the meeting place at Aust, near the River Severn, Augustine remained seated. The was judged as being too arrogant, and the leaders returned home without further discussion.[17]

For the next 61 years the Roman Church negotiated for a unification between the two churches. This was finally resolved at the Synod of Whitby in 664, when the power of the Pope finally extended itself to the Celtic fringe. Here the weak Abbot Colman submitted to Rome and apparently surrendered the beliefs of the Celtic Church – its calendar, its distinctive Druidic tonsure and its other practices. Early in the next century, Bede, the Church historian, recorded a set of minutes of this meeting, reporting that:

15 Bryce, D.: *Symbolism of the Celtic Cross*, Llanerch, 1989
16 Marsden, J.: *The Tombs of the Kings, An Iona Book of the Dead*, Llanerch, 1994
17 Edward, H.T.: *Wales and the Welsh Church*, Rivingtons, 1898

And when discussions arose on the questions of Easter, the tonsure and various other church matters, it was decided to hold a synod to put an end to this dispute.[18]

The actual discussions are interesting. Wilfred, the representative of the Roman view, started a slanging match by asserting that anybody who disagreed with the way things were done in Rome had to be stupid:

The only people who are stupid enough to disagree with the whole world are these Scots and their obstinate adherents the Picts and the Britons, who inhabit only a portion of these two islands in the remote ocean.

The argument took a strange turn when the subject of circumcision was introduced. The Roman Church representative, Wilfred argued:

But today it is unnecessary and undesirable for the faithful to be circumcised or to offer animals to God in sacrifice.

This was a most unusual digression in a discourse about the date of Easter. Do we take it from this statement that the Celtic Church was still observing the Jewish law too closely? Did the Church of Columba still practise circumcision and animal sacrifice? (If they had kept to the teachings of Jermiah – possibly bought to Ireland as we saw in Chapter Thirteen – they might well have done.) Wilfred followed up this point by saying Colman was following a Jewish practice of fixing Passover to celebrate Easter, and that he was wrong in saying the Council of Nicaea had been trying to change the date of Easter away from the date of the Passover:

This is the true and only Easter to be observed by the faithful. It was not newly decreed by the Council of Nicaea, but reaffirmed by it as Church history [NB Roman Church history] records.

In response, Colman invoked Columba to support his case:

Are we to believe that our most revered Father Columba and his successors, acted contrary to the Holy Scriptures when they followed these customs?

18 Bede: *A History of the English Church and People*, Penguin Classics

The Roman Church was not used to being questioned and Wilfred now started to lose his temper. He then introduced the false Pauline proof of papal authority, which tried to assert that Peter, and not James, was the leader of the Jerusalem Church after Jesus:

> *And even if your Columba was a Saint of most potent virtues, can he take precedence before the most blessed Prince of the Apostles, to whom our Lord said, 'Thou art Peter. and upon this rock I will build my Church and the gates of Hell shall not prevail against it, and to thee I will give the keys of the kingdom of heaven'?*

Given this news, King Oswy of Northumbria, who was chairing the meeting, became concerned he might not get passed St Peter into heaven, and asked Colman:

> *Is it true, Colman, that these words were spoken to Peter by our Lord?*

Colman admitted these words were in the Romanized gospel. On this basis King Oswy then ruled in favour of Rome, giving this news about Peter as his reason:

> *Then Peter is the guardian of the gates of heaven and I shall not contradict him. I shall obey his commands in everything to the best of my knowledge and ability, otherwise, when I come to the gates of heaven, he who holds the keys may not be willing to open them.*

The Celtic Church had lost. Ian Findley regrets that Colman did not inherit Columba's political skills:

> *Columba himself must have foreseen the inevitable confrontation. His learning and eloquence would have been hard to match in such a contest and even if they had prevailed his proud temper would have yielded no more ground than the Welsh clerics did to Augustine.*[19]

[19] Findley, I.: *Columba*, Victor Gollancz, 1979

However, we do not believe that Celtic Christianity was ever *fully* subsumed by the Roman Church. There is, for example, a telling confirmation of the Scottish perception of Iona as a site with a Jewish tradition recorded in *The Scottish Chronicle*, a ninth-century document dealing with the early MacAlpin kings of Scotland. It has an entry for AD 806 which says:

> *The community of Iona was slain by the gentiles, that is, to the number of sixty eight.*[20]

The word 'gentiles' is only used by Jews about non-Jews; the uncircumcised.

Many writers, including Findley, believe that the Culdees – a religious movement in Scotland – took on the traditions of the Celtic Church which were to emerge in Scotland's later religious and political thinking.

As a strange echo of this debate, whilst checking out the origins of the Jewish rite of Brit Milah (circumcision), we found this statement on Rabbi Malka's Brit Milah website:

> *It is noteworthy to mention, that, following the tradition of the Royal House of England, which requires circumcision of all male children, it was the Jewish Mohel of London rather than the Royal Physician who was called to circumcise the son of Princess Elizabeth. Rabbi Jacob Snowman, official Mohel of the London Jewish Community, circumcised Prince Charles, heir to the throne, at Buckingham Palace.*

Elsewhere the Rabbi says:

> *The moment of the Brit Milah has a great spiritual effect upon the child. Therefore Jewish Law specifies that one should choose a Mohel who is noted not only for his technical skills, but also for his level of piety and religious observance.*

We feel sure that a Mohel (rabbi specializing in circumcision) of the standing of Rabbi Snowman would not have compromised on the religious observances associated with Brit Milah.

[20] Donaldson, G.: *Scottish Historical Documents*, Neil Wilson Publishing, 1970

Whilst this practice seems to have died out in the general populace, it is an interesting thought that the line of descent of the English Crown, which can be traced back through the Scottish kings to Columba (through its Stewart, rather than its Hanoverian line), still use the king-making stone Columba is said to have brought from Ireland, and they are still observing his Jewish customs with their male children.

THE RISE OF THE SONS OF LIGHT

As the Enochian traditions of the Jews and the Druids were being welded together into Celtic Christianity, the families of the surviving Enochian-Zadokite priests were prospering in Europe.

We have already noted that the Book of Revelation appears to have been written by someone from the Enochian tradition who was probably witness to the destruction of Jerusalem in AD 70. The writer was a contemporary of James, evidently shared similar beliefs, could even have known him at first-hand, and might well have been old enough to remember Jesus and John the Baptist. This final book of the New Testament contains apocalyptic visions of a very Enochian nature that refer to the next destruction of the Earth by cometary impact, apparently based on an ancient cultural memory of the seven impacts of the earlier strike.

The author of Revelation describes how the martyrs who died defending Jerusalem from the Romans ('the beast'), would be with the messiah for a 1,000 years after which time they would be resurrected. At the end of the first millennium, he tells us, the reign of the messiah will be attacked by heathen nations, led by 'Gog and Magog'.

Rather strangely, the prophecy contained in Revelation came true, because 1,000 years and a few months after the destruction of Jerusalem by Titus (i.e. 1071), the Seljuk Turks arrived and devastated the city.

The families of Zadokite priests who escaped from Jerusalem had become highly influential by this time and took this Seljuk attack as confirmation of the old prophecy. As we described in *The Second Messiah*, these families secretly identified themselves under the generic title of Rex Deus. We now believe that this title was adopted to reflect the two lines of hereditary power; that of the king (in Latin, *Rex*) and priesthood signifies by the Latin word for God (*Deus*).

The principal families involved were: the Counts of Champagne, Lords of Gisors, Lords of Payen, Counts of Fontaine, Counts of Anjou, de Bouillon,

St. Clairs of Roslin, Brienne, Joinville, Chaumont, St Clair de Gisor, St Clair de Neg, the Dukes of Normandy and the Hapsburgs.

We had received information about these families from a man who claimed to be a living family member – to his knowledge – the only surviving member of Rex Deus. Whilst we found what he had to say was completely consistent with our existing findings, we would have ignored his evidence as being far too unreliable – except for the fact that we later found old Masonic rituals that confirmed his words.

Amongst other things, he had told us that at the time of Christ, the priests of the Jerusalem Temple were known by the names of angels, such as Michael, Gabriel and *Melchizedek*. At the time, the inclusion of Melchizedek with the only two angels mentioned in the Old Testament did not seem to us strange, but we now realise how important this issue is. As we explained in Chapter Twelve, Solomon's father, David, acquired both his kingly and priestly authority from Melchizedek, the Canaanite king-priest of Jerusalem.

We believe that these later Zadokite priestly families, now called 'Rex Deus', carefully laid the ground and then seeded the idea for a holy Crusade to Pope Urban II. It was this man who eventually launched an appeal for an invasion of the Holy Land in the French city of Clermont-Ferrand on Tuesday, 27 November 1095.

A year later, the assembled armies of Europe arrived at Constantinople, and in the following May they attacked their first major target: the Anatolian Turkish capital at Nicaea – the very city where Christianity had been formalized. The Crusaders enjoyed rapid success and met with little resistance during the rest of their campaign in Asia Minor. The next major obstacle was the city of Antioch in northern Syria, which they besieged for almost eight months until its fall on 3 June 1098. By May 1099 the Crusaders had reached the northern borders of Palestine; on the evening of 7 June they camped within sight of the walls of the holy city of Jerusalem. On Friday, 15 July 1099, with the aid of newly constructed siege machines, the Crusading army captured Jerusalem and, with an efficiency not seen since Roman times, massacred the entire Jewish and Muslim population.

A week later, the Crusaders elected Godfrey of Bouillon, Duke of Lower Lorraine, to rule the newly won city as governor. Strangely, the 39-year-old Godfrey appears to have died at this precise moment of triumph, because his brother was crowned King of Jerusalem under the title of Baldwin I in the year 1100. As we explained in detail in *The Second Messiah*, the Rex Deus families did not take full control of the situation for another 18 years, when

Baldwin II came to the throne of Jerusalem, immediately giving nine knights permission to excavate below the ruins of the holy Temple.

The Order of the Poor Soldiers of Christ and the Temple of Solomon, otherwise known as the Knights Templar, was formed in 1128 after the nine founding members had spent nine years digging under the ruins of the Herodian Temple. We found that other researchers had come to similar conclusions about the true motive of the Templars:

> *The real task of the nine knights was to carry out research in the area in order to obtain certain relics and manuscripts which contain the essence of the secret traditions of Judaism.*[21]

We even found that disused Masonic rituals state that the descendants of the Jerusalem high priests who had survived the destruction in AD 70 were pre-eminent in the Crusades, and that they formed the Knights Templar. These rituals go on to say that the Templars removed documents from beneath the Temple, which they took to Scotland in AD 1140.

THE KNOWLEDGE OF THE BRUCES AND THE ST CLAIRS

The invasion of Jerusalem by the Seljuk Turks may have been fortuitous for the Rex Deus families, because it gave them, as the 'resurrected Sons of Zadok', the excuse to call for a full-scale Christian war to retake the Holy Land. We say this because it seems that their interest lay not just in Jerusalem, but in *all* of the ancient megalithic sites from the Orkneys to the Holy Land.

For 1,000 years after the death of James, the brother of Jesus, a state of balance had been maintained until about AD 1062, when a number of Norman knights arrived in Scotland and Ireland. Amongst them was one, William 'the Seemley' St Clair, whose son Henri joined the Crusade as the battle partner of Hugh de Payen, the founder of the Knights Templar. Henri also became the first Earl of Roslin and founder of the St Clair line which built Roslin Chapel (now known as Rosslyn) and became the hereditary Grand Master Masons of Scotland.

In 1066 Rex Deus family member William, Duke of Normandy, invaded

[21] Delaforge, G.: *The Templar Tradition in the Age of Aquarius*

England and after defeating Harold at the battle of Hastings, installed himself as King William I of England.

The Norman conquest of England and Ireland broke up the line of the Ur Neill Kings of Tara and destabilized the Welsh kings. Battles were fought to gain control over the megalithic sites of the Boyne Valley in Ireland and of Anglesey in North Wales. The Vikings were permanently battling for control of the eastern seaboard of Ireland, twice losing control of Dublin in 1052 and 1075. In 1071, William I destroyed the cathedral at Bangor, North Wales, which had been established by Maelgwn, and Anglesey was attacked in the Battle of the Menai Straits in 1095.

Anglesey seems to have been a desirable domain to control because yet another battle was fought over it a few years later. Known as the Battle of Aber Menia it was fought between two brothers, Cadwaladr and Owain, grandsons of Cynan (a descendant of Maelgwyn). Cadwaladr wanted to make Anglesey into a separate kingdom, but his elder brother did not intend to allow the split. This battle is interesting because Cadwaladr used Scottish merceneries from Lothian supplied by the St Clairs, who at that time had designs on extending their domains into Orkney, Ireland and Anglesey.

By the time of Edward I, in the late 13th century, much of Ireland and Wales had been annexed and their rightful kings suppressed. Edward had also tried to take Scotland, but had been repulsed. Robert de Bruce, who became King of Scotland in 1306, saw his chance and set about reuniting the old kingdom of Dalriada by sending the following letter to the subjugated kings of Ireland.

> *The King sends greetings to all the kings of Ireland, to the prelates and clergy, and to the inhabitants of all Ireland, his friends.*
>
> *Whereas we and you and our people share the same national ancestry and are urged to come together more eagerly and joyfully in friendship by a common language and by common custom, we have sent you our beloved kinsman, the bearers of this letter, to negotiate with you in our name about permanently strengthening and maintaining inviolate the special friendship between us and you, so that with God's will your nation may be able to recover her ancient liberty.*[22]

[22] Scott, R.M.: *Robert the Bruce, King of Scots*, Canongate, 1982

The Ur Neils, the surviving line of Columba, responded by asking for military aid against the English, in return offering the High Kingship of Ireland to Edward Bruce, Robert's brother. Robert sent an expeditionary force under the command of Edward and they landed at Carrickfergus, from where they marched south immediately securing the area of the Boyne Valley and its megalithic sites. With a base established in Ireland, Robert sent Thomas Dun to attack the English harbour at Holyhead, and on 12 September 1315 Dun took it. Historian Ronald Scott comments:

> *A rumour spread that Edward Bruce was about to cross from Ireland and restore the ancient liberties of Wales, and the Welsh rose under Llewellyn Bran. Edward II had to countermand the Welsh levies who were being pressed to join the army he was preparing against Scotland.*[22]

This attempt to restore the Welsh monarch against the English failed and King Robert and his brother never did take more than Anglesey, although he did make the traditional Royal Progress of a High King of Tara around Ireland. Ronald Scott continues the story:

> *There was an ancient custom that whoever became High King of Ireland should make a royal progress through all the provinces of Ulster, Meath, Leinster, Munster and Connaught. To conform to this usage and thereby stamp the legitimacy of Edward Bruce's coronation on the minds of the native Irish chieftains and win their adherence, it was decided that the two brothers should make their way with their whole host through Ireland from one end to the other.*[24]

At this time Edward II mounted an attack on Dunfermline but was repulsed by Bishop William St Clair of Dunkeld, brother to the then Sir William St Clair Roslin.[25]

From the mid 11th century, the Rex Deus family of St Clair had been building their power base until they became the most powerful family in Scotland. By the 15th century they owned more of Scotland than the de Bruce line of the kings of Scotland, and when William St Clair died on 3 July

[23] Scott, R.M.: *Robert the Bruce, King of Scots*, Canongate, 1982
[24] Scott, R.M.: *Robert the Bruce, King of Scots*, Canongate, 1982
[25] Scott, R.M.: *Robert the Bruce, King of Scots*, Canongate, 1982

1480, his holdings were forcibly broken up between his 16 children by order of King James III, who had already forced him to give up Orkney in 1471. As well as a large proportion of Scotland, these holdings had included large parts of Dublin and the Orkneys.[26]

We had noticed when we wrote *The Hiram Key* that Robert de Bruce seemed to have taken a clear political decision to adopt Celtic practices to gain the support of the Scots in his battle against Edward I, and now we also knew that he had done exactly the same in Ireland, as well as using similar tactics to encourage opposition to Edward's oppression in Gwynedd.

He seemed to have realized that certain beliefs ran strongly in the traditions of the Celtic countries. We now understand that the belief systems he was tapping into were Druidic, with the Enochian tradition of the Celtic Church and its successors the Culdees. Robert I was a Rex Deus family member from the Norman line of de Bruce, but he was *also* a direct descendant of the MacAlpin line of Scotland, which had grown to be kings of Scotland from the time of Columba's decision to change the line of succession of the kingdom of Dalriada.

This made the Bruce family a doubly powerful force of kingship, and Robert had been crowned King of Scotland standing on the Stone of Scoon on the week of the spring equinox in 1306. When King Robert failed to produce a male heir, his daughter's son ended up founding the line of the Stewarts, who named no less than eight of their kings James, after the brother of Jesus and in honour of the Jacobite Church. It could be no accident that it was a Bruce (indeed a James Bruce), who successfully recovered the *Book of Enoch* after it had been lost to the world for 1,500 years (as we saw in Chapter Two). Had his Freemasonic training alerted him to the importance of this lost book? Had his family knowledge enabled him make a sensible guess as to where he might find it?

The St Clairs had arrived from Normandy and for many years posed a threat to the line of David I of Scotland. From the time that the Knights Templar were excavating under the Temple in Jerusalem, the St Clairs had taken the title, Earls of Roslin. This name in the Gaelic means 'Ancient Knowledge passed down the generations'.[27]

The first Knight Templar preceptory outside the Holy Land was built on St Clair land at a place called Temple near Edinburgh, and when the scrolls

[26] Saint-Clair, R.W.: *The Saint-Clairs of the Isles*, H. Brett, 1898
[27] Knight, C. and Lomas, R.: *The Second Messiah*, Century, 1997

of the Jerusalem Church were removed from under the Jerusalem Temple they were brought to Killwinning, which was also St Clair-controlled.

By 1440, William St Clair was concerned for the safety of the ancient Jewish scrolls in his safekeeping and decided to build a replica of the ruined Jerusalem temple to house them, next to his castle at Roslin, near Edinburgh.[28] The scroll sanctuary at Roslin is now called Rosslyn Chapel although, as Biblical scholars have confirmed, the building is a blend of Celticism and Judaism with nothing Christian about it.[29]

We have been able to prove from the carvings in the building that the first degree of Freemasonry was known to the builders of Rosslyn over 550 years ago.[30]

William St Clair, the chapel builder, was the most powerful of the St Clair dynasty and in a position to make a play for the Crown of Scotland. The building of Roslin may even have been an attempt to establish a seat of spiritual authority to challenge the right to rule of the old king, James II.

When James II died in 1460, his son James III took up this challenge, and immediately stripped William of his lands in Orkney, and then forced his successors to break up the St Clair lands so they no longer a posed a threat to the Royal Stewart line. The St Clairs, however, retained the loyalty of the Order of Freemasonry that they had created, and when James VI tried to take this away from them in 1600, the lodges of Scotland rallied to the support of the St Clairs and rejected a move to make the king Grand Master Mason.[31]

However, James VI took Freemasonry to England when he was made James I of England in 1603. The St Clairs remained Grand Master Masons until 1736 when another William St Clair resigned his office so that Freemasonry in Scotland could be led by a democratically elected leader. We feel that the strain of Freemasonry in England has viewed negatively calls for greater democracy to this day.

In 1715 the Jacobite army of the Scots invaded England and almost succeeded in toppling Hanoverian control. This made the Freemasons in London very nervous, as they were a Jacobite organization brought to

28 Knight, C. and Lomas, R.: *The Hiram Key*, Century, 1996, and *The Second Messiah*, Century, 1997

29 Private conversations with Professor Philip Davies and the Revd Professor James Charlesworth

30 Knight, C. and Lomas, R.: *The Second Messiah*, Century, 1997

31 Stevenson, D.: *The Origins of Freemasonry: Scotland's Century 1590-1710*, Cambridge Uuniversity Press, 1988

England by a previous Jacobite king. By 1717 they had almost dwindled out of existence, but finally saved themselves from extinction by suddenly denying any knowledge of their own history, forming a Grand Lodge of London, and swearing loyalty to the Hanoverian crown.

At first, this change was only to disassociate themselves from their Scottish roots, but it eventually turned into a rolling programme of reworking their own rituals to suppress the 'illogical' Enochian elements and introduce Pauline 'Christian' ideas.

But, like all censors, they could not suppress enough to hide its true origins.

THE ENOCHIAN TEMPLE OF FREEMASONRY

The Masonic temple is said to be based on King Solomon's Temple in Jerusalem, and it therefore has the astronomical characteristics of an Enochian temple.

The room that is the temple faces east, with a door that is usually either north or south of west. In the centre of the eastern end sits the worshipful master representing the sunrise at the equinox, and either side of him are two pillars, said to represent the pillars of Boaz and Jachin which stood at the porchway of King Solomon's Temple.

Opposite the worshipful master in the west, sits the senior warden, who represents the setting sun at the equinox, and in the south sits the junior warden representing moon.

In the centre of the ceiling of an English Masonic temple is a blazing star with the letter 'G' at its centre. This is said to represent the sun at noon, which is God most high. Around the blazing sun is a five-pointed star which has no explanation within Freemasonry, but it is certainly a representation of Venus' movements around the sun as viewed from Earth. The Grooved Ware People knew that an understanding of the 40-year cycle of Venus, through five of these five-pointed star cycles, was a perfect calendar/clock. In fact, until atomic clocks were invented a few years ago, there was no more accurate means of checking the passage of time than studying the position of Venus against the backdrop of the stars.

There are two other key figures in the Masonic temple who are designated as deacons (a word which comes from the Greek, *diakonos* meaning 'attendant'). The senior of these officers is stationed in the north-east and the junior in the south-west, and it is their job to escort the candidate around the temple during the various ritual. Each carries a six-foot-high staff that is usually termed a 'wand' in English Freemasonry.

These 'wands' are the measuring rods that the Canaanites and first Jews called Asherah; named after the goddess who was the mother of the dawn and the dusk. As with the gigantic prehistoric carving of the chalk man at Wilmington in Sussex, the purpose of these *asherah* is to determine the angles of the sunrise and sunset indicated by the shadows cast from the vertically held staffs.

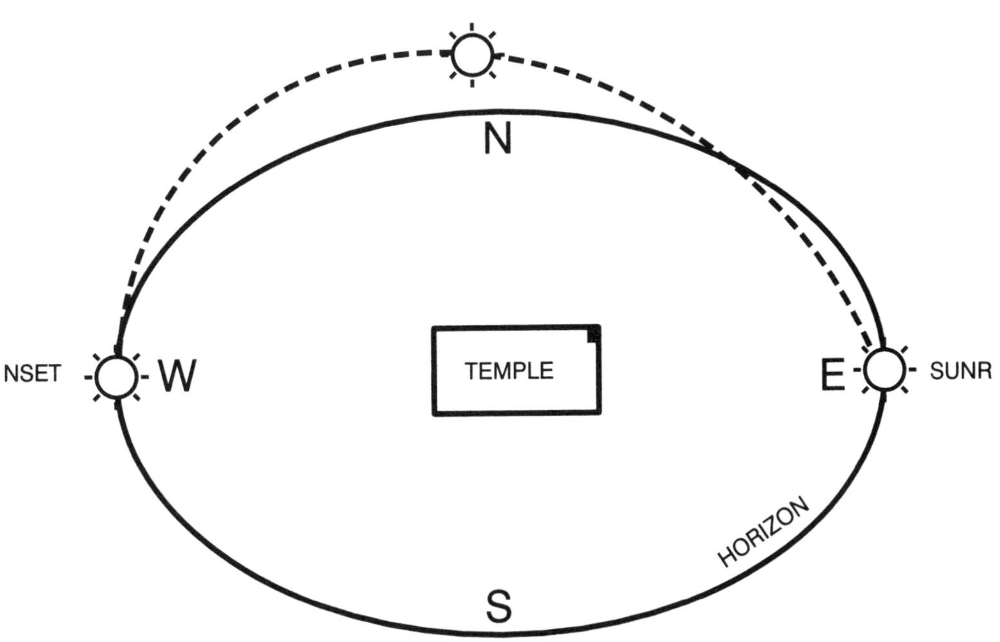

Figure 49. *The astronomical alignment of Solomon's Temple.*

These deacons were essential for orientating the temple (the word orient meaning 'east' comes from the Latin *oriens*, meaning rise). This was, of course, done by finding the two days a year when the shadow of the rising sun was perfectly aligned with the shadow of the setting sun, which are the equinoxes.

Jachin and Boaz are freestanding pillars placed in the north of east and the south of east, and they represent the two standing stones called 'messebhoth' by the Canaanites, that Solomon had erected in front of the porchway of his

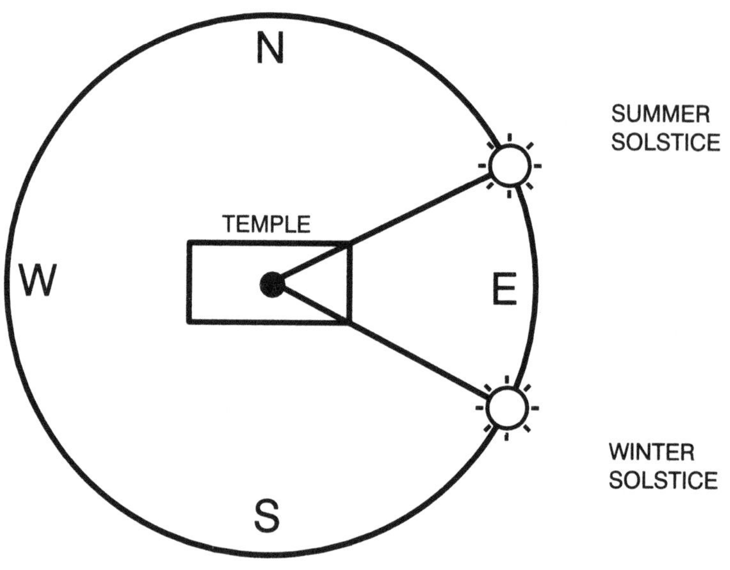

Figure 50. *The astronomical alignment of Solomon's Temple.*

Temple. Jachin marked the northern extremity of the rising sun at the summer solstice, and Boaz the southern extremity of the rising sun at the winter solstice.

The two most important feast days in the Masonic calendar are both St John's days. One is dedicated to John the Baptist, on or around the summer solstice, and the other to John the Divine, on or around the winter solstice. These two days therefore represent the celebration of the two solstices, marked by the sunrise lines of Jachin and Boaz in the Enochian temple of Freemasonry.

There are three degrees through which a man must pass to become a full member, known as a master mason. In the first degree, the candidate is conducted through a ritual before being made an 'entered apprentice' Freemason. He is then placed in the north-east corner of the lodge, with the deacon holding the candidate in one hand and his asherah in the other. In this place he is standing on the summer solstice sunrise line marked by the shadow of the Jachin messebhoth.

The basic tools of his emblematic craft are explained to him whilst he is in this position

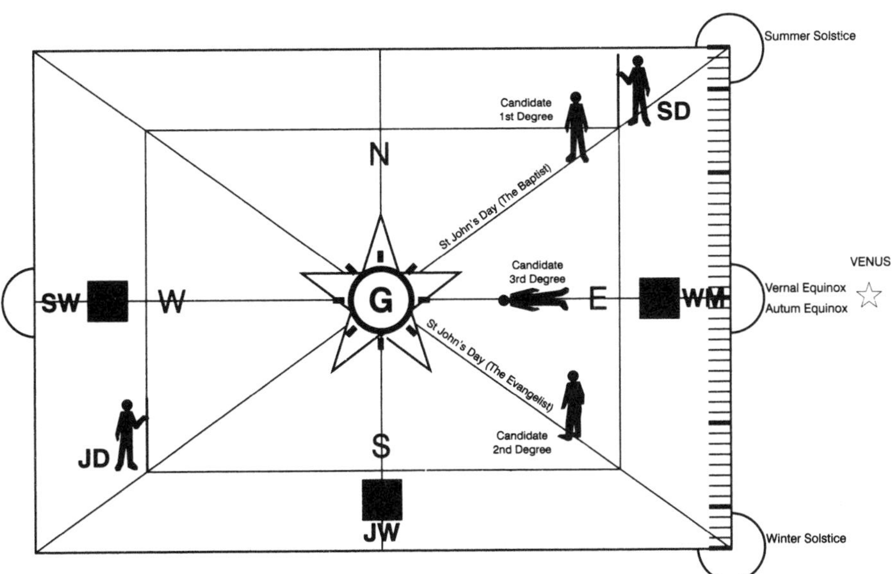

Figure 51. *The astronomical layout of a Masonic Temple.*

When the entered apprentice Freemason is ready to be put through his second degree, that of a 'fellowcraft mason', he is placed in the south-east corner to 'mark the progress he has made in the science'. The place that he stands at this moment is on the winter solstice sunrise line delineated by the shadow of the Boaz messebhoth.

The fellowcraft is next put forward for his third degree in Freemasonry, which is a very special rite indeed.

The candidate is told that the subject of this degree is death. And for the crucial part of this degree, he is placed on the centre-line of the temple, which designates the perfect east-west line of the equinoxes.

The first part of the ritual takes place in the dark and its dramatic climax arrives with the candidate being symbolically murdered and laid 'lifeless' on the floor wrapped in a death shroud. The ritual continues in the blackness until a method is applied that allows the candidate to be raised from his 'tomb' and resurrected to live once again. At the moment of resurrection, a light in the shape of a small five-pointed star is illuminated in the east, and the worshipful master draws the candidate's attention to the light of the 'bright morning star' that heralds his return to life.

In the first chapter of our first book, at the outset of our quest to find the origins of Freemasonry, we were puzzled by the description given for this degree during ceremony:

> . . . .*points to the darkness of death and to the obscurity of the grave as a forerunner of a more brilliant light, which shall follow at the resurrection of the just, when these mortal bodies which have been long slumbering in the dust shall be awakened, reunited to their kindred spirit, and clothed with immortality* . . .

Then it had made no sense. But after ten years of constant delving into the origins of the ritual, we now believe that it makes perfect sense.

We could now imagine Newgrange, some 5,000 years ago. The remains of the dead king or priest have been brought into the pitch black chamber which is representative of the *darkness of death*. But they knew that this darkness is a *forerunner of a more brilliant light*, which (as described in the Masonic ritual) is the rising of Venus. Then *the resurrection of the just* occurs as the light of the morning star stabs into the chamber. This only happens at Newgrange once every eighth year, so much time may have passed before the moment when *mortal bodies which have been long slumbering in the dust shall be awakened*. This reawakening causes them to be *reunited to their kindred spirit*. The spirit of the departed one has entered their kindred, a related offspring. This process then causes the individual concerned to be; *clothed with immortality*.

It is a perfect description of the Enochian belief that, we believe, sprang from the megalithic Grooved Ware People and survived via the Canaanites into Zadokite Judaism.

This passage from death to life might not have been thought easy for the deceased one. The Masonic ritual then continues with a prayer addressed to the great Architect of the Universe:

> ... *we beseech Thee to impart Thy grace to this Thy servant who seeks to partake with us the mysterious secrets of a Master Mason. Endue him with such fortitude that, in the hour of trial he fail not, but passing safely under Thy protection, through the dark valley of the shadow of death he may finally rise from the tomb of transgression to shine as the stars, for ever and ever.*

These rituals were originally held inside natural caves or man-made caverns, and the Qumran Community appears to have continued the tradition. It seems that some 18th-century Freemasons may have also recaptured the full effect. A certain Lord Dashwood of West Wycombe, in the English county of Buckinghamshire, was noted for conducting strange rites in caves under an old church, which local people believed to be some kind of devil worship. However, it is almost certain that they had a Masonic connection, because amongst the many visitors he received there was the leading American statesman, scientist and Freemason, Benjamin Franklin.

We found that the Freemasons' skill with the asherah was put to practical use in the period of the Templars and the early years of Freemasonry.

We believe that when the Knights Templar built their cathedrals and churches across Europe, they would use asherah to measure the angle of the sun's first shadow when they were laying the foundation stone in the north-east corner. The resulting angle would be dependent on time of year and surrounding topology, but this would define the line of the north and south walls of the building, so that it faced the rising sun one of two specific days of the year. (Only the solstices have only one day with a given angle; all other days share an angle with one other.) The church would then be dedicated to a saint whose feast day fell on that day. In this way, a Templar-period church that is named after St Mary Magdalene will face the rising sun, at that particular spot on 22 July (the feast of St Mary Magdalene).

We found a reference which told us that this technique had survived the demise of the Templars to become associated with the early practices of Scottish Freemasonry. In 1925 Alfred Watkins wrote a book called *The Old Straight Track*, in which he discusses a connection between the alignment of old tracks he called 'leys' and the orientation of old churches:

> *Freemasonry affords a most striking link between ley sighting methods and orientation of buildings; for their lodges were formally oriented and annals of some of the Scotch lodges describe the exact procedure followed for the alignment of churches.*
>
> *The site of the Altar having been decided upon, a pole was thrust in to the ground and a day appointed for the building to be commenced. On the evening previous, the Patrons, Ecclesiastics, and Masons assembled, and spent the night in devotional exercises; one being placed to watch the rising of the sun gave notice when his rays appeared above the horizon. When fully in view, the Master Mason sent out a man with a rod, which he ranged in line between the altar and the sun, and thus fixed the line of orientation.*[32]

This shows that old Enochian ideas had survived into Freemasonry, but as this book neared completion we were given another fascinating confirmation of the links between knowledge of the heavens and Freemasonry. David Ovason, a researcher in arcane subjects, had become interested in the unusually high proportion of astronomical symbolism in the city of Washington DC. He found no less than 20 zodiacs on public display in the centre of the city, and commented, 'I know of no other city in the world with such a multitude of public zodiacs displayed in so small a place.'

Reading his manuscript, we were excited to realise that he had confirmed what we suspected. As we saw earlier, we had been told by Fred Olsen, the Norwegian shipping magnate, that George Washington had bought his ranch because it had upon it an ancient pyramid which was aligned with the equinoxes, and we knew that Brother Washington, who had been made a Mason in Fredericksburg on 4 November 1752, had conceived the city.

[32] Watkins, Alfred: *The Old Straight Track*, 1925 (reprinted: Abacus, 1974)

As he was made a Mason, Washington would have been told during the ceremony that '*The proper business of a Mason is astronomical, chemical, geological and moral science, and more particularly that of the ancients, with all the mysteries and fables founded upon it.*'

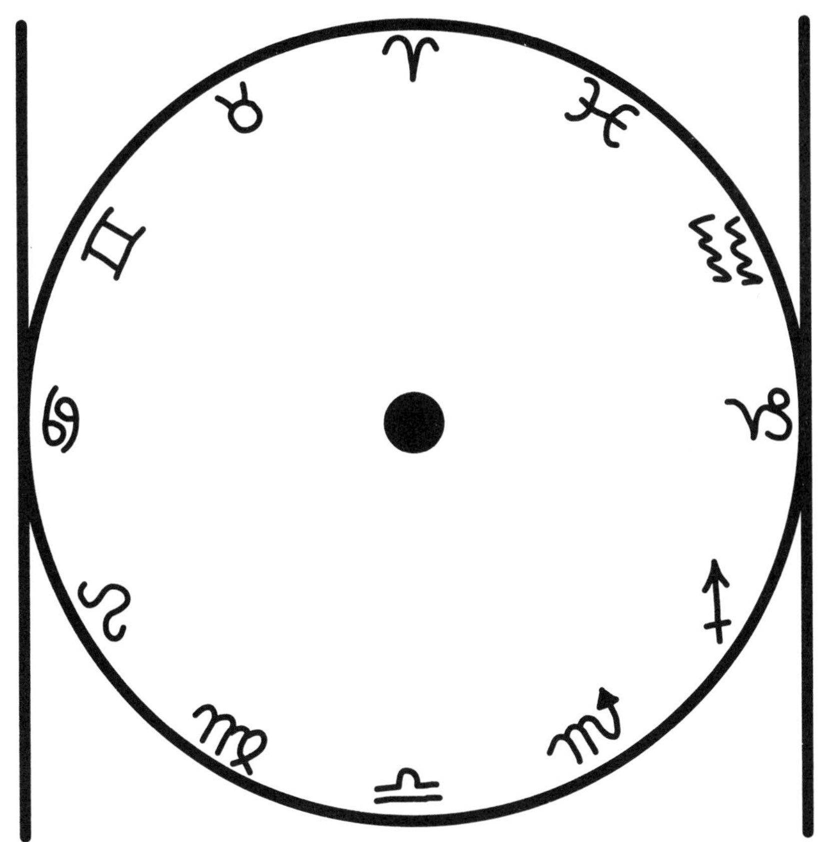

Figure 52. *The Masonic symbol of the zodiac between two sighting sticks.*

This is still the introduction to the Noachite Degree which continues to be so important in American Law, and at the time Washington was made a Mason was part of the basic introduction to Craft Freemasonry.

Non-Freemason Ovason has come to exactly the conclusion that the Masons who built and developed Washington were obsessed with the heavens. He has found that the layout of the city corresponds to solar alignments that were still being added to as recently as the late 19th century:

> *Who, in Washington DC during the 1880s, had the power to arrange and disseminate such arcane astrological symbolism, and to ensure that the statuary of the city should reflect the starry cosmos with such precision? . . . The extraordinary answer to my question carries us back to the very beginnings of the federal city, when it was still little more than an idea in the mind of George Washington. Under his persistent and far-sighted direction the city was surveyed, planned, designed and built largely by Masons.*[33]

The knowledge held by Uriel's people has survived in the temples of Freemasonry and has even been embodied into the capital city of the most powerful nation on earth.

THE END OF THE BEGINNING

Ten years ago, we set out to find some answers concerning the origins of the oddball rituals used by Freemasonry. We have found many answers, most of them to questions that we could never have imagined would arise.

We believe that we have glimpsed a history of humankind that has become lost and confused over time – a history that spans tens of thousands of years and includes the greatest disaster to have befallen our planet.

Human development is not to be plotted as some relentless upwards curve along which we progress from ignorance to knowledge, for there must be much that we have forgotten. There was once a time when priests were scientists who understood why God had made the universe, and they built their theology around knowledge. But over the last 2,000 years, religion has forgotten science to become an empty husk of mantra and baseless superstition. The priesthood once led humankind's search for the hidden mysteries of nature and science, but today clings to a remote relevance trying to be guardians of an assumed social morality in a changing world.

So what has our quest achieved?

We have come to understand that human development is much older than is generally accepted. There is evidence of a manufacturing economy in

[33] Ovason, D.: *The Secret Zodiacs of Washington DC*, Century, 1999

Europe 26,000 years ago and clear proof that the megalithic structures of Europe predate the cities of Sumer and Egypt. But civilization arrived not by a steady upwards progression, instead, it appears to have been subjected to catastrophic setbacks. Geological evidence shows that the cause of these reverses was the Earth being hit by *two* comets: one in 7620 BC and the other in 3150 BC.

The wide variety of current languages seems to have developed from a single global language that may have still existed 15,000 years ago.

The *Book of Enoch*, which had been lost until the 18th century, contains the story of a man who was warned about the effects of cometary impacts ad taught survival skills by an advanced group of people known as the Watchers.

Astronomical data in the *Book of Enoch* reveal it to have been written between the latitudes of 52° and 59° North, which is exactly where an astronomically advanced group of people known as the Grooved Ware People lived until 2600 BC. An earlier people had been decimated by the comet of 7640 BC, but the survivors then developed astronomy as a means of protection.

They built a complex of temples which were carefully engineered to allow the light of Venus to shine into dark chambers just before sunrise, or just after sunset, once every eight years. They appear to have believed that this ritual allowed the soul of a dead person to be transferred to a newly born child (who thus became a 'Son of Light'), and to this end they held fertility rites at the spring equinox so that their children would be born at the winter solstice. As their observational astronomy developed, they invented a sophisticated measurement system (the megalithic yard) which came into common use throughout their lands, and they built hundreds of huge stone circles to act as horizon declinometers, providing accurate calendars and cometary early-warning systems. The megalithic 'art' the Grooved Ware People used to decorate many of their structures is an early form of writing, and we learned to read some of their symbols as we recreated the calendar machine that Uriel descibed to Enoch.

Some time prior to 3150 BC, the Grooved Ware People saw *another* comet on a collision course and decided to spread their survival knowledge as widely as possible. One of the people they took to the British Isles from the Middle East, to learn the secrets of their astronomy, was Enoch. The *Book of Enoch* clearly decribes his visit to the White Crystal Wall of Newgrange, hundreds of years before the building of the pyramids of Egypt.

It seems possible that the Sumerian city-builders could have been an offshoot of these Grooved Ware People, and that another sub-group could have travelled to China.

Traces of the beliefs of the Grooved Ware People survived in two major strands: the teachings of Enochian Judaism, and the Celtic legends of the Druids. These two strands recombined – some time around 580 BC – at the time of the fall of Solomon's Temple, when a princess of the line of David was taken to Ireland for safety, and established the royal line of the High Kings of Tara by marrying the native king. The Roman Empire tried, unseccessfully, to destroy both these strands of Enochian belief in the first century AD.

When Jacobite Christianity came first to Wales, and later to Ireland and Scotland, it was easily accepted. The remnants of the native Druidism readily mutated into Celtic Christianity. This Enochian form of Christianity survived well into the sixth century AD, and we traced it through the teachings of the early Celtic saints and the poems of Taliesin.

The sites of the Grooved Ware People have always been held sacred, and for the last 3,000 years have been the object of battles between the various lines of the royal houses of Britain and the descendants of the Priests of the Jerusalem Temple.

This, then, is the tangled story we uncovered. But what of our quest? At the outset of this book we had asked ourselves three questions:

1. Is it physically possible for the entire world to flood, and if so what evidence is there that such a terrible thing has happened within human racial memory?

2. The oral traditions of Freemasonry claim that there was an advanced civilization before the coming of the Flood. Are these accounts just myth, or do they record a memory of a lost people?

3. Could all of this help us to construct a new paradigm of prehistory?

Yes, the world was all but destroyed by a flood caused by a cometary impact less than 10,000 years ago. Such events appear to be frighteningly frequent, with a significant later impact occurring again around 3150 BC.

Yes, the oral traditions of Freemasonry do record real events and there was an advanced group of people in the British Isles who appear to had a major influence in the Middle East and even in China.

Yes, there is a new paradigm of prehistory to construct. We have just started to shed a little light on a new way to explain how we arrived at the world we live in today.

However, we think that any answers we may have provided are less important than the many questions we have raised. For so long the world seems to have been fixated by patently incorrect information about the past, and every time someone has introduced a new idea that contradicts old dogmas, they are ignored or ridiculed. But today there is hope, because leading intellectuals have learnt that today's heterodoxy is tomorrow's othodoxy.

We have found the origin of Professor Thom's megalithic yard.

We have made tentative inroads into the understanding of megalithic art as a form of writing. And we hope that the good work in this area will continue.

We have found the pivotal role of Venus in the science and theology of the ancient world. Above all, we hope that we have uncovered enough to convince people that our distant ancestors deserve respect.

Through the science of Uriel and the oral traditions of Enoch, we have evidence of the terrible disasters that are unleashed upon the world when small lumps of ice from outer space hit our oceans.

Archaeology tells us that our species has not changed for around 115,000 years, and yet we have apparently developed civilization only during the last 10,000 years, from the time when the last global flood occurred.

So, what happened for the 105,000 years *before* the comet hit? Did our ancestors stagnate, or could there have been a technologically developed civilization that was washed from the face of the Earth?

Yes, we have to conclude that it is entirely possible that our species has developed and regressed more than once. It took us little more than 100 years to move from wooden sailing ships to spaceships on the moon; so why could humankind not have achieved rapid development before?

The flash-floods from cometary impacts are catastrophic beyond imagination. The tsunamis that swept the Earth would have wiped away all evidence of any preceding civilization, as surely as sandcastles dissolve on the beach at high tide.

Above all, we must take notice that the great message from Uriel is not about history. It is about the future.

Think the unthinkable, says Uriel – the Earth will be hit again.

We may have enjoyed a lucky run with relatively small impacts hitting us for the last 10,000 years. But can it last? Surely we have been lucky for too long not to take the problem very, very seriously.

If we do not invest in finding the technology to protect our planet, perhaps we too will become a memory, with as little remaining of our civilization as remains now of the Grooved Ware People.

We will become a fuzzy oral tradition of an ancient people who could fly like birds, who had buildings that reached to the sky and who possessed the power to communicate to the four corners of the world. These people, they will say, existed before the stars fell to earth and God punished them for their evil ways.

Perhaps the survivors will grow and hear the ancient echo before it is too late. But maybe they will also fail to hear the message of the past.

> ***Behold destruction is coming, a great flood and it will destroy all living things.***
>
> The *Book of Enoch*

TIME LINE

2,600,000 BC	First tools manufactured
180,000 BC–360,000 BC	'Mitochandrial Eve'
115,000 BC	Modern humans existed
26,000 BC	First known 'factory'
25,000 BC	Last Neanderthals die out
16,000 BC	Scotland under a mile of ice
11,000 BC	Orkney separated from Scotland by rising sea level
10,000 BC	Scotland ice free, giant fallow deer, elk and reindeer living
9000 BC	Cold snap of Loch Lomond Stadial
8075 BC	First sighting posts established at Stonehenge
7640 BC	Seven-part comet strike
7500 BC	Agriculture begins
7100 BC	New sighting posts established at Stonehenge
7000 BC	Settlements on Rum in Hebrides and Mount Sandal in Ireland
6500 BC	Scotland warms up and becomes attractive habitat
6500 BC	Settlement at Inverness
6000 BC	North Sea floods northern plains
6000 BC	Settlements at Islay, Jura, Arran, Oban and Loch Doon
5500 BC	Baltic sea flood
4900 BC	Skaill freshwater loch flooded by sea to become Skaill Bay
3930 BC	Bank at Maes Howe established
3600 BC	House built at Knap of Howar
3500 BC	Food-producing communities established on Orkney

3420 BC	First burial at Quanterness
3250 BC	Sumerians arrive in Sumer
3215 BC	First houses built at Skara Brae
3215 BC	Tomb of the Eagles, Isbister built
3200 BC	Newgrange in use
3200 BC	Bryn Celli Ddu chamber built
3150 BC	Mediterranean comet impact
3080 BC	Domestic cattle grazed on Knowe of Ramsay
3040 BC	Stones of Stennes set up, henge dug in bedrock
3035 BC	Domestic cattle grazed on Knowe of Rowiegar
3020 BC	Houses 2, 7 and 8 added to Skara Brae
3020 BC	Henge started at Stonehenge
2990 BC	Human burial at Quoyness
2895 BC	Central setting of stones of Stennes built
2830 BC	Structure built at Peirowall Quarry with spiral stones
2820 BC	Structure built at Maes Howe
2700 BC	Silbury Hill built
2700 BC	Bronze artefacts in Wiltshire but not in Scotland
2700 BC	First ziggurat built in Iraq
2700 BC	Old Kingdom of Egypt ends
2670 BC	Agga defeated by Mesanepada, King of Ur
2655 BC	Skara Brae abandoned
2650 BC	First pyramid in built at Seqqara
2650 BC	Reign of Gilgamesh ended
2650 BC	Agga, last ruler of Etana, dies
2638 BC	Khufu becomes King of Two Lands of Egypt
2600 BC	First large temple mounds built in Peru
2500 BC	Avebury stones set up
2500 BC	Megalithic building stops in Orkney
2000 BC	Bronze artefacts appear in Scotland
2000 BC	Climate in northern Scotland starts to deteriorate
1200 BC	Population of Scotland declines, possible plague
1159 BC	Hekla erupts, causing ten years of poor summers in Scotland
1020 BC	Saul became first king of Israel
1002 BC	David King of Israel
972 BC	Solomon builds his Temple
586 BC	Destruction of Solomon's Temple
539 BC	Start of Zerubbabel's Temple

155 BC	Zedikite Priests move to Qumran
7 BC	Jesus born

AD

AD 32	John the Baptist killed
AD 33	The Crucifixion of Jesus
AD 58	Bran takes Christianity to Wales
AD 60	Saul becomes Paul and redirects Christianity
AD 60	Battle of Castell Ior, Druid Massacre on Anglesey
AD 62	James brother of Jesus killed
AD 66	Jewish Revolt begins
AD 70	Destruction of Jerusalem and its Temple
AD 78	Final defeat of Anglesey Druids
AD 79	Agricola builds fort in Ireland
AD 84	Agricola defeats Scottish Druids
AD 132	Bar Kochba revolt begins
AD 432	Patrick goes to Ireland
AD 525	Maelgwn Gwynedd establishes Bangor Cathedral
AD 547	Maelgwn Gwynedd dies
AD 563	Columba sails to Scotland
AD 1095	First Crusade starts
AD 1118	Nine knights excavate the ruined Temple
AD 1307	Templars destroyed in France
AD 1314	Battle of Bannockburn
AD 1329	Pope accepts Robert I as King of Scotland
AD 1601	James VI made a Mason at Lodge of Perth and Scoon
AD 1603	James VI made King of England
AD 1641	Sir Robert Moray made a Mason at Newcastle
AD 1691	James VII defeated at Battle of the Boyne
AD 1715	First Jacobite Campaign to restore Stewart Line
AD 1717	London Masons break away from Scottish Tradition
AD 1725	Formation of First National Grand Lodge in Ireland
AD 1736	Grand Lodge of Scotland Formed
AD 1745	Second Jacobite Campaign to restore Stewart Line
AD 1757	George Washington made a Mason
AD 1813	Formation of United Grand Lodge of England

Appendix 1

A MESSAGE TO ENGLISH FREEMASONRY

A NEW PARADIGM OF FREEMASONRY

We believe that a number of Freemasons who have found fault with our findings may have done so because they measured what we said against existing views of Masonic history. Some have raised genuine points where we have got some detail wrong, or have wanted to enter into healthy debate. However, in our view, there are also those who may believe they have a duty to protect long-established dogma, created largely by the London Masons of the early 18th century. The more 'expert' they consider themselves to be, the less prepared most of them are to consider a new way of looking at the whole subject.

What we have put forward in our three books amounts to such a radical reappraisal of Freemasonic origins that it is simply not possible to dismiss elements of our findings on the grounds that they conflict with established assumptions. Our explanation for the existence of Freemasonry and its current rituals has to be discussed on its own merits, and then compared (as a complete alternative) to the standard theories.

Our efforts over the last ten years differ from those of most modern Masonic researchers in that we have looked at a total context rather than restricting ourselves to Masonry alone. It is our view that you cannot understand a fish without studying the sea.

To use another analogy, we feel a little like Galileo trying to persuade the establishment that the world is a sphere orbiting the sun. Existing authority figures have always had a major problem adjusting to new ideas, although today serious academics often thrive on the rapid and radical changes that occur in the hard sciences. Back in the early 17th century, there was no evidence that the sun and other heavenly bodies orbit around a flat and stationary earth, just as there is not a jot of evidence to support the improbable idea that the aristocrats of 18th-century speculative Freemasonry adopted the rituals of simple stonemasons.

But old nonsense is robust nonsense.

We consider that the Grand Lodge of England's own explanation of the Craft's origin is wholly untenable, as are its claims that all explanations are just theories whilst it proceeds to promote the stonemasons explanation.

As we finished this book we were pleased to receive, with the compliments of the Grand Secretary of the United Grand Lodge of England (UGLE), two booklets entitled *Your Questions Answered* and *Freemasonry: An Approach to Life*.

These mini-booklets are a good attempt to start to dispel some of the sillier ideas about Freemasonry that exist in the world today. Indeed, at least one of the ideas contained in these booklets was suggested by ourselves to the Grand Lodge.

However, these little documents do contain some of the same old information, some of which is, in our view, highly debatable or demonstrably wrong.

One leaflet asks, 'How and when did Freemasonry start?' It then states that it is not known how and when Freemasonry started, and that the earliest recorded 'making' of a Freemason in England is that of Elias Ashmole in 1646.

Even in this detail they are wrong.

In a meticulously researched book, entitled *The Origins of Freemasonry: Scotland's Century 1590 -1710*, published by Cambridge University Press in 1988, Professor David Stevenson, then Professor of Scottish History at the University of St Andrews, produced the original lodge minutes which showed two of the leading covenantors were made Freemasons at a meeting of Edinburgh Cannongate Lodge held at Newcastle in 1641. This makes Elias Ashmole the third recorded `making' of a Freemason in England. And it shows clearly that Freemasonry started in Scotland at least 50 years before Brother Ashmole's initiation into what can only have been a Scottish lodge.

One of the Masons made at Newcastle in 1641 was Sir Robert Moray, a founder member of the Royal Society, along with Ashmole. One of the three leading Scottish lodges of research is named Lodge Sir Robert Moray in honour of this great man. When Professor Stevenson, a non-Mason, addressed these Scottish research lodges, he was treated with the respect due to his academic position, and his findings were welcomed and discussed widely. At a later date, when he addressed the `primary' English lodge of research called 'Quator Corinarti', the learned professor's presentation was coolly received. We recommend that all members of the Craft read Stevenson's evidence for themselves.

The leaflets also state that The Grand Lodge of England was the first grand lodge in the world, being established in 1717, but that was only a London-based organization of just four lodges. Lodges in the towns and cities of Scotland had been working together for centuries before this date; they just did not choose to adopt the rather presumptuous title of 'grand'.

Despite the hard proof that we and others have put forward about the origin of Scottish Freemasonry lying with the Knights Templar, it appears to us that UGLE continues to turn a blind eye. These leaflets repeat the odd idea that English gentlemen and aristocrats of the 17th century suddenly decided to ask the guilds of stonemasons if they could adopt their craft-based rituals for their own betterment. The reality is almost the reverse. The stonemasons of Europe were accepted into the lower levels of Templar rituals when the Knights Templar instigated their famous programme of medieval cathedral-building across the whole of the continent. When the power of the Templars was suddenly extinguished in the early 14th century, these high grade stonemasons kept the rituals that Templars had given them and formed guilds in mainland Europe, but not in England, Ireland, Wales or Scotland. In *circa* 1440, William St Clair of Roslin brought in these continental master masons, rather than use local Scottish masons to build Rosslyn. He and his descendants were thereafter Grand Master Masons of Scotland.

William St Clair called in these masons because his family were the guardians of Templar rituals and documents, and from 1440 onwards the operating masons were reunited with the spiritual, or speculative, masons.

OUR STARTING POINT

The utter implausibility of the old stonemason theory of origin was what first prompted us to start our quest into the origins of the rituals used by Freemasons. Indeed, we had both joined Freemasonry out a sense of curiosity.

Nobody we asked could tell us where the order came from. Most members seemed to simply accept that it is some sort of amateur dramatics with moral overtones, and a chance to have a meal and a drink afterwards; a gentlemen's dinning club with charitable objectives and a chance to dress up in strange regalia that includes elaborate leather aprons, white gloves, ornamental collars and cuffs.

We knew that non-members viewed it quite differently. After the First World War, Freemasonry took to ignoring all external comment about itself and its purpose. Non-Masonic, Christian opponents to Freemasonry, such as writer Walton Hannah, realized that they could say what they liked about the Craft without anybody answering their assertions and misunderstandings. Hannah discovered this lack of defence when he wrote an article in *Theology* (January 1951), published by the Christian pressure group the Society for Promoting Christian Knowledge, entitled, 'Should a Christian be a Freemason?'. Hannah was pleasantly surprised at the considerable controversy this article generated and at the number of private letters he had from practising Freemasons, which he describes as `full of courtesy and forbearance'. But it did not change his opinion that Freemasonry was an evil organization which needed to be destroyed, citing as his reason 'the necessarily evasive answers of Masons'.[1] In this manner were planted the seeds of the present widespread belief, espoused even by the present Government, that Freemasons are not to be trusted, even under oath.

We set out to discover the origins of the rituals contained within Freemasonry, which led us in to totally unexpected areas. What we found was so important that we wrote down the story of our quest and, seven years after starting out, we published *The Hiram Key*. In this book we told how we had come to the considered view that Freemasonry is a repository of ancient teaching that could be traced back to the Jerusalem Church during the times of Jesus and James.

Those rituals had, we said, been resurrected by the medieval order of the Knights Templar and brought to Scotland, where the order was turned into Freemasonry during the 14th and 15th centuries. Our motivation to publish our first book was three-fold:

1. To share the excitement we felt at finding the fabulous history that lay behind the Order.

[1] Hannah, W.: *Darkness Visible, A Revelation and Interpretation of Freemasonry*, The Augustine Press, 1952

2. To show to the world in general that Freemasonry was an unfairly ignored source of historic knowledge.

3. To combat the rising tide of ill-informed books that attack Freemasonry as some sort of evil conspiracy against society.

We felt that the leaders of English Freemasonry were not prepared to defend themselves adequately against authors such as the late Stephen Knight and Martin Short whom we felt portrayed Freemasonry as a vast sprawling network with undesirable tentacles in every area of public life.

Ignoring the fact that Freemasonry is not a 'secret society', Martin Short wrote in 1989:

> *What action should be taken? [about Freemasonry]. I suggest it should be more than would appeal to the Tory MP who says, `if people wish to belong to secret societies, that is their own business,' but probably less than required by the Labour man who feels it `should be illegal'.*
>
> *The only proper way would be to put a `disclosure' bill to the vote. This bill should also give full public access to full and up-to-date membership list of all Masonic lodges.'*[2]

These writings, and our perception of the failure of the leadership of United Grand Lodge of England to adequately address their accusations, did enormous damage to what is a benign, and charitable, if somewhat eccentric order.

THE FUTURE

The world is changing and everybody is entering a new information age, an age which questions traditional practices and modes of authority. Today, most of the Westernized world has a democratic view of authority which is reflected in all levels of society. Even in England, hereditary authority is no longer simply accepted; the monarchy is called to account for its morals and extravagances, the House of Lords is set to be abolished; even the unelected and unaccountable commissioners of the European Union have been toppled

[2] Short, M.: *Inside the Brotherhood*, Grafton Books, 1989

from their gravy-train by public opinion. The traditional view of authority being passed down from on high to the grateful underlings is no longer acceptable to anyone. The nature of authority is changing, but Freemasonry is only just beginning to change with it.

In the information age, knowledge is power, and the only members worth having are those with many other choices for their loyalty and sources of entertainment. Bright, informed people bore very easily, particularly if they are not challenged. Occasionally, authority can command compliance, but it can never command commitment. The generation which will be the next generation of Freemasons is as unconvinced by assumed authority as any in history. With no positional and hereditary authority to command, how can the Rulers of the Craft build any legitimacy into their decisions? How can they encourage membership now they can no longer command obedience?

The most capable future Freemasons will not think of themselves as loyal soldiers, but more as sought-after assets. It's not longer acceptable to say, 'become worshipful master of your lodge, keep your nose clean and in ten years or so you'll get to be a provincial grand officer, with some gold braid'. This false carrot of conferred status is of little value to people who can achieve real status in their own professions and want to spend what little spare time they have doing something interesting and useful. How do you motivate these sorts of people to become masons, and if they join, how to you keep them?

Threats are no use, for what possible sanctions can be applied to professionals who are not prepared to be cowed by anyone, let alone a local butcher, or a retired bank manager, in a fancy apron? How can the 'rulers' of the Craft exercise authority over the brightest and best new members, in the absence of dependency? Certainly they cannot continue as they have done, and unless they change, Freemasonry will die with them.

When the people who now control English Freemasonry were young, control was everything. Senior brethren were allergic to surprises. Everybody asked permission for everything and did exactly what they were told. This led to a illusion of power on the part of some of the previous occupants of UGLE, but this sense of control was not real. It is no longer possible to restrict debate when there are so many sources of information available.

Gary Hamel, Visiting Professor of Strategic and International Management at the London Business School, has commented on the changing environment for authority in general, saying:

> *'It was once the case that unless you were caught with your hand in the till, or publicly slandered your boss, you could count on a job for life in many large organizations. Loyalty was valued more than capability, and there was always a musty corner where mediocrity could hide. Entitlement produced a reasonably malleable work force, and dependency enforced a begrudging kind of loyalty. That was then, this is now.*
>
> *Talk all you like about building a high commitment organisation, but isn't commitment reciprocal? No wonder loyalty ain't what it used to be.'*[3]

Experience brings with it authority, and in the past hierarchical superiority has rested on the supposition that the people at the top know more than the people at lower levels. In a system which has seemed to be based on promoting people by the 'Buggins's turn' principle, this can never be true. The danger is that the people running Freemasonry may come to know less and less about it. It does not take any bright young man, joining a local lodge, very long to notice a lack of knowledge in some senior members. If the next generation cannot respect Freemasonry, they will neither join nor support it.

Freemasonry was a protected environment. It was seen by outsiders as a high-status club to belong to, and if the price of preferment was not to ask difficult questions, then in an age which accepted assumed authority, perhaps that was considered a fair price for the social status Freemasonic rank conferred in society. But the territory has changed dramatically . . .

Gary Hamel also suggested a solution for companies which had this problem:

> *Shouldn't authority be as much a function of foresight as hindsight? In a world of discontinuous change, shouldn't authority rest not only on experience, but also on the capacity to learn and adapt?*[4]

Personal computers, networks and the Internet are creating an information democracy. The information boundaries that once allowed senior brethren

[3] Hamel, G.: 'Managing Out of Bounds', *FT Mastering Management Overview*, Oc92.html
[4] Hamel, G.: 'Managing Out of Bounds', *FT Mastering Management Overview*, Oc92.html

to seek to restrict the debate amongst junior brethren can easily be breached. If relevant facts are broadly accessible, then every decision can be challenged. Authority can no longer be idiosyncratic and capricious. When junior Masons are in possession of all the facts, and capable of making their own judgments, they are more than willing to challenge the judgment of those they pay to administer what is, after all, only a hobby organization.

An organization which cannot imagine the future will have no place in it, but John F. Kennedy also reminded us that anybody who forgets their history will not have any future either. Here, then, are the three main challenges that we believe English Freemasonry faces today:

1. Preserve the ancient teaching and re-instate the old rituals so we can learn from the past.

2. Attract intelligent and thoughtful young people into your lodges, both male and female, so that they can learn the true purpose of the Order and share in its beliefs and values.

3. Move to a system of authority which is acceptable to today's society. This will involve a change to election rather than appointment.

Then English Freemasonry will have a future.

Appendix 2

REFLECTIONS ON MAES HOWE

The name of Maes Howe, given to the chambered structure near Stromness on Orkney, had intrigued us for a long time. We knew that the Irish, Manx and Scots languages are branches of two closely related tongues, the first identified today as Goidelic (Q-Celtic) or, more commonly, Gaelic; and the second called Brythopic (P-Celtic) which connects the Welsh, or Cymric, language with Cornwall and Brittany. The standard line on all of these languages is that their very oldest forms came into use around the sixth century AD. It had been our feeling that a language does not pop out of nowhere, any more than a new religion is suddenly created out of nothing; they are always reworkings of more ancient ideas. This seemed to be confirmed by Dr W. Nicolaison, who found considerable evidence of Welsh words being used as place names in Scotland.

> *It is a striking fact that P-Celtic names are found not just in Wales but much further north in Scotland . . . such place names could only have been coined if a P-Celtic language akin to modern Welsh was spoken thoughout the lowland of eastern Scotland, stretching from the Scottish borders to the Moray Firth and beyond, where these place-names are found. As Gaelic-speaking Scots from Dalriada colonised Scotland north of the Forth, starting in the eight century, if not earlier, such a language can only have been spoken by the Picts. These place names could only be preserved if they were adopted by the Gaelic-speaking incomers, who took to using them even as the older language*

> *died out, so arguing for a lengthy period of bilingualism between the Picts and the Scots.*[1]

So perhaps the story of Maelgwn fathering King Brude was not such a far-fetched story, if his mother spoke Welsh! But this information caused us to reconsider the meaning of the name Maes Howe – could it be related to the phonetically near-identical Welsh words *Maes Hwyr*, which translates as – 'the field of the evening after the sun has set'?

Victor Reijs, the Dutch astronomer whose work we discussed in Chapter Seven, had shown that the sun rises and sets behind Ward Hill 20 days before the winter solstice and 20 days afterwards. He set up a video camera in the Maes Howe chamber and published exact timings of every occasion when the sunlight entered. The result was a fairly hit-and-miss pattern of sunlight falling on the back wall of the chamber over a period of 60 days. Reijs therefore concluded that Maes Howe was simply a Yule building, with a general indication of the winter season.[2]

Euan Mackie has said that it is time to think again about Maes Howe:

> *A generation ago, inquiries into the astronomical and mathematical knowledge of the standing stone-erectors of prehistoric Britain dealt largely with statistical patterns. Since then, the great passage grave at Newgrange, eastern Ireland, has proved to be engineered to address the midwinter sunrise. It is time once more to look at another great chamber-tomb, Maes Howe in northernmost Scotland, with these concerns in mind.*[3]

We knew that Bryn Celli Ddu has an appearance of Venus, as the evening star, and we applied Robert's 'virtual-aperture' technique to the sun light timings provided by Victor Reijs. There are two virtual apertures which caused the sun to appear, to set, and apparently rise again – so could there be a Venus alignment as well as a solar one?

There was! One year in every eight, the calculation shows that Venus will

[1] Roberts, J.L.: *Lost Kingdoms, Celtic Scotland and the Middle Ages*, Edinburgh University Press, 1997

[2] Reijs, V.: 'Megalithic Month Alignment at Maes Howe', *Third Stone*, October-December 1998, pp.18-20

[3] Mackie, E.W.: 'Maes Howe and the Winter Solstice'; *Antiquity*, 71, June, 1997, pp.338-359

make a double flash on the back wall of the chamber in the evening, after the sun has set at the winter solstice.

At around 2:35 p.m. on the winter solstice, the sun shines on the back of the chamber for 17 minutes and then sets at 3.20 p.m. At 5.00 p.m. the light of Venus enters the first slot, lighting the Chamber, and then at 5.15 p.m. it sets behind Ward Hill. But 15 minutes after its first setting, Venus reappears beyond Ward Hill, and the light enters the chamber for a further two minutes, before setting for a second and last time.

So, every eight years Venus causes a double flash of light into the chamber of Maes Howe, 'the field of the evening after the sun has set' – how appropriate a name for a structure aligned with the evening star. This last happened in 1996 and will happen again in 2004.

Mackie was right when he suspected that there was more to Maes Howe than meets the eye. The solar alignment might be accidental, but the Venus alignment combined with it cannot be. Once again, we discovered the extent of the engineering expertise of these long-gone scientist priests.

Appendix 3

HOW DID THE GROOVED WARE PEOPLE DEVELOP AN ADVANCED CIVILIZATION?

THE CHARACTERISTICS OF THE BOYNE VALLEY COMMUNITY

Many people who look at the ancient past feel the need to explain the existence of certain knowledge. The sudden emergence of civilizations would seem to imply that some groups knew exactly what they were doing when they introduced farming and domestic animals. Some ascribe the sudden developments to Atlanteans, others to alien interventions; but they seem to miss the point that everything has to start somewhere – whether on a mythical land in the ocean, on Mars or somewhere near Dublin – and that this location may provide the key to understanding the anomalies.

Newgrange and its surrounding structures involved a profound social commitment over a long period of time, covering many generations. This represented an enormous investment of the resources of what has, until recently, been assumed to be a simple hunter-gatherer population just starting to develop farming. To succeed, it would have required the sort of specialization of labour which has previously been associated only with city cultures.

After completing his excavations, Professor Michael O'Kelly speculated that there were at least six different skilled gangs working on various aspects of the construction work.[1] These skilled people who built and decorated

[1] O'Kelly, M.J.: *Newgrange, Archaeology, Art and Legend*, Thames & Hudson, 1982

Newgrange would have needed to be fed and housed during the years of construction.

Who were these early builders, and how organized was their megalithic culture?

As we have said in the main text, the skills required to produce the structures built by the Grooved Ware People around the Irish Sea demonstrate a degree of maturity in economic development far in advance of their usual image of savages. They were capable of successfully planning and implementing massive civil engineering projects which consumed a very large proportion of their available labour force. Furthermore, they were a relatively short-lived people with an extremely high infant mortality rate, which makes their achievements all the more astonishing. Euan Mackie makes an important point:

> *There must have been specialized, proto-urban or urban stratified societies in existence before the earliest megaliths appeared.*[2]

Professor Eogan found evidence of settlements on various sites that predated the building of the main Boyne structures.

> *No unequivocal settlement of passage-tomb people has come to light but the excavation of some tombs has revealed evidence for domestic activity underneath them. One such site is Townleyhall 2 [just to the north of Newgrange and Knowth] . . . the area was unprotected, roughly oval, at most 1,575 m long and 11 m wide. There were 142 stake holes but it was impossible to disentangle a plan of a structure from these – although the use of stakes would suggest less substantial constructions like a tent.*[3]

He also found evidence for a domestic settlement on the site of Knowth which predated the construction of the mound.

> *On the western part of the ridge, there are features consisting of the remains of a sub-rectangular structure, palisade trenches, pits,*

[2] Mackie, E.: *The Megalithic Builders*, Phaidon Press, 1977
[3] Eogan, G.: *Knowth and the Passage-Tombs of Ireland*, Thames & Hudson, 1986

> *fireplaces and areas of pebbling. Not all the features were in use at the same time. The sub-rectangular structure had a trench dug into the subsoil around all sides, with eleven post holes in the base on one side.*[4]

The population studies we discussed in Chapter Eleven suggested about 1,200 people lived in the Boyne Valley Basin,[5] giving an estimate of the available male workforce between the ages of 15 and 30 years as about 240. Was this enough people to develop the specialization of labour that Eogan had observed?

As we also discussed in Chapter Eleven Professor Eogan, (who excavated Knowth) said of the Grooved Ware People.

> *It is possible that they worked out some method of calculating and measuring, especially lengths . . . these people had almost achieved a true arch; . . . an awareness of the effects of stress and the ways of counteracting it must have been acquired. . . . they were undoubtedly a thinking and conscious people, intellectually as well as spiritually motivated, and were developing a body of knowledge which could have laid the foundations of scientific development. . . . their deliberate selection of a hard rock, like greywacke, as the main building material [shows] An elementary grasp of geology . . . the tomb structures clearly demonstrate architectural and engineering abilities.*[6]

They were also skilful in exploiting local resources to feed themselves, as a large proportion of the population was not concerned with food production. We have already posed the question, 'How had they developed these skills of a type which previously had always been associated with development of the cities of Sumer?'.

Furthermore, we have also already listed Professor Eogan's account of the four possible ways in which these people could have acquired their skills;[7] but we need to repeat them here:

4 Eogan, G.: *Knowth and the Passage-Tombs of Ireland*, Thames & Hudson, 1986
5 Mitchell, F.: *The Irish Landscape*, Collins, 1976
6 Eogan, G.: *Knowth and the Passage-Tombs of Ireland*, Thames & Hudson, 1986
7 Eogan, G.: *Knowth and the Passage-Tombs of Ireland*, Thames & Hudson, 1986

1. The acquisition of a knowledge of farming by chance, through a source and means of transmission which are unknown.

2. Indigenous development due to local adaptive processes by the Mesolithic people.

3. Irish Mesolithic people travelling abroad, acquiring a knowledge of farming and introducing it at home.

4. The arrival of agricultural foreigners either by accident, such as farmer-fishermen blown off course, or by virtue of a more positive and intentional immigration.

Professor Eogan then went on to develop these possibilities. We now give a fuller version of his deliberations before we discuss the puzzle further:

> *The view has already been expressed that this society need not have been of local origin, but emerged as part of a spread – which is not yet fully understood – of agriculture into Ireland . . . there is enough evidence to indicate that Ireland was a recipient of ritual practices and possibly of people, from Brittany, and in particular the Morbihan region, as well as from Iberia and the lower Tagus area. However, one fact about the passage-tomb society is clear: it was not a prisoner of inherited ideas, but an innovative organism that played a key role in the shaping of society as a whole, in the development of landscape, in the evolution of Neolithic Ireland, and in forging links with Britain and continental Europe.*
>
> *The theory has been advanced that the passage tomb builders of Ireland were part of a wider Atlantic economic and ritual community . . . While there is a relationship between the Scottish and Irish passage tombs, this was not as close as were those with northern Wales. Nonetheless, the Irish contribution to the Scottish passage tomb series is fundamental.*[8]

Was there any mechanism which could explain how their skills developed,

[8] Eogan, G.: *Knowth and the Passage-Tombs of Ireland*, Thames & Hudson, 1986

without assuming they had imported them from the Eastern city states? As we now knew, the culture of the Grooved Ware People predated Sumer and Ancient Egypt, so the imported skills option looks very unlikely.

We decided to look more closely at the economics of early cities and, in particular, at the work of economist Dr Jane Jacobs. She has argued that it was not the new wealth of agriculture in Neolithic times which allowed cities be built, instead, the cities created and spurred on the agriculture around them. We wondered whether her work could have implications for understanding the settlement of around 1,200 people who built the mounds of the Boyne Valley. She based her argument on a detailed study of the city of Catal Huyuk, so we decided to consider that site more closely.

THE ECONOMICS OF FARMING

In the Turkish province of Anatolia at a site called Catal Huyuk, archaeologist James Mellaart excavated a city which extended over 100 acres. Mellaart estimated that it had once supported a population of more than 7,000 people. It was a sophisticated city with square-built terraced houses featuring timber-supported flat roofs, with access holes that enabled them to be used as roof-top verandas. On the wall of one of the buildings he found a detailed map of the town in its prime, showing its terraced housing, and behind it a picture of a twin-peaked active volcano, which has long since become extinct. The importance of this volcano was as a source of obsidian, a variety of black volcanic glass highly prized for making stone tools and mirrors. Indeed, Mellaart investigated the economy of the city and found that it seemed to have been an importance trading centre for obsidian and artifacts made from it. The city also had an agricultural infrastructure based on the farming of barley, wheat and cattle. It was clear from a detailed study of the rubbish heaps that the people of Catal Huyuk also ate the meat of wild animals.

The level of workmanship demonstrated in the artefacts he dug up – woven fabrics, jewellery, tools, pottery and obsidian mirrors – was extremely high. The craftsmen of the city were evidently well skilled in their various professions. They obviously spent most of their time on manufacture to develop such a high level of craftsmanship, which implies specialization of skills. Mirror grinders still have to eat, and so they had to be able to trade their mirrors for food. This specialization also suggests that the society they were living in was a peaceful one. Societies which have to fight to survive can not afford the luxury of artists and craftsmen working on non-essential items such as jewellery and mirrors.

What is most surprising about this site is its date. It flourished between 7000 and 6000 BC – about as long after the 7640 BC cometary impact as we are from the destruction of the Knights Templar. That is long enough for some sort of civilization to start to rebuild itself after the devastation of the impact, provided the builders had retained some knowledge. Mellaart noted of the site.

> *Neolithic civilization revealed at Catal Huyuk shines like a supernova among the rather dim galaxy of contemporary peasant culture . . . [It represents] a link between the remote hunters of the Upper Palaeolithic and the new order of food-production that was the basis of all our civilization.*[9]

From the shrine and statues that he found, Mellaart concluded that the inhabitants of the city worshipped a Great Goddess. Pre-historian Richard Rudgley said of Catal Huyuk:

> *Neither the earlier cultures which gave birth to this remarkable civilization nor the reasons for its death are known. The decline and fall of Catal Huyuk are shrouded in mystery.*[10]

Jane Jacobs was puzzled by the implications of this site. As she said:

> *The dogma of agricultural primacy says: agriculture first, cities later. Behind the dogma lies the notion that in pre-Neolithic times hunting men lived only in small and economically self sufficient groups, finding their own food, making their own weapons, tools and other manufactured goods. Not until some of these primitive groups learned to cultivate grain and raise livestock, it is thought, did settled and stable villages emerge, and not until after the villages were built did complex divisions of labour become possible, large economic projects and intricate social organisation become possible. These advances,*

[9] Mellaart, J.: *Catal Huyuk: a Neolithic Town in Anatolia*, Thames & Hudson, 1967.
[10] Rudgley, R.: *Lost Civilisations of the Stone Age*, Century, 1998

> *coupled with a surplus of agricultural food, are supposed to have made cities possible.*[11]

Looking first at Japan after the Second World War she notes that 'It created rural productivity upon a foundation of city productivity.' She commented:

> *Modern productive agriculture has been reinvented by the grace of hundreds of innovations that were exported from the cities to the countryside, transplanted to the countryside or imitated in the countryside . . . The agricultural revolution occurred first in cities and later in agriculture . . . there is no way to increase rural productivity first and city productivity later . . . Because we are so used to thinking of farming as a rural activity, we are especially apt to overlook the fact that new kinds of farming come out of cities.*
>
> *In very ancient times, too, cities were engaged in developing agriculture and animal husbandry. In the Egyptian cities of the Old Kingdom, for example, many experiments with animal domestication were tried: records of the efforts have been left in pictures. . . . during Old Kingdom times hyenas were tied up and force-fed until fat enough for slaughter; pelicans were kept to lay eggs; mongooses tamed to kill rats and mice and there is a suggestion that Dorcas gazelles were herded in flocks. Pictures show ibex, and two of the large kinds of antelope, addax and oryx stabled and wearing collars. The ass and the common house cat were domesticated in the ancient cities of the Nile; they are city animals distributed into the rural world.*[12]

To develop her argument, she takes the city of Catal Huyuk and puts forward a detailed economic argument to show how the city could develop from the need for a specialized commodity which was only available at that one place – obsidian. She speculates how a camp might be set up to trade in obsidian, and to meet that need local craftsmen produce more and more obsidian artifacts and trade them for food. The traders bring in goods to trade obsidian objects and in time other products develop, such as leather

[11] Jacobs; J.: *The Economy of Cities, Pelican*, 1968
[12] Jacobs; J.: *The Economy of Cities, Pelican*, 1968

bags to carry trade goods. When the people of the city want special treasures like copper, shells or pigments which they do not find in their own territories, they send out traders to swap obsidian objects for what they want.

> *The economy of the city divides into an export-import economy on the one hand, and a local or internal economy on the other. As time passes the settlement adds many new exports from its own local economy. For example the hide bags in which obsidian is carried down from its source are sometimes bartered to hunters or traders from other settlements who have come to purchase obsidian. Fine, finished obsidian knives, arrow heads, spearheads and mirrors of the kind produced in the settlement for its own use are also coveted by those who come for raw obsidian. The potent religion of the prospering settlement becomes an object of trade too; its common local talismans are bought . . . the food [of the settlement] is derived in two ways. Part of it comes from the old hunting and gathering territory – which is still hunted, foraged and patrolled . . . . but a large proportion of food is imported from foreign hunting territories. This food is traded for obsidian and other exports of the settlement. Wild food of the right kind commands a good exchange . . . the right kind of wild food is non-perishable.*[13]

Only non-perishable food is traded because it stands the trip to the settlement best and it can be stored by the settlement. The major types of non-perishable food will be live animals and hard seeds. With a successful settlement, large quantities of live animals and seeds accumulate in what has now become a small city. The settlement will quickly develop specialized individuals, whose job is to look after the stores of food. Those who look after wild animals will slaughter the most dangerous animals first, and the more docile species that can eat grass will be stored until they are needed for food, and will probably end up breeding. As Jacobs says, 'the stewards are intelligent men and fully capable of solving problems and catching insights from experience. But they are not trying to domesticate animals, they are simply trying to manage the city's wild food imports to the best of their abilities.'

[13] Jacobs; J.: *The Economy of Cities, Pelican*, 1968

The only reason that second or third generation captives live long enough to breed yet another generation is that they happen to be the easiest to keep during times of plenty.[14]

In this way, sheep, goats and cattle become domesticated over many generations. Jacobs then goes on to investigate the economics of seed storage.

The seed stewards of the settlement have no reason to prefer saving one kind of seed over another, and they do not do so. The dry seed are all mingled together in storage and are also eaten as a mixture. Seeds of many different kinds of wild grasses . . . come from the territories of scores of tribes who do not harvest one anther's territories except during war and raids, when the raiders eat quickly what they have seized. But in the city the seeds flow together for storage. Seeds that have never been juxtaposed are tumbled into baskets and bins, husked, pounded and cooked they are further jumbled with peas, lentils and nut meats. When seeds remain after winter, they are used for wild patch sowing, a practice not productive of much food, it just makes gathering wild seeds more convenient.[15]

It is no problem to get grain crosses, or even crosses with beans or peas, in this environment; indeed, such crosses cannot be avoided. The hybrids and crosses will be noticed as the settlement attracts people who are expert in recognizing varieties and estimating the worth of barter seeds.

Mutations occur no more commonly than they would in the wild, but they are not unnoticed either, as they most likely would be in the wild; nor do occasional batches of mutant seeds go unnoticed. But crosses and hybrids and the rare mutants are not deliberately put to use in selective breeding . . . .Selection happens because some patches of sown seeds yield much more heavily than others. The particular households with the lucky patches are more often than not, the ones with seed left for sowing.[16]

[14] Jacobs; J.: *The Economy of Cities, Pelican*, 1968
[15] Jacobs; J.: *The Economy of Cities, Pelican*, 1968
[16] Jacobs; J.: *The Economy of Cities, Pelican*, 1968

The people of the settlement do not know why their strains of seed are the best, but they realize they are. In time, the process of selection becomes purposeful. Jacobs points out the conditions needed for the development of sophisticated cultivated grain crops – such as the spelt found at Newgrange and Knowth – are threefold.

> 1. *Seeds that normally do not grow together must come together, frequently and consistently, over considerable periods of time.*
>
> 2. *In that same place variants must consistently be under the informed and close observation of people able to act relevantly in response to what they see.*
>
> 3. *That same place must be well-secured against food shortages so that in time the seed grain can become sacrosanct, otherwise the whole process of selective breeding will be repeatedly aborted before it can amount to anything. In short, property is a prerequisite. Although time is necessary, time in itself does not bestow cultivated grains on the settlement.*[17]

Here is suggested a incremental way in which the Grooved Ware People could have originally developed their 'proto-urban' civilization to the stage where their economy was productive enough to allow the luxury of scientific speculations. We couldn't help thinking back to the ancient city of Dolni Vestonice near to the town of Mikulov in the Czech Republic, which, as we noted in Chapter One, is the site of a 26,000-year-old factory and we remembered that the Vinca symbols, so similar to the megalithic art of the Boyne Valley, had been found near Turdas in Transylvania. Had the arts of civilization first developed 26,000 years ago in central Europe, before impact of the 7640 BC comet, and been reborn 5,000 years ago around the Irish Sea by a people who were determined not to be caught unaware again by a cometary impact?

Were, then, the people of the Boyne Valley living in a 'city' economy but without the permanent buildings we expect to see in a modern city? We had noticed that Eogan had commented that they seemed to live in wooden-

[17] Jacobs; J.: *The Economy of Cities, Pelican*, 1968

framed tent houses, where the covering fabric has long since decayed to nothing,` and the population studies of Mitchell showed that they were enough of them (1,200) to sustain the range of economic activities which Jacob's work shows will arise in areas with a high enough density of population.

Dr Julian Thomas of Southampton University had noticed that there had seemed to be a rapid rise in the establishment of enclosed farms in the Middle Bronze Age which marked a change in the way in which people lived, and he warned that we should not expect the way that Neolithic people made use of land to be simply a less intensive version of the Bronze-Age pattern. What he said made enormous sense in the context of the development of the Boyne Valley complex. He pointed out that there was not much evidence for permanent domestic buildings in Neolithic Britain, and a possible reason for the lack of such structures might be because the bulk of the populations lived in flimsy or temporary dwellings, of exactly the type that Professor Eogan had noticed at Knowth. He speculated that it is a relatively modern idea that people want to live in houses, and the outlook of Neolithic Britons might have favoured wooden or tent-type structures, which have in most cases have not survived.[18] He warned against accepting unthinkingly that that all societies progress gradually from being 'simple' to a state of 'complexity'.

Professor Childe, when he excavated Skara Brae, speculated along similar lines when saying that the only reason the village was constructed of stone was because of a lack of wood as building material – suggesting that the Grooved Ware People of Skara Brae were only doing in stone what all other Neolithic Britons were doing in wood, if it was available.[19]

So perhaps the Grooved Ware People had developed a city economy without the city hardware. The economic forces Jacobs describes need only enough people to be settled in an area with sufficient resources for the processes to occur. Her theory does not require the people involved to live in any particular type of house. So it seems that Jane Jacobs provides the mechanism for the means by which the Bru na Boinne – the Boyne Valley complex – became established.

Now that we have investigated the extent of the Grooved Ware Culture,

[18] Thomas, J.: 'Neolithic Houses in Mainland Britain and Ireland: a Sceptical View, in Darvill, T. and Thomas, J. (eds) *The Neolithic House in Britain and Beyond*, Oxford, Oxbow, 1996

[19] Childe, V.G.: 'Neolithic House-Types in Temperate Europe', *Proceedings of the Prehistoric Society* 15, 1949, pp.77-86

we also inclined to believe that the Grooved Ware People saw their domains as the seas and rivers, rather than the land-masses set within the sea. They were enormously successful navigators and utilized the transportation facilities of boats extensively. All their sites are either by the sea or within easy reach of a navigable river. When the Celtic Irish founded the kingdom of Dalriada which, being made up of what is now Ulster and Argyll, spanned the Irish Sea – they were not doing something unusual, but were simply reverting to form of community which the Grooved Ware People had developed to a high level of sophistication.

Appendix 4

ROSSLYN CHAPEL

In *The Hiram Key* and *The Second Messiah* we explained how the building called Rosslyn Chapel, in the village of Roslin, seemed to be a Jewish/Celtic structure based on Ezekiel's vision of the new Jerusalem and on the ruins of Herod's Temple.

When we compared the plan of Rosslyn to that of Herod's Temple we could see that they were identical, with the two pillars of Boaz and Jachin perfectly in place, and a massive engrailed St Clair cross on the ceiling even pointed down at the exact spot where the 'Holy of Holies' was kept in the Jerusalem Temple.

In particular,` we argued that the oversized west wall was a copy of the ruined remains of the Herodian structure and not, as the standard theory suggested, an aborted attempt to build a huge collegiate church. Our contention was, and remains, that the scrolls removed from under the Jerusalem Temple between 1118 and 1128 are now under Rosslyn.

The launch of *The Hiram Key* was held in Rosslyn and Baron St Clair Bonde, the direct descendant of the 15th-century builder – William St Clair – addressed the assembled crowd in his capacity as one of the trustees of Rosslyn. He stated that the trustees also believed that Rosslyn contained something very special, and they would support a application for an archaeological investigation from a properly constituted group of appropriately qualified scholars. We were also led to believe that 'Historic Scotland', the governing body for all national monuments, would be very sympathetic to any such application.

After completing *The Hiram Key* we had the great pleasure of meeting

Professor Philip Davies, the well-known biblical and Dead Sea Scrolls scholar. Philip visited Rosslyn with us and met his old friend Professor Graham Auld of Edinburgh University, and both men agreed that the architecture of the west wall was indeed recognizably Herodian in its style. When looking at the building in more depth, Philip Davies came to the opinion that there appeared to be nothing Christian about the building, except for the Victorian additions. His immediate impression was that it had been constructed to conceal some medieval secret.

Some months later we took Dr Jack Miller, a head of studies in geology from Cambridge University, to see the building. Jack pointed out that the west wall could not possibly be the beginnings of an intended collegiate church because the stones were not tied into the main building. It was, he told us, quite simply 'a folly'. He even pointed out that the stones of the unfinished ends had been chiselled to make them look worn, like a ruin.

Jack Miller said that he would like to bring up a small team to conduct some non-invasive ground-scans and, after discussing it with the Rosslyn project manager, he organized for the best equipment to be supplied, and for a world-class expert to fly in from the Colorado School of Mines – the world's finest underground investigators.

Unfortunately, with just days to go, permission to examine Rosslyn was withdrawn. The trustees told us in writing that any such permission would only be given if the people concerned signed a confidentiality agreement, which might even require them to deny that an investigation had taken place at all.

We refused to have any involvement under such anti-academic conditions.

In February 1998 we took two more specialist visitors to Rosslyn. Joe Peeples, President of the Jerusalem Historical Society; and the Reverend Professor James Charlesworth, Head of the Dead Sea Scrolls Project at Princeton University, and also the 1998 Albright Professor of Archaeology in Jerusalem.

Both men had broken into a very busy schedule to fly into the UK, but when they saw Rosslyn they did not seem in the least disappointed. Pointing out the imitation 'robbed stones' of false doorways, James Charlesworth quickly spotted the clues which indicated that the west wall was a painstaking copy of the remains of Herod's temple. As a minister himself he had intended to attend the Sunday service, but after commenting that it was clearly not a Christian building, he cancelled that idea as wholly inappropriate.

Jim's view was that the building was decaying rapidly, and he felt that anything underneath it should be investigated quickly, because it would be deteriorating at a much faster rate.

That evening we had dinner with Baron Bonde, while listening to Professor Charlesworth's assessment, and we advised that he should meet with Andrew Russell, another trustee, without delay. We are told that this meeting took place, and that Professor Charlesworth was invited to submit a proposal for an investigation of Rosslyn that should include leading Scottish scholars.

By a happy coincidence, Professor Charlesworth had spend several years at Edinburgh University, and so knew many of the countries leading experts who would be required to make the case for an archaeological investigation.

Having brought together the people best qualified to investigate Rosslyn, we stepped back to let the experts proceed as they wish. It has been our good fortune to find the real meaning of Rosslyn; however, we did not feel qualified to make further input at that time.

Some months later, we were informed that a detailed proposal had been submitted to the Trustees of Rosslyn Chapel. But we have heard nothing further since.

There is evidence of older buildings under Rosslyn and it is claimed by some that there was a Roman temple of Mithras on the site. This may well be true, but we now have good reason to believe that Rosslyn is built on the site of a megalithic chamber which involves a natural cavern well below the present building. From knowledge of detailed records from ancient Masonic sources, we think that we can give good guidance on where to look for the Zadokite scrolls that rest beneath this medieval shrine.

We can only hope that people will listen. Rosslyn is ready to yield its secret.

BIBLIOGRAPHY

Agenbroad L.D., ed: *Megafauna and Man*, Flagstaff University, Hot Springs, 1990

Aitken, M.J: *Science-Based Dating in Archaeology*, Longman, 1990

Allen, J.R: *Celtic Crosses of Wales*, Archaeoliga Cambiensis, 1899

Anderson, G.W: 'The Religion of Israel', *Peake's Commentary on the Bible*

Andrews, H.T: 'Daniel', *Peake's Commentary on the Bible* (1920 Edition)

Baigent, M: *Ancient Traces,* Viking 1998

Bailey, C: *The Legacy of Rome,* Oxford University Press

Bailey, H: *The Lost Language of Symbolism*, 1998

Balfour, M: *Stonehenge and its Mysteries*, Macdonald and Jane's, 1979

Bancroft, quoted in Howarth, H.H: *The Mammoth and the Flood*, Sampson Low, Marston, Searle and Rivington, London 1887

Barber, E.W: *The Mummies of Urumchi*, Macmillan, 1999

Barr, J: 'Daniel', *Peake's Commentary on the Bible* (1962 edition)

Bede, *A History of English Church and People*, Penguin Classics

Bellamy, H.S: *Before the Flood: The Problem of the Tiahuanaco Ruins,* Faber & Faber, 1943

Bennett, W.H: *Symbols of our Celto-Saxon Heritage*, Covenant Books, 1976

Berndt and Berndt: *The Speaking Land*, Penguin, 1989

Black, M: *The Book of Enoch or I Enoch, A New English Edition*, E.J. Brill, 1985

Blackett, A.T. and Wilson, A: *Arthur and the Charters of the Kings*, M.T. Byrd and Co, 1980

Boccaccini, G: *Beyond the Essenes*, Eerdmans, Grand Rapids, 1998

Bodge, T.J: *The Tradition of the The Old York T J Lodge of Mark Master Masons*, Bronte Lodge Haworth, 1912

Boobyer, G.H: 'Jude', *Peakes Commentary on the Bible*

Book of the Year: Anthropology and Archaeology, *Britannica Online.* <http://www.eb.com/, 1998

Bowen, E.G: *The Settlements of the Celtic Saints of Wales*, University of Wales Press, 1956

Bradley, I: *Columba, Pilgrim and Penitent*, Wild Goose Publications, 1996

Brennan M: *The Stones of Time*, Inner Traditions International, 1994

Britannica Online. www.eb.com

Bromwich, R: *Trioedd Ynys Prydein*, University of Wales Press, 1961

Bromwich, R: *The Triads of the Island of Britain*, University of Wales Press, 1978

Bruce, J: *Travels to Discover the Source of the Nile*, Vol IV, Edinburgh University Press 1804

Bryce, D: *Symbolism of the Celtic Cross*, Llanerch, 1989

Butler, A: *The Bronze Age Computer Disc*, W. Foulsham and Co, 1999

Caesar, J: *The Conquest of Gaul*, translated by Handford, S.A., Penguin, 1951

Caesar, J: *The Conquest of Gaul*, Penguin Classics, 1964

Campbell, J.Y: 'The Origin and Meaning of the Term Son of Man', *JThS* XL VIII, 1947, p.148

Ceremonial of the Red Cross of Babylon, Grand Council of the Allied Masonic Degrees, Ritual No. 2

Ceremony of Installation, Order of the Royal and Select Masters, Ritual No 2, The Grand Council

Chadwick, N.K: *The Celts*, Penguin, 1971

Chadwick, N.K: *The Druids*, University of Wales Press, 1966

Charles, R.H: *The Book of Enoch*, Oxford University Press, 1912

Childe, V.G: 'The Orient and Europe', *American Journal of Archaeology*, vol. 43, 1939, p 10

Clark, E.E: *Indian Legends of the Pacific Northwest*, Berkeley, University of California Press, 1963

Clarke, D.V and Sharples, N: 'Settlements and Subsistence in the 3rd Millennium BC', in *The Prehistory of Orkney*, ed. Renfrew, C., Edinburgh University Press

Clayton, P: *Chronicle of the Pharaohs*, Thames & Hudson, 1994

Cohen, A: *The Soncino Chumash*, The Soncino Press, London, 1962

Connelly, M. and Condit T., 'Ritual Enclosures in the Lee Valley, Co. Kerry,' *Archaeology Ireland*, vol. 12, No. 6, issue 46, Winter 1998

Cunliffe, B: *Prehistoric Europe*, Oxford University Press, 1965

Cusack, M.E: *An Illustrated History of Ireland*, Dublin, 1869

Davidson, D.A and Jones, R.L: 'The Environment of Orkney', in *The Prehistory of Orkney*, ed. Renfrew, C., Edinburgh University Press, 1985

Davies, P: *New Scientist*, 12 September 1998

Delaforge, G: *The Templar Tradition in the Age of Aquarius*

Doble, G.H: *Lives of the Welsh Saints*, University of Wales Press, 1971

Dolgopolsky, D: 'Linguistic Prehistory,' *Cambridge Archaeological Journal, 5/2* 1995, 268-71

Donaldson, G: *Scottish Historical Documents*, Neil Wilson, 1970

Drummond, J: *Sculptured Monuments in Iona and the West Highlands*, Society of Antiquaries of Scotland, 1831

Dubrovo, I: 'The Pleistocene Elephants of Siberia', in: *Megafauna and Man*, Agenbrod, L.D., ed., University of Flagstaff, 1990, pp.1-8

Duncan, D.E: *The Calendar*, Fourth Estate, 1998

Edward, H.T: *Wales and the Welsh Church*, Rivingtons, 1898

Edwards, G.T: *A Short History of the Churches and Neighbourhood of Llanbadrig, Llanfechell, Llanfflewin and Bodewryd*, Oriel Cemaes, 1997

Edwards, H.T: *The Eisteddfod*, University of Wales Press, 1990

Eisenman, R: *James the Brother of Jesus*, Faber & Faber, 1997

Eisenman, R: *The Dead Sea Scrolls and the First Christians*, Element, 1996

Eisenman, R: and Wise, M: *The Dead Sea Scrolls Uncovered*, Element, 1992

Eogan, G: *Knowth and the Passage-Tombs of Ireland*, Thames & Hudson, 1986

Fellows, J: *Mysteries of Freemasonry*, W.M. Reeves

Finlay, I: *Columba*, Victor Gollancz, 1979

Fohrer, G: *The History of Israelite Religion*, SPCK, 1973

Gardener, L: *Bloodline of the Holy Grail*, Element, 1996

Gaster, M: *The Chronicles of Jarahmeel*, 1899

Gault, D.E. and Sonet, C.P: 'Laboratory Simulation of Pelagic Astroidal Impact,' *Spec, Papers Geol. Soc. A.*, 190, pp. 69-92

Geikie, A: *'Text-book of Geology'*, quoted in Filby, F.A: *The Flood Reconsidered*, Zondervan, 1971

Gerber, P: *Stone of Destiny*, Canongate Books, 1997

Glass, B.P: 'Australasian Microtektites and the Stratigraphic Age of the Australites,' *Bull. Geol. Soc. Am.* 89, 1978, pp. 1455-58

Glazebrook, M.F: *Anglesey and the North Wales Coast*, Brookland and Co., 1962

Gould and Eldridge: *Punctuated Equilibria: an Alternative to Phyletic*

Gradualism, Models in Paleobiology, 1990, p. 42

Grady, M: *Astronomy Now*, November, 1997, p. 45-49

Graves, R: *The White Goddess*, Faber & Faber, 1948

Gribbin, J. and Plagemann, S: *The Jupiter Effect*, New English Library, 1980

Grimal, N: *History of Ancient Egypt*, Blackwell, Cambridge 1992

CD-Rom *Grolier Encyclopaedia*

Gutzlaff, A: *Journal of the Asiatic Society*, Vol. xvi, no. 79

Hackwell, W.J: *Signs, Letters, Words, Archaeology Discovers Writing*, Macmillan, 1987

Hadingham, E: *Circles and Standing Stones*, Heinemann, 1975

Hale, R.B: *The Magnificent Gael*, Mom, Ottawa, 1976

Hallo, W.W: *Journal of Cuneiform Studies*, vol. 23, No. 3, 1971, pp. 57-67

Hamel, G: 'Managing Out of Bounds,' *FT Mastering Management Overview*, Oc92.html

Hancock, G. and Bauval, R: *Keepers of Genesis*, Heinemann, 1996

Hancock, G: *Fingerprints of the Gods*, Heinemann, 1995

Hawkins, G.S: *Stonehenge Decoded*, Souvenir Press, 1966

Hedges, J.W: *Tomb of the Eagles*, Tempvs Reparavm, 1992

Heggie, D.C: *Megalithic Science*,Thames & Hudson, 1981

Henshall, A.S: *The Chambered Cairns in The Prehistory of Orkney*, Edinburgh University Press, 1993

Heyerdahl, T: *The Tigris Expedition*, George Allen & Unwin, 1980

Higham, M: Letter to the *Halifax Courier*, April 1996

Hodder, E: *On Holy Ground*, William P. Nimmo, 1876

Holmes, A: *Principles of Physical Geology*,Thomas Nelson & Sons, 1978

Hooke, S.H: 'The Religious Institutions of Israel,' *Peake's Commentary on the Bible*

Hooke, S.H: 'Genesis', *Peake's Commentary on the Bible* (1962 edition)

Howarth, H.H: *The Mammoth and the Flood*, Sampson Low, Marston, Searle and Rivington, London 1887

Hughes, D: 'Focus: Visitors from Space,' *Astronomy Now*, November 1997, pp.41-44

Hyde, D: *A Literary History of Ireland*, T. Fisher Unwin, 1899

Imbrie, J. and Imbrie, K.P: *Ice Ages*, Harvard University Press, 1986

Imbrie, J and Imbrie, K.P: 'Modeling the Climate Response to Orbital Variations,' *Science*, 207, 1980 pp.943-953

Isbell, D and Hardin, M: *Chain of Impact Craters Suggested by Spaceborne Radar Images*, http:/www.jpl.nasa.gov/sl19/news80.html

Izokh, E.P: 'Age-paradox and the Origin of Tektites', *Sec. Int. Conf. Nat. Glasses,* Charles University, Prague, 1987, pp.379-384

Jackson, K: 'The Dawn of the Welsh Language,' *Wales Through the Ages*, vol. 1, Christopher Davies, 1959

Jacobs, J: *The Economy of Cities*, Pelican, 1968

Josephus Flavius: *The Jewish Wars*

King, L.C: *The Morphology of the Earth*

Klee, K: *La Deluge*, quoted in *The Words of Sir Wm Jones*, London, 1880

Knez, Eugene I: 'Ainu,' *Microsoft (R) Encarta, 97*

Knight, C. and Lomas, R: *The Second Messiah*, Century, 1997

Knight, C. and Lomas, R: *The Hiram Key*, Century, 1996

Kromer, B. and Becker, B: 'Tree Ring Carbon 14 Calibration at 10,000 Bp' *Proc. NATO Advanced Research Workshop*, Erice, 1990

Krupp, E.C: *Echoes of the Ancient Skies*. Oxford University Press, 1983

Lamy, L: *Egyptian Mysteries*, Thames & Hudson, 1981

Lang, A: *Custom and Myth*, London, 1860

Laplace, P.S: *Exposition du système du Monde*, 1796

Larousse Encyclopaedia of Astronomy, 1959 ed.

Leake, J and Howard S: 'Bronze-Age Script?' *The Sunday Times*, 16 June, 1996, p.17

Lenormant, L. quoted in Howarth, H.H: *The Mammoth and the Flood*, Sampson Low, Marston, Searle and Rivington, London, 1887

Libby, W.R: *Radiocarbon Dating*, University of Chicago Press, 1955

Lockyer, N: 'Some questions for Archaeologists,' *Nature*, vol.73, 1906, p.280

Lockyer, N: *Stonehenge and other British Stone Monuments Astronomically Considered*, Macmillan, 1909

Long, D, Wickham-Jones, C, and Ruckley, NA: *Studies in the Upper Palaeothic of Britain and Northwest Europe*, pp.55-62, S296, 1986

Macalister, R.A.S: Armstrong, E.C.R and Praeger, R.L, 'Bronze Age Cairns on Carrowkeel Mountain Co. Sligo,' *PRIA*, 29C 1912, pp.311-347

Mackie, E.W. 'Maes Howe and the Winter Solstice'; *Antiquity*, 71, June 1997 pp.338-359

Mackie, E.W: *The Megalith Builders*, Phaidon Press, 1977

Manual of Freemasonry, Reeves and Turner

Margary, I.D: *Roman Roads in Britain*, John Barker, 1973

Marsden, J: *The Illustrated Life of Columba*, Macmillan, 1991

Marsden, J: *The Tombs of the Kings, and Iona Book of the Dead*, Llanerch, 1994

Marshack, A: *The Roots of Civilisation*, McGraw-Hill, 1972
Matthews, J. and C.: *British and Irish Mythology,* The Aquarian Press, 1988
Mattingly, H: *Roman Imperial Civilization*, Oxford University Press, 1956
May, H.G: 'Joshua', *Peake's Commentary on the Bible*
May, H.G: 'History of Israel - 1', *Peake's Commentary on the Bible*
Melosh, H.J: Schneider, N.M., Zahnle, K.J and Latham, D: 'Ignition of Global Wildfires at the Cretaceous/Tertiary Boundary'. *Nature*, 348, 1990
Microsoft (R) Encarta (R) Encyclopedia CD-Rom
Milankovitch, M.M: *Canon of Insolation and the Ice-Age Problem*, Koniglish Serbisch Akademie Beograd, 1941
Mitchell, F: *The Irish Landscape*, Collins, 1976
Moore, P and Mason, J: '*The Return of Halley's Comet*, Patrick Stephens, 1984
Neugebauer, O: Appendix A, Matthew Black: *The Book of Enoch or I Enoch, A New English Edition*, Leiden, E.J. Brill, 1985
Neugebauer, O: *Ethiopic Astronomy and Computus*, Akad d Wiss, 1979
Newell, E.J: *A History of the Welsh Church,* Elliot Stock, 1895
North, J: *Stonehenge, Neolithic Man and the Cosmos*, HarperCollins, 1996
Nyland, Edo : http://www.islandnet.com/~edonon
O'Kelly, C: *Concise Guide to Newgrange*, C. O'Kelly, Cork, 1984
O'Kelly, M: *Newgrange, Archaeology, Art and Legend*, Thames & Hudson, 1982
Oliphant, M: *Atlas of the Ancient World*, Ebury Press, 1992
Oram, R: *Scottish Prehistory*, Birlinn, 1997
Osborne, H: *South American Mythology*, Hamlyn Press, 1968
Ovason, D: *The Secret Zodiacs of Washington DC*, Century, 1999
Oxford Companion to the Bible, Oxford University Press
Papke, W: *Die Sterne von Babylon*
Parry, T: *The Oxford Book of Welsh Verse*, Clarendon Press, 1962
Peake's Commentary on the Bible, 1962 edition
Picard, L: *Structure and Evolution of Palestine*, Bull Geological Department, Hebrew University, Jerusalem, 1943
Pinker, Steven: *The Language Instinct*, HarperPerennial Library, 1995
Pohl, E.J: *Prince Henry Sinclair*, Nimbus, 1967
Prasad, N.Sh. and Rao, P.S: 'Tektites Far and Wide', *Nature*, 347, 1990, p.340
Preston, W: *Illustrations of Masonry*, G. and T. Wilkie, 1746
Prestwich, J: *On Certain Phenomena of the last Geological Period*, quoted in Filby, F.A: *The Flood Reconsidered*, Zondervan, 1971
Ray, T.P: *Nature*, vol.337, no. 26, January 1989, pp.345-346

Reed, A.W: *Myths and Legends of Australia*, London, 1889

Reijs, V.M.M: 'Maes Howe's Megalithic Month Alignment,' *Third Stone*, October-December 1998

Renfrew, C: *Before Civilization*, Jonathan Cape, 1973

Renfrew, C: *Investigations in Orkney*, Penguin, 1979

Renfrew, C: 'Investigations in Orkney,' *Report Research Comm, Soc. Antiq. London*, no. 38, 1979

Richards, C: 'The Later Neolithic Settlement Complex at Barnhouse Farm, Stenness,' in *The Prehistory of Orkney*, Edinburgh University Press, 1993

Ritchie, A: 'The First Settlers in the Prehistory of Orkney,' ed. Renfrew, C. Edinburgh University Press, 1985

Ritchie, A: *Prehistoric Orkney*, Historic Scotland, 1995

Ritual of Freemasonry, Reeves & Turner

Ritual of St Lawrence the Martyr, Knight of Constantinople, Grand Tilers of Solomon, The Order of Allied Masonic Degrees

Ritual of the Degree of the Noahites or Prussian Knights, Reeves & Turner, 1812

Rituals of the Supreme Grand Royal Arch Chapter of Scotland, Dunedin, Chapter No. 703

Roberts, J.L: *Lost Kingdoms, Celtic Scotland and the Middle Ages*, Edinburgh University Press, 1997

Rolleston, T.W: *Myths and Legends of the Celtic Race*, G.G. Harrap and Co., 1911

Rose, A: *The Director of Ceremonies His Duties and Responsibilities*, Kenning and Son, 1932

Ross, A: *Druids Gods and Heroes from Celtic Mythology*, Peter Lowe, 1986

Rudgley, R: *Lost Civilizations of the Stone Age*, Century, 1998

Ruhlen, M: 'Linguistic Evidence for Human Prehistory', *Cambridge Archaeological Journal, 5/2*, 1995, pp.265-8.

Schmandt-Besserat, D: *Before Writing, Volume One: From Counting to Cuneiform*, University of Texas Press, 1992

Schultz, J: *Movements and Rhythms of the Stars*, Floris, 1986

Schwarcz, H.P: 'ESR Dates for the Hominid Burial Site of Qafzeh in Israel', *Journal of Human Evolution*, 17, 1988

Scott, R.M: *Robert the Bruce*, Canongate, 1993

Scott, W: *The Pirate*, T. Nelson & Sons Ltd

Senior, M: *Gods and Heroes in North Wales*, Gwasg Carreg Gwalch, 1993

Shreeve, James: *The Neanderthal Enigma*, William Morrow & Co., 1995

Sitchin, Z: *The Wars of God and Men*

Slyman, A.L. 'A Battle of Bones,' *Archaeology*, vol. 40 no. 1, January-February 1997

Snaith N.H: 'Numbers', *Peake's Commentary on the Bible* (1962 edition)

Sobel, D: *Longitude*, Fourth Estate, 1996

Spence, L: *Mysteries of Celtic Britain*, Nelson & Sons, 1890

Springett, B.H: *The Mark Degree: its Early History, its Variations in Ritual, its Symbolism and Teaching*, A. Lewis, 1931

Squire, C: *Celtic Myth and Legend, Poetry and Romance*, Gresham Publishing Co. 1890

Steiner, R: *The Festivals and Their Meaning*, Rudolf Steiner Press, 1981

Stendahl, K: 'Matthew', *Peake's Commentary on the Bible*

Stevenson, D: *The Origins of Freemasonry: Scotland's Century 1590-1710*, Cambridge University Press, 1988

Stewart, R.J: *Celtic Gods, Celtic Goddesses*, Blandford, 1990

Stoker, J.J: *Water Waves, The Mathematical Theory with Applications*, John Wiley & Sons, 1992

Strauss, W.L. and Cavge A.J.E: 'Pathology and Posture of Neanderthal Man,' *Quarterly Review of Biology*, 32, 1957, pp.348-363

Suess, H.E: and Berger, R: *Radiocarbon Dating,* University of California Press, 1970

Tacitus: *The Agricola* and *The Germania*, Penguin Classics, 1948

Tacitus: *The Histories,* Penguin Classics, 1962

Temple, R: *He Who Saw Everything*, Century, 1991

The Ceremonies of a Chapter of Princes Rose Croix of Heredom of the Ancient and Accepted Rite for England And Wales, The Supreme Council

The Ceremonies of the Degrees of Selected Master, Royal Master, Most Excellent Master and Super-Excellent Master, Ritual No.1, The Grand Council

The Ceremonies of the Masonic and Military Order of the Red Cross of Constantine, Ritual No 2, The Grand Imperial Conclave

The Degrees of the Captivity, 1920 Edition, Scottish Workings

The Freemason's Vade Mecum, A. Lewis

The Holy Order of the Grand High Priest, Ritual No 3, Executive Committee of the Order of Allied Masonic Degrees

The Masonic and Military Order of the Red Cross of Constantine and the Appendant Orders of the Holy Sepulchre and of St John the Evangelist

The Perfect Ceremonies of The Supreme Order of the The Holy Royal Arch, A. Lewis

The Ritual of the Three Degrees of Craft Freemasonry, Imperial Printing Co.

The Scottish Ritual of Craft Freemasonry, John Bethune, Edinburgh

The Universal Book Of Craft Freemasonry, Toye and Co. 1912

The Universal Book of Craft Freemasonry, Toye, Kenning and Spencer, 1968

Thom, A: *Megalithic Sites in Britain*, Oxford University Press, 1968

Thom, A.S: *Walking in All of the Squares*, Argyll Publishing, 1995

Thom, A. and A.S: *Megalithic Rings*, *BAR* British Series 81, 1980

Thompson, S: *Tales of the North American Indians*, Bloomington, Indiana University Press, 1966

Tollmann, E. and A: *Terra Nova*, 6, 1994, pp.209-217

Tri-City Herald, 9 September 1996

Turco, R.P., Toon, O.B. *et al.*: 'Nuclear Winter: Global Consequences of Multiple Nuclear Explosions,' *Science*, 222, 1983

Twohig, E.S: *Irish Megalithic Tombs*, Shire Archaeology, 1990

Walk, L: 'Das Flut-Geschwisterpaar als Ur und Stammelternpaar der Menschheit,' *Mitt osterr Gesz, Anthropol Ethon, Prahist*, v. 78/79, 1941

Walker, Alan and Shipman, Pat: *The Wisdom of the Bones*, Alfred A. Knopf, Inc., 1996

Ward, J.S.M: *Freemasonry and the Ancient Gods*, Gresham and Co., 1921

Wickham-Jones, C.R: *Scotland's First Settlers*, Historic Scotland, 1994

Wilkinson, R.J.L: *The Cryptic Rite, An Historical Treatise*, Grand Council of the Royal and Select Masters of England and Wales

Williams, G.A: *When was Wales?* Penguin, 1985

Williams, I: *Canu Taliesin*, Caeroydd, 1960

Wills, Christopher: *The Runaway Brain*, Flamingo, 1994

Wilson, H: *Understanding Hieroglyphics*, Michael O'Mara Books, 1993

Winn, S.M.M: *Pre-writing in Southeastern Europe: The Sign System of the Vinca Culture Circa 4000 BC*, Western Publishers, 1981

Wise, M, Abegg, M. and Cook, E: *The Dead Sea Scrolls, a New Translation,* Harper San Francisco, 1996

Woolley, L: *Ur of the Chaldees, Seven Years of Excavation*, Pelican, 1929

INDEX